Redesigning Organizational Information Systems for Productivity and Digital Well-Being

Houssem Chemingui
https://orcid.org/0000-0002-3351-250X
Brest Business School, France

IGI Global
Scientific Publishing
Publishing Tomorrow's Research Today

Vice President of Editorial	Melissa Wagner
Director of Acquisitions	Mikaela Felty
Director of Book Development	Jocelynn Hessler
Production Manager	Mike Brehm
Cover Design	Jose Rosado

Published in the United States of America by
IGI Global Scientific Publishing
701 East Chocolate Avenue
Hershey, PA, 17033, USA
Tel: 717-533-8845 | Fax: 717-533-7115
Website: https://www.igi-global.com E-mail: cust@igi-global.com

Library of Congress Cataloging-in-Publication Data

LCCN: 2026017830 (CIP Data Pending)
ISBN13: 9798260001110
Isbn13Softcover: 9798260001127
EISBN13: 9798260001134
British Cataloguing in Publication Data
A Cataloguing in Publication record for this book is available from the British Library.

Table of Contents

Detailed Table of Contents

This conceptual chapter argues that organizational information systems (OIS) should be redesigned around a dual objective: sustained productivity and digital well-being. Many enterprise systems still privilege speed, visibility, and continuous availability, yet research on information overload, interruption, technostress, cognitive load, and recovery suggests that these same conditions can degrade judgment quality, focus, and long-term performance. The chapter synthesizes these literatures and proposes the Cognitive Shield: an AI-enabled architectural layer that filters noncritical interruptions, summarizes communication streams, supports priority orchestration, and protects recovery boundaries. The chapter contributes a human-centered design framework, an implementation roadmap, and governance principles for organizations seeking to balance technological performance with psychological sustainability.

This chapter examines the tension between AI driven productivity gains and employee well being in African organizations undergoing digital transformation. Using a conceptual and integrative review of literature and contextual analysis, it develops a socio technical framework for sustainable AI enabled information systems. The study finds that unregulated automation increases precarity, algorithmic management heightens technostress, and skills gaps constrain inclusive productivity. It recommends human centered design, responsible governance, and continuous capacity building to align AI adoption with sustainable organizational development.

Organizational information systems (OIS) have historically prioritized operational efficiency over employee experience. The emergence of Industry 5.0, with its emphasis on human centricity, sustainability, and resilience, compels a fundamental rethinking of how digital workplaces are designed. This chapter argues that existing OIS frameworks inadequately address the relational and psychological dimensions of work, contributing to technostress, disengagement, and organizational fragility. Drawing on sociotechnical systems theory, human-centric design, and organizational resilience frameworks, it proposes the RECS (Resilient, Employee-Centric Systems) framework comprising four interconnected dimensions: Adaptive Intelligence, Well-Being Integration, Organizational Agility, and Participatory Governance. Applied across manufacturing, knowledge-work, and healthcare contexts, including Indian case examples, the framework offers researchers and practitioners a structured pathway for redesigning OIS that genuinely serves the humans who depend on them.

The rapid expansion of artificial intelligence, algorithmic systems, and digitally mediated workplaces has transformed organizational information systems into behavioral environments that shape employee productivity, cognition, and psychological well-being. Existing organizational information systems literature mainly emphasizes technological efficiency and system adoption while providing limited integration of behavioral psychology, digital well-being, and human-centered workplace design. This chapter addresses this gap by proposing a Behavioral-by-Design framework integrating digital psychology, behavioral design, and organizational information systems to support sustainable digital transformation in AI-mediated workplaces. The proposed framework extends behavioral information systems perspectives toward adaptive and psychologically informed organizational systems while offering strategic recommendations for ethical AI governance and sustainable digital well-being practices.

functioning depends equally on forms of contribution that resist measurement such as informal mentoring, discretionary judgment, and relational care. Recognizing this residue is essential for sustaining organizations that are efficient, morally responsible, and capable of supporting meaningful collective work in the algorithmic age.

The integration of artificial intelligence (AI) into organizational information systems (IS) has fundamentally altered the landscape of workplace productivity, decision-making, and data governance. While AI-enabled IS offer unprecedented capabilities for automating complex tasks, augmenting human cognition, and accelerating information flows, they simultaneously introduce profound ethical, privacy, and governance challenges that cannot be resolved through purely technical solutions. This chapter explores the confluence of these dimensions, arguing that sustainable productivity in AI-enabled environments must be defined and measured through an ethical lens. It develops a comprehensive framework for understanding how ethical principles, privacy regulations, and governance architectures interact with productivity outcomes in modern organizations.

Libraries have long served as the custodians of knowledge, playing a pivotal role in the preservation and dissemination of information throughout human history. They have evolved over time, adapting to meet community needs. This research aims to explore how modern libraries have evolved from traditional physical spaces to dynamic digital entities. It will examine the integration of digital technologies in library services, the impact on user engagement and access to information, and the challenges and opportunities this transformation presents. The study will focus on several key areas: digital collections and archives, online library services, virtual reference systems, and the role of libraries in promoting digital literacy. By investigating these aspects, the research seeks to provide a comprehensive understanding of the modern library's function and significance in the digital age, emphasizing that libraries are no longer confined to their physical buildings but have become integral components of the global information infrastructure. This study offers an original contribution by repositioning the contemporary library not merely

Preface

The accelerating integration of Artificial Intelligence (AI), digital transformation technologies, and intelligent organizational systems is profoundly reshaping the modern workplace. Organizations today operate in increasingly complex digital ecosystems where productivity is no longer measured solely by efficiency and automation, but also by adaptability, employee well-being, ethical governance, resilience, cognitive sustainability, and human-centered innovation. As enterprises continue to adopt AI-enabled information systems, a critical challenge emerges: how can organizations harness the power of intelligent technologies while preserving human values, meaningful work, privacy, and sustainable productivity?

This book, *AI-Enabled Organizational Information Systems for Sustainable Productivity and Digital Well-Being*, addresses this important question by exploring the evolving relationship between AI technologies, organizational information systems, human work, and digital well-being. The chapters included in this volume collectively investigate how organizations can design intelligent systems that support productivity while simultaneously fostering resilience, cognitive sustainability, ethical governance, human-centered work environments, and responsible digital transformation.

The subject matter of this book is highly relevant within the context of contemporary organizational transformation. The rise of generative AI, algorithmic management systems, intelligent analytics, process mining, digital platforms, and Industry 5.0 has introduced new opportunities for improving organizational performance and operational intelligence. At the same time, these developments have raised significant concerns regarding employee well-being, cognitive overload, privacy, surveillance, ethical governance, and the future of meaningful work. Organizations are increasingly required to balance technological innovation with social responsibility and human-centered system design.

This volume situates itself at the intersection of Organizational Information Systems, Artificial Intelligence, Digital Transformation, Human–Technology Interaction, Cognitive Ergonomics, Organizational Psychology, Process Optimization, and Sustainable Enterprise Management. It contributes to ongoing academic and professional discussions surrounding responsible AI adoption, human-centered digital ecosystems, sustainable productivity, and intelligent organizational transformation.

The target audience of this book includes researchers, academics, doctoral students, practitioners, consultants, digital transformation leaders, organizational strategists, human resource specialists, and policymakers interested in AI-enabled organizational systems and the future of work. Scholars in Information Systems, Management, Organizational Behavior, Digital Innovation, and Human–Computer Interaction will find theoretical and applied perspectives relevant to contemporary research challenges. Industry professionals and enterprise leaders will benefit from practical insights into designing resilient, ethical, and sustainable digital workplaces.

OVERVIEW OF CHAPTERS

Chapter 1: AI-Enabled Organizational Information Systems for Sustainable Productivity and Digital Well-Being

This conceptual chapter argues that organizational information systems (OIS) should be redesigned around a dual objective: sustained productivity and digital well-being. Many enterprise systems still privilege speed, visibility, and continuous availability, yet research on information overload, interruption, technostress, cognitive load, and recovery suggests that these same conditions can degrade judgment quality, focus, and long-term performance. The chapter synthesizes these literatures and proposes the Cognitive Shield: an AI-enabled architectural layer that filters noncritical interruptions, summarizes communication streams, supports priority orchestration, and protects recovery boundaries. The chapter contributes a human-centered design framework, an implementation roadmap, and governance principles for organizations seeking to balance technological performance with psychological sustainability.

Chapter 2: AI, Work, and Well-Being: Rethinking Organizational Information Systems for Sustainable Productivity in Africa

This chapter examines the tension between AI driven productivity gains and employee well being in African organizations undergoing digital transformation. Using a conceptual and integrative review of literature and contextual analysis, it develops a socio technical framework for sustainable AI enabled information systems. The study finds that unregulated automation increases precarity, algorithmic management heightens technostress, and skills gaps constrain inclusive productivity. It recommends human centered design, responsible governance, and continuous capacity building to align AI adoption with sustainable organizational development.

Chapter 3: Beyond Automation: Designing Resilient, Human-Centric Organizational Information Systems in the Age of Industry 5.0

Organizational information systems (OIS) have historically prioritized operational efficiency over employee experience. The emergence of Industry 5.0, with its emphasis on human centricity, sustainability, and resilience, compels a fundamental rethinking of how digital workplaces are designed. This chapter argues that existing OIS frameworks inadequately address the relational and psychological dimensions of work, contributing to technostress, disengagement, and organizational fragility. Drawing on sociotechnical systems theory, human-centric design, and organizational resilience frameworks, it proposes the RECS (Resilient, Employee-Centric Systems) framework comprising four interconnected dimensions: Adaptive Intelligence, Well-Being Integration, Organizational Agility, and Participatory Governance. Applied across manufacturing, knowledge-work, and healthcare contexts, including Indian case examples, the framework offers researchers and practitioners a structured pathway for redesigning OIS that genuinely serves the humans who depend on them.

Chapter 4: Behavioral-by-Design: Integrating Digital Psychology Into Organizational Information Systems for Productivity and Wellness

The rapid expansion of artificial intelligence, algorithmic systems, and digitally mediated workplaces has transformed organizational information systems into behavioral environments that shape employee productivity, cognition, and psychological well-being. Existing organizational information systems literature mainly emphasizes technological efficiency and system adoption while providing limited integration of behavioral psychology, digital well-being, and human-centered workplace design. This chapter addresses this gap by proposing a Behavioral-by-Design framework integrating digital psychology, behavioral design, and organizational information systems to support sustainable digital transformation in AI-mediated workplaces. The proposed framework extends behavioral information systems perspectives toward adaptive and psychologically informed organizational systems while offering strategic recommendations for ethical AI governance and sustainable digital well-being practices.

Chapter 5: Cognitive Sustainability and Algorithmic Ergonomics: Re-Architecting Organizational Information Systems for Human-Centered Productivity

Organizational Information Systems that are powered by Artificial Intelligence have become more efficient but also cause more cognitive workload by making people constantly connected and always monitored by algorithms and overloaded with information. In this chapter, the author presents the concept of Cognitive Sustainability as the design idea that helps safeguard long-term attention, decision-making, and emotional stability at digital workplaces. It offers Algorithmic Ergonomics to make intelligent systems conform to human mental capacity through minimizing interruptions, workload adaptation, and privacy-by-design protection. The idea of a conceptual architecture and dual-outcome measurement model illustrate how productivity and digital well-being may be maximized at the same time. Case-based observations indicate that sustainable performance arises when AI frameworks stabilize the attention as opposed to increasing the speed of digital intensity.

Chapter 6: Designing Smarter Systems for Better Work: Reducing Cognitive Load in Digital Workplaces

This chapter examines the impact of modern Information Systems on cognitive performance in digitally intensive work environments. It identifies key challenges such as the toggle tax, attentional residue, cognitive overload, and decision fatigue, which collectively reduce productivity and increase mental strain. Drawing on cognitive ergonomics and behavioral research, the chapter proposes a human-centered design approach that aligns system architecture with the limitations of human cognition. It explores solutions including unified digital hubs, intelligent notification management, focus shielding, and automation of routine tasks. The chapter further introduces concepts such as strategic friction, adaptive interfaces, and the right to disconnect as mechanisms to support sustained attention and well-being. It concludes by proposing new metrics for sustainable productivity that prioritize cognitive health, task quality, and long-term performance over superficial activity measures.

Chapter 7: Designing the Attention-Resilient Enterprise: A Socio-Technical Framework for Productivity and Digital Well-Being in AI-Enabled Organizational Systems

The rapid implementation of Artificial Intelligence, predictive analytics, and always-on collaborative platforms have added cognitive burdens to the modern organizations. The chapter suggests a socio-technical model named Attention-Resilient

Enterprise in which the strategic asset of the organization is attention. The framework integrates the emphasis on technology development, ethical AI regulation, and behavioral orientation to demonstrate that sustainable productivity does not conflict with digital health. Using the existing evidence in the cases, the chapter provides the particular quantifiable metrics of attention and architecture to ensure that the AI-based systems can help in creating continuity of the focus, decreasing overload, and increasing the sustainability of the stability within an organization.

Chapter 8: Algocracy, Ethical Residue, and the Quest for Meaningful Work in the Age of Algorithmic Management

This chapter explores the human and ethical implications of algorithmic management and the possibility for meaningful work in an age of algocracy. Algocracy refers to organizational environments where algorithms function as central regulatory mechanisms. The growing reliance on algorithmic decision-making introduces challenges related to agency, transparency, responsibility, and autonomy. The reign of algocracy also leads to "ethical residue", referring to the gap between quantified organizational performance metrics and the lived experience of value produced through everyday collegial acts of support. Contemporary organizations privilege outputs and performance indicators as primary indicators of success. Yet, organizational functioning depends equally on forms of contribution that resist measurement such as informal mentoring, discretionary judgment, and relational care. Recognizing this residue is essential for sustaining organizations that are efficient, morally responsible, and capable of supporting meaningful collective work in the algorithmic age.

Chapter 9: Ethics, Privacy, and Governance in AI-Enabled Information Systems: Measuring Productivity

The integration of artificial intelligence (AI) into organizational information systems (IS) has fundamentally altered the landscape of workplace productivity, decision-making, and data governance. While AI-enabled IS offer unprecedented capabilities for automating complex tasks, augmenting human cognition, and accelerating information flows, they simultaneously introduce profound ethical, privacy, and governance challenges that cannot be resolved through purely technical solutions. This chapter explores the confluence of these dimensions, arguing that sustainable productivity in AI-enabled environments must be defined and measured through an ethical lens. It develops a comprehensive framework for understanding how ethical principles, privacy regulations, and governance architectures interact with productivity outcomes in modern organizations.

Chapter 10: The Evolution of Libraries in the Digital Age: Beyond Brick and Mortar

Libraries have long served as the custodians of knowledge, playing a pivotal role in the preservation and dissemination of information throughout human history. They have evolved over time, adapting to meet community needs. This research aims to explore how modern libraries have evolved from traditional physical spaces to dynamic digital entities. It will examine the integration of digital technologies in library services, the impact on user engagement and access to information, and the challenges and opportunities this transformation presents. The study will focus on several key areas: digital collections and archives, online library services, virtual reference systems, and the role of libraries in promoting digital literacy.

Chapter 11: The Institutional Data Supply Chain in Multi-Ranking Systems: A Case Study of a Turkish Research University

This chapter explores how colleges balance the demands of international rankings with their own data. Research typically focuses on how rankings affect university tactics. The daily grind, how teams actually collect, arrange, and present data, gets less attention. The paper examines how information moves between departments prior to reaching ranking agencies using an example from a Turkish research institution. Not everything is going smoothly. Different teams employ different approaches, which results in a lot of headaches and repetitive effort. Nonetheless, informal cooperation is how people manage to get things done. The research refers to this as a "institutional data supply chain", a novel perspective that not only clarifies the procedure but also provides some useful suggestions for improving data management.

Collectively, the chapters included in this volume demonstrate that the future of organizational information systems cannot be defined solely by technological sophistication or automation capabilities. Instead, the next generation of intelligent organizational systems must prioritize ethical governance, human-centered design, cognitive sustainability, resilience, digital well-being, and meaningful work. The book highlights the importance of integrating technological innovation with psychological, organizational, and societal considerations in order to create balanced and sustainable digital ecosystems.

This volume contributes to the advancement of knowledge in Organizational Information Systems by bridging multiple disciplines, including Artificial Intelligence, Information Systems, Organizational Behavior, Human–Computer Interaction, Digital Psychology, Cognitive Ergonomics, and Sustainability Studies. It offers both conceptual foundations and applied perspectives for understanding the evolving role of AI in shaping future workplaces and intelligent enterprises.

As organizations continue to navigate the challenges of digital transformation, the discussions presented in this book aim to support researchers, practitioners, and decision-makers in designing intelligent systems that not only improve organizational performance but also enhance human well-being and sustainable productivity.

Ultimately, this book advocates for a future in which AI-enabled organizational systems serve not merely as instruments of automation, but as enablers of resilient, ethical, sustainable, and human-centered digital transformation.

Acknowledgment

The editors would like to express their sincere appreciation to all authors who contributed to this book. Their valuable research, commitment, and interdisciplinary perspectives have greatly enriched this volume and advanced the discussion surrounding AI-enabled organizational information systems, sustainable productivity, digital well-being, and human-centered digital transformation.

We are also deeply grateful to the reviewers for their thoughtful evaluations, constructive feedback, and academic expertise. Their contributions played an essential role in strengthening the quality, rigor, and relevance of the chapters included in this book.

Special thanks are extended to the publishing and editorial teams for their continuous guidance, professionalism, and support throughout the preparation and publication process of this volume.

We further acknowledge the broader academic and professional communities working in the fields of Artificial Intelligence, Information Systems, Organizational Studies, Human–Computer Interaction, Digital Transformation, and Industry 5.0. Their ongoing research and innovation continue to inspire new perspectives on the design of ethical, resilient, and human-centered organizational systems.

Finally, we would like to thank our colleagues, institutions, collaborators, and families for their encouragement and support during the development of this book.

It is our hope that this volume contributes meaningfully to future research and practice by promoting intelligent organizational systems that balance technological innovation with human well-being, ethical responsibility, and sustainable productivity.

Chapter 1
AI-Enabled Organizational Information Systems for Sustainable Productivity and Digital Well-Being

Sevil Işık Özder
http://orcid.org/0000-0003-2665-7177
Gebze Technical University, Turkey

ABSTRACT

This conceptual chapter argues that organizational information systems (OIS) should be redesigned around a dual objective: sustained productivity and digital well-being. Many enterprise systems still privilege speed, visibility, and continuous availability, yet research on information overload, interruption, technostress, cognitive load, and recovery suggests that these same conditions can degrade judgment quality, focus, and long-term performance. The chapter synthesizes these literatures and proposes the Cognitive Shield: an AI-enabled architectural layer that filters noncritical interruptions, summarizes communication streams, supports priority orchestration, and protects recovery boundaries. The chapter contributes a human-centered design framework, an implementation roadmap, and governance principles for organizations seeking to balance technological performance with psychological sustainability.

DOI: 10.4018/979-8-2600-0111-0.ch001

INTRODUCTION

Organizational Information Systems (OIS) have long occupied a strategic position in modern organizations because they coordinate activities, structure information, standardize routines, and make large-scale management possible. Traditional enterprise systems were designed to reduce uncertainty, accelerate transactions, and improve organizational control. In that model, success was typically associated with more data, more visibility, shorter response times, tighter workflow integration, and increasingly measurable forms of performance. Such assumptions made sense in industrial and early digital settings where access to timely information was scarce and where the principal challenge was to connect fragmented tasks across organizational units. Today, however, the problem has changed. In many digital workplaces, the limiting resource is no longer access to information. It is the human capacity to process, prioritize, and act on incessant streams of information without losing focus, judgment, motivation, or well-being.

The contemporary organization is characterized by an unprecedented density of digital interactions. Employees navigate collaboration platforms, enterprise dashboards, project boards, messaging applications, mobile devices, and AI-supported services simultaneously, and the cumulative burden of these channels has become a central concern in research on information overload, interruption, and technostress (Eppler & Mengis, 2004; Mark et al., 2005; Tarafdar et al., 2007).

This chapter begins from a tension that now defines many digital workplaces. Many OIS still reflect an efficiency logic that made sense when information was scarce: more activity, more connectivity, more data exposure, and faster response were treated as signs of better performance. In hyper-connected environments, that assumption is harder to sustain. Digital abundance can become counterproductive when it exceeds human processing limits. Information overload undermines decision quality (Eppler & Mengis, 2004). Frequent interruptions increase stress and frustration even when workers compensate by accelerating their pace (Mark et al., 2008). Technostress emerges when information and communication technologies create overload, invasion, complexity, or uncertainty in users' work lives (Ayyagari et al., 2011; Tarafdar et al., 2007). Mobile and connected technologies produce paradoxical experiences in which empowerment and control coexist with dependency and pressure (Jarvenpaa & Lang, 2005; Mazmanian et al., 2013). Digital platforms also intensify behavioral visibility and algorithmic forms of control that can narrow autonomy and distort how performance is recognized (Kellogg et al., 2020; Leonardi & Treem, 2020).

The consequences of this shift are organizational as much as individual. When employees are exposed to excessive alerts, overlapping channels, constant coordination requests, and ambiguous priorities, the result is not simply inconvenience but reduced decision quality, impaired recovery, and a higher probability of chronic strain over time (Ayyagari et al., 2011; Mark et al., 2008; Sonnentag & Fritz, 2015).

The chapter argues that OIS should be redesigned around a broader and more durable conception of productivity. In digital organizations, productivity is better understood as the sustained capacity of people and systems to produce valuable outcomes without degrading the cognitive and emotional conditions that make such outcomes possible. This view is consistent with work on cognitive load, flow, and sustainable recovery (Csikszentmihalyi, 1990; Sonnentag & Fritz, 2015; Sweller, 1988).

AI has an important place in this argument. Public and managerial discourse often presents AI in organizations through the lenses of automation, surveillance, and efficiency gains. Such uses are real and consequential, but they are incomplete. AI can also be conceptualized as an augmentative infrastructure that reduces unnecessary cognitive burden and helps restore fit between technological complexity and human capacity (Raisch & Krakowski, 2021). This chapter develops that view. It proposes that AI should be repositioned as a "Cognitive Shield": a provisional design concept for an AI-enabled coordination layer that classifies incoming signals, bundles or defers noncritical interruptions, summarizes fragmented communication, supports priority orchestration, and protects recovery boundaries. From the outset, then, the term does not refer to a single standalone application. It refers to a family of interoperable design capabilities that could be embedded across enterprise platforms so that OIS become not only faster and more visible, but also more selective, more intelligible, and more humane in the timing and form of digital demands. In this conception, AI becomes an architecture of protection and augmentation rather than a mechanism of compression and control.

The chapter develops this argument by diagnosing the structural pathologies of contemporary OIS, especially the ways notification density, communication fragmentation, behavioral visibility, and expectation escalation intensify cognitive strain and technostress (Eppler & Mengis, 2004; Kellogg et al., 2020; Leonardi & Treem, 2020; Tarafdar et al., 2007). It then reframes productivity as sustainable cognitive performance, treats flow as a relevant design target for enterprise systems, and proposes the Cognitive Shield as a theory-informed AI layer for filtering, sequencing, and summarizing digital demands. The discussion closes by outlining managerial and governance implications for organizations seeking a more human-centered digital infrastructure.

CONCEPTUAL APPROACH AND CHAPTER CONTRIBUTIONS

The chapter adopts a conceptual integration approach rather than an empirical one. It links research on information overload and interruption from HCI, technostress and digital work from MIS, socio-technical systems thinking, organizational studies on behavioral visibility and algorithmic management, and psychological work on cognitive load, flow, and recovery. These strands are not reviewed exhaustively. They are combined because each explains a distinct failure mechanism in contemporary OIS and together support a move from diagnosis to design.

The contribution is threefold, but the argument is developed as an integrated whole. The chapter reframes productivity as sustainable cognitive performance linked to attention, judgment quality, and recovery. It also introduces the Cognitive Shield as a design vocabulary for AI as a protective and augmentative layer within enterprise systems, while connecting that architecture to policy, ethics, and role-sensitive deployment choices through an implementation and governance roadmap.

Because the chapter is conceptual, its architectural claims remain provisional rather than validated.

METHODOLOGICAL POSITION OF THE CONCEPTUAL SYNTHESIS

The chapter's conceptual approach synthesizes established research streams rather than testing a new empirical model. Its evidentiary logic is integrative. It draws on studies of information overload, interruption, technostress, behavioral visibility, algorithmic control, cognitive load, flow, recovery, and augmentation-oriented AI to identify a recurring socio-technical problem: many enterprise systems increase the speed and visibility of work while externalizing the cognitive and emotional costs of digital abundance to users. The contribution is not a statistical estimate of effect size. It is a theory-informed design argument that connects dispersed findings into a coherent framework for redesigning OIS around sustainable cognitive performance.

This methodological position also clarifies the strength and limits of the chapter's claims. Claims about overload, interruption, technostress, recovery, and digital visibility are grounded in prior empirical and theoretical literature. Claims about the Cognitive Shield remain more provisional because the Shield is presented as a design concept rather than as a validated product or implemented system. The chapter treats the Cognitive Shield as a researchable architectural hypothesis: if digital strain emerges partly from fragmented signals, unclear priorities, and weak boundary protection, then AI-enabled curation, sequencing, summarization, and explanation may improve both performance quality and digital well-being when they are governed appropriately.

A conceptual synthesis is appropriate here because the problem crosses disciplinary boundaries. No single literature fully explains how OIS, AI mediation, cognitive load, flow, recovery, behavioral visibility, and organizational governance interact. Conceptual integration helps clarify mechanisms, formulate design principles, and identify conditions that future empirical work can test. The structure is meant to avoid overclaiming while still offering a practical framework for organizational leaders, IT architects, and scholars who need language for evaluating AI-enabled systems beyond narrow efficiency metrics.

THE PRODUCTIVITY PARADOX OF HYPER-CONNECTED OIS

The dominant narrative of digital transformation assumes that increasing connectivity produces increasing performance. Enterprise systems promise faster communication, shorter cycle times, more apparent visibility, and better managerial oversight. Yet studies of mobile work and information abundance show that more connectivity can also produce contradiction, overload, and declining quality of attention when systems privilege immediacy over cognitive fit (Eppler & Mengis, 2004; Jarvenpaa & Lang, 2005).

This paradox becomes clear in the move from information scarcity to information abundance. Earlier enterprise systems addressed a genuine problem: people often lacked timely access to relevant data. Today, dashboards, inboxes, chat channels, and algorithmic alerts generate more signals than workers can realistically interpret, rank, and use. Under these conditions, performance depends less on sheer access to information than on the capacity to discriminate between what deserves immediate attention and what can be deferred or ignored (Eppler & Mengis, 2004; Mark et al., 2005).

Research on information overload helps explain why more information is not always better information. Eppler and Mengis (2004) show that overload emerges from the interaction between information characteristics, task complexity, personal processing limits, and organizational conditions. In OIS terms, overload develops when systems multiply dashboards, alerts, channels, and coordination requests faster than users can convert them into meaningful action. The cost is not only delay. Overload can push people toward superficial scanning, simplified judgment, and reactive decision making.

Interruption is another part of the same paradox. Most digital tools are built to optimize immediacy. Collaboration platforms privilege real-time exchange, mobile devices extend access across space and time, and notification systems turn passive information into active demand. Immediacy is valuable for truly urgent work, yet it also imposes a persistent cognitive tax. Interruptions force people to stop, reorient, and later reconstruct task context. Mark et al. (2008) found that interrupted work may be completed more quickly only because workers compensate by accelerating their pace, and this speed comes with greater stress, frustration, and effort. Response speed alone is a poor measure of success. A tool may accelerate visible action while invisibly increasing mental strain.

The architecture of control is also changing. Contemporary OIS do not only record transactions; they shape the observability of behavior. Leonardi and Treem (2020) describe behavioral visibility as a defining feature of organizing in digitalized environments, where systems make it easier to see what others are doing and when they are doing it. Visibility can support coordination and accountability, but it can also intensify comparison, performative busyness, and pressure to remain visibly engaged. Kellogg et al. (2020) show that algorithmic systems extend this dynamic by encoding managerial priorities into rules, metrics, rankings, and automated evaluative processes. Employees may end up working not only to perform well, but to perform in ways the system can recognize.

This matters because what is measurable in digital systems is not always what is valuable. Complex knowledge work often depends on activities that generate few visible traces, such as reflection, synthesis, deliberate problem framing, and uninterrupted analysis. Research on algorithmic control and behavioral visibility offers an important warning: digital traceability can displace substantive value when systems overreward visible responsiveness and underrecognize deep work (Kellogg et al., 2020; Leonardi & Treem, 2020).

The paradox of hyper-connectivity also manifests in employee autonomy. Mobile and flexible technologies are often celebrated for expanding freedom over where and when work can be performed. Yet research on connected work shows that this flexibility can generate a norm of continual accessibility. Mazmanian et al. (2013) describe this as an autonomy paradox: the same devices that appear to grant control over time and location can intensify expectations to remain available. Jarvenpaa and Lang (2005) similarly identify mobile technology paradoxes in which empowerment coexists with dependency. Applied to OIS, these studies suggest that flexibility tools can quietly transform optional connection into moralized availability.

The consequences extend beyond immediate strain. Constant connectivity erodes recovery opportunities, making it harder for employees to psychologically detach from work. Recovery research shows that detachment during nonwork time is essential for replenishing depleted resources and maintaining long-term functioning (Sonnentag & Fritz, 2015). When OIS extend alerts, tasks, and communication into evenings and weekends, they compress the boundaries that make recovery possible. Over time, this contributes to fatigue, lower engagement, and weaker judgment.

These dynamics place many OIS between two competing design philosophies. One approach escalates connectivity, responsiveness, measurement, and immediacy. A more humane approach preserves focus, sequences demands intelligently, and recognizes that sustainable performance depends on bounded attention and periodic recovery rather than uninterrupted availability (Csikszentmihalyi, 1990; Sonnentag & Fritz, 2015; Sweller, 1988).

DIAGNOSING THE STRUCTURAL PATHOLOGIES OF CONTEMPORARY OIS

The most important problems in contemporary OIS rarely arise from one tool in isolation. They arise from the combined ecology of platforms, norms, and data-rich interfaces that together shape how work is distributed, signaled, and interpreted. Research on fragmented work and digital traceability suggests that cumulative system effects rather than any single application often create the most serious burdens on attention and sensemaking (Leonardi & Treem, 2020; Mark et al., 2005).

Notification inflation is one recurring pathology. In many organizations, every platform claims the right to issue alerts because each system is optimized locally around its own service deadlines. Messaging applications announce mentions and replies, project tools signal status changes, enterprise systems generate workflow events, and email remains a catch-all for background coordination. When alerts are not differentiated by urgency or task dependence, the result is a continuous, low-grade attentional tax that accumulates across the day (Bailey & Konstan, 2006; Eppler & Mengis, 2004; Mark et al., 2008).

Communication fragmentation is another pathology. Knowledge work often requires assembling understanding from multiple conversational traces scattered across threads, meeting notes, project boards, and informal messaging. The same issue may be discussed in several places with slightly different language and slightly different contextual assumptions. Under such conditions, reconstruction work grows while coherence declines, and people expend energy not on analysis but on reassembling context (Eppler & Mengis, 2004; Mark et al., 2005).

Priority ambiguity adds another burden. In many digital environments, systems generate tasks effectively but do little to rank them in relation to strategic importance, temporal dependence, or human cognitive limits. Workers face queues composed of heterogeneous demands: some are urgent but low value, some are important but deferrable, some are socially visible, and some are analytically vital but opaque. In the absence of intelligent triage, workers often respond to the most recent or most visible demand rather than to the one that best advances organizational goals (Eppler & Mengis, 2004; Sweller, 1988).

Visibility pressure is equally important. Digital systems generate extensive traces of activity: login times, message counts, response speeds, task statuses, revision histories, and platform presence indicators. These traces can create implicit expectations of constant demonstration and can shift organizational attention toward visible responsiveness rather than substantive contribution. The problem is not visibility per se but the incentive structure it creates when workers feel compelled to maximize observable activity even at the expense of uninterrupted problem solving (Kellogg et al., 2020; Leonardi & Treem, 2020).

Boundary erosion is the final pathology considered here. Because digital platforms travel with users across devices and locations, the formal end of the workday no longer guarantees a practical end to work demands. After-hours pings, asynchronous messaging, and weakly enforced response norms can gradually transform flexibility into expanded availability. Research on mobile devices and work-life balance shows that this spillover increases the difficulty of psychological detachment and recovery, both of which are essential for sustained performance (Mazmanian et al., 2013; Sarker et al., 2012; Sonnentag & Fritz, 2015).

These pathologies reinforce one another. Notification inflation increases fragmentation by distributing information across more micro-events and threads. Fragmentation intensifies priority ambiguity because workers cannot easily determine what is central or consequential. Visibility pressure then rewards rapid response behavior, which further normalizes interruption and boundary erosion. Many organizations are dealing not with isolated annoyances but with a reinforcing system of digital strain (Ayyagari et al., 2011; Mark et al., 2005; Tarafdar et al., 2007).

The organizational cost of these pathologies is often underestimated because it is distributed and partly hidden. Firms can count tickets, messages, response times, and logged activity, but they often cannot easily observe the reconstructed context-switching costs, the quality losses caused by interruption, or the recovery deficits caused by chronic digital spillover. When these hidden costs are ignored, organizations can mistakenly interpret high digital traffic as evidence of high performance (Ayyagari et al., 2011; Mark et al., 2008; Tarafdar et al., 2007).

These burdens are also unevenly distributed. Frontline service workers, managers, analysts, healthcare staff, designers, educators, and remote teams all experience digital strain differently because their work rhythms, accountability structures, and temporal constraints differ. Even so, research on fragmented work and role-specific mobile expectations suggests that overload is rarely uniform across roles and that system redesign must be sensitive to occupational differences rather than assuming a single ideal pattern of digital responsiveness (Mark et al., 2005; Sarker et al., 2012).

A further problem lies in the moral language surrounding digital strain. Organizations often frame overload as an issue of resilience, preference, or personal boundary setting. This framing obscures the role of architecture. A worker who receives hundreds of prompts each week is not simply failing at focus; they may be operating within a system that has no coherent logic of notification governance, no prioritization support, and no protection for deep work. Diagnosing these conditions clarifies the direction of redesign. Contemporary OIS often optimize for visibility, immediacy, and traceability while underinvesting in curation, coherence, and recovery. The user is asked to function as their own filter, integrator, prioritizer, and boundary manager under conditions of escalating digital complexity. This is the design gap that the Cognitive Shield seeks to address.

THEORETICAL FOUNDATIONS FOR HUMAN-CENTERED REDESIGN

The structural pathologies described above require a theoretical explanation, not only a list of symptoms. A meaningful redesign needs a framework that explains why notification inflation, communication fragmentation, visibility pressure, and boundary erosion become so costly in digital work. For much of the history of enterprise technology, systems were evaluated primarily in terms of efficiency, standardization, and control. These criteria remain important, but they are insufficient in environments where the key constraints on performance are increasingly cognitive, temporal, and psychological. A human-centered redesign benefits from a framework that connects system architecture to the dynamics of attention, motivation, autonomy, and recovery. This chapter draws together five particularly relevant lenses: socio-technical thinking, cognitive load theory, flow theory, technostress research, and research on digital visibility and algorithmic control.

Socio-technical thinking provides the broadest foundation. Its central insight is that organizational performance emerges from the joint optimization of social and technical systems rather than from technical optimization alone. In practice, systems should be designed around how people actually coordinate, interpret information, and exercise judgment, not merely around what technologies can technically deliver (Trist & Bamforth, 1951).

Cognitive load theory deepens this argument by specifying limits on information processing. Sweller (1988) distinguishes between the cognitive resources available to a person and the demands placed on those resources during learning and problem solving. Although the theory was originally developed in educational contexts, its relevance to digital work is considerable. Knowledge work relies heavily on working memory, selective attention, and schema activation. When organizational systems require workers to monitor many channels, interpret large volumes of information, or continually switch tasks, they increase extraneous load that competes with the resources needed for core work. A human-centered OIS should be evaluated partly by how effectively it reduces extraneous cognitive load and preserves attentional resources for higher-value reasoning.

Flow theory adds a motivational and experiential dimension to this view. Csikszentmihalyi (1990) describes flow as a state of deep involvement in which attention is intensely focused, goals are clear, feedback is immediate, and action feels coherent rather than fragmented. In organizational settings, flow matters because many forms of valuable work require sustained immersion: strategic analysis, design, writing, diagnosis, coding, and complex problem solving. Yet most contemporary OIS are poorly aligned with the preconditions of flow. They expose workers to continual notifications, ambiguous priorities, communication sprawl, and interface switching. If flow is accepted as a relevant benchmark for sustainable productivity, then system design must include the protection of uninterrupted focus and the reduction of avoidable fragmentation.

Technostress research helps explain the costs of failing to do so. Tarafdar et al. (2007) demonstrate that information and communication technologies can create stressors that contribute to role stress and reduced productivity. Ayyagari et al. (2011) expand this line of work by showing how technology characteristics such as overload, complexity, invasion, uncertainty, and pace can produce strain in users. These studies are valuable because they name the organizational consequences of design choices that are often normalized. Overloaded inboxes, unclear cross-platform coordination, always-on expectations, and rapidly changing interfaces are not trivial inconveniences. They are antecedents of strain that affect mood, concentration, self-efficacy, and performance.

Research on mobile and connected work further shows that digital systems produce paradoxical experiences rather than linear improvements. Jarvenpaa and Lang (2005) identify several mobile technology paradoxes, including experiences of empowerment alongside enslavement and independence alongside dependence. Mazmanian et al. (2013) show that technologies associated with flexibility can simultaneously reinforce expectations of constant accessibility. These paradoxes caution against simplistic claims that more mobility or more access always benefits users. The same capability can be experienced as supportive or oppressive depending on how norms, metrics, and system defaults are configured.

Behavioral visibility and algorithmic management research adds a power-sensitive perspective. Leonardi and Treem (2020) argue that digital systems make behavior increasingly visible in organizational life, changing how workers learn from one another and coordinate. Visibility can have real benefits, but it can also intensify performative pressure. Kellogg et al. (2020) show that algorithmic systems reshape workplace control through mechanisms that classify, direct, evaluate, and sanction work. Such systems may reduce discretion, narrow the meaning of contribution, and create a contested terrain between organizational goals and worker autonomy.

A human-centered redesign must ask not only how to make systems smarter, but also how to prevent intelligence from being translated into overcontrol.

Behavioral visibility also needs careful definition. In Leonardi and Treem's (2020) formulation, the term describes what digitalized organizational environments make newly observable: activities, response patterns, interactions, and traces of coordination that were previously less visible. The term is not inherently negative. It becomes problematic when visibility is coupled with performance cultures, metrics, or monitoring practices that convert observability into pressure, comparison, or coercive responsiveness. That distinction matters because the redesign problem is not visibility itself, but the institutional and architectural conditions under which visibility drifts into performative exposure and intensified control.

These literatures share a common point: organizational systems should be judged by the fit they produce between digital demands and human capacities. When the volume, speed, and fragmentation of digital signals exceed working memory, erode recovery time, and encourage performative visibility, system efficiency at the technical layer can coexist with dysfunction at the human layer (Ayyagari et al., 2011; Csikszentmihalyi, 1990; Sweller, 1988).

A human-centered redesign reverses that logic. Instead of requiring individuals to continually adapt themselves to the escalating complexity of enterprise systems, the system should adapt to the attentional, temporal, and recovery needs of the user. This view is also compatible with augmentation-oriented perspectives on AI, which argue that intelligent systems create greater value when they complement human judgment rather than merely replacing or intensifying it (Raisch & Krakowski, 2021).

Across these theoretical lenses, the pathologies diagnosed in the previous section are not isolated annoyances. They are predictable consequences of a misfit between digital system logics and human cognitive, motivational, and recovery limits. The redesign challenge is to develop OIS that reduce this misfit rather than externalize it onto workers. That challenge motivates the reframing of productivity developed in the next section.

REFRAMING PRODUCTIVITY: FROM THROUGHPUT TO SUSTAINABLE COGNITIVE PERFORMANCE

The preceding sections establish the problem space and the theoretical lenses needed to understand it. The next question is what a more appropriate productivity model would look like. The central argument of this chapter is that organizational productivity in digital environments should be reframed as sustainable cognitive performance. The phrase brings together three concerns: productivity involves judgment, coherence, creativity, and error avoidance, not only volume or speed;

these outcomes depend on attentional continuity, manageable information load, and opportunities for recovery; and because those conditions are shaped by systems, productivity must be treated as an architectural and governance issue rather than as a purely individual trait.

Traditional productivity metrics remain useful for certain tasks. Throughput, response time, utilization, and output counts can still be valuable indicators in transactional settings. The difficulty arises when those metrics become the sole basis of organizational judgment. Under those conditions, productivity is often redefined as visible activity rather than durable contribution, and systems begin to reward the fastest response instead of the highest-quality response (Kellogg et al., 2020; Leonardi & Treem, 2020).

A sustainability perspective corrects this distortion by incorporating temporal durability. A work pattern should not be considered productive if it delivers short-term output while producing long-term fatigue, rising error probability, degraded attention, or weakened recovery. This view follows logically from cognitive load theory and recovery research, both of which stress that performance depends on bounded mental capacity and opportunities for detachment and replenishment (Sonnentag & Fritz, 2015; Sweller, 1988).

Digital well-being should move from the margins of organizational discourse to the center of systems design. In many institutions, well-being is treated as a welfare or culture concern. Yet interruption density, ambiguous priorities, and after-hours digital spillover directly shape whether employees can think clearly, sustain engagement, and maintain high-quality judgment during complex work. Digital well-being is not a soft add-on but a precondition for cognitive performance (Csikszentmihalyi, 1990; Tarafdar et al., 2007).

This view has practical implications for evaluation. Organizations need broader indicators that capture whether their systems are supporting or degrading attention. These indicators might include average uninterrupted focus time, the volume of after-hours digital activity, rates of context switching, perceived autonomy, time spent reconstructing fragmented information, and the frequency of user-initiated overrides to AI triage. Such measures make it easier to evaluate whether systems are genuinely reducing cognitive friction rather than simply accelerating visible activity (Mark et al., 2008; Sonnentag & Fritz, 2015).

It also changes how organizations should think about optimization. In conventional system design, optimization often means removing friction that slows transactions. In a human-centered design, some frictions are functional because they create time for reflection, reduce unnecessary interruption, or limit low-value escalation. System designers need to distinguish between productive friction and destructive friction rather than assuming that all delay is wasteful (Bailey & Konstan, 2006; Sweller, 1988).

Digital well-being can be understood through four interrelated dimensions: cognitive clarity, attentional continuity, temporal boundary integrity, and agency over interruption and sequencing. Cognitive clarity means that users can identify what matters without constant reconstruction effort. Attentional continuity means that systems preserve meaningful blocks of focused work. Temporal boundary integrity means that work demands do not routinely spill into recovery periods. Agency means that users can understand and influence how digital signals reach them. These dimensions align digital well-being with measurable conditions of sustainable performance (Csikszentmihalyi, 1990; Sonnentag & Fritz, 2015; Sweller, 1988).

Reframing productivity also requires revising managerial assumptions about responsiveness. Fast response is sometimes necessary, but when it becomes the default expectation it creates a hidden organizational tax. Workers learn that acknowledging signals quickly matters more than engaging with them deeply. In organizations built on such norms, managers inadvertently encourage shallow processing, anxiety, and performative speed at the expense of durable contribution. A more appropriate norm is calibrated responsiveness: reply expectations should vary by role, task criticality, and time horizon (Mazmanian et al., 2013; Sarker et al., 2012).

The same argument applies to organizational measurement design. If a firm says it values sustainable productivity but still relies almost exclusively on response speed, task completion counts, and visible activity traces, the measurement system will continue to reward interruption-heavy behavior. A more coherent scorecard would combine operational indicators with human-centered ones: uninterrupted work intervals, escalation ratios, after-hours spillover, perceived clarity of priorities, and rates of rework caused by fragmented coordination. These measures would not replace conventional metrics, but they would help organizations judge whether apparent efficiency gains are being purchased at the expense of the cognitive conditions on which knowledge work depends. Measurement is not a neutral afterthought; it is one of the main ways an organization decides what kind of productivity its systems are actually designed to produce.

This argument provides the normative basis for the design framework proposed in the next section. If sustainable productivity depends on protecting attention, clarifying priorities, preserving autonomy, and supporting recovery, then enterprise systems should include active mechanisms for doing precisely those things. The issue is no longer whether organizations should care about digital well-being in the abstract. The issue is how they can build it into system architecture. The answer advanced in this chapter is the Cognitive Shield: an AI-enabled layer that translates the principles of sustainable cognitive performance into concrete design capabilities embedded within OIS themselves.

THE COGNITIVE SHIELD: AN AI-ENABLED ARCHITECTURE FOR DIGITAL WELL-BEING

The idea of a Cognitive Shield begins with a simple design inversion. Instead of assuming that the worker must continually absorb and regulate digitally generated demands, the system should assume part of that regulatory burden. In this model, enterprise technologies no longer act merely as channels for information transmission; they could also function as mediators that help preserve attention and sequence demands according to cognitive and organizational relevance (Raisch & Krakowski, 2021; Sweller, 1988).

The Cognitive Shield can be understood as an architectural layer that sits across the enterprise application ecosystem. It would not replace core business systems such as ERP, CRM, workflow management, or collaboration platforms. Rather, it would orchestrate signals from those systems into a form better aligned with human attention, recovery, and judgment. In doing so, the Shield extends sociotechnical and augmentation-oriented design principles into the infrastructure of everyday digital work (Raisch & Krakowski, 2021; Trist & Bamforth, 1951).

The architecture rests on six design principles: context sensitivity, proportionality, explainability, reversibility, boundary protection, and role-based adaptation. Context sensitivity recognizes that the relevance and interruptive value of a signal depend on the user, the task, the moment, and the surrounding workload. Proportionality requires that signals be presented in ways matched to their urgency and consequence. Explainability gives users a way to understand why a signal was surfaced, deferred, or summarized. Reversibility gives users meaningful override mechanisms. Boundary protection helps preserve recovery time rather than colonize it. Role-based adaptation prevents the system from assuming a universal work rhythm across occupations (Csikszentmihalyi, 1990; Mazmanian et al., 2013; Sonnentag & Fritz, 2015).

The Cognitive Shield can be represented as five interacting layers. A signal ingestion layer would collect metadata from communication tools, enterprise applications, and workflow systems. A classification layer would estimate urgency, task dependence, sender relevance, and likely cognitive cost. An orchestration layer would determine whether information should be delivered immediately, deferred, bundled, or summarized. An interface layer would present outputs through dashboards, summary panes, focus modes, or low-interruption notifications. A governance layer would set policies for explainability, auditability, override rights, retention, and fairness (Kellogg et al., 2020; Leonardi & Treem, 2020; Raisch & Krakowski, 2021). Figure 1 visualizes how these layers connect from enterprise inputs to user-facing intervention under governance constraints.

Figure 1. Conceptual Architecture of the Cognitive Shield

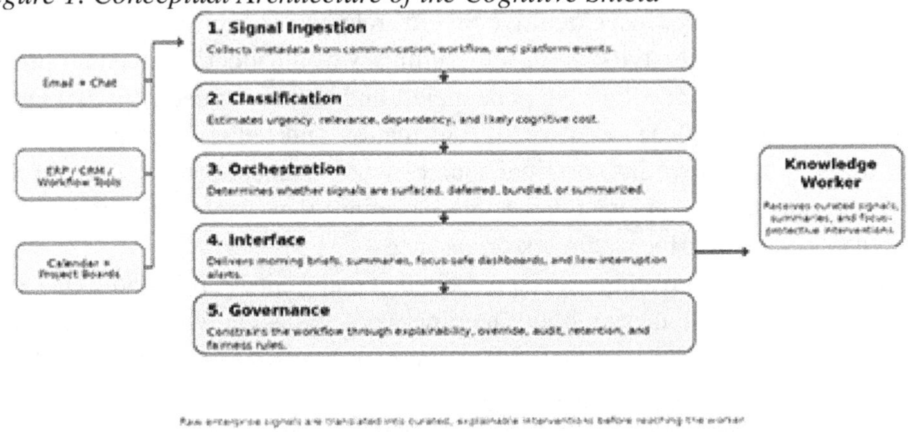

Note. Developed by the author based on the chapter's synthesis of Trist and Bamforth (1951), Sweller (1988), Csikszentmihalyi (1990), Tarafdar et al. (2007), Leonardi and Treem (2020), Kellogg et al. (2020), Raisch and Krakowski (2021), and Brown et al. (2020).

Because this architecture is conceptual, the capabilities described below should be read as plausible design functions rather than empirically settled solutions. Their value will depend on role demands, organizational norms, technical quality, and governance safeguards. The point is not to claim that AI mediation necessarily improves digital work, but to specify how it might do so while preserving worker agency, source transparency, and override. Framed in this way, the Cognitive Shield becomes a researchable design hypothesis: if interruption, fragmentation, and boundary erosion are structural drivers of digital strain, then enterprise systems that selectively curate and sequence demands may improve both performance quality and digital well-being.

Context-aware notification filtering is one of the most valuable functions of this architecture. Most enterprise tools treat every event as self-justifying. A Cognitive Shield would instead apply a triage logic: signals that clearly require immediate response would be surfaced, time-sensitive but noncritical items could be bundled into periodic digests, and low-value interruptions might be delayed or muted. Such filtering may reduce context switching and support longer blocks of concentrated work, which is especially important for cognitively demanding tasks (Bailey & Konstan, 2006; Mark et al., 2008).

Communication summarization is another key function. Workers increasingly confront long email threads, repeated updates across channels, dense meeting transcripts, and parallel conversations about related topics. Large Language Models (LLMs) are relevant here because recent work has shown that large-scale language models can perform a wide range of text synthesis tasks and that LLM research now treats summarization as one of their central application domains (Brown et al., 2020; Zhao et al., 2023). In a Cognitive Shield architecture, summarization should be structured, not merely stylistic. A useful summary would identify decisions made, unresolved questions, deadlines, dependencies, and recommended next actions. It should distinguish between confirmed information and tentative discussion and allow users to drill down into original sources when nuance matters. Used in this way, LLMs would not replace human interpretation; they may reduce the cost of regaining context after focused work or absence.

Priority orchestration addresses a problem that many enterprise systems leave to the user. They generate tasks without helping workers decide which ones deserve attention now, which can wait, and which are merely visible. A Cognitive Shield might rank demands using deadlines, strategic importance, role relevance, and cognitive cost. Rather than assuming that all incoming tasks are equally urgent, the architecture could help users and teams distinguish between genuine dependencies and merely visible demands. This function is particularly important in environments where workers face queues of mixed importance and limited attentional capacity (Eppler & Mengis, 2004; Sweller, 1988).

Flow protection is another essential function. If flow is treated as a legitimate organizational resource, systems should explicitly defend the conditions that make it possible. A Cognitive Shield could create protected focus windows, suppress noncritical alerts during cognitively demanding work, and bundle routine messages into periodic digests. Used carefully, such features would not prevent collaboration; rather, they may reduce the unnecessary fragmentation that undermines deep engagement, analytic quality, and creative problem solving (Csikszentmihalyi, 1990; Mark et al., 2005; Mark et al., 2008).

Boundary management and recovery support are also necessary. Many organizations acknowledge the importance of reducing after-hours pressure, yet their communication systems often operate as if workers have no nonwork time. A Cognitive Shield could embed calendar-aware and policy-aware rules so that noncritical messages are delayed outside agreed working hours, recovery periods, or focus-protected time blocks. In doing so, the system would translate research on recovery and psychological detachment into everyday system behavior (Mazmanian et al., 2013; Sarker et al., 2012; Sonnentag & Fritz, 2015).

Load balancing and coordination support bring the argument to the team level. Digital overload is not only an individual problem; it also emerges from poorly distributed work, repeated requests for the same input, unclear ownership, or coordination concentrated on a few central actors. The Shield could generate team-level diagnostics showing where bottlenecks, duplication, and interruption hotspots are located. Here, AI would be used not to intensify surveillance but to identify systemic patterns that can be redesigned at the workflow level (Kellogg et al., 2020; Leonardi & Treem, 2020).

Illustrative Use Case: A Day in the Life of a Knowledge Worker

A brief scenario helps translate the architecture into practice. Consider a product manager in a hybrid technology firm who begins the day with overnight emails, messages from a global team, project-board updates, and analytics alerts. In a conventional OIS environment, these demands arrive as a largely undifferentiated stream, forcing rapid decisions about urgency, ownership, and timing before higher-value planning can begin.

Under a Cognitive Shield model, the day would look different. Before the work session begins, the system could generate a short brief that clusters overnight messages by project, identifies urgent dependencies, and suppresses low-value duplication. During the protected work block, only genuinely time-critical items would surface immediately; other messages could be bundled into a later digest.

This scenario should not be read as full algorithmic substitution. The worker would still inspect sources, override priorities, and decide which items warrant action. The system's role would be to reduce avoidable fragmentation, not replace human judgment.

Sectoral Contexts

The same logic also travels across sectors. In multinational technology teams, the Shield could separate truly time-zone-sensitive dependencies from routine overnight traffic, reducing the pressure to remain effectively on call across regions. In healthcare administration, the same triage logic would need a stricter threshold: patient-safety or care-coordination alerts should surface immediately, whereas routine scheduling, billing, and documentation prompts could be bundled. In both settings, shielding works by differentiating criticality rather than suppressing visibility indiscriminately.

The Cognitive Shield is best understood not as a single feature but as a design philosophy instantiated through several capabilities. Table 1 contrasts the dominant logic of conventional OIS with the logic of a human-centered, shielded architecture.

Table 1. Conventional OIS Versus the Cognitive Shield Model

Design Dimension	Conventional OIS Logic	Cognitive Shield Logic
Notification Design	Each platform pushes events according to its own local urgency model.	Signals are triaged across platforms so interruption is reserved for genuinely critical events.
Information Flow	Users receive raw streams and reconstruct meaning themselves.	AI summarizes, clusters, and sequences information to reduce context-rebuilding costs.
Productivity Assumption	More visibility, speed, and connectivity are treated as inherently beneficial.	Performance is tied to sustainable attention, clarity, and high-quality output over time.
User Role	Workers act as their own filter, prioritizer, and boundary manager.	The system shares responsibility for curation, prioritization, and protection of focus.
Control and Evaluation	Behavioral traces can drift toward surveillance and performative busyness.	Governance limits data use and favors augmentation, explainability, and user agency.
Temporal Logic	Immediate responsiveness becomes the default norm.	Response expectations are calibrated by role, context, and recovery needs.

Note. Table 1 is author-developed and synthesizes arguments from Sweller (1988), Csikszentmihalyi (1990), Tarafdar et al. (2007), Leonardi and Treem (2020), Kellogg et al. (2020), Raisch and Krakowski (2021), Brown et al. (2020), and Zhao et al. (2023).

Failure Modes and Safeguards

Any persuasive account of the Cognitive Shield must also address the possibility of failure. Misclassification is the most immediate risk. A system that defers or bundles the wrong signal may create more damage than the interruption it was designed to prevent. In high-tempo environments, a low-frequency but high-consequence event may be difficult to distinguish from a routine update. Triage models should be calibrated conservatively, configured by role, and continuously audited against downstream errors rather than evaluated only for average efficiency gains. Human override and sender-designated escalation channels are essential safeguards, not optional features (Bailey & Konstan, 2006; Mark et al., 2008).

Summary distortion presents another risk. LLM-generated summaries may compress nuance, omit minority positions, overstate consensus, or reproduce inaccuracies present in source material. These risks are especially important in organizational contexts because a misleading summary can change not only comprehension but also accountability, timing, and perceived agreement. Summaries in a Cognitive Shield environment should remain source-linked, confidence-qualified, and easy to inspect. The correct design norm is assistive compression, not authoritative replacement. Brown et al. (2020) and Zhao et al. (2023) are useful reminders here: the same capabilities that make LLMs powerful for text generation also make careful evaluation, contextual grounding, and human verification indispensable.

Governance drift is a more institutional risk. Even a system introduced in the language of well-being can be repurposed into a more refined surveillance apparatus if leaders treat triage logs, summary behaviors, or override patterns as new performance metrics. Such drift would undermine the legitimacy of the architecture and reproduce the very visibility pressures the chapter seeks to reduce. To guard against this outcome, organizations need explicit purpose limitation, role-sensitive data minimization, audit trails for policy changes, and worker representation in governance processes. If a Shield is allowed to become a covert instrument for ranking responsiveness or monitoring micro-behavior, it ceases to be a shield at all (Kellogg et al., 2020; Leonardi & Treem, 2020).

Over-personalization can also undermine the design. A highly individualized system may learn a user's habits so well that it stabilizes existing patterns rather than challenging dysfunctional ones. For example, if a worker has adapted to chronic after-hours activity, the system may incorrectly infer that such activity is acceptable or even preferred. Participatory calibration is crucial. Users should be able to inspect and adjust preference settings, but organizational policy must also establish baseline protections that do not depend solely on individual self-advocacy. Good design requires both personalization and normative limits (Mazmanian et al., 2013; Sarker et al., 2012; Sonnentag & Fritz, 2015).

For these reasons, trust cannot be treated as a soft adoption issue that appears after design. It must be built into the architecture from the beginning. Workers will only accept AI mediation if they believe the system serves their interests rather than merely making them easier to govern. Transparency, meaningful override rights, limited data collection, clear governance boundaries, and visible channels for contesting system behavior are conditions of legitimacy for augmentation-oriented AI at work (Kellogg et al., 2020; Raisch & Krakowski, 2021).

MANAGERIAL, ETHICAL, AND GOVERNANCE IMPLICATIONS

Any attempt to redesign OIS for sustainable productivity will fail if it is treated purely as a technical upgrade. Digital strain is produced not only by interfaces but also by norms, incentives, managerial rhetoric, and role expectations. Human-centered OIS require institutional change as well as interface change (Ayyagari et al., 2011; Tarafdar et al., 2007).

Leaders must redefine what they publicly treat as evidence of good performance. If managers continue to reward instant responsiveness, visible busyness, and perpetual availability, employees will rationally optimize for those signals. A more sustainable model requires leaders to value judgment quality, coherent prioritization, and focused completion alongside responsiveness (Kellogg et al., 2020; Leonardi & Treem, 2020).

Policy is also needed. Human-centered OIS require explicit organizational rules about interruption, availability, and data use. Without policy, even carefully designed interfaces will be weakened by informal expectations of constant reachability. The right to disconnect should be treated not only as an HR principle but as compliance by design: systems can encode quiet hours, escalation exceptions, channel rules, and role-based override paths so boundary protection becomes operational rather than rhetorical, especially where such expectations are becoming more formalized (Mazmanian et al., 2013; Sarker et al., 2012).

Ethics and privacy deserve equal attention. A Cognitive Shield relies on data about communication patterns, workloads, schedules, and interaction timing in order to judge relevance. The use of such data creates real governance risks unless limits are defined in advance. Organizations should articulate clear principles of data minimization, purpose limitation, retention, and employee oversight, with special caution against repurposing supportive infrastructure into covert monitoring systems (Kellogg et al., 2020; Raisch & Krakowski, 2021).

Explainability is equally important. Users must understand why the system classified a signal as urgent, why a message was deferred, why a summary emphasized certain points, and why a particular recommendation was made. Explainability supports trust, accountability, and learning; it also makes AI mediation subject to critique and revision rather than hidden automation (Raisch & Krakowski, 2021).

Fairness across roles and groups must also be addressed. If triaging features are designed mainly around managerial or professional roles, the organization may unintentionally create a new hierarchy of who receives protection and who remains exposed to digital noise. Fair implementation requires role-sensitive design, participatory testing, and systematic review of whether shielding benefits are distributed equitably across occupations, locations, and employment arrangements (Kellogg et al., 2020).

Change management is part of the governance problem. Introducing a Cognitive Shield changes not only interfaces but also habits and expectations. Users may initially fear that algorithmic mediation will hide information or reduce autonomy. Managers will need to model new practices, provide training, and establish feedback loops so that employees can question, refine, and help shape the rules of mediation. Effective adoption depends as much on communication and participatory governance as it does on technical capability (Raisch & Krakowski, 2021).

An additional managerial implication concerns participatory governance. Because the Cognitive Shield changes how signals are received, interpreted, and sometimes delayed, implementation should involve users early and repeatedly. Cross-functional groups including operations leaders, HR, IT, legal staff, and employee representatives can define acceptable uses, review error cases, and revise escalation policies as work rhythms change. Such participation is one of the main ways organizations ensure that supportive infrastructure remains supportive after deployment (Kellogg et al., 2020; Leonardi & Treem, 2020; Raisch & Krakowski, 2021).

These governance principles also require a more explicit user-facing transparency layer, especially because the Cognitive Shield would actively defer, bundle, or summarize workplace signals (Kellogg et al., 2020; Raisch & Krakowski, 2021).

AI Transparency for Users

For the Cognitive Shield to be trusted, transparency must be visible to workers in everyday use, not only stated as a general governance principle. When the system defers, bundles, or summarizes a set of notifications, the worker should be able to see a short and understandable explanation of that decision. For example, a bundled digest might state: "These messages were grouped because they were not time-critical and arrived during a protected focus period." A delayed notification might indicate whether the decision was based on urgency, sender role, task dependency, calendar status, or the user's selected focus settings (Kellogg et al., 2020; Leonardi & Treem, 2020; Raisch & Krakowski, 2021).

This form of user-facing transparency protects worker agency. Workers should be able to inspect the reasoning behind system decisions, correct mistaken classifications, and override the system when necessary. It also reduces the risk that the Cognitive Shield becomes another opaque layer of algorithmic control. A system designed to protect attention should not leave workers uncertain about how their attention is being managed. For this reason, user-facing explanations, override options, and feedback channels should be treated as core governance requirements rather than optional interface features (Kellogg et al., 2020; Raisch & Krakowski, 2021).

Evaluation Logic for the Cognitive Shield

Because the Cognitive Shield is presented as a conceptual architecture, organizations should evaluate it through staged and role-sensitive pilots rather than assuming that AI mediation automatically improves work. A useful evaluation design would compare conditions before and after implementation and, where possible, compare teams using the Shield with similar teams that continue to use conventional notification and communication settings. The evaluation should not rely only on operational indicators such as response time or task completion. Those indicators are important, but they can hide the very costs the Shield is intended to reduce. A more appropriate evaluation logic would combine operational performance with measures of attention, autonomy, recovery, trust, and perceived legitimacy (Bailey & Konstan, 2006; Mark et al., 2008; Sonnentag & Fritz, 2015).

At the individual level, organizations could examine interruption frequency, average uninterrupted focus intervals, perceived cognitive load, perceived autonomy over work sequencing, after-hours digital activity, and user satisfaction with summaries and prioritization. At the team level, relevant indicators include duplication of requests, escalation patterns, coordination delays, distribution of interruption burdens, and the extent to which urgent issues still reach the right people quickly. At the governance level, the most important evidence may come from override logs, user feedback, explanation requests, disputed classifications, summary-correction records, and audit reviews of whether the system treats roles and groups proportionately. These indicators would help determine whether the Shield reduces strain or merely redistributes it across less visible parts of the organization (Ayyagari et al., 2011; Kellogg et al., 2020; Mark et al., 2008).

Evaluation should also include failure signals. A high override rate may show that the system is misclassifying urgency or misunderstanding local work rhythms. A decline in after-hours alerts may be positive, but only if urgent issues are still handled appropriately and if delayed messages are not simply concentrated into more stressful morning backlogs. Positive productivity metrics should be interpreted cautiously unless they are accompanied by evidence of preserved agency, clearer priorities, improved recovery, and user trust. Evaluation is part of governance rather than a separate technical afterthought. The Shield should be judged by whether it produces sustainable cognitive performance, not only by whether it accelerates visible digital activity (Kellogg et al., 2020; Leonardi & Treem, 2020; Sonnentag & Fritz, 2015).

An effective implementation roadmap can be described in four stages. Diagnostic mapping identifies where notification volume, fragmented communication, and after-hours expectations are most costly. Policy and governance alignment clarifies response expectations, privacy boundaries, override rights, and escalation rules before automation is introduced. Design prototyping and controlled piloting test triage rules, focus modes, summary interfaces, and override mechanisms with representative users, assessing them not only for efficiency but also for fairness and perceived legitimacy. Governance scaling formalizes policies for transparency, auditability, data minimization, and role adaptation before broader deployment (Bailey & Konstan, 2006; Raisch & Krakowski, 2021; Sonnentag & Fritz, 2015).

To make this sequence more concrete, Table 2 translates the implementation logic into a staged roadmap for organizations and aligns each stage with its primary activities and expected outputs (Bailey & Konstan, 2006; Raisch & Krakowski, 2021; Sonnentag & Fritz, 2015).

Table 2. Four-Stage Roadmap for Implementing a Cognitive Shield

	Focus	Typical Activities	Key Outputs
1	Diagnostic Mapping	Analyze notification density, fragmentation, meeting load, and after-hours activity through trace data and interviews.	Digital strain baseline and priority pain points
2	Policy and Governance Alignment	Clarify response expectations, privacy boundaries, escalation rules, and acceptable use principles. Include user-facing explanation requirements for deferred, bundled, or summarized signals.	Governance charter and communication norms, plus AI transparency rules for users.
3	Technical Piloting	Pilot message bundling, AI summaries, focus protection, and overload analytics in selected units. Test whether users understand and can override bundling or deferral decisions.	Usability evidence, trust feedback, and feature refinement, including explanation usability feedback.
4	Scaling and Evaluation	Extend successful features while monitoring productivity, interruption load, autonomy, and well-being indicators.	Scaled deployment and continuous evaluation model

Note. Table 2 is author-developed and summarizes the staged implementation logic proposed in the chapter.

Evaluation should be multi-dimensional. Organizations should examine not only throughput or deadline adherence but also interruption frequency, time spent in focused work, after-hours digital activity, perceived autonomy, summary accuracy, override frequency, and quality of coordination. These data can show whether AI mediation is improving sustainable performance instead of merely accelerating visible activity. They can also surface a more difficult but essential question: whether the system is reducing digital strain equitably across roles rather than simply moving strain to less powerful groups.

The governance challenge is especially important because AI-enabled enterprise systems are entering organizations at a time when many firms are already expanding monitoring capabilities. There is a real risk that the language of well-being could be used to justify new forms of behavioral visibility. A Cognitive Shield should be evaluated not only by whether it improves speed or coordination but also by whether it preserves worker agency, proportionality, and dignity in the use of digital data (Kellogg et al., 2020; Leonardi & Treem, 2020).

FUTURE RESEARCH DIRECTIONS

The framework presented in this chapter is conceptual, and that creates an important agenda for future research. Scholars need stronger instruments for measuring sustainable productivity, especially indicators that capture interruption intensity, attentional fragmentation, recovery quality, and the hidden coordination work generated by digital sprawl. The literature already provides useful building blocks, including measures of technostress, interruption cost, and recovery, but additional work is needed to integrate them into enterprise-system evaluation (Ayyagari et al., 2011; Mark et al., 2008; Sonnentag & Fritz, 2015).

Intervention research is especially important. The field needs empirical studies that test specific design features associated with the Cognitive Shield model. Experimental or quasi-experimental studies could compare bundled notification regimes with continuous alerts, structured AI summaries with unsummarized streams, or protected focus windows versus unrestricted push communication. Such research would help clarify which combinations of design features produce the strongest gains in attention, performance quality, and well-being (Bailey & Konstan, 2006; Mark et al., 2008).

Future research should also examine differential effects across occupations and organizational contexts. Not all work is equally disrupted by interruption, nor does all work benefit from the same form of shielding. High-tempo environments, frontline service roles, distributed teams, and knowledge-intensive professions may each require different design patterns and policy combinations. Future studies should examine how role structure, task interdependence, and accountability conditions shape the effectiveness and acceptability of AI-mediated shielding (Kellogg et al., 2020; Sarker et al., 2012).

Governance and legitimacy also need further study. Future research should examine how workers interpret AI mediation when it is framed as support rather than surveillance. Under what conditions do employees trust algorithmic triage, summarization, and recommendation? Which forms of explanation and override increase trust without creating new burdens? Such questions are especially important because supportive infrastructures can be converted into monitoring systems if governance protections are weak (Kellogg et al., 2020; Raisch & Krakowski, 2021).

Collective dynamics deserve more attention as well. Much research on digital overload focuses on the individual user, yet many burdens are generated by team norms, interdependence, and shared platforms. Future research should investigate how collective communication patterns, coordination protocols, and managerial signaling generate digital strain and how redesign at the workflow level can reduce those burdens more effectively than individual coping strategies alone (Leonardi & Treem, 2020; Mark et al., 2005).

Future work should also examine the relationship between human-centered OIS and broader digital transformation. If the next phase of organizational technology is expected to be more resilient, ethical, and human-centered, then redesign principles such as those proposed here should not remain niche concerns. They should become part of enterprise architecture, leadership development, and digital governance. The most important contribution of future research may be to demonstrate, with empirical rigor, that systems protecting digital well-being are not a luxury or concession. They are a foundation for resilient organizational performance in an environment where attention has become one of the most valuable and vulnerable resources (Raisch & Krakowski, 2021; Trist & Bamforth, 1951).

LLM-mediated summarization and triage also require dedicated evaluation in enterprise contexts. Existing NLP benchmarks can demonstrate that LLMs summarize text, but they do not by themselves show whether summaries are organizationally useful, whether deferred signals were correctly deprioritized, or whether users come to trust the system over time. Future research should combine technical evaluation with workplace outcomes such as coordination quality, escalation accuracy, cognitive effort, and perceptions of procedural fairness. Without such mixed evaluation, organizations risk mistaking fluent summarization for reliable decision support (Brown et al., 2020; Zhao et al., 2023).

Cross-level and cross-jurisdictional variation is another important direction. The same shielding architecture may work differently across national regulatory contexts, public and private organizations, high-autonomy versus tightly scripted forms of work, and roles with different availability expectations. Comparative research would clarify which design principles travel well and which depend on local norms, privacy expectations, and occupational conditions (Kellogg et al., 2020; Mazmanian et al., 2013; Sarker et al., 2012).

CONCLUSION

This chapter has argued that Organizational Information Systems must be redesigned to address a defining contradiction of digital work: systems created to improve coordination and performance can also degrade the attentional and recovery conditions on which sustainable performance depends. The chapter reframed productivity as sustainable cognitive performance and showed why digital well-being is not peripheral to organizational effectiveness but foundational to it (Ayyagari et al., 2011; Sonnentag & Fritz, 2015; Sweller, 1988).

By synthesizing insights from socio-technical thinking, cognitive load theory, flow theory, technostress research, and studies of behavioral visibility and algorithmic management, the chapter showed that sustainable productivity requires more than faster systems. It requires systems that fit human cognitive limits, protect recovery opportunities, and resist the drift toward performative hyper-visibility (Csikszentmihalyi, 1990; Kellogg et al., 2020; Leonardi & Treem, 2020; Trist & Bamforth, 1951).

To make this argument concrete, the chapter introduced the concept of the Cognitive Shield: an AI-enabled architectural layer that filters, sequences, summarizes, and times information flows in ways that support attention, judgment, and recovery. The core claim is not that AI will automatically solve digital strain, but that AI can be repurposed from acceleration and surveillance logics toward augmentation, protection, and humane systems design when it is embedded within clear governance boundaries (Kellogg et al., 2020; Raisch & Krakowski, 2021).

The broader implication is that next-generation OIS should not merely ask how to move more information faster. They should ask how to deliver the right information, to the right people, at the right moment, in the right form, while protecting the finite human resources of attention, autonomy, and recovery. In an era of permanent connectivity, the most advanced organizational systems may be those that know when not to interrupt. Designing for that restraint is not a retreat from innovation. It is a necessary step toward a more resilient, ethical, and genuinely human-centered digital workplace (Bailey & Konstan, 2006; Mark et al., 2008; Sonnentag & Fritz, 2015).

The chapter's final claim is deliberately modest and ambitious at the same time. It does not suggest that the Cognitive Shield has already been empirically validated across settings. It does argue that the central design question for next-generation OIS is no longer only how to increase digital throughput, but how to govern attention, interpretation, and recovery in humane and sustainable ways. If that claim is correct, the redesign of OIS will depend not only on more capable AI, but on stronger institutional commitments to augmentation, proportionality, explainability, and worker agency (Kellogg et al., 2020; Leonardi & Treem, 2020; Raisch & Krakowski, 2021).

Seen in this light, the chapter is not simply a plea for kinder interfaces. It is an argument that the design of enterprise systems has become inseparable from the design of contemporary work itself. When information systems govern the timing, visibility, and interpretation of digital demands, they also govern the conditions under which people can think, coordinate, recover, and contribute. A future-oriented OIS agenda must treat digital well-being as a constitutive design criterion rather than a downstream remediation strategy (Ayyagari et al., 2011; Tarafdar et al., 2007; Trist & Bamforth, 1951).

REFERENCES

Ayyagari, R., Grover, V., & Purvis, R. (2011). Technostress: Technological antecedents and implications. *Management Information Systems Quarterly*, *35*(4), 831–858. DOI: 10.2307/41409963

Bailey, B. P., & Konstan, J. A. (2006). On the need for attention-aware systems: Measuring effects of interruption on task performance, error rate, and affective state. *Computers in Human Behavior*, *22*(4), 685–708. DOI: 10.1016/j.chb.2005.12.009

Brown, T. B., Mann, B., Ryder, N., Subbiah, M., Kaplan, J., Dhariwal, P., Neelakantan, A., Shyam, P., Sastry, G., Askell, A., Agarwal, S., Herbert-Voss, A., Krueger, G., Henighan, T., Child, R., Ramesh, A., Ziegler, D. M., Wu, J., Winter, C., & Amodei, D. (2020). *Language models are few-shot learners* (Vol. 33). Advances in Neural Information Processing Systems, https://arxiv.org/abs/2005.14165

Csikszentmihalyi, M. (1990). *Flow: The psychology of optimal experience*. Harper & Row.

Eppler, M. J., & Mengis, J. (2004). The concept of information overload: A review of literature from organization science, accounting, marketing, MIS, and related disciplines. *The Information Society*, *20*(5), 325–344. DOI: 10.1080/01972240490507974

Jarvenpaa, S. L., & Lang, K. R. (2005). Managing the paradoxes of mobile technology. *Information Systems Management*, *22*(4), 7–23. DOI: 10.1201/1078.10580530/45520.22.4.20050901/90026.2

Kellogg, K. C., Valentine, M. A., & Christin, A. (2020). Algorithms at work: The new contested terrain of control. *The Academy of Management Annals*, *14*(1), 366–410. DOI: 10.5465/annals.2018.0174

Leonardi, P. M., & Treem, J. W. (2020). Behavioral visibility: A new paradigm for organization studies in the age of digitization, digitalization, and datafication. *Organization Studies*, *41*(12), 1601–1625. DOI: 10.1177/0170840620970728

Mark, G., Gonzalez, V. M., & Harris, J. (2005). No task left behind? Examining the nature of fragmented work. *Proceedings of the SIGCHI Conference on Human Factors in Computing Systems*, 321-330. DOI: 10.1145/1054972.1055017

Mark, G., Gudith, D., & Klocke, U. (2008). The cost of interrupted work: More speed and stress. *Proceedings of the SIGCHI Conference on Human Factors in Computing Systems*, 107-110. DOI: 10.1145/1357054.1357072

Mazmanian, M., Orlikowski, W. J., & Yates, J. (2013). The autonomy paradox: The implications of mobile email devices for knowledge professionals. *Organization Science*, *24*(5), 1337–1357. DOI: 10.1287/orsc.1120.0806

Raisch, S., & Krakowski, S. (2021). Artificial intelligence and management: The automation-augmentation paradox. *Academy of Management Review*, *46*(1), 192–210. DOI: 10.5465/amr.2018.0072

Sarker, S., Xiao, X., Sarker, S., & Ahuja, M. (2012). Managing employees' use of mobile technologies to minimize work-life balance impacts. *MIS Quarterly Executive*, *11*(4), 143–157. https://ir.library.louisville.edu/faculty/359/

Sonnentag, S., & Fritz, C. (2015). Recovery from job stress: The stressor-detachment model as an integrative framework. *Journal of Organizational Behavior*, *36*(S1), S72–S103. DOI: 10.1002/job.1924

Sweller, J. (1988). Cognitive load during problem solving: Effects on learning. *Cognitive Science*, *12*(2), 257–285. DOI: 10.1207/s15516709cog1202_4

Tarafdar, M., Tu, Q., Ragu-Nathan, B. S., & Ragu-Nathan, T. S. (2007). The impact of technostress on role stress and productivity. *Journal of Management Information Systems*, *24*(1), 301–328. DOI: 10.2753/MIS0742-1222240109

Trist, E. L., & Bamforth, K. W. (1951). Some social and psychological consequences of the longwall method of coal-getting: An examination of the psychological situation and defences of a work group in relation to the social structure and technological content of the work system. *Human Relations*, *4*(1), 3–38. DOI: 10.1177/001872675100400101

Zhao, W. X., Zhou, K., Li, J., Tang, T., Wang, X., Hou, Y., Min, Y., Zhang, B., Zhang, J., Dong, Z., Du, Y., Yang, C., Chen, Y., Chen, Z., Jiang, J., Ren, R., Li, Y., Tang, X., Liu, Z., & Wen, J.-R. (2023). A survey of large language models. arXiv. https://arxiv.org/abs/2303.18223

ADDITIONAL READING

Carayon, P., Hancock, P. J., Leveson, N., Noy, I. Y., Sznelwar, L., & van Hootegem, G. (2015). Advancing a sociotechnical systems approach to workplace safety: Developing the conceptual framework. *Ergonomics*, *58*(4), 548–564. DOI: 10.1080/00140139.2015.1015623 PMID: 25831959

Walker, G. H., Stanton, N. A., Salmon, P. M., & Jenkins, D. P. (2008). A review of sociotechnical systems theory: A classic concept for new command and control paradigms. *Theoretical Issues in Ergonomics Science*, *9*(6), 479–499. DOI: 10.1080/14639220701635470

Weinmann, M., Schneider, C., & vom Brocke, J. (2016). Digital nudging. *Business & Information Systems Engineering*, *58*(6), 433–436. DOI: 10.1007/s12599-016-0453-1

KEY TERMS AND DEFINITIONS

Organizational Information Systems (OIS).: Digital infrastructures that coordinate work, information, communication, and decision processes across an organization.

Sustainable Productivity.: A form of performance that maintains high-quality output over time without chronically exhausting the cognitive and emotional resources of workers.

Digital Well-Being.: The condition in which digital technologies support effective work while minimizing overload, fatigue, stress, and unhealthy boundary erosion.

Cognitive Shield.: An AI-enabled architectural layer that filters, sequences, summarizes, and times information flows to protect attention and reduce unnecessary digital strain.

Technostress.: Stress experienced when information and communication technologies create overload, invasion, complexity, uncertainty, or rapid pace in work.

Cognitive Load.: The amount of mental effort required to process information and perform a task within the limits of working memory.

Flow.: A state of deep, focused, and goal-directed involvement in an activity in which attention is fully engaged and performance feels coherent.

Behavioral Visibility.: The degree to which digital systems make workers' actions, interactions, and response patterns observable to others in the organization.

Algorithmic Management.: The use of data-driven rules, rankings, and automated decision systems to direct, evaluate, and coordinate work.

Right to Disconnect.: A policy principle that protects employees from routine expectations of responding to work demands outside agreed working times.

Attention Management.: The deliberate regulation of digital demands so that users can allocate focus to tasks that matter most.

Focus Protection.: System and policy mechanisms that preserve uninterrupted blocks of time for cognitively demanding work.

Boundary Erosion.: The weakening of distinctions between work time and nonwork time caused by persistent digital reachability and spillover.

Algorithmic Triage.: The classification and sequencing of digital demands according to urgency, dependence, relevance, and cognitive cost.

Chapter 2
AI, Work, and Well-Being: Rethinking Organizational Information Systems for Sustainable Productivity in Africa

Tola Benjamin Kehinde
http://orcid.org/0009-0004-9963-5029
Redeemer's University, Nigeria

ABSTRACT

This chapter examines the tension between AI driven productivity gains and employee well being in African organizations undergoing digital transformation. Using a conceptual and integrative review of literature and contextual analysis, it develops a socio technical framework for sustainable AI enabled information systems. The study finds that unregulated automation increases precarity, algorithmic management heightens technostress, and skills gaps constrain inclusive productivity. It recommends human centered design, responsible governance, and continuous capacity building to align AI adoption with sustainable organizational development.

INTRODUCTION

Artificial intelligence is transforming organizational knowledge systems throughout the world, redefining the organization of work, its management, and its assessment. More and more, advanced analytics, machine learning apps, intelligent automation, and generative systems are integrated into enterprise platforms, human resource, customer relationship management tools, and decision support infrastructures (Ledro et al., 2022). Such developments hope to bring efficiency, the accuracy of decisions, and novel value creation. However, they also leave some

DOI: 10.4018/979-8-2600-0111-0.ch002

very deep questions concerning the essence of work, autonomy of the employee, mental wellbeing, and long-term productivity. As an organization adopts artificial intelligence as part of its core operations, there is a need to re-evaluate the manner in which information systems are developed and managed in order to strike a balance between performance benefits and human wellbeing. Artificial intelligence and productivity have been discussed in the context of optimization and cost cut (Ismanov et al., 2024; Ojika et al., 2022). The use of AI driven systems by organizations aims at automating repetitive processes, speeding data processing, and improving predictability. Although these results can boost quantifiable output, productivity in the modern digital economy cannot be measured by only efficiency indicators. Sustainable productivity must have in place systems that promote long term organizational resilience, employee involvement, skill improvement and moral accountability. Short term benefits can be gained at the cost of the workforce stability and wellbeing when algorithmic systems deepen work, increase monitoring or produce cognitive overload. This tension accentuates the necessity to re-examine organizational information systems as socio technical infrastructures that do not only influence economic but also human results.

African setting is a particularly useful environment to study these dynamics. Digital transformation is becoming faster across the continent in the sectors of finance, telecommunications, agriculture, healthcare, public administration, and entrepreneurship. There has been a rapid growth in the use of mobile technologies, digital financial platforms and data driven service delivery models making the African economies a place of innovation as opposed to adoption. Simultaneously, structural realities including infrastructural inequalities, informal labor markets, unemployment among the youth and skills gaps shape the experience and implementation of artificial intelligence. The current situation in most African nations is that organizations are in a dual jump that encompasses the digital modernization as well as the overall economic and institutional reform. This poses opportunities and risks to the adoption of AI in the information systems of organizations. Artificial intelligence in African organizations is not just an upgrade in technology. It is inculcated in the larger socio economic factors that influence the work practices, the control of managers, and the expectations of the employees. Formal sectors are also employing AI facilitated systems in reducing financial processes, streamlining supply lines, and improving service delivery. Startups are currently using data analytics and machine learning to solve problems locally in new technology ecosystems (Razaghzadeh Bidgoli et al., 2024). Nonetheless, the advent of algorithmic decision making also comes with some issues of job replacement, online monitoring, discrimination in the automated systems, and unequal accessibility to technological infrastructure. These issues are exaggerated in the situations when labor rights might be changing and when digital literacy differs greatly. The aims of productivity gains by using AI should thus be well-balanced with inclusive development and employee welfare.

Digital wellbeing has been revealed as an essential aspect of modern organizational discourse. The presence of constant connectivity, platform based performance monitoring, and data driven evaluation systems have the potential to exert pressure and erase the boundaries between personal and professional life. Within the context of artificial intelligence determining the distribution of responsibilities, the evaluation of performance, and control of managers, workers can feel a lack of autonomy or an increase in technostress. On the other hand, properly constructed AI systems may also improve the job quality by decreasing routine workload, helping in decision making and allowing flexible working patterns. The form and management of organizational information systems consequently are at the center of either empowerment or strain with AI.

This chapter postulates sustainable productivity in Africa needs reconfiguration of organizational information systems that incorporates artificial intelligence in a context sensitive and human centred structure. Organizations should treat AI as a socio technical system, which is part of a wider socio technical system, including institutional norms, leadership practices, workforce capabilities, and ethical standards. Redesigning organizational information systems entails integrating transparency, accountability, inclusivity and digital wellbeing considerations in system architecture and implementation. It must also be in line with national development objectives and local realities. This chapter is intended to serve three purposes. First, it focuses on the changing role of artificial intelligence in transforming the work and organizational information systems in African settings. Second, it examines the consequences of AI implementation on the wellbeing of the employees and sustainable output. Third, it suggests a conceptual framework of reconstructing the organizational information systems in such a manner that would encourage performance and human flourishing. Situating artificial intelligence in the context of a larger debate on digital transformation and socio technical systems, the chapter can also be used to continue the scholarly and policy debate on the topic of responsible innovation in emerging economies.

CONCEPTUAL FOUNDATIONS

The implementation of artificial intelligence in organizational information systems needs a clear conceptual basis that puts technological innovation in a much larger organizational, economic, and human interaction. The absence of a robust theoretical framework likely makes the discussion of AI overly technical or focused on efficiency of operation. This chapter takes socio technical approach because organizational information systems have not been viewed as just technological artifacts but intricate systems of individuals, processes, institutional rules, and digital infrastructures. In this context, artificial intelligence does not only transform the workflow and decision-making, but also the power structure, skill demands, and work experiences.

Information Systems based on Artificial Intelligence in Organizations

Artificial intelligence is defined as any computational system that can perform computations that human thought processes would normally undertake such as processing data through learning, pattern recognition, prediction, and the creation of insights. Regarding the organizational information systems, AI is integrated into enterprise resource planning systems, human resource management systems, customer relationship management systems, supply chain systems, and business intelligence dashboards. The current AI enabled systems have expanded the past role of information systems beyond data storage and reporting into predictive analytics, automated decision support and adaptive process management.

Artificial Intelligence in Organizational Information Systems

Organizational information systems have traditionally been created to enhance coordination, standardization of processes, and managerial control. The introduction of AI makes these systems dynamic platforms that can continuously learn and optimize on a real time basis. Algorithms are being availed or at least partially implemented to support decision making processes that previously were centralized and driven by human beings. This change means that it transforms organizational arrangements and shifts cognitive work between machines and people. It casts significant doubts on accountability, transparency and the degree to which the decision-making powers should be devolved to automated systems.

One significant difference that appears in literature is between automation and augmentation. Automation focuses on substituting human labor in de-skilling or repetitive work and may be accompanied by increased efficiency and reduced costs (Willcocks, 2024). Augmentation on the other hand is about augmenting human abilities by offering analytical knowledge, recommendations and decision support (Hassan et al., 2025). The decision between automation and augmentation has a big socio economic impact in the context of African organization where the labor markets are diverse and highly affected by skill shortages and excess unemployment. A moderate solution combining focus on augmentation will encourage skill and inclusive development and enhance organizational performance.

Sustainable Productivity

Traditional measurement productivity has been traditionally defined by output to unit of input and conventionally in monetary terms of financial performance, operational efficiency and short term returns. Such metrics are important but not enough to reflect the general effects of AI driven change. Sustainable productivity is based on the combination of economic performance and social responsibility, involvement of employees and long term institutional resilience. It recognizes that organizations exist in ecosystems that comprise workers, communities, regulators, as well as technological infrastructures.

Productivity increase can also occur in AI enabled environments, through increased speed in processing data, predictive maintenance, automated customer service, and increased efficiency in resource allocation. But when such gains are obtained at the expense of excessive surveillance, intensified work or workforce displacement without reskilling opportunities, then they can be counterproductive to long term sustainability. Unethical AI practices can undermine the productivity gains that organizations aim to obtain by burning employees, lowering their morale, and putting their reputations at risk (Al Naqbi et al., 2024). Sustainable productivity then necessitates the need to harmonize technological innovation and human development. Sustainable productivity also overlaps with national development priorities in the African context which include employment creation, digital inclusion and capacity building. Information systems that incorporate AI in the organization should be crafted to accommodate these wider purposes. This can be through investment in digital skills, creation of local centers of innovation, and promoting equitable distribution of technological benefits across regions and sectors.

Digital Well Being in the Workplace

Digital wellbeing can be defined as the level, to which digital technologies are helpful rather than harmful to the psychological, social, and professional well-being of people. Digital wellbeing issues within the organizational institution include workload balance, autonomy, privacy, cognitive demand, technology mediated quality human interaction (Vanden Abeele, 2021). The role of artificial intelligence on the wellbeing of employees is more vital as artificial intelligence is being integrated into the performance management systems, algorithms in task allocation and real time monitoring tools.

Technostress is one of the key issues that can be addressed in relation to AI enabled systems because of the constant connectivity, the speed of technological evolvement, and the necessity to use new digital tools. It could be aggravated by algorithmic management systems continuously monitoring performance metrics and creating automated reviews. There is a risk that employees lose control of their working process when opaque algorithms are influential in the decisions that are made. The issue of data privacy and surveillance may also add anxiety and mistrust to the organizations. Meanwhile, AI can develop digital wellbeing as long as it is developed in a responsible way. Intelligent systems have the ability to minimize routine demands, allow flexible work arrangements and offer individualized learning and development prospects. They would help the employees to prioritize tasks and cope with information overload. The success of the organizational information systems relies much on the conceptualization of information systems, their implementation and governance. The approach of human centred designing, including employee nature of input and ethical protection is necessary in ensuring that AI works towards the benefit of wellbeing in the workplace.

Collectively, these theoretical backgrounds point to the necessity to shift away from overly technical accounts of artificial intelligence. Organizational information systems should be perceived as both socio technical systems that influence productivity, power and well being at a time. This combined vision will be especially relevant to guarantee that AI-based change leads to an increase in the performance of organizations and sustainable development in Africa.

OPPORTUNITIES AND STRUCTURAL REALITIES IN AFRICA

The implementation of artificial intelligence in organizational information system in Africa has to be interpreted within the specific socio economic, demographic, and institutional environment of the continent. Although global discourse tends to discuss AI diffusion as a homogeneous wave of technology, its application and its effects are closely determined by the contextual realities. Digital transformation in Africa is also taking place in the context of more general economic restructuring, institutional change and demographic transformation. Such dynamics provide a complicated setting where AI driven systems will be able to produce important developmental possibilities as well as increase structural vulnerabilities.

In most African economies, the digital infrastructure has grown significantly in the last two decades. The increase in mobile connectivity, broadband connectivity, digital payment systems, and cloud services to enhance the operations has made organizations modernize and expand their market reach. Countries like Kenya, Nigeria, Rwanda, Ghana and South Africa have created technology hubs that encourage data analytics, fintech, health technologies and agritech platforms. These advances offer a platform on which AI may be incorporated in organizational information systems in both the public and private sectors. Nevertheless, the difference in infrastructures between urban and rural regions, and large enterprises and small and medium sized organizations are still sharp. Lack of access to good and stable electricity, high speed internet, and digital infrastructure has an uneven impact on the speed and accessibility of AI (Atiase et al., 2020). The nature of the labor market also forms the consequences of AI induced change. Economies in Africa are marked by the high informal sector, a large number of young people, and digital illiteracy. Formal organizations can also improve productivity with the use of AI by automatizing processes and predictive analytics. However, in informal or semi formal settings, resource constraints, regulatory ambiguity and skills gaps can prevent the implementation of the AI systems. The young demographics profile of the continent is an opportunity and a challenge. On the one hand, the increase in the number of workers presents opportunities in the development of digital skills and innovation. Conversely, in the event of AI adoption, where labor substitution is the most significant outcome, and no evidence of increased investment in reskilling and job creation, current unemployment strains may also escalate.

The institutional and regulatory systems are also significant aspects that influence the implementation of AI. The legislation of data protection, cybersecurity, labor, and the national digital strategies are diverse in the African countries (Effoduh et al., 2024). Other governments have expressed bold agendas of digital transformation that focus on innovation and technological entrepreneurship. Others continue to come up with holistic regulatory strategies to solve problems like algorithmic bias, data governance, and ethical AI implementation. Lack of clear guidelines in some situations can result in uncertainty among the organizations and the possibility of inconsistency or imbalance of system design. Empowering the governance systems is thus the main focus in making sure that AI integration is in line with the values of accountability, transparency and inclusion (Kiemde & Kora, 2022). The perception and use of AI is also affected by cultural and organizational norms. The styles of leadership, hierarchical frameworks, and perceptions towards adopting technologies influence engagement of the employees and their confidence in AI facilitated systems. Some environments have hierarchical cultures where top down adoption of new technology can be speedy but inputs cannot be participatory. In others, the collaboration methods can be helpful in increasing acceptance but would need a more proactive change management plan. It is necessary to understand such dynamics and create organizational information systems that are sensitive and responsive to workforce expectations.

Notably, Africa is not a passive recipient of technologies imported. Context specific AI applications being developed by local entrepreneurs, researchers and technology communities are capable of confronting issues in agriculture, healthcare delivery, financial inclusion, education and in public administration. The innovations can show that AI has the potential to help develop inclusively in areas where AI is deployed in conjunction with local needs and knowledge systems. The information systems of organizations that include the inclusion of locally relevant information and culturally informed design principles have higher chances of creating sustainable productivity gains. Meanwhile, there is a threat of digital divide due to structural inequalities between and within countries. More competitive AI may be used faster by more financially strong organizations, which have access to more global networks and have a higher chance of staying ahead of the game. Smaller organizations and government institutions having tightened budgets might not manage to keep up. Digital disparities, STEM disparities, and gender disparities, are also determiners of the beneficiary of AI driven transformation. To solve these disparities, there is need to invest in capacity building, education and inclusive innovation policies. The high pace of digital growth, the young population, and the growing innovation ecosystems are good platforms that can facilitate revolutionary change. Nonetheless, the infrastructural constraints, workforce pressures, and the diversity in regulations and social disparities make this course of action complicated. These structural realities can only be successfully restructured through a subtle comprehension that would enhance sustainable productivity and digital wellbeing in various African contexts in relation to organizational information systems.

AI, WORK REDESIGN, AND ORGANIZATIONAL TRANSFORMATION

Artificial intelligence deployment in organizational information systems goes beyond the technological improvement. It is the work that is being fundamentally transformed to redefine the idea of work, modify organizational structures and change the way managers are working. With AI integrated into the main functional and strategic processes, organizations have to re-examine the ways in which the tasks are distributed, how performance is evaluated, and how human capacities are trained. In the African case, where economic change and digital modernization are both occurring at the same time, AI inspired work redesign bears extensive implications on productivity, quality of employment, and the resilience of institutional forms. Reorganization of work tasks is one of the most obvious impacts of the integration of AI. Intelligent systems are becoming common in automating routine and repetitive tasks whether it is in data entry, processing transactions, customer queries, and basic analysis. This change alters the skill mix that is demanded in organizations. The workers are supposed to take part in higher level of cognitive activities like interpretation, problem solving, innovation, and strategic management. As a result, there is the increased need in digital literacy, data competence, and adaptive learning. In the context of unequal access to opportunities of advanced training, this change demonstrates the relevance of the ongoing professional growth and the investment of the organization in the human factor.

The redesign of work in AI facilitated systems frequently implies the replacement of the task execution with the supervision and cooperation with smart devices. The outputs of algorithms can be supervised by human employees, and automated decisions are to be validated, whereas in the cases when the contextual judgment or ethical aspects are to be taken into consideration, human employees may intervene (Tsamados et al., 2025). This model of collaboration between humans and AI refutes the conservative beliefs and premises concerning authority and expertise. Decision making gets decentralized between human participants and computerized systems and necessitates proper accountability frameworks. Companies should establish limits of algorithmic autonomy and make sure that human control is not a formalism. There is also transformation of leadership practices in the atmosphere of AI. Predictive analytics and data enriched dashboards enable managers to get real time information on performance metrics, employee productivity and operational risks. These tools could be useful in terms of increasing the strategic planning and responsiveness, but they can also stimulate over-monitoring when managed in an irresponsible manner. Employee monitoring via algorithmic management systems capable of tracking employee activity and creating metrics of performance may increase pressure and decrease perceived autonomy. Successful organizational change thus relies on the leadership strategies that are balanced in terms of data driven management and trust, transparency, and participatory engagement.

In the process of ensuring AI enabled transformation is successful, the organizational culture assumes a central role. Organizations that support experimentation, learning, and cross functional collaboration in their cultures will be in a better option to harness AI in terms of innovation. On the other hand, strict hierarchies and change no-fly zones can impede integrating operations. Change management in African organizations that are moving towards digital transition, should be able to deal with both technological change and mindset change. To understand the purpose behind the adoption of AI, the expected benefits, and its impacts on the role of the employees, they should be clear. The anxiety in this context can be countered by open communication and inclusive decision making processes to promote the feeling of shared ownership of the transformation initiatives. The ethical issues cannot be separated by the work redesign in AI driven systems. Algorithms bias, automated decision making fairness, privacy of data and transparency pose direct challenges on employee confidence and organizational legitimacy. With regulatory frameworks that are still developing, organizations have a big role to play towards setting internal standards of governance. The implementation of AI ethically needs impact assessment, bias reduction measures, and means of challenging automated decisions. These controls can be integrated into the organizational information systems and therefore enhance compliance and sustainability.

Notably, organizational transformation that is mediated by AI cannot be associated only with workforce reduction. Although the automation process can change the pattern of employment, it provides new jobs in the fields of data analysis, system maintenance, cybersecurity, and digital strategy. The overall effect on employment is contingent on complementary sources of investment in skills, ecosystems of innovation and conducive public policies. In the African economies where the number of youth grows, it is crucial to be proactive in matching the use of AI and the skill development programs to ensure that technological advancements are translated into economic growth that is not exclusive to the youth. AI mediated work redesign can be defined as a pivotal point in the growth of the organization. It promises the possibility of efficiency improvement and decision quality improvement and innovation. This, however, does not mean that without a conscious focus on human factors, systems of governance, and the realities on the ground, it can only increase inequality, tension, and fragility of institutions. A socio technical perspective of rethinking organizational transformation is the sure way of having the artificial intelligence complementing and not diminishing sustainable productivity and digital wellbeing within African organizations.

RISKS AND WELL BEING CHALLENGES IN AI DRIVEN SYSTEMS

Although Artificial intelligence has a transformational potential towards the productivity and innovation of an organization, its application in information systems has also come with serious threats as well as threats to wellbeing. These difficulties are not technical only but social, psychological and institutional. With more AI systems involved in the processes of decision making, performance review and task delegation, the lived experience of working is transformed in such a way that it can either benefit or harm the welfare of the employees. With the dynamics in labor markets and regulatory systems that are changing in the African region, these risks must be looked into keenly to ensure that organizational development is sustainable. Among the concerns is a question of job displacement and employment precarity. Routine and semi routine tasks can be automated and this could lead to the reduction of the need of some type of labor, specifically with regard to the administrative, clerical and transactional labor. Though Artificial Intelligence is capable of creating new jobs within the technology direction, the process of the displaced jobs and the new one is not often smooth. The lack of skills, access to higher-level training, and varying levels of digital skills can make certain groups of the workforce susceptible.

Uncontrolled automation may widen social and economic disparities in economies that are already struggling to cope with elevated rates of unemployment especially among the youth. There must be a conscious workforce transition and reskilling strategy in order to achieve sustainable productivity.

One of the most important threats is the emergence of algorithmic management and online surveillance. Smart systems are capable of monitoring the activity of employees, tracking in real time the performance indicators, and creating automatic assessments. Although they might increase transparency and efficiency of operations, they can also increase work pressure and perceived loss of autonomy. Constant surveillance can also result in a state of hyper vigilance and stress as well as low job satisfaction. Uncertainty and mistrust are other negative effects that can manifest in employees whose performance is not well understood through the algorithms. Honest communication about data collection, assessment criteria and decision rationale is thus very vital in building trust in an organization. Technostress is another danger to AI based workplaces. The high pace of technology demands an employee to constantly adjust to new platforms, interfaces, and workflow (Chang et al., 2024). Cognitive load may also be added with the interpreting of algorithmic outputs, large amounts of information, and responding to automated alerts (Puppala, 2025). In situations where there is less training and technical support, the staff might become overpowered or unprepared. This dilemma is especially relevant in organizations where the digital transformation process is fast-moving, and no investments in capacity building are made. The technostress problem is not something that can be solved with simple technical training, but it takes a careful design of the systems that put usability and human centered interfaces on the forefront.

The privacy of data and the ethical issue also makes AI implementation in the organizational information system harder. The artificial intelligence (AI) systems usually presuppose the usage of massive datasets that contain personal and behavioural data on the staff and clients. Poor information governance systems can put an organization at risk of breach, information misuse, and damage to reputation. Additionally, the algorithmic bias may lead to unfair or discriminatory results of the recruitment process, promotion or evaluation, performance. When regulatory regulation is still in its infancy, the organizations are recommended to practice proactive ethical principles that uphold fairness, accountability and inclusivity. The redistribution of the decision authority between human beings and machines also has a role to play in psychological wellbeing. Employees can lose agency when they feel that algorithms are taking away their professional discretion or interfering with their professional judgment. This may long term demoralize motivation and interest. On the other hand, employees will have a more positive perception of AI systems in situations when the latter are presented as complementary resources, which augment instead of substitute expert knowledge. The psychological effect of AI is therefore determined by how it is framed and implemented into organizational culture.

The existence of such risks highlights the need to consider wellbeing issues during the design and governance of AI enabled organizational information systems. It is impossible to have sustainable productivity when efficiency gains are coupled by burnout, mistrust, or social exclusion. The African institutions in the digital transformation process should thus take a middle ground between technological innovation and sound ethical protection strategies, employee training programs, and the participative engagement system. However, by responding to these wellbeing issues before they arise, organizations will be able to utilize the opportunities of artificial intelligence and reduce the risks of its harmful impact.

RETHINKING ORGANIZATIONAL INFORMATION SYSTEMS FOR SUSTAINABLE PRODUCTIVITY

The above discussion shows one of the main contradictions of the modern digital transformation. Artificial intelligence holds the potential to make the organization more efficient, precise, and strategic, but, unless integrated carefully, can cause further inequality, stress, and organizational vulnerability. To solve this paradox, the organizational information systems need to be rethought fundamentally. These systems need to be reimagined as socio technical infrastructures, which deliberately combine productivity, ethics, and human wellbeing as opposed to seeing them as mere technical infrastructures with the objective of maximizing output. A reformulated organizational information system commences with human oriented design philosophy. Human centered systems focus on usability, transparency and inclusivity during the preliminary stages of development. The workers are neither seen as passive consumers of technology but as active stakeholders whose experience and insights influence the functionality of the system. The consultations, pilot testing, and iterative feedback mechanisms are part of consultancy-based approach of design which allows organizations to align AI capabilities with actual workplace requirements. In African settings that have various literacy levels, cultural beliefs, and hierarchies, inclusive design is especially relevant in ensuring fair uptake and reducing opposition.

It is also necessary that sustainable productivity requires AI systems to have an augmentation orientation instead of blind automation. Although automation may be effective in terms of lowering the cost and speed, the use of augmentation strategies aims at improving the human judgment and creativity. The employees can be empowered to make informed decisions without taking away the agency through intelligent decision support tools, predictive analytics dashboards, and adaptive learning systems. This will maintain meaningful human control and enhance the development of skills. In dynamic African economies, where the growth of workforce, and the utilization of youth is a top policy consideration, augmentation oriented system design can reconcile technological development with the growth of an inclusive economy.

Another platform of redesigned organizational information systems is the responsible governance structures. The decision making processes that are AI based should be transparent, explainable and accountable (Dafoe, 2018). The way data are collected, stored and analyzed should be defined using clear protocols. The employees must know the impacts of the algorithmic outputs on the performance reviews, task distribution and promotion. Contest mechanisms and mechanisms to receive grievances on automated outcomes must be in place to ensure trust. The institutional credibility and resilience can be enhanced through the establishment of internal ethics committees, impact assessment, and compliance with the national and international data protection standards. Digital wellbeing should be parted of system architecture, as well. This includes creating interfaces and processes that minimize cognitive load, minimize avoidable notifications, and encourage work-life balance. Technostress can be overcome by the availability of features that enable employees to control the digital borders, including customizable alerts or set-offline hours. One can even use AI to facilitate wellbeing by detecting imbalances related to workloads, suggesting training materials, or even allowing flexible schedules. Once wellbeing metrics are added to organizational measures of performance, productivity is redefined as a multidimensional performance outcome and not a quantitative and measurable outcome.

Capacity building is one more element of sustainable system redesign. Introducing AI in successful integration is possible only under the conditions of constant learning opportunities, training in digital skills, and leadership. To make sure that employees know how to use AI tools, organizations have to invest in not only technical competence but also ethical literacy to be able to interpret and question their results. In African contexts where digital skills disparities may limit change initiatives, collaboration with universities, vocational education, and technology centers can facilitate labor preparedness. Lastly the concept of rethinking organizational information system is the alignment of the technological strategies with long term developmental and societal goals. Digital transformation in Africa is tightly connected with economic diversification, financial inclusion, the improvement of services to the citizens, and social equity. Companies that develop AI-permitted systems that are sensitive to local issues and the impact on the community not only promote internal productivity but also national developmental trends. This convergence enhances sustainability at the long term since it instills organizational success in a broader ecosystem of inclusive development. Sustainable productivity in the artificially intelligent age cannot be attained using gradual technological improvements only. It involves a conscious re-architecturing of information systems in organizations that incorporates human centered values, accountable governance, digital wellbeing protection, and situational awareness. African organizations can turn AI into an agent of resilient, ethical, and inclusive performance by taking a holistic perspective and transforming AI as an instrument of narrow efficiency.

A PROPOSED FRAMEWORK FOR SUSTAINABLE AI ENABLED ORGANIZATIONAL SYSTEMS IN AFRICA

Based on the above discussion, the section suggests a combination conceptual framework on how to design and govern AI enabled organizational information systems to facilitate sustainable productivity and digital wellbeing in African settings. The framework is a response to the necessity of an organized method that brings together technology innovation and human development, ethical responsibility and institutional resiliency. The framework does not view artificial intelligence adoption as a technical and linear process of upgrading, but conceptualizes a complex transformation process such as the contextual, organizational, and human factors.

This framework is based on four pillars which are interconnected and which are; technological integration, development of human capability, ethical and governance structures and well being based performance measurements. These pillars exist in a greater contextual environment that is determined by national digital infrastructure, regulatory, labour market conditions, and socio cultural norms. When these dimensions are not only strategically aligned, but also sought after together, sustainable productivity should develop.

The first pillar is technological integration whereby it focuses on the strategic alignment of AI tools to organizational goals and operational realities. In this dimension, the readiness is evaluated based on the quality of data, the capacity of the infrastructure, the preparedness to the cybersecurity, and the compatibility with the already existing systems. It also necessitates articulation about the purpose of AI, it can be either automation, augmentation or hybrid cooperation. The proper prioritization is a key factor in the African organizations where resources limits might be the determining factor of the technology selection, so that AI investments can bring measurable values without stretching the capacity of the institution. Human capability development is the second pillar which emphasizes the primary importance of skills, leadership and organizational culture. The employment of AI-driven systems is certain to need workers capable of perceiving the information outputs, critical thinking, and adjusting to the changes in the working process. Digital competence should be developed through continuous training programs, mentorship systems, and knowledge sharing platforms. Inclusive transformation commitment by leaders is also essential. Managers need to explain the reasons behind the adoption of AI and respond to the concerns of employees and create a collaborative learning culture instead of a culture of fear. In a setting such as working with young demographics and growing workforce, the connection between AI implementation and systematic reskilling programs can provide increased productivity and economic sustainability in employment.

The third pillar, ethical and governance structures, is accountable and trusts AI driven decision making. This aspect brings in open data management policies, mitigation of bias measures, and oversight and redress mechanisms. Organizations should come up with explicit rules that specify the extent of algorithms control and the human supervision. The AI systems should be audited regularly to ensure that unintended consequences and disparities are minimized. Due to the dissimilarity between the regulatory settings in various African nations, internal governance standards are especially significant in keeping the level of ethical consistency and safeguarding the interests of the stakeholders.

Wellbeing centered performance metrics is the fourth pillar, which transforms the evaluation of organizational success. The classical productivity metrics like output volume, cost reduction are accompanied by the employer metrics of employee engagement, workload balance, skill development, and psychological safety. Including these metrics in performance dashboards will be an indicator of institutional investment in whole outcomes. Even AI tools may be utilized to track the workloads and determine the patterns of burnout risk. Organizations integrate human sustainability and technological efficiency by putting the consideration of wellbeing into their performance evaluation systems. These four pillars are dynamic. Indicatively, integration of technology in the absence of the human capability building might lead to a situation of underutilisation of the systems or resistance to the system by the employees. Moral leadership that lacks proper technical systems can curtail the capacity of control system. In the same manner, wellbeing measures that lack the commitment of leaders can be symbolic, as opposed to being transformative. The paradigm thus focuses on the systemic consistency and iterative adjustment. Organizations are advised to reevaluate cross-pillar alignment regularly due to the changes in technologies and changing contextual factors.

On the contextual level, the external partnerships help in the implementation of the framework. Knowledge sharing and harmonisation of regulations can be helped through partnerships with universities, research centres, technology centres and policy agencies. These collaborations are especially important in African innovation ecosystems where there exists an equal influence of both public and private stakeholders on the direction of digital transformation. The coordination of organizational AI plans with the national digital plans reinforces the legality of the social sustainability in the long term. The framework can be operationalized in real life by using a step by step method of implementation. The first stage is readiness assessment and consultations with the stakeholders. The second stage is pilot integration and specific training. The third stage is focused on the institutionalization of governance and monitoring of performance. Ongoing assessment will be done to make sure that lessons learnt are used to refine the system. This cyclic process identifies that sustainable AI adoption is a process and not a one-time intervention.

The current framework adds to the existing discussion of the redesign of the organization information systems as it combines the factors of productivity, ethics, and well being into one analytic framework. It offers a framework but flexible roadmap to African organizations wishing to use artificial intelligence in a responsible manner. The framework links AI not only as an efficiency driver but also as an inclusive and resilient organizational change agent by foregrounding contextual awareness and human centered principles.

PRACTICAL IMPLICATIONS

The artificial intelligence of organizational information systems has important implications to various stakeholders. The conversion of conceptual understanding into practice-based strategies is critical in achieving sustainable productivity results and in protecting digital well being through the AI driven transformation. This part will provide practical implications of the research to organizational leaders, policy makers, system designers and researchers in the African contexts.

To organizational leaders, the key implication is that there should be strategic intentionality. Having clear objectives articulated is the key to use AI adoption to map technological capabilities to the long term organization vision and workforce development objectives. Instead of focusing on cost-saving stories, the leaders should adopt a balanced scorecard that involves an employee engagement process, adherence to ethics, and innovation ability. Open communication is essential. It is important that employees are aware of the purpose of introducing AI systems, of how the decisions made will be shaped by the outputs of algorithms, and whether they have the opportunity to improve their skills. Digital literacy and ethical AI governance competencies also should be introduced into leadership development programs to enable managers to make data informed yet human centered decisions.

The findings highlight to system designers and technology managers the need to apply directly the wellbeing principles into system architecture. The design of the user interface, automation processes in the workflow and performance dashboards must focus on being clear, easily accessible, and easy to think about. Increased system acceptance and functionality can be achieved by use of participatory design methods which engages employees at various levels within an organization. Designers should also have guiding features that enable users to have a feel of how these algorithmic recommendations are produced. Training modules and continuous technical support should be seen as the part of the system deployment instead of the add-on in situations when the level of digital literacy varies.

The policymakers have a significant role to play in the formation of a larger ecosystem where organizations work. The development of AI should be combined with the employment policy, educational reform, and the protection of data as national digital strategies. The innovation ecosystems can be enhanced in the continent through investment in digital infrastructure, research, and public-private partnerships. Regulations concerning accountability of algorithms, data confidentiality, and equity are fundamental towards the establishment of trustworthiness among the population. Procedures to maintain small and medium sized enterprises should also be considered by policy makers since they might not have the resources to install the responsible AI systems independently and yet are the key drivers of economic growth.

The changing nature of AI facilitated organizational transformation challenges provide strong avenues to empirical research and theory building. The context specific insights could be formed through longitudinal studies of the connection between the adoption of AI, employee well being, and productivity outcomes within organizations in Africa. Relative study over industries and nations can shed some light on the differences observed on the effectiveness of governance and acculturization. Scholars are also placed to play a role in building locally based theoretical frameworks that bring to bear African realities of the institution as opposed to the use of models that have already been developed elsewhere.

CONCLUSION

Artificial intelligence is another revolution in the history of organizational information systems. The fact that it has been integrated into working processes provides a big potential to achieve efficiency, innovation and strategic capability. The quest of productivity enhancement based on AI though could not be separated of employee wellbeing, moral responsibility, and situational reality. This balance is especially important in African organizations, which are exposed to the digital transformation and are facing larger developmental issues. This chapter has stated that sustainable productivity necessitates a re-design of the organizational information systems on a holistic basis based on socio technical principles. The strategies of implementing AI have to be integrated with human centered design, accountable governing structures, capacity building programs and wellbeing performance measures. Organizations can reduce the risks of automation, surveillance and inequality by locating technological innovation in the context of local institutions and socio economic factors.

The recommended framework will provide an organisation of integrating technological integration, advancement of human potential, ethical supervision and wellbeing-based analysis. When these dimensions work together, artificial intelligence will not only be the means of improving the efficiency of operations but the driver of the impactful and sustainable organizational change. The decisions that are being made in the present-time concerning the design and governance of AI will determine the future of work in the African continent as the African economies grow in terms of digital capacities. Stakeholders can utilize the power of artificial intelligence by reevaluating organizational information systems through the prism of sustainable productivity and digital wellbeing to shape it in manners that will improve economic performance and human flourishing.

REFERENCES

Al Naqbi, H., Bahroun, Z., & Ahmed, V. (2024). Enhancing work productivity through generative artificial intelligence: A comprehensive literature review. [Publisher Full Text.]. *Sustainability (Basel)*, *16*(3), 1166. DOI: 10.3390/su16031166

Atiase, V. Y., Kolade, O., & Liedong, T. A. (2020). The emergence and strategy of tech hubs in Africa: Implications for knowledge production and value creation. *Technological Forecasting and Social Change*, *161*, 120307. DOI: 10.1016/j.techfore.2020.120307

Dafoe, A. (2018). AI governance: a research agenda. *Governance of AI Program, Future of Humanity Institute, University of Oxford: Oxford, UK, 1442*, 1443.

Effoduh, J. O., Akpudo, U. E., & Kong, J. D. (2024). Toward a trustworthy and inclusive data governance policy for the use of artificial intelligence in Africa. *Data & Policy*, *6*, e34. DOI: 10.1017/dap.2024.26

Ismanov, I., Qayumov, N., Mukhamadjonova, D., & Akhmadaliyev, B. (2024, April). AI and cost management: Strategies for reducing expenses and improving profit margins in business. In *2024 International Conference on Knowledge Engineering and Communication Systems (ICKECS)* (Vol. 1, pp. 1-7). IEEE. DOI: 10.1109/ICKECS61492.2024.10616761

Kiemde, S. M. A., & Kora, A. D. (2022). Towards an ethics of AI in Africa: Rule of education. *AI and Ethics*, *2*(1), 35–40. DOI: 10.1007/s43681-021-00106-8

Ledro, C., Nosella, A., & Vinelli, A. (2022). Artificial intelligence in customer relationship management: Literature review and future research directions. *Journal of Business and Industrial Marketing*, *37*(13), 48–63. DOI: 10.1108/JBIM-07-2021-0332

Ojika, F. U., Owobu, W. O., Abieba, O. A., Esan, O. J., Ubamadu, B. C., & Daraojimba, A. I. (2022). The role of artificial intelligence in business process automation: A model for reducing operational costs and enhancing efficiency. *International Journal of Multidisciplinary Research and Growth Evaluation*, *3*(1), 842–860.

Puppala, A. (2025). Cognitive Load Analysis in AI-Augmented BI Dashboards: Understanding the Impact of Artificial Intelligence on User Comprehension, Trust, and Decision-Making Efficiency. *Journal of Computer Science and Technology Studies*, *7*(6), 207–213.

Razaghzadeh Bidgoli, M., Raeesi Vanani, I., & Goodarzi, M. (2024). Predicting the success of startups using a machine learning approach. *Journal of Innovation and Entrepreneurship*, *13*(1), 80. DOI: 10.1186/s13731-024-00436-x

Tsamados, A., Floridi, L., & Taddeo, M. (2025). Human control of AI systems: From supervision to teaming. *AI and Ethics*, *5*(2), 1535–1548. DOI: 10.1007/s43681-024-00489-4 PMID: 40352578

Willcocks, L. P. (2024). Automation, digitalization and the future of work: A critical review. *Journal of Electronic Business & Digital Economics*, *3*(2), 184–199. DOI: 10.1108/JEBDE-09-2023-0018

Chapter 3
Beyond Automation:
Designing Resilient, Human-Centric Organizational Information Systems in the Age of Industry 5.0

Satya Subrahmanyam
http://orcid.org/0000-0003-0441-2742
Holy Spirit University of Kaslik, Lebanon

ABSTRACT

Organizational information systems (OIS) have historically prioritized operational efficiency over employee experience. The emergence of Industry 5.0, with its emphasis on human centricity, sustainability, and resilience, compels a fundamental rethinking of how digital workplaces are designed. This chapter argues that existing OIS frameworks inadequately address the relational and psychological dimensions of work, contributing to technostress, disengagement, and organizational fragility. Drawing on sociotechnical systems theory, human-centric design, and organizational resilience frameworks, it proposes the RECS (Resilient, Employee-Centric Systems) framework comprising four interconnected dimensions: Adaptive Intelligence, Well-Being Integration, Organizational Agility, and Participatory Governance. Applied across manufacturing, knowledge-work, and healthcare contexts, including Indian case examples, the framework offers researchers and practitioners a structured pathway for redesigning OIS that genuinely serves the humans who depend on them.

DOI: 10.4018/979-8-2600-0111-0.ch003

1. INTRODUCTION

1.1 From Industry 4.0 to Industry 5.0: A Paradigm Shift in Technology Philosophy

The fourth industrial revolution redrew the boundaries of what machines could accomplish. Enterprise resource planning systems, robotic process automation, the Internet of Things, and cloud-based data infrastructure became standard instruments of organizational life over the first two decades of the twenty-first century. Organizations that embraced these technologies discovered measurable gains in throughput, cost reduction, and supply chain coordination. Yet by the early 2020s, a disquieting counternarrative had emerged. The same systems that increased output were also identified as contributors to elevated stress, surveillance anxiety, and a creeping erosion of employee agency (Carayon et al., 2021). The optimization logic of Industry 4.0, it appeared, had a shadow side.

Industry 5.0, a term formally introduced by the European Commission in 2021, does not repudiate technological progress. Rather, it reorients the purpose of that progress. Where Industry 4.0 asked how technology could make organizations more efficient, Industry 5.0 asks how technology can make organizations more human (European Commission, 2021). The three pillars of this paradigm, namely human centricity, sustainability, and resilience, constitute not merely rhetorical additions to industrial policy but a substantive philosophical shift with deep implications for how organizational information systems are designed, deployed, and governed.

1.2 The Evolving Role of Organizational Information Systems in the Digital Workplace

Organizational information systems are the technological nervous systems of contemporary enterprises. They mediate communication, coordinate workflow, store institutional knowledge, facilitate decision-making, and increasingly generate the data that drives organizational strategy. The transition to remote and hybrid work, accelerated dramatically by the COVID-19 pandemic, expanded the reach of OIS into the domestic spaces of employees, blurring boundaries that had previously regulated the relationship between work and personal life (Wang et al., 2021).

This expansion has not been without cost. Research consistently demonstrates that poorly designed information systems increase cognitive load, generate information overload, and contribute to what scholars describe as technostress, a form of occupational stress arising directly from the use of digital technology at work (Pothuganti et al., 2025). The design choices embedded in OIS, from notification architectures to workflow sequencing to the degree of human override permitted in algorithmic processes, are not neutral. They shape behavior, affect health, and ultimately determine whether a system empowers or diminishes the employee.

1.3 The Productivity-Well-Being Paradox

Central tension animates contemporary debates about OIS design. Organizations pursue productivity as a primary metric, while mounting evidence from occupational psychology, human-computer interaction research, and organizational behavior suggests that sustained productivity is impossible when employee well-being is structurally neglected (Giorgi et al., 2020). The paradox is self-defeating: systems designed to maximize output through intensification of work often produce the burnout, turnover, and reduced creativity that undermine the very productivity they were designed to enhance.

This chapter argues that resolving the productivity-well-being paradox requires not incremental system adjustment, but a principled redesign of OIS grounded in the values of Industry 5.0. That redesign must be theoretically coherent, practically implementable, and empirically testable.

1.4 Chapter Objectives, Scope, and Contribution

This chapter pursues three interconnected objectives. First, it synthesizes the theoretical landscape relevant to Industry 5.0 and OIS redesign. Second, it presents the RECS framework as an original conceptual contribution that integrates human-centric, resilience-oriented, and participatory principles into a structured design architecture. Third, it grounds the framework in real organizational vignettes, including examples from Indian enterprises and public institutions, to demonstrate how its dimensions manifest in practice. The chapter does not claim to offer a prescriptive blueprint; organizational contexts are too varied for universal prescription. It offers instead a principled framework and a set of testable propositions that can guide both future empirical research and practitioner decision-making.

1.5 Chapter Structure Overview

The chapter proceeds as follows. Section 2 establishes the theoretical foundations. Section 3 reviews the relevant literature and identifies research gaps. Section 4 elaborates the Industry 5.0 imperatives that bear on OIS design. Section 5 presents the RECS framework in full. Section 6 applies the framework across three sector-specific vignettes. Section 7 discusses implications for researchers, practitioners, and policymakers. Section 8 concludes.

2. THEORETICAL FOUNDATIONS

2.1 Industry 5.0 Defined

The European Commission's 2021 report on Industry 5.0 defined the concept as a vision in which industry serves societal goals beyond jobs and growth, providing prosperity by making production respectful of the limits of our planet and placing the well-being of the industry worker at the center of the production process (European Commission, 2021, p. 4). Three pillars structure this vision. Human centricity places the needs, competencies, and welfare of people at the core of technological deployment. Sustainability demands that industrial processes operate within planetary boundaries. Resilience requires that production systems maintain continuity and adaptive capacity in the face of disruption.

These pillars carry direct implications for OIS. A human-centric OIS would be co-designed with employees rather than imposed on them. A sustainable OIS would minimize digital waste, unnecessary notifications, and cognitive pollution. A resilient OIS would sustain functionality under crisis conditions while preserving employee agency throughout.

2.2 Sociotechnical Systems Theory

Sociotechnical systems (STS) theory, originating in the Tavistock Institute studies of British coal mines in the 1950s, holds that technical and social subsystems within organizations must be jointly optimized rather than designed independently (Ang et al., 2025). The theory challenges the dominant logic of technological determinism, which assumes that human work processes should be adapted to whatever technology makes possible. STS insists on the reverse: technology design should be shaped by the social and relational demands of work.

In the context of OIS, STS theory provides the conceptual license to evaluate system design not only by technical performance metrics but by the quality of working life it enables. Recent scholarship has extended STS frameworks to digital workplaces, arguing that algorithmic management systems represent a new frontier of sociotechnical tension because they frequently optimize for measurable output while rendering invisible the tacit, relational, and creative dimensions of knowledge work (AgoteGarrido et al., 2023).

2.3 Human-Centric Design

Human-centric design (HCD), as formalized in ISO 9241-210, defines a design philosophy in which systems are shaped by the needs, goals, and contexts of their intended users throughout the entire development lifecycle. Vial (2019) argues that digital transformation efforts that fail to embed HCD principles consistently produce systems that are technically sophisticated but experientially alienating. The gap between system capability and user experience is, in many organizations, the primary driver of adoption failure and productivity loss.

HCD in the OIS context demands participatory methods: co-design workshops, iterative prototyping with employee panels, usability testing across demographic groups, and ongoing feedback loops embedded in post-deployment governance. The principle of inclusivity extends this agenda further, requiring that system design account for employees with disabilities, varying digital literacy levels, and culturally diverse interaction preferences (Subrahmanyam, 2025).

2.4 Organizational Resilience Theory

Organizational resilience refers to the capacity of an enterprise to anticipate, prepare for, respond to, and adapt to incremental change and sudden disruptions in order to survive and prosper (Conz & Magnani, 2020, p. 4). In the digital workplace, resilience has both a technical dimension, which concerns system continuity and redundancy, and a human dimension, which concerns employee adaptive capacity and psychological safety.

Jia et al. (2020) distinguish between reactive resilience, which involves recovery after disruption, and proactive resilience, which involves building organizational structures that prevent disruption from becoming catastrophic. OIS design participates in both. Systems with modular architectures, interoperable components, and crisis-mode workflow triggers embody proactive resilience. Systems with rapid reconfiguration capabilities and human override provisions enable reactive resilience.

2.5 Digital Well-Being Frameworks

Digital well-being, as a scholarly construct, encompasses both the positive dimensions of technology use, such as connection, capability, and creativity, and its negative correlates, such as technostress, digital fatigue, surveillance anxiety, and work-life boundary erosion (Vanden Abeele et al., 2022). Pothuganti et al. (2025) identify five technostress creators that are directly attributable to OIS design: techno-overload (systems demanding more work), techno-invasion (systems intruding into personal time), techno-complexity (systems requiring excessive learning), techno-insecurity (fear of replacement), and techno-uncertainty (constant system change).

Reducing these stressors through deliberate design choices is not merely a welfare concern; it is a productivity imperative. Meta-analytic evidence reviewed by Giorgi et al. (2020) demonstrates that technostress is significantly and negatively associated with job satisfaction, organizational commitment, and cognitive performance.

2.6 Synthesis: A Unified Theoretical Lens

Taken together, these five theoretical traditions converge on a coherent set of principles for OIS redesign. Systems should be co-produced with their users (STS and HCD), should incorporate well-being signals as first-class design considerations (digital well-being frameworks), should maintain operational continuity under disruption (resilience theory), and should serve societal goals that extend beyond organizational profit (Industry 5.0). Table 1 summarizes the contrast between the prevailing Industry 4.0 logic and the emerging Industry 5.0 orientation that this theoretical synthesis demands.

Table 1. Comparison of Industry 4.0 and Industry 5.0 Orientations for Organizational Information Systems

Dimension	Industry 4.0	Industry 5.0
Primary focus	Efficiency and automation	Human dignity and collaboration
Role of AI	Replace human labor	Augment human capabilities
Value orientation	Profit maximization	Societal and environmental value
OIS design priority	Data throughput and scalability	Employee experience and resilience
Employee role	Operational input	Creative and ethical agent
Risk framing	Technical and cybersecurity risk	Human and systemic risk
Organizational goal	Lean and agile production	Resilient and sustainable enterprise

Note. OIS = organizational information system. Sources: European Commission (2021); Carayon et al. (2021); Xu et al., 2021.

Table 2 maps the five theoretical frameworks onto their specific contributions to the OIS redesign agenda pursued in this chapter.

Table 2. Theoretical Frameworks and Their Contributions to OIS Redesign

Framework	Core proposition	Relevance to OIS redesign	Key scholar(s)
Sociotechnical Systems Theory	Technology and people must be jointly optimized	Guides co-design of IS and work roles	Trist & Bamforth; Ang et al., 2025
Human-Centric Design	Systems should be shaped by user needs and contexts	Frames participatory IS development	ISO 9241-210; Vial, 2019
Organizational Resilience Theory	Organizations absorb, adapt, and transform under disruption	Justifies flexible IS architectures	Conz & Magnani, 2020
Digital Well-Being Framework	Technology use affects cognitive and emotional health	Grounds the well-being integration dimension	Vanden Abeele et al., 2022; Twenge & Campbell, 2019
Technology Acceptance Model (TAM)	Perceived usefulness and ease of use drive adoption	Predicts OIS uptake among employees	Venkatesh et al., 2016

Note. Sources: Ang et al. (2025); Vial (2019); Conz & Magnani (2020); Vanden Abeele et al. (2022); Venkatesh et al. (2016).

3. LITERATURE REVIEW

3.1 Existing OIS Design Paradigms

The dominant tradition in enterprise IS design has been unambiguously efficiency-first. Systems such as ERP platforms, business process management suites, and workflow automation tools have been architected primarily to reduce transaction costs, eliminate redundancy, and generate real-time data for managerial decision-making (Praharaj & Chhatoi, 2025). The employee appears in this tradition primarily as a source of input data and a potential source of error to be minimized through standardization.

An alternative tradition, traceable through the participatory design movement of the 1970s and the usability research of the 1980s and 1990s, has advocated for a fundamentally different orientation. This tradition holds that the legitimacy and effectiveness of information systems depends on the degree to which they reflect and respect the lived realities of their users (Bodker et al., 2022). The tension between these traditions remains unresolved in most contemporary organizations, where enterprise IS decisions are made by technology procurement teams using vendor scorecards that privilege functionality and cost over employee experience.

The Technology Acceptance Model, as mapped in Table 2, traditionally frames adoption through perceived usefulness and ease of use as the twin anchors of system uptake (Venkatesh et al., 2016). However, when systems incorporate digital well-being features such as mandatory notification throttling or focus mode protocols, these conventional anchors shift in important ways. Employees no longer evaluate usefulness solely through the lens of task efficiency; they weigh whether a system actively protects their cognitive and emotional resources. Similarly, ease of use expands beyond interface simplicity to encompass whether a system's defaults and behavioral nudges reduce rather than amplify digital overload. TAM-informed research on Industry 5.0 OIS must therefore revisit these foundational constructs and measure acceptance in terms that capture well-being outcomes alongside performance outcomes.

3.2 The Human Cost of Poorly Designed Information Systems

The scholarly literature on the negative consequences of OIS for employee health and performance has expanded substantially since 2020. A comprehensive review by Molino et al. (2020) found that technostress was significantly associated with emotional exhaustion, reduced job performance, and higher turnover intention across knowledge-work occupations. Specific OIS design features were identified as drivers: notification architectures that interrupt deep work, performance monitoring systems that generate surveillance anxiety, and collaboration platforms that blur the boundary between working hours and personal time.

Research conducted in the Indian context amplifies these global findings. A study examining software engineers at IT firms in Bengaluru and Hyderabad found that always-on communication expectations embedded in OIS were the single strongest predictor of work-family conflict, outperforming individual demographic variables including gender and tenure (Balakrishnan et al., 2025). A separate study of administrative workers in Delhi found that perceived lack of control over digital workflows was associated with significantly elevated cortisol levels, a physiological marker of chronic stress (Narayanan et al., 2025).

3.3 Resilience Engineering in Digital Workplaces

The application of resilience engineering principles to OIS design remains a relatively nascent scholarly field, though interest has accelerated considerably since the disruptions of the COVID-19 pandemic demonstrated the fragility of many enterprise systems under crisis conditions (Li et al., 2024). Ponomarov and Holcomb's (2009) framework for supply chain resilience, extended to the digital domain by Bruckler et al. (2024), identifies absorptive capacity (the ability to withstand disruption), adaptive capacity (the ability to reconfigure in response), and restorative capacity (the ability to return to or exceed pre-disruption performance) as the three core dimensions of a resilient system architecture.

For OIS, these dimensions translate into specific design requirements. Absorptive capacity demands redundancy in data storage and processing, fail-safe communication channels, and crisis-mode workflow templates. Adaptive capacity requires modular system architecture that enables rapid reconfiguration without system-wide redeployment. Restorative capacity depends on institutional learning mechanisms that capture and embed lessons from disruption events into system design iterations.

3.4 Industry 5.0 in Organizational Research

Empirical research directly examining Industry 5.0 as an organizational phenomenon remains limited, reflecting the relative novelty of the concept. However, a growing body of work has begun to operationalize its principles. Subrahmanyam (2026b) conducted a systematic review of 87 papers on human-robot collaboration and found that worker acceptance and performance outcomes were significantly better in contexts where collaborative robots were designed to respond to human preferences rather than requiring humans to adapt to robot constraints. This finding illustrates a central Industry 5.0 insight: technology serves humans rather than the reverse.

In India, early Industry 5.0 implementations have been documented in the manufacturing sector. Research on the Pune automotive corridor found that firms integrating cobots with operator-controlled interfaces reported higher worker satisfaction scores and lower injury rates than firms deploying fully automated systems with passive human monitoring roles (Rajkumar et al., 2024). These findings, while preliminary, support the RECS framework's emphasis on adaptive intelligence as a design priority.

3.5 Gaps in Literature

Despite the richness of these individual streams, several important gaps remain. First, the literature on OIS design rarely engages directly with Industry 5.0 as a theoretical framework, tending instead to treat employee well-being and system efficiency as independent optimization targets rather than as integrated design goals. Second, the resilience literature in IS tends to focus on technical resilience, the survivability of systems under load, with insufficient attention to the human dimension of organizational resilience. Third, empirical studies from Global South contexts, and particularly from India, which hosts the world's largest IT sector workforce, remain underrepresented relative to their practical importance. The RECS framework presented in Section 5 is explicitly designed to address these gaps.

4. INDUSTRY 5.0 IMPERATIVES FOR ORGANIZATIONAL INFORMATION SYSTEMS REDESIGN

4.1 Human-Machine Collaboration: Co-Design Principles

The foundational imperative of Industry 5.0 for OIS is that technology and humanity must collaborate rather than compete. In the IS design context, this imperative materializes as a commitment to genuine co-design: processes by which employees at all organizational levels contribute meaningfully to system requirements, architecture, and interface decisions. Bodker et al. (2022) distinguish between tokenistic participation, in which employees are consulted after key design decisions have been made, and substantive participation, in which employees exercise real influence over system specification from the outset.

Co-design in hybrid work environments introduces particular challenges. Remote employees may lack access to design workshops, and synchronous participation may be difficult across time zones. However, digital ethnography methods, asynchronous design sprint tools, and AI-assisted preference aggregation platforms offer viable pathways for inclusive co-design that does not require physical co-presence (Subrahmanyam, 2026c).

4.2 Moving From Surveillance-Oriented to Empowerment-Oriented Architectures

One of the most consequential design decisions embedded in contemporary OIS is the choice between surveillance-oriented and empowerment-oriented monitoring architectures. Surveillance-oriented systems collect granular data about employee behavior, location, and productivity metrics, and present that data primarily to managers. Empowerment-oriented systems make equivalent data available to employees themselves, enabling self-regulation, skill development, and meaningful dialogue with supervisors about workload and performance (Schafheitle et al., 2020).

The distinction matters enormously for well-being outcomes. A large-scale study of warehouse workers in the United Kingdom found that monitoring systems perceived as surveillance tools were associated with significantly higher anxiety levels and lower organizational commitment, whereas systems perceived as developmental feedback tools produced the reverse pattern (Ball, 2021). For Indian IT firms, where performance monitoring has intensified dramatically during the hybrid work era, this distinction between architectures carries immediate practical relevance.

4.3 Sustainable OIS: Reducing Digital Overload

The sustainability pillar of Industry 5.0 has an inward-facing dimension that applies to organizational information systems: the reduction of digital waste. Digital waste takes multiple forms including redundant notifications, parallel communication platforms that duplicate rather than complement each other, data collection that serves no decision-making purpose, and reporting requirements that consume employee time without generating organizational value (Finbite, 2024).

Lean information flow principles, adapted from lean manufacturing, offer a systematic methodology for identifying and eliminating digital waste. Value stream mapping applied to information workflows reveals which data flows genuinely serve organizational decisions and which persist solely through institutional inertia. Organizations that have applied such methodologies report reductions in the time employees spend on system administration of between 20% and 35%, with corresponding improvements in creative and substantive work time (HorsthoferRauch et al., 2024).

4.4 Embedding Resilience Into OIS

The resilience pillar of Industry 5.0 requires OIS architectures to be explicitly designed for disruption tolerance. This means moving beyond the assumption that systems will operate under normal conditions and designing instead for a range of disruption scenarios: cyberattacks, natural disasters, pandemic-induced remote work transitions, and leadership crises that disrupt coordination norms. Modular architecture, in which system components can be redeployed or substituted without triggering cascading failures, is the technical foundation of OIS resilience (Weill & Woerner, 2018).

At the human level, resilient OIS must preserve employee agency under pressure. Systems that lock employees into predefined workflows during a crisis, when improvisation and judgment are most necessary, actively undermine the organizational resilience they claim to support. Crisis-mode workflow templates that relax routine constraints while maintaining data integrity offer one design pathway for reconciling system structure with human adaptability.

4.5 Inclusive and Accessible System Design

Inclusivity is not an afterthought in Industry 5.0 but a foundational design requirement. OIS that function well for digitally fluent employees in urban settings but poorly for employees with lower digital literacy, disabilities, or intermittent connectivity fail the human-centricity test on their own terms. In India, the demographic diversity of the workforce, spanning multiple languages, educational backgrounds, urban and rural contexts, and varying degrees of digital access, makes inclusive OIS design a particularly urgent imperative (Dubey et al., 2024).

Web Content Accessibility Guidelines (WCAG 2.1) provide a minimum standard, but genuine inclusivity requires ethnographic understanding of the specific populations who will use a system. Screen reader compatibility, multilingual interface options, low-bandwidth modes for intermittent connectivity environments, and alternative input modalities for employees with physical disabilities are design features that expand the radius of OIS benefit.

Figure 1. Designing Resilient Information Systems

Source: Author, (2026)

5. A CONCEPTUAL FRAMEWORK: THE RECS MODEL

5.1 Presenting the RECS Framework

The RECS framework integrates four dimensions of OIS design that together operationalize the Industry 5.0 imperatives articulated in Section 4. The acronym stands for Resilient, Employee-Centric Systems, and the four dimensions are: Adaptive Intelligence (AI-D), Well-Being Integration (WBI), Organizational Agility (OAG), and Participatory Governance (PGov). The framework is not a checklist of features but a set of design orientations, each of which manifests differently depending on organizational context, sector, and workforce characteristics.

The dimensions are theoretically distinct but practically interdependent. Adaptive Intelligence without Participatory Governance risks producing technically sophisticated systems that employees distrust or circumvent. Organizational Agility without Well-Being Integration may produce flexible systems that are experienced as destabilizing rather than empowering. The RECS framework treats each dimension as a necessary but not sufficient condition for holistic OIS redesign.

Table 3 presents the framework's four dimensions, their definitions, design principles, measurable OIS indicators, and testable propositions.

Table 3. The RECS Framework: Dimensions, Principles, Indicators, and Propositions

Dimension	Definition	Design principle	OIS indicator	Proposition
Adaptive Intelligence (AI-D)	AI-assisted decision support that preserves human judgment	Explainability and human override	Transparent algorithm dashboards	P1: AI-D positively predicts employee autonomy perceptions
Well-Being Integration (WBI)	Embedding health signals into system workflows	Cognitive load reduction	Notification throttling; workload alerts	P2: WBI reduces technostress and improves engagement
Organizational Agility (OAG)	System capacity to flex during disruption	Modular and interoperable architecture	Crisis-mode workflows; remote failover	P3: OAG strengthens organizational resilience scores
Participatory Governance (PGov)	Employees co-design and iterate system features	Inclusive sprint cycles	Employee IS advisory panels	P4: PGov improves IS satisfaction and adoption rates

Note. RECS = Resilient, Employee-Centric Systems. AI-D = Adaptive Intelligence; WBI = Well-Being Integration; OAG = Organizational Agility; PGov = Participatory Governance.

5.2 Dimension 1: Adaptive Intelligence

Adaptive Intelligence refers to the deliberate design of AI-assisted OIS in ways that augment rather than supplant human judgment. The distinction between augmentation and replacement is not merely semantic; it has profound consequences for employee experience, cognitive development, and the quality of organizational decisions. Systems that present algorithmic recommendations as inviolable directives diminish the epistemic agency of employees. Systems that present the same recommendations with explanations, confidence intervals, and explicit override mechanisms enable employees to develop their own expertise while benefiting from machine processing power (Jarrahi, 2019).

The requirement for explainability is increasingly recognized in regulatory frameworks, including the European Union's proposed Artificial Intelligence Act, which mandates that high-risk AI systems used in employment contexts provide meaningful explanation of their outputs to human operators. Indian regulatory frameworks have been slower to develop in this area, but the National Institution for Transforming India Aayog's National Strategy for Artificial Intelligence (2018) emphasizes human-centric AI development as a policy priority.

Operationally, the AI-D dimension requires that OIS dashboards display the data inputs and weighting logic underlying algorithmic outputs, that employees have clearly accessible mechanisms for flagging algorithmic errors, and that organizational processes exist for incorporating employee feedback into model retraining cycles.

5.3 Dimension 2: Well-Being Integration

Well-Being Integration represents the embedding of digital well-being signals directly into OIS workflows and interfaces, rather than relegating well-being concerns to separate wellness applications or human resource programs. This approach treats employee health not as a personal responsibility to be managed outside the system but as a systemic outcome that system design can actively shape.

Concrete manifestations of the WBI dimension include notification throttling mechanisms that regulate the frequency and timing of system alerts based on employee-defined preferences; workload visibility dashboards that display aggregate cognitive load indicators to both employees and supervisors; mandatory rest period enforcement within task management systems; and focus mode protocols that temporarily disable non-urgent communications. Microsoft's Work Trend Index (2022) reported that employees who used digital tools with built-in well-being features reported 23% lower burnout scores than those who did not, illustrating the potential of this design orientation.

The WBI dimension also has a data governance implication. Well-being data generated by OIS is among the most sensitive personal information an organization holds. Its collection must be voluntary, its use transparent, and its governance subject to robust employee oversight. The risk of well-being data being repurposed for performance surveillance represents a genuine ethical hazard that RECS-compliant design must explicitly guard against.

5.4 Dimension 3: Organizational Agility

Organizational Agility in the RECS framework refers specifically to the capacity of OIS to support organizational responsiveness under conditions of disruption. This includes both the technical architecture of the system and the degree to which the system preserves human decision-making authority when normal operating procedures are suspended.

From an architectural perspective, agility requires modular system design in which core functional components, such as communication, workflow management, data storage, and reporting, can be independently updated, substituted, or reconfigured without triggering system-wide failure. Application programming interface (API)-first design philosophies facilitate this modularity by ensuring that individual components communicate through standardized, interoperable interfaces rather than proprietary integration schemes.

From a human perspective, agility requires that OIS contain explicit crisis-mode workflow templates that have been co-designed with employees before disruption occurs. The experience of organizations during the COVID-19 pandemic demonstrated repeatedly that systems without such templates forced managers and employees to improvise workarounds that were both inefficient and inequitably distributed across the workforce (Sull et al., 2022).

5.5 Dimension 4: Participatory Governance

Participatory Governance is the dimension that bridges the design phase and the operational life of OIS. It concerns the ongoing processes by which employees exercise meaningful influence over system evolution after initial deployment. Most enterprise IS governance frameworks concentrate decision-making authority in IT departments, vendor relationships, and senior management, with employees playing at most an advisory role (Sunyaev et al., 2026). The PGov dimension of the RECS framework challenges this arrangement.

Employee IS advisory panels, with genuine decision-making power over feature prioritization and interface design, represent one institutional mechanism for PGov. Participatory agile sprint cycles, in which employees serve as product owners for specific OIS modules relevant to their work, represent another. The key criterion is not the specific mechanism but the genuine redistribution of design authority to those who bear the consequences of design decisions.

Research from Scandinavian organizations with long-established traditions of participatory IS governance demonstrates that employee-led governance structures produce significantly higher system satisfaction, lower circumvention rates, and faster adoption of system updates than top-down governance models (Subrahmanyam, 2026a). These findings provide empirical grounding for the PGov dimension's proposition that participatory governance improves IS satisfaction and adoption rates.

5.6 Framework Propositions and Testable Hypotheses

The RECS framework generates four primary propositions, corresponding to each dimension, that can guide future empirical research. These propositions are stated at a level of generality appropriate for a conceptual chapter and are intended to be operationalized through survey instruments, field experiments, and longitudinal case studies.

Proposition 1 (AI-D): Organizational information systems incorporating explainable AI features and human override mechanisms will be positively associated with employee perceptions of autonomy and negatively associated with technostress, relative to systems without such features.

Proposition 2 (WBI): Organizational information systems that embed well-being signals, including notification management, workload visibility, and focus mode protocols, into core workflow architecture will be associated with lower burnout, higher job satisfaction, and improved cognitive performance among employees.

Proposition 3 (OAG): Organizations whose information systems exhibit modular architecture and contain pre-designed crisis-mode workflow templates will demonstrate higher organizational resilience scores and faster recovery from disruption events than organizations with monolithic, non-modular OIS.

Proposition 4 (PGov): Organizations that establish formal employee IS advisory panels with genuine decision-making authority over system evolution will achieve significantly higher OIS satisfaction scores and lower system circumvention rates than organizations with IT-only governance structures.

Figure 2. Resilient Employee-Focused Systems Framework

Source: Author, (2026)

6. APPLIED ILLUSTRATIONS AND CASE VIGNETTES

6.1 Case 1: Manufacturing Sector — Tata Steel, India

Tata Steel, one of India's largest integrated steel manufacturers, provides a compelling illustration of the OAG and AI-D dimensions of the RECS framework in a complex, safety-critical manufacturing environment. The company's experience demonstrates how legacy information system architectures can become organizational liabilities when they are structured in ways that exclude frontline workers from the data flows most relevant to their daily decisions. It also demonstrates how deliberate redesign, grounded in co-creation with the workforce, can unlock both operational and human-centered gains that neither management nor technology alone could have produced.

Following the disruptions of the pandemic era, Tata Steel initiated a systematic audit of its operational technology and enterprise information system architecture across its Jamshedpur and Kalinganagar plants. The audit revealed that legacy ERP systems used for production scheduling and maintenance management were structured in ways that prevented frontline operators from accessing real-time process data, creating a systematic dependency on supervisory chains that slowed both routine decision-making and emergency response. When a sensor indicated an anomaly in blast furnace temperatures or rolling mill pressure, the information traveled upward through multiple management layers before returning downward as an instruction, a design that introduced latency at precisely the moments when speed of response mattered most. The audit also uncovered a related problem: because operators lacked access to system data, they had developed extensive informal workarounds, including personal logbooks, informal messaging chains, and unrecorded manual overrides, that were invisible to organizational managers and therefore impossible to incorporate into system improvement.

Between 2021 and 2023, Tata Steel implemented a co-bot integration program that placed intelligent operator workstations directly on the production floor, providing workers with real-time sensor data, predictive maintenance alerts, and production scheduling information in visual formats designed through a series of co-design workshops involving operator teams. These workshops were not superficial consultations; they involved operators spending structured sessions identifying which data they needed to do their jobs well, which alerts were useful and which were noise, and how information should be displayed to remain legible in the physically demanding conditions of a steel plant. The resulting interface designs reflected genuinely operator-driven specifications, including large-format displays readable from a distance, color-coded priority indicators calibrated to plant-specific risk thresholds, and audio alerts differentiated by urgency level.

Critically, the system was architected to present algorithmic recommendations as advisory inputs rather than directives, with a simple override mechanism accessible to any operator without supervisory authorization. This design choice, directly aligned with the AI-D dimension of the RECS framework, reflected the recognition that frontline workers possessed tacit knowledge about plant conditions that no algorithm could fully capture (Tata Steel Sustainability Report, 2023). An operator who knew from experience that a particular sensor reading behaved anomalously when ambient humidity was high could exercise judgment that the algorithm, lacking that contextual knowledge, would not. Preserving the space for that judgment was not a concession to tradition; it was considered recognition of where machine intelligence had limits.

The outcomes reported over the first 18 months of the program included a 25% reduction in system-related production downtime, a measurable improvement in operator confidence scores on internal engagement surveys, and a 40% reduction in the number of maintenance emergencies escalated to senior engineering staff, suggesting that operator-level system access genuinely enabled better real-time decision-making. The reduction in escalations carried a secondary benefit that the original program designers had not fully anticipated: supervisor time previously consumed by routine emergency coordination was freed for higher-value coaching and strategic planning activities.

The program also revealed tensions that speak directly to the challenges of implementing RECS principles at scale. Scaling co-design workshops across the company's global workforce of over 80,000 employees required significant investment in facilitation capacity and raised difficult questions about the consistency of design principles across geographically and culturally diverse plant populations. The participatory process that worked well in Jamshedpur, where operators had long-established relationships with plant management and a strong informal culture of process knowledge sharing, produced somewhat different dynamics at other sites where those cultural conditions did not hold. Tata Steel's experience thus illustrates both the power and the limits of participatory design in large, heterogeneous organizations: the principles travel, but their implementation must be adapted to local relational and cultural realities.

6.2 Case 2: Knowledge Work — Infosys, India

Infosys, one of India's most globally prominent information technology services companies, confronted a well-being crisis that was simultaneously a system design crisis. By 2021, internal data from employee engagement surveys and exit interviews consistently identified communication overload and blurred work-life boundaries as the primary drivers of voluntary attrition, particularly among mid-career employees in the age range of 30 to 40 years. These employees, typically carrying the heaviest client delivery responsibilities and navigating the dual pressures of career development and family commitments, were the population whose retention the company most needed to prioritize and the population the existing OIS architecture was most systematically failing.

The company's collaboration platforms, primarily Microsoft Teams and an internal project management system, had been configured to enable always-on visibility into employee availability and activity. This design choice, while intended to facilitate distributed coordination across the time zones that characterize global

IT service delivery, had created a culture of ambient surveillance that employees found psychologically exhausting. The persistent awareness that a manager or client could see their availability status at any moment, combined with an implicit organizational norm that response times under one hour were expected regardless of the hour, produced a pattern of boundary erosion that employees described in qualitative interviews as feeling permanently at work. The technical configuration of the OIS had, in effect, dissolved the temporal boundary between professional and personal life for a significant portion of the workforce.

Infosys responded by convening cross-functional employee panels to co-design a revised OIS configuration. The panels, which included representatives from software development, project management, human resources, and client delivery functions, were given explicit authority to recommend system changes, not merely to advise. This distinction in governance structure proved consequential for the quality of the recommendations that emerged. When employees understood that their proposals would actually be implemented, the discussions moved quickly from generic complaints about workload to specific, actionable system configuration choices. The panels identified three specific system changes as priorities.

The first change was the introduction of notification throttling that limited non-urgent alerts to defined windows aligned with employee-set preferences. Employees could specify the hours during which they were available for real-time communication and the hours during which only designated emergency contacts could reach them. The system enforced these preferences technically rather than relying on individual managers to respect them, removing the relational awkwardness that had made employees reluctant to enforce boundaries informally. The second change was the removal of real-time activity indicators from manager-facing dashboards and their replacement with outcome-based progress tracking. Rather than showing whether an employee was actively engaged with their device, the revised dashboard showed task completion rates, milestone progress, and client deliverable status. This shift in what the system made visible represented a philosophical move from monitoring presence to measuring contribution. The third change was the creation of protected focus blocks within the scheduling system that employees could reserve without seeking managerial approval. These blocks, capped at four hours per working day, appeared as unavailable in the scheduling system and could not be overridden by meeting invitations from colleagues at the same or lower organizational level.

These changes, implemented between 2022 and 2023, directly instantiated the WBI and PGov dimensions of the RECS framework. The notification throttling and focus mode features embodied WBI by embedding well-being protection into system architecture rather than leaving it to individual self-management. The co-design panels and the governance authority they carried embodied PGov by giving employees genuine influence over the system environment in which they worked.

A follow-up survey conducted by Infosys's internal people analytics team 12 months after implementation found a 17% reduction in self-reported technostress, a 9-point improvement in eNPS (Employee Net Promoter Score), and a measurable reduction in voluntary attrition among the cohort of employees who had participated in the co-design panels. This last finding deserves particular attention. The employees who participated in the co-design process showed stronger retention outcomes not only because the system changes benefited them materially but also because the act of participation itself generated a stronger sense of organizational belonging and agency. The process was, in other words, an intervention in its own right, separate from and additive to the technical changes it produced.

The sustained challenge, consistent with the literature on participatory IS governance, was maintaining the cultural momentum of co-design as the organization returned to growth-oriented OIS expansion and the urgency of the well-being crisis receded from executive attention. Several co-design panel members interviewed in a follow-up study reported that subsequent system updates had been implemented without panel consultation, suggesting that the participatory governance structure had not been institutionalized with sufficient formality to survive the transition from crisis response to business-as-usual. This finding underlines one of the central lessons of the Infosys vignette: PGov requires institutional embedding, not merely the establishment of temporary panels during a period of acute organizational concern.

6.3 Case 3: Healthcare — AIIMS New Delhi, India

The All India Institute of Medical Sciences in New Delhi represents one of the most demanding contexts for OIS redesign: a high-stakes, high-volume clinical environment where information system failures can have direct consequences for patient safety. AIIMS operates as both a premier tertiary care hospital and a leading medical research and education institution, serving a patient population that is among the most complex in South Asia. Its clinical staff work under conditions of extreme cognitive demand, managing caseloads that often exceed global benchmarks by substantial margins while navigating an organizational culture that prizes clinical expertise and professional autonomy. Any OIS intervention in this environment must be designed with exceptional sensitivity to the cognitive realities of clinical work and the professional identity of clinical practitioners.

AIIMS has been engaged in a multiyear digital transformation effort, central to which is the implementation of a hospital information system (HIS) and a clinical decision support system (CDSS) that assists physicians and nurses with diagnosis, drug interaction checking, and treatment protocol adherence. The ambition behind the CDSS was laudable and clinically justified: by embedding evidence-based protocols and pharmacological safety checks directly into the clinical workflow, the system was intended to reduce preventable medication errors, flag drug-drug interactions before prescriptions were finalized, and support junior residents in applying complex treatment guidelines accurately. The design intent was to make the accumulated evidence of clinical science available at the point of care, in real time, without requiring clinicians to interrupt their workflow to consult reference materials.

The initial implementation of the CDSS, completed in 2020, produced a well-documented phenomenon in clinical informatics known as alert fatigue: a condition in which the volume and frequency of system-generated alerts is so high that clinicians begin systematically overriding them without reading them, defeating the purpose of the system (Dubey et al., 2024). At AIIMS, a study of resident physicians found that 68% of CDSS alerts were being overridden within the first three seconds of their appearing on screen, a response time so brief as to preclude genuine reading or deliberation. The system was generating noise rather than signal, and in doing so it was creating a risk profile arguably worse than no system at all: clinicians who had learned to dismiss alerts reflexively might override a genuinely critical warning with the same automatic motion they used to dismiss the irrelevant ones.

Qualitative interviews with residents and attending physicians revealed that the alert problem was rooted in three specific design failures. First, the alert system made no distinction between clinical urgency levels; a flag for a minor drug interaction of theoretical concern appeared in the same format and with the same visual prominence as a warning for a potentially lethal contraindication. Second, alerts provided no explanatory context; they stated that a problem existed without explaining why the algorithm had flagged it or what clinical evidence supported the warning, making it impossible for clinicians to evaluate the alert's relevance to their specific patient's circumstances. Third, the system provided no straightforward pathway for recording a clinician's reasoning when overriding an alert, meaning that override decisions were technically invisible and therefore neither auditable nor learnable from.

A subsequent redesign initiative, led by a joint committee of clinicians, medical informaticists, and user experience researchers, applied principles directly aligned with the AI-D and WBI dimensions of the RECS framework. The committee's work began with a six-month ethnographic study of how clinicians actually interacted with the CDSS during clinical shifts, a methodological choice that produced insights unavailable from log data alone. Researchers observed that alert interruptions were most disruptive when they occurred during the particularly cognitively demanding transitions between patient consultations, a finding that informed a new alert timing protocol that suppressed non-urgent notifications during the three minutes following the initiation of a new patient encounter.

Alerts were stratified by clinical urgency, with only the highest-urgency alerts requiring immediate acknowledgment. Moderate-urgency alerts were queued for review at the next natural pause in clinical activity, and low-urgency informational alerts were routed to an asynchronous review queue accessible between consultations. All alerts were redesigned to include a brief explanatory rationale stating the clinical evidence underlying the flag, a clearly visible contextual override pathway that required the physician to select from a structured list of clinical reasons for the override, and a free-text field for documentation of patient-specific factors not captured in the structured list. The volume of low-priority alerts was reduced by 60% through algorithm recalibration based on clinician feedback about which alert categories generated the most clinically irrelevant triggers.

The redesigned system showed meaningful improvements in alert acknowledgment rates, which increased from 32% to 71% in the six months following implementation, and in clinician-reported cognitive load, which declined significantly on validated measurement scales administered to the same cohort before and after the redesign. Patient safety indicators also showed improvement, though the complexity of attributing patient outcomes to specific system changes in a high-acuity clinical environment requires interpretive caution.

Importantly, the introduction of the mandatory override rationale field, while adding a small time cost of approximately eight seconds to each override interaction, created a data stream of considerable clinical value. The medical informatics team used the accumulated override rationale data to identify systematic errors in the algorithm: categories of clinical presentation for which the alert logic was consistently triggering inappropriately, and categories of genuine risk that the algorithm was missing because it lacked access to relevant clinical context. This iterative feedback loop between clinical practice and algorithmic design exemplifies the AI-D principle of human-algorithm collaboration as an ongoing, bidirectional process rather than a one-time deployment event. The system improved because clinicians taught it; and the system taught clinicians, through better-calibrated alerts, what kinds of drug interactions deserved their closest attention.

The ethical tensions surfaced by the AIIMS experience deserve explicit acknowledgment. The override rationale data, while invaluable for system improvement, also constituted a record of individual clinician judgment decisions that could, in principle, be used for performance evaluation or disciplinary purposes. Clinicians who became aware of this possibility might become reluctant to record honest override rationales, introducing a distortion that would undermine the data's value for system learning. The governance framework around the override data, which restricted access to the medical informatics team and prohibited use in any individual performance review process, was therefore as important a design decision as any technical feature of the system itself. The AIIMS case thus illustrates with particular clarity that OIS redesign in sensitive institutional environments is always simultaneously a technical challenge and an ethical governance challenge, and that the two must be addressed together.

6.4 Cross-Vignette Analysis: Patterns, Tensions, and Transferable Lessons

Examined together, the three vignettes illuminate several recurrent patterns that both validate the RECS framework and reveal its limits. Table 4 presents a structured comparison across the cases.

Table 4. Cross-Vignette Comparative Analysis

Criterion	Tata Steel (Manufacturing)	Infosys (Knowledge Work)	AIIMS Delhi (Healthcare)	Transferable lesson
RECS Dimension emphasized	OAG and AI-D	WBI and PGov	AI-D and WBI	All four dimensions interact; none operates in isolation
Primary OIS challenge	Legacy system inflexibility	Notification overload and burnout	Cognitive load on clinicians	OIS complexity grows faster than human adaptive capacity
Intervention type	Co-bot integration with operator control panels	AI-curated communication and flexible work OIS	Clinical decision support with human override	Participatory redesign yields higher adoption than top-down rollout
Outcome reported	25% reduction in system-related downtime; improved operator confidence	17% drop in reported technostress; improved retention	Reduced alert fatigue; clinician satisfaction improved	Well-being metrics should be embedded in OIS dashboards from day one
Remaining challenge	Scaling co-design across all 80,000 employees globally	Sustaining cultural change after initial IS redesign	Data privacy in AI-assisted diagnostics	Ethical governance of data must accompany every RECS implementation

Note. eNPS = Employee Net Promoter Score. Sources: Tata Steel Sustainability Report (2023); Infosys Annual Report (2023); Dubey et al. (2024).

Three transferable lessons emerge from this analysis. First, the RECS dimensions are mutually reinforcing: none of the three organizations achieved its redesign goals by focusing on a single dimension in isolation. Tata Steel's AI-D improvements required the PGov structures of co-design workshops to succeed. Infosys's WBI changes required PGov legitimacy to produce cultural as well as technical change. AIIMS's AI-D redesign produced WBI benefits as a direct consequence of improving alert calibration and reducing cognitive load. In each case, the dimension that appears primary in Table 4 was enabled and sustained by one or more of the other three dimensions operating simultaneously. This finding carries a practical implication for organizations beginning RECS-inspired redesign: interventions that address a single dimension without attending to the others are likely to produce partial improvements that fail to compound into the systemic change the framework envisions.

Second, the cases demonstrate that well-designed OIS can achieve simultaneous improvements in organizational performance and employee well-being, directly challenging the assumption that these goals trade off against each other. Tata Steel's downtime reduction and operator confidence improvement were achieved together, not at the expense of one another. Infosys's retention improvement was accompanied by productivity stability. AIIMS's alert acknowledgment improvement enhanced both patient safety outcomes and clinician experience. The evidence from these three organizations, taken alongside the broader literature reviewed in Section 3, makes the case for the RECS framework not as a welfare concession made by enlightened employers but as a performance strategy grounded in the recognition that employee capacity is an organizational asset that poorly designed systems systematically erode.

Third, all three cases revealed the limits of technical intervention in the absence of cultural and governance change. The Tata Steel system improved plant operations measurably, but its benefits were unevenly distributed across plant sites with different cultural relationships to participatory management. The Infosys changes improved well-being metrics substantially, but the governance structures required to sustain those improvements were not sufficiently institutionalized to survive the return to normal organizational priorities. The AIIMS redesign improved clinical practice but required robust data governance commitments to prevent the same data that improved the system from being repurposed in ways that would have undermined clinical trust. In each case, the system improved; in each case, the surrounding organizational and governance context determined whether the improvement was lasting and equitable.

7. IMPLICATIONS AND FUTURE DIRECTIONS

7.1 Implications for Information Systems Researchers

The RECS framework points toward a rich agenda for empirical IS research. The four propositions articulated in Section 5 generate hypotheses that can be tested through a variety of methodological approaches. Survey-based studies can operationalize the framework's constructs, measuring each RECS dimension through validated scales and examining their relationships to well-being and performance outcomes. Longitudinal case studies can track the evolution of OIS governance structures and their consequences for employee experience over time. Field experiments can compare redesigned system configurations with control conditions to establish causal rather than merely associative evidence.

The Indian context offers particularly valuable research opportunities. The scale and diversity of India's technology sector workforce, combined with the availability of rich administrative data from large IT firms, creates conditions for natural experiments that would be difficult to construct elsewhere. The intersection of Industry 5.0 principles with India's specific regulatory context, demographic characteristics, and cultural attitudes toward technology and hierarchy represents fertile ground for cross-cultural IS research that challenges the implicit universalism of frameworks developed primarily in European and North American organizational settings (Balakrishnan et al., 2025).

7.2 Implications for Organizational Practitioners and IS Architects

For practitioners, the RECS framework offers a structured starting point for OIS redesign conversations that move beyond feature checklists and vendor marketing materials. The framework's four dimensions provide a language for articulating design priorities that are often implicit and therefore contested. Organizations beginning an OIS redesign effort can use the framework's dimensions as evaluation criteria for vendor proposals, as organizing principles for co-design workshops, and as metrics categories for post-deployment assessment.

IS architects specifically should note the framework's implications for technical specification. The AI-D dimension translates into requirements for explainability APIs, override logging, and feedback ingestion pipelines. The WBI dimension translates into notification management modules, cognitive load dashboards, and privacy-preserving data architectures for well-being data. The OAG dimension translates into API-first modular design, crisis workflow templates, and reconfiguration testing protocols. The PGov dimension translates into governance structures, advisory panel charters, and participatory sprint frameworks that must be established alongside rather than after technical implementation.

7.3 Policy-Level Recommendations

At the policy level, the RECS framework suggests several regulatory and standards-based interventions. First, government procurement frameworks for public sector IS should require vendors to demonstrate compliance with minimum well-being integration standards, analogous to existing requirements for accessibility compliance. India's Digital India initiative, which drives large-scale OIS deployment across government ministries and public services, could incorporate RECS-aligned criteria into its vendor evaluation scorecards.

Second, corporate governance frameworks should require organizations above a threshold size to establish formal employee IS advisory structures as a condition of digital transformation funding or incentives. Third, national occupational health and safety regulations should be updated to explicitly recognize technostress as a recognized occupational health risk, creating a legal foundation for employee claims related to OIS design that demonstrably contributes to psychological harm.

7.4 Limitations of the Current Chapter

This chapter has several limitations that future research should address. The RECS framework is conceptual rather than empirically validated, and while the propositions it generates are theoretically grounded, they remain untested. The case vignettes, while drawn from published organizational reporting and peer-reviewed literature, do not constitute primary research and are subject to the limitations of selective organizational self-disclosure. The framework's applicability across industrial sectors, organizational sizes, and national contexts requires systematic empirical examination. Micro-enterprises and organizations in low-connectivity environments may face constraints that render some RECS dimensions aspirational rather than immediately actionable.

7.5 Future Research Directions

Priority research directions include: the development and validation of a RECS scale instrument for quantitative cross-organizational research; longitudinal studies tracking the relationship between RECS implementation and organizational resilience over disruption cycles; comparative studies examining RECS applicability across Indian, European, and East Asian organizational contexts; and action research collaborations between IS researchers and organizations actively engaged in OIS redesign. The intersection of RECS principles with emerging technologies, including generative AI, extended reality, and ambient computing, also warrants attention, as these technologies will reshape the OIS landscape significantly over the next decade.

8. CONCLUSION

The argument of this chapter is simple in its logic, though demanding in its implications. Organizational information systems are not neutral tools. They embody values, distribute power, shape experience, and determine whether work is a source of meaning or a source of exhaustion. The emergence of Industry 5.0 as a paradigm for industrial development provides the philosophical grounding and the practical mandate for a new generation of OIS that is genuinely designed around the humans who use them.

The RECS framework offered here, comprising the dimensions of Adaptive Intelligence, Well-Being Integration, Organizational Agility, and Participatory Governance, translates this mandate into actionable design orientations. The framework is grounded in five decades of sociotechnical theory, contemporary digital well-being research, and organizational resilience scholarship. It is illustrated through the experiences of organizations as varied as a steel manufacturer in Jamshedpur, a technology services company in Bengaluru, and a clinical institution in New Delhi.

What the vignettes reveal, perhaps most powerfully, is that the choice between productivity and well-being is a false one. Organizations that redesign their information systems around human needs do not sacrifice performance. They build the foundation for a more sustained, more creative, and more resilient kind of performance, one that serves not only organizational shareholders but the employees, communities, and ecosystems on which every organization ultimately depends. Designing systems worthy of the humans who use them is not a gesture of organizational philanthropy. It is, under the logic of Industry 5.0, the central task of twenty-first-century management.

REFERENCES

Agote-Garrido, A., Martín-Gómez, A. M., & Lama-Ruiz, J. R.AgoteGarrido. (2023). Manufacturing system design in Industry 5.0: Incorporating sociotechnical systems and social metabolism for humancentered, sustainable, and resilient production. *Systems, 11*(11), 537. DOI: 10.3390/systems11110537

Ang, K. C. S., Sankaran, S., & Liu, D. (2025). Advancing sociotechnical systems theory: New principles for human-robot team design and development. *Applied Ergonomics, 129*, 104604. Advance online publication. DOI: 10.1016/j.apergo.2025.104604 PMID: 40753964

Balakrishnan, S., Arunkumar, A., John, E. P., Savitha, S., Chandra, K., & Subrahmanyam, S. (2025). Exploring the influence of family supportive benefits on work-life balance and job embeddedness through internal motivation in IT sectors. *Revista Latinoamericana de la Papa, 26*(1), 441–453. https://dialnet.unirioja.es/servlet/articulo?codigo=10627881

Ball, K. (2021). *Electronic monitoring and surveillance in the workplace: Literature review and policy recommendations*. Publications Office of the European Union., DOI: 10.2760/451453

Bodker, S., Dindler, C., Iversen, O. S., & Smith, R. C. (2022). *Participatory design*. Springer., DOI: 10.1007/978-3-031-02235-7

Bruckler, M., Wietschel, L., Messmann, L., Thorenz, A., & Tuma, A. (2024). Review of metrics to assess resilience capacities and actions for supply chain resilience. *Computers & Industrial Engineering, 192*, 110176. DOI: 10.1016/j.cie.2024.110176

Carayon, P., Hoonakker, P., & Hundt, A. S. (2021). Human factors and ergonomics in health care and patient safety. In Salvendy, G. (Ed.), *Handbook of human factors and ergonomics* (5th ed., pp. 1674–1700). Wiley. DOI: 10.1002/9781119636113.ch53

Conz, E., & Magnani, G. (2020). A dynamic perspective on the resilience of firms: A systematic literature review and a framework for future research. *European Management Journal, 38*(3), 400–412. DOI: 10.1016/j.emj.2019.12.004

Dubey, A., Sinha, A., & Raj, A. (2024). Navigating the digital divide in India: A comprehensive guide. *Humanities & Social Sciences Reviews, 12*(2), 16–24. DOI: 10.18510/hssr.2024.1223

European Commission. (2021). *Industry 5.0: Towards a sustainable, human-centric and resilient European industry*. Publications Office of the European Union., DOI: 10.2777/308407

Finbite. (2024). *Sustainable development & digital waste reduction.* Finbite. https://finbite.eu/en/digital-waste/

Giorgi, G., Lecca, L. I., Alessio, F., Finstad, G. L., Bondanini, G., Lulli, L. G., Arcangeli, G., & Mucci, N. (2020). COVID-19-related mental health effects in the workplace: A narrative review. *International Journal of Environmental Research and Public Health, 17*(21), 7857. DOI: 10.3390/ijerph17217857 PMID: 33120930

Horsthofer-Rauch, J., Guesken, S. R., Weich, J., Rauch, A., Bittner, M., Schulz, J., & Zaeh, M. F.HorsthoferRauch. (2024). Sustainability-integrated value stream mapping with process mining: State of the art and future directions. *Production & Manufacturing Research, 12*(1), 2334294. DOI: 10.1080/21693277.2024.2334294

Infosys. (2023). *Infosys integrated annual report 2022-23.* Infosys Limited.

Jarrahi, M. H. (2019). In the age of the smart artificial intelligence: AI's dual capacities for automating and informating work. *Business Information Review, 36*(4), 178–187. DOI: 10.1177/0266382119883999

Jia, X., Chowdhury, M., Prayag, G., & Hossan Chowdhury, M. M. (2020). The role of social capital on proactive and reactive resilience of organizations post-disaster. *International Journal of Disaster Risk Reduction, 48*, 101614. DOI: 10.1016/j.ijdrr.2020.101614

Li, M., Cheng, S., & Lu, M. (2024). Impact of information technology capabilities on organizational resilience: The mediating role of social capital. *Humanities & Social Sciences Communications, 11*(1), 1424. DOI: 10.1057/s41599-024-03951-0

Microsoft. (2022). *Microsoft Work Trend Index 2022: Great expectations — Making hybrid work work.* Microsoft Corporation. https://www.microsoft.com/en-us/worklab/work-trend-index/great-expectations-making-hybrid-work-work

Molino, M., Cortese, C. G., & Ghislieri, C. (2020). The promotion of technology acceptance and work engagement in industry 4.0: From personal resources to information and training over time. *International Journal of Environmental Research and Public Health, 17*(7), 2438. DOI: 10.3390/ijerph17072438 PMID: 32260142

Narayanan, H., & Shankar, S. L. (2025). Cortisol levels and their association with workplace stress in IT workers. *National Journal of Community Medicine, 16*(8), 824–830. Advance online publication. DOI: 10.55489/njcm.160820255534

National Institution for Transforming India Aayog. (2018). *National strategy for artificial intelligence* (#AIforAll). Government of India. https://www.niti.gov.in/sites/default/files/2023-03/National-Strategy-for-Artificial-Intelligence.pdf

Ponomarov, S. Y., & Holcomb, M. C. (2009). Understanding the concept of supply chain resilience. *International Journal of Logistics Management, 20*(1), 124–143. DOI: 10.1108/09574090910954873

Pothuganti, S. K., Ramachandra, G. P., & Devi, V. R. (2025). The impact of technostress on employee engagement and wellbeing: The moderating role of perceived organizational support. *Personnel Review, 44*(5). Advance online publication. DOI: 10.1177/01672533251331503

Praharaj, A., & Chhatoi, B. P. (2025). Enterprise resource planning (ERP) in business: A contextual snapshot. *Global Knowledge, Memory and Communication*. Advance online publication. DOI: 10.1108/GKMC-07-2024-0453

Rajkumar, N., Nachiappan, B., Mathews, A., Radha, V., Viji, C., & Kovilpillai, J. A. (2024). Industry 5.0: The human-centric future of manufacturing. In Sharmila, V. (Eds.), *Challenges in information, communication and computing technology* (pp. 562–567). CRC Press., https://www.taylorfrancis.com/books/9781003559085/chapters/10.1201/9781003559085-97 DOI: 10.1201/9781003559085-97

Schafheitle, S. D., Weibel, A., Ebert, I. L., Kasper, G., Schank, C., & Leicht-Deobald, U. (2020). No stone left unturned? Toward a framework for the impact of datafication technologies on organizational control. *Academy of Management Discoveries, 6*(3), 455–487. DOI: 10.5465/amd.2019.0002

Subrahmanyam, S. (2025). AI and Automation: The Intersection of Human Autonomy and Machine Learning. In Tsvasman, L. (Ed.), *Cybernetic Leadership for Sustainable Innovation* (pp. 237–262). IGI Global Scientific Publishing., DOI: 10.4018/979-8-3373-2484-5.ch009

Subrahmanyam, S. (2026a). Building Applied Models From Multiple Sources. In Hai-Jew, S. (Ed.), *Building Applied Models for Problem Solving* (pp. 27–62). IGI Global Scientific Publishing., DOI: 10.4018/979-8-3373-3301-4.ch002

Subrahmanyam, S. (2026b). Building Trust in the Age of Intelligent Machines: Rethinking Human-Robot Synergy. In Anshari, M., Ordóñez de Pablos, P., & Almunawar, M. (Eds.), *Driving Organizational Transformation Through Human-Robotic Collaboration* (pp. 237–272). IGI Global Scientific Publishing., DOI: 10.4018/979-8-3373-3404-2.ch008

Subrahmanyam, S. (2026c). Entrepreneurship and Startup Business in the Age of AI. In Almasradi, R., & Awad, A. (Eds.), *Innovative Approaches to AI-Supported Hybrid and Remote Workplaces* (pp. 159–192). IGI Global Scientific Publishing., DOI: 10.4018/979-8-3373-7416-1.ch007

Sull, D., Sull, C., & Zweig, B. (2022). Toxic culture is driving the great resignation. *MIT Sloan Management Review*, *63*, 1–9. https://sloanreview.mit.edu/article/toxic-culture-is-driving-the-great-resignation/

Sunyaev, A., Avital, M., & Lacity, M. C. (2026). From ideology to design: Toward purposeful decentralization of information systems governance. *Journal of Information Technology*, *41*(1), 2–14. Advance online publication. DOI: 10.1177/02683962261430919

Tata Steel. (2023). *Tata Steel integrated report and annual accounts 2022-23*. Tata Steel Limited. https://www.tatasteel.com/investors/integrated-report-2022-23/

Vanden Abeele, M. M. P., & Nguyen, M. H. (2022). Digital wellbeing in an age of mobile connectivity: An introduction to the special issue. *Mobile Media & Communication*, *10*(2), 174–189. Advance online publication. DOI: 10.1177/20501579221080899

Venkatesh, V., Thong, J. Y. L., & Xu, X. (2016). Unified theory of acceptance and use of technology: A synthesis and the road ahead. *Journal of the Association for Information Systems*, *17*(5), 328–376. DOI: 10.17705/1jais.00428

Vial, G. (2019). Understanding digital transformation: A review and a research agenda. *The Journal of Strategic Information Systems*, *28*(2), 118–144. DOI: 10.1016/j.jsis.2019.01.003

Wang, B., Liu, Y., Qian, J., & Parker, S. K. (2021). Achieving effective remote working during the COVID-19 pandemic: A work design perspective. *Applied Psychology*, *70*(1), 16–59. DOI: 10.1111/apps.12290 PMID: 33230359

Weill, P., & Woerner, S. L. (2018). *What's your digital business model?: Six questions to help you build the next generation enterprise*. Harvard Business Review Press.

KEY TERMS AND DEFINITIONS

Algorithmic Bias: Systematic and unfair discrimination embedded in AI systems due to biased data, flawed design, or opaque decision-making processes, potentially leading to inequitable workplace outcomes.

Digital Resilience: The ability of organizations and employees to withstand, adapt to, and recover from digital disruptions, including cyber risks, technological changes, and remote work challenges.

Digital Well-Being: The state in which individuals can effectively manage digital technologies to maintain psychological health, productivity, and work-life balance, minimizing stress, overload, and burnout.

Employee-Centric Workplace: A work environment intentionally designed to prioritize employee needs, well-being, engagement, and autonomy, while aligning organizational goals with human values and capabilities.

Human-Centered Design (HCD): A design approach that places users' needs, experiences, and limitations at the core of system development, ensuring technologies are usable, ethical, and supportive of human performance and satisfaction.

Human-Technology Collaboration: A synergistic interaction between humans and intelligent systems in which human judgment, creativity, and emotional intelligence complement machine speed, precision, and data-processing capabilities.

Hybrid Intelligence: A collaborative intelligence model combining human cognitive abilities and artificial intelligence, enabling superior decision-making and problem-solving compared to either humans or machines acting independently.

Industry 5.0: A socio-technical paradigm that extends Industry 4.0 by emphasizing human-centricity, resilience, and sustainability, focusing on the integration of human creativity and advanced technologies to create value beyond efficiency and automation.

Organizational Information Systems (OIS): Integrated digital systems designed to collect, process, store, and disseminate information within organizations, increasingly evolving toward supporting employee experience, collaboration, and well-being.

Organizational Resilience: The capacity of an organization to anticipate, adapt, and recover from disruptions, leveraging digital capabilities, flexible structures, and continuous learning mechanisms.

Chapter 4
Behavioral-by-Design: Integrating Digital Psychology Into Organizational Information Systems for Productivity and Wellness

Doni Sugianto Sihotang
http://orcid.org/0009-0008-5222-4475
Universitas Negeri Jakarta, Indonesia

Usep Suhud
http://orcid.org/0000-0002-1728-0737
Universitas Negeri Jakarta, Indonesia

Agung Wahyu Handaru
Universitas Negeri Jakarta, Indonesia

Yulian Sri Lestari
UIN Datokarama Palu, Indonesia

ABSTRACT

The rapid expansion of artificial intelligence, algorithmic systems, and digitally mediated workplaces has transformed organizational information systems into behavioral environments that shape employee productivity, cognition, and psychological well-being. Existing organizational information systems literature mainly emphasizes technological efficiency and system adoption while providing limited integration of behavioral psychology, digital well-being, and human-centered workplace design. This chapter addresses this gap by proposing a Behavioral-by-Design framework integrating digital psychology, behavioral design, and organizational information

DOI: 10.4018/979-8-2600-0111-0.ch004

systems to support sustainable digital transformation in AI-mediated workplaces. The proposed framework extends behavioral information systems perspectives toward adaptive and psychologically informed organizational systems while offering strategic recommendations for ethical AI governance and sustainable digital well-being practices.

INTRODUCTION

1. The Digital Workplace Transformation

The digital workplace transformation represents a profound reconfiguration of how organizations manage work processes, communication systems, and employee interactions in increasingly technology-mediated environments. In the era of generative artificial intelligence, algorithmic mediation, and advanced analytics, organizational information systems are no longer passive infrastructures but active behavioral environments that shape cognition, decision-making, and employee behavior. Digital systems increasingly influence how employees prioritize tasks, interact with colleagues, and respond to organizational expectations. Consequently, digital transformation is not solely a technological transition but also a behavioral and psychological one that requires organizations to reconsider the relationship among productivity, employee well-being, and human-centered system design.

Digital technologies have significantly enhanced operational efficiency through automation, remote collaboration, and real-time decision-making capabilities. Hybrid work systems, cloud-based collaboration platforms, and AI-assisted organizational tools provide greater flexibility and accessibility, enabling organizations to maintain productivity across geographically distributed workforces (Sihotang, 2026). However, these technological advancements have simultaneously intensified organizational dependence on algorithmic systems and automated decision-making processes. As firms increasingly rely on digital infrastructures to coordinate work activities, employees face rising expectations for continuous responsiveness, perpetual connectivity, and accelerated performance. This dependency creates a paradox in which digital technologies improve efficiency while simultaneously contributing to technostress, cognitive overload, and emotional exhaustion (Han et al., 2025).

The rise of hybrid and remote work environments has further intensified behavioral fragmentation within digital workplaces. Employees frequently navigate multiple communication channels, notifications, and digital tasks simultaneously, resulting in divided attention and reduced cognitive focus. Constant digital interruptions often undermine deep work, increase mental fatigue, and weaken long-term engagement. Moreover, algorithmic productivity monitoring and AI-driven surveillance systems have introduced additional psychological pressures into organizational environments. Performance-tracking technologies, predictive analytics, and behavioral monitoring systems may improve organizational control and operational visibility. However, they can also diminish employee autonomy, increase anxiety, and foster perceptions of digital surveillance. These developments demonstrate the growing tension between technology-driven productivity and employee well-being in contemporary workplaces (Walenta & Koppe, 2025).

Human-centered design has therefore become increasingly critical in organizational information systems. Digital workplaces must support psychological needs such as autonomy, competence, and relatedness to sustain motivation and engagement. Employees are more likely to adopt digital technologies when systems are perceived as supportive rather than intrusive or behaviorally controlling. Consequently, integrating behavioral insights into organizational system design is essential for reducing digital fatigue, mitigating technostress, and fostering sustainable digital well-being (Meske, 2019). Leadership and organizational culture also play vital roles in managing this transformation. Supportive leadership, ethical AI governance, and psychologically safe organizational cultures enable firms to balance technological efficiency with employee welfare, ensuring that digital transformation contributes not only to organizational productivity but also to sustainable human performance and long-term organizational resilience (Diniz et al., 2025).

2. THE EMERGENCE OF DIGITAL PSYCHOLOGY IN ORGANIZATIONAL SYSTEMS

The emergence of digital psychology in organizational systems reflects a significant interdisciplinary shift in understanding how digital environments influence employee cognition, emotion, motivation, and workplace behavior. Digital psychology may be defined as the study of psychological processes, behavioral responses, and patterns of human interaction within digitally mediated environments, particularly those shaped by algorithmic systems, artificial intelligence, and interactive technologies. In organizational contexts, digital psychology examines how employees perceive, adapt to, and behave within digital infrastructures that increasingly influence communication, collaboration, and decision-making processes (Suhud et al., 2026). This perspective extends beyond conventional organizational behavior research by emphasizing the psychological consequences of technologically embedded work systems and AI-mediated interactions (Walter, 2024).

Conceptually, digital psychology intersects with several established disciplines, including organizational behavior, behavioral information systems, cyberpsychology, and human–computer interaction. Organizational behavior traditionally examines employee attitudes, leadership, and workplace dynamics, whereas behavioral information systems research focuses on user behavior and technology adoption within organizational environments. Cyberpsychology primarily investigates psychological experiences in online and virtual settings, while human–computer interaction emphasizes usability, interface design, and user experience. Digital psychology integrates these perspectives into a broader framework that explains how algorithmic systems and intelligent technologies shape behavioral patterns, emotional responses, and organizational culture in digitally mediated workplaces. Consequently, digital psychology provides a more comprehensive lens for understanding employee experiences in environments increasingly governed by automation and AI-driven decision architectures (Vargas-Hernandez & Vargas-González, 2025).

Despite extensive literature on organizational information systems, existing research remains insufficient for explaining the growing behavioral complexity associated with AI-mediated work environments. Traditional organizational information systems literature primarily emphasizes technological adoption, system efficiency, and operational performance, often underestimating the psychological implications of constant connectivity, algorithmic surveillance, and behavioral manipulation. Similarly, many technology acceptance and information systems studies focus predominantly on usability and functional outcomes rather than long-term cognitive and emotional consequences. As digital systems evolve into adaptive and predictive infrastructures, employees are increasingly exposed to behavioral fragmentation, digital fatigue, reduced autonomy, and technostress. These emerging conditions reveal a significant theoretical gap regarding how organizational systems actively shape employee psychology and behavioral outcomes in the era of generative artificial intelligence (Ochoa Pacheco & Coello-Montecel, 2023).

Recent developments in AI-mediated organizational behavior further intensify these debates. AI-driven collaboration systems, predictive analytics, and intelligent monitoring platforms increasingly influence communication patterns, performance evaluation, and workplace interactions. Although such systems can improve efficiency and organizational agility, they may also create concerns regarding autonomy, trust, ethical governance, and psychological well-being. This chapter addresses these gaps by conceptually positioning Behavioral-by-Design as an integrative framework that combines digital psychology, behavioral insights, and human-centered organizational information systems. Through this perspective, the chapter contributes to ongoing theoretical debates concerning the balance between technological efficiency and employee well-being in digitally transformed workplaces (Lathabhavan & Keisham, 2025).

3. OBJECTIVES OF THE CHAPTER

The rapid expansion of organizational information systems in the era of generative artificial intelligence, algorithmic mediation, and advanced digital infrastructures has fundamentally transformed how employees interact with technology, perform organizational tasks, and manage workplace productivity. As digital environments increasingly shape communication patterns, behavioral responses, and decision-making processes, organizations must adopt more behavior-informed approaches that integrate psychological principles into system design and implementation. Existing organizational information systems literature has predominantly focused on operational efficiency, technological adoption, and performance optimization. At the same time, comparatively limited attention has been given to the psychological and behavioral implications of AI-mediated work systems. Therefore, this chapter aims to address this theoretical and practical gap by developing a Behavioral-by-Design perspective that integrates digital psychology into organizational information systems to improve both productivity and employee well-being.

The first objective of this chapter is to conceptually examine the role of digital psychology within organizational information systems and digitally mediated workplaces. This objective seeks to explain how algorithmic systems, AI-driven platforms, and digital infrastructures influence employee cognition, motivation, engagement, and workplace behavior. In doing so, the chapter bridges the domains of behavioral psychology, organizational behavior, and behavioral information systems by positioning digital psychology as a critical theoretical lens for understanding human–technology interaction in contemporary organizations. This objective also contributes to extending current organizational information systems literature beyond purely technical and operational perspectives toward more human-centered and psychologically informed approaches (Gephart Jr, 2002).

The second objective is to identify and critically analyze the behavioral challenges emerging from digital workplace transformation. Specifically, the chapter investigates issues such as technostress, cognitive overload, digital fatigue, behavioral fragmentation, and organizational dependency on algorithmic systems. This objective emphasizes the growing contradiction between technology-driven productivity and employee well-being in AI-mediated work environments. By explicitly examining these behavioral and psychological tensions, the chapter contributes to ongoing theoretical debates regarding the sustainability of digitally transformed workplaces and the long-term consequences of algorithmic organizational systems (Tudose, 2025).

The third objective is to develop an integrative conceptual framework termed Behavioral-by-Design for organizational information systems. This framework seeks to combine behavioral insights, motivational theories, adaptive technologies, and human-centered design principles into a unified organizational approach. Through this framework, the chapter proposes strategic implementation pathways for designing organizational systems that simultaneously enhance productivity, reduce cognitive strain, and foster digital well-being. The framework also aims to support organizations in aligning technological innovation with employee psychological needs and sustainable organizational performance (Borsato et al., 2025).

Finally, this chapter aims to provide strategic and organizational recommendations for implementing Behavioral-by-Design approaches within digital workplaces. This includes proposing organizational strategies related to leadership, ethical AI governance, digital well-being initiatives, and adaptive system development. By integrating systems thinking and digital transformation perspectives, the chapter contributes to future discussions concerning sustainable digital transformation, organizational resilience, and human-centered AI implementation in organizational ecosystems (Casalino et al., 2021).

BACKGROUND

1. Digital Psychology and Behavioral Design

Digital psychology and behavioral design have emerged as critical interdisciplinary approaches for understanding how digital technologies influence human cognition, motivation, emotional responses, and workplace behavior within organizational environments. As organizations increasingly depend on algorithmic systems, artificial intelligence, and adaptive digital platforms, organizational information systems no longer function solely as technical infrastructures but also as behavioral environments that shape employee experiences and decision-making processes. Digital psychology may be understood as the study of psychological processes and behavioral responses within digitally mediated environments. In contrast, behavioral design refers to the intentional application of psychological and behavioral principles to influence user interaction and organizational outcomes. Together, these perspectives establish a theoretical foundation for Behavioral-by-Design approaches that seek to improve productivity while preserving employee well-being in AI-mediated workplaces (Walter, 2024).

Several theoretical perspectives contribute to understanding behavioral dynamics in organizational information systems. Behavioral Design emphasizes how technological environments intentionally shape employee behavior through interface structures, feedback systems, and digital interaction patterns (Gram-Hansen, 2021). Persuasive Technology extends this perspective by examining how digital systems use behavioral triggers, rewards, and persuasive mechanisms to encourage desired actions and sustained engagement. Similarly, Nudge Theory explains how subtle modifications in digital environments can influence decision-making without restricting user choice. However, persuasive and behavioral technologies remain controversial because excessive behavioral influence may contribute to dependency, behavioral manipulation, and reduced autonomy within organizational settings (Morato & Nunes, 2023).

Human-Centered AI provides an alternative perspective by emphasizing transparency, usability, and employee empowerment in intelligent systems. This approach aligns closely with Self-Determination Theory, which holds that employee motivation and well-being depend on the fulfillment of psychological needs such as autonomy, competence, and relatedness. In organizational contexts, digital systems that undermine autonomy through excessive monitoring or algorithmic surveillance may increase technostress and disengagement. Cognitive Load Theory further contributes to this discussion by explaining how excessive information processing demands, multitasking, and continuous notifications create cognitive overload and fragmented attention. Consequently, behavioral design in digital workplaces must balance productivity enhancement with cognitive and psychological sustainability (Supriyadi et al., 2025).

Despite growing literature on digital workplaces and organizational information systems, several theoretical gaps remain unresolved. Existing studies frequently emphasize technological efficiency, usability, and system adoption while offering limited integration of behavioral psychology with organizational information systems. Furthermore, prior research often examines technostress, persuasive technology, or digital engagement separately rather than synthesizing these concepts into a comprehensive framework. Contradictions also persist between organizational goals of maximizing productivity and growing evidence of digital fatigue, cognitive strain, and diminished employee well-being. Therefore, this chapter contributes by proposing Behavioral-by-Design as an integrative conceptual perspective that bridges digital psychology, behavioral design, and organizational information systems within AI-mediated workplaces. Table 1 presents the theoretical synthesis of major perspectives on Behavioral-by-Design, including their primary focus, limitations, and relevance to organizational information systems.

Table 1. Theoretical Synthesis Related to Behavioral-by-Design

Theory	Focus	Limitation	Relevance to Behavioral-by-Design
Behavioral Design	Shaping user behavior through system design	May become behaviorally manipulative	Supports adaptive workplace system design
Persuasive Technology	Encouraging engagement and action	Risks of dependency and excessive digital engagement	Explains behavioral influence mechanisms
Nudge Theory	Indirectly influencing decision-making	Limited focus on long-term psychological effects	Supports subtle behavioral interventions
Human-Centered AI	Human empowerment and ethical AI interaction	Often lacks behavioral implementation strategies	Promotes ethical and employee-centered AI
Cognitive Load Theory	Managing cognitive processing demands	Focuses primarily on cognition rather than organizational behavior	Explains digital fatigue and fragmented attention
Self-Determination Theory	Psychological needs and intrinsic motivation	Less emphasis on algorithmic workplaces	Supports employee well-being and autonomy

2. Organizational Information Systems and Employee Productivity

Organizational Information Systems (OIS) have become essential infrastructures that shape employee productivity, organizational performance, and behavioral dynamics within digitally mediated workplaces. In the era of algorithmic mediation, artificial intelligence, and advanced analytics, organizational information systems no longer operate merely as administrative or operational tools but also function as behavioral environments that influence employee autonomy, decision-making, communication patterns, and emotional experiences. Contemporary organizations increasingly depend on digital platforms, workflow automation, and data-driven monitoring systems to coordinate work activities and improve operational efficiency. Consequently, understanding the relationship between organizational information systems and employee productivity requires a broader perspective that incorporates both technological performance and behavioral implications in digitally transformed organizations.

Organizational information systems can significantly enhance productivity by improving communication efficiency, accelerating access to information, automating repetitive tasks, and facilitating collaborative work processes. These systems enable organizations to standardize workflows, reduce operational errors, and improve decision-making quality through real-time information processing. Knowledge management systems and collaborative digital infrastructures also support organizational learning and innovation by enabling employees to efficiently access and exchange relevant knowledge. When aligned with organizational objectives and employee capabilities, organizational information systems can improve individual productivity, organizational flexibility, and operational responsiveness in dynamic business environments (Sylqa, 2025; Zhang, 2005).

However, the relationship between organizational information systems and employee productivity is increasingly complex and paradoxical. While digital systems improve efficiency and accessibility, they may simultaneously diminish employee autonomy and increase psychological strain. Algorithmic management systems, AI-assisted performance monitoring, and predictive analytics are increasingly used to supervise employee activities, measure productivity, and optimize organizational control. These monitoring systems often intensify performance pressure, reinforce constant connectivity, and reduce perceived autonomy in digital workplaces. Such developments resemble forms of digital Taylorism, where employee behavior becomes increasingly quantified, standardized, and algorithmically regulated. Consequently, employees may experience emotional exhaustion, technostress, and behavioral fatigue despite improvements in organizational efficiency (Bala & Bhagwatwar, 2018).

The productivity paradox further illustrates these tensions within organizational information systems. Although organizations continue to invest heavily in digital infrastructure and advanced technologies, productivity gains are not always proportional to these investments. Research on the information technology productivity paradox suggests that technological efficiency alone cannot guarantee improved organizational performance without considering human capabilities, organizational culture, and behavioral adaptation processes. Excessive dependence on digital systems may also contribute to fragmented attention, information overload, and cognitive exhaustion, reducing employee engagement and long-term productivity (Faryabi & Tajvidi, 2012).

Furthermore, organizational information systems increasingly operate as mechanisms of algorithmic control within contemporary workplaces. AI-driven evaluation systems, productivity dashboards, and digital surveillance platforms can create environments characterized by continuous monitoring and behavioral regulation. While such systems may improve managerial visibility and operational accountability, they also raise concerns regarding employee trust, psychological well-being, and sustainable work practices. Therefore, organizations must adopt more human-centered approaches that balance productivity enhancement with employee autonomy, emotional well-being, and ethical digital governance. Integrating behavioral insights into organizational information systems is essential for developing adaptive digital workplaces that support both organizational performance and sustainable employee productivity.

3. Digital Well-Being in the Workplace

Digital well-being in the workplace has emerged as a critical concept for understanding the behavioral, psychological, and organizational consequences of digital transformation in contemporary work environments. As organizations increasingly adopt artificial intelligence, automated systems, digital collaboration platforms, and algorithmic management technologies, employees experience continuous exposure to digitally mediated work conditions that significantly affect productivity, mental health, and organizational sustainability. Digital well-being refers to the extent to which digital technologies support psychological health, cognitive balance, work satisfaction, and sustainable work engagement while minimizing negative effects such as technostress, cognitive overload, burnout, and emotional exhaustion. Consequently, digital well-being has become an essential dimension of human-centered organizational information systems in the era of generative artificial intelligence and algorithmic mediation (Illgen & Thomas, 2025).

Digital well-being encompasses several measurable dimensions that influence employee experiences within digital workplaces. These dimensions include cognitive well-being, emotional well-being, social well-being, and behavioral sustainability. Cognitive well-being refers to employees' ability to maintain concentration, stable attention, and a manageable cognitive workload while interacting with digital systems. Emotional well-being involves psychological resilience, reduced anxiety, and the ability to manage stress associated with constant connectivity and the demands of digital performance. Social well-being concerns healthy communication patterns, the quality of collaboration, and psychological safety within digitally mediated organizational environments. Behavioral sustainability reflects employees' capacity to maintain long-term productivity without experiencing burnout, disengagement, or digital dependency. These dimensions collectively demonstrate that digital well-being extends beyond technological usability toward broader psychological and organizational outcomes (Li et al., 2025).

A major challenge within digital workplaces is the increasing prevalence of technostress and cognitive fatigue. Employees are frequently exposed to excessive notifications, multitasking requirements, information overload, and uninterrupted digital communication, all of which contribute to cognitive strain and emotional exhaustion. Burnout indicators commonly associated with digitally intensive work environments include reduced concentration, emotional fatigue, declining motivation, irritability, and decreased work engagement. Research further indicates that prolonged digital exposure may undermine psychological safety, particularly when employees perceive excessive monitoring, algorithmic surveillance, or unrealistic productivity expectations within organizational systems. These conditions often weaken employee autonomy and increase workplace anxiety, ultimately affecting organizational performance and long-term well-being (Rahmi et al., 2025; Marsh et al., 2024).

Despite these challenges, organizational information systems can also support digital well-being when developed through human-centered and behaviorally informed approaches. Human-centered digital workplace design emphasizes autonomy, competence, relatedness, and supportive interaction patterns to reduce cognitive burden and enhance employee engagement. Interface simplicity, adaptive feedback systems, manageable communication structures, and psychologically safe digital environments can significantly improve employee well-being and sustainable productivity (Asha & Kumar, 2025). Figure 1 illustrates the conceptual relationships among digital systems, behavioral design, productivity, and employee well-being in digitally mediated workplaces.

Figure 1. Conceptual Relationship

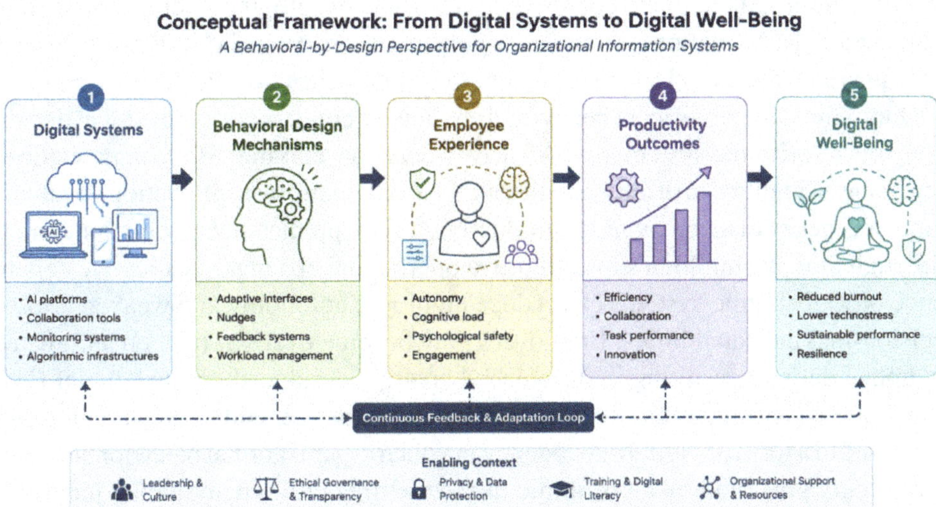

Furthermore, organizations that prioritize digital well-being alongside technological efficiency are more likely to foster innovation, resilience, and sustainable organizational performance. Integrating behavioral insights into organizational information systems, therefore, represents a strategic necessity for balancing productivity enhancement with employee well-being in contemporary digital workplaces (Li et al., 2025).

MAIN FOCUS OF THE CHAPTER

Issues, Controversies, Problems

1. Behavioral Challenges in Organizational Information Systems

The growing integration of artificial intelligence, algorithmic infrastructures, and advanced organizational information systems has created increasingly complex behavioral challenges within digitally mediated workplaces. Contemporary organizational systems no longer function solely as operational technologies but also act as behavioral architectures that influence employee cognition, emotional responses, communication patterns, and workplace conduct. As organizations intensify their reliance on algorithmic systems for workflow coordination, decision-making, and productivity management, employees are exposed to new forms of behavioral pressure, digital surveillance, and cognitive strain. These developments demonstrate that organizational information systems are deeply intertwined with behavioral dynamics, requiring more analytical and human-centered approaches to digital transformation.

One of the most significant behavioral challenges concerns organizational dependency on algorithmic systems and AI-driven decision-making. Many organizations increasingly employ artificial intelligence to automate task allocation, evaluate employee performance, monitor productivity, and predict behavioral outcomes. Although these technologies may improve operational efficiency, excessive dependence on algorithmic systems can reduce employee autonomy and weaken critical decision-making capabilities. Employees may become overly reliant on automated recommendations, resulting in diminished creativity, reduced organizational flexibility, and passive compliance with system-generated decisions. Such conditions contribute to a form of digital dependency in which organizational behavior becomes increasingly governed by algorithmic infrastructures rather than human judgment and collaborative reasoning (Whitney et al., 2009).

Digital surveillance and productivity monitoring systems also represent major behavioral concerns in contemporary organizations. AI-assisted monitoring technologies, predictive analytics, and digital tracking platforms are increasingly used to measure employee performance, communication frequency, screen activity, and behavioral patterns. While organizations justify these systems as mechanisms for improving productivity and accountability, employees often perceive them as intrusive and psychologically controlling. This form of algorithmic oversight resembles digital Taylorism, where employee activities are fragmented, quantified, and continuously evaluated through data-driven monitoring systems. Consequently, constant digital surveillance may intensify productivity pressure, increase emotional exhaustion, and undermine psychological safety within organizational environments (Åberg et al., 2021).

Another critical issue involves behavioral manipulation and AI bias within organizational systems. Behavioral nudges, persuasive interfaces, and adaptive algorithms are frequently embedded within digital platforms to shape employee behavior and optimize organizational outcomes. However, these mechanisms may unintentionally manipulate decision-making processes or reinforce algorithmic biases. AI systems trained on incomplete or biased datasets may produce discriminatory evaluations, unequal task allocation, or unfair performance assessments. Contemporary workplace trends demonstrate growing organizational concerns regarding ethical AI, transparency, and behavioral fairness in algorithmic management systems. For example, AI-assisted recruitment platforms and productivity analytics systems have faced criticism for reproducing demographic bias and reinforcing workplace inequalities. These developments illustrate the urgent need for ethical governance frameworks within organizational information systems (Mago et al., 2022).

Furthermore, behavioral challenges in organizational systems increasingly manifest through technostress, cognitive overload, and fragmented work behaviors. Employees operating in highly connected digital environments frequently experience constant interruptions, excessive demands for multitasking, and persistent pressure to remain available at all times. Such conditions contribute to emotional fatigue, declining engagement, and reduced long-term productivity. Insider threats and insecure digital behaviors may also emerge when employees experience stress, fatigue, or disengagement in digitally intensive work environments. Consequently, organizations must integrate behavioral insights, ethical AI governance, and adaptive human-centered system design into organizational information systems to balance technological efficiency with sustainable employee well-being and organizational resilience (Warkentin & Mutchler, 2014).

2. Ethical Concerns in Behavioral-by-Design Approaches

Behavioral-by-Design approaches in organizational information systems increasingly utilize behavioral analytics, artificial intelligence, persuasive technologies, and adaptive digital infrastructures to shape employee behavior, optimize productivity, and enhance organizational efficiency. Although these systems offer significant operational advantages, they also raise complex ethical concerns regarding autonomy, transparency, accountability, privacy, and behavioral manipulation. In the era of generative artificial intelligence and algorithmic mediation, organizational systems are becoming progressively capable of predicting, influencing, and regulating employee behavior through real-time data analysis and adaptive interventions. Consequently, ethical governance has become a central requirement to ensure that Behavioral-by-

Design systems support employee well-being rather than create digitally coercive organizational environments.

One of the primary ethical concerns involves the tension between behavioral influence and employee autonomy. Persuasive technologies frequently employ nudges, adaptive interfaces, feedback loops, and behavioral triggers to encourage desired organizational behaviors. While these mechanisms may improve engagement and productivity, they may also unintentionally undermine employees' freedom of choice when implemented without transparency or informed consent. Adaptive systems that continuously modify interfaces and recommendations based on behavioral data may subtly shape decisions that employees do not fully recognize. This issue raises ethical concerns about the boundaries between supportive behavioral guidance and manipulative digital interventions within organizational systems (Stock et al., 2016).

Transparency and explainability are, therefore, essential principles within ethical Behavioral-by-Design frameworks. Employees increasingly interact with algorithmic systems that influence recruitment, task allocation, productivity evaluation, and workplace communication. However, many AI-driven organizational systems operate as "black boxes," where employees cannot clearly understand how algorithmic decisions are generated or how behavioral data are interpreted. The absence of explainability may weaken organizational trust, intensify perceptions of unfairness, and reduce psychological safety within digital workplaces. Ethical AI governance requires organizations to establish transparent mechanisms that explain how behavioral analytics, predictive models, and AI-assisted evaluations influence organizational decisions. In this context, explainable AI and responsible AI frameworks are becoming increasingly important components of ethical organizational information systems (Aboshi et al., 2025).

Privacy and informed consent also represent significant ethical challenges in Behavioral-by-Design approaches. Organizational systems frequently collect extensive behavioral data, including communication patterns, productivity metrics, digital interactions, and emotional indicators. Although these data can support organizational optimization and employee well-being initiatives, excessive surveillance and opaque data practices may create intrusive and psychologically stressful environments. Contemporary governance frameworks, including the European Union Artificial Intelligence Act (EU AI Act), emphasize the importance of risk-based AI governance, transparency obligations, human oversight, and protections against manipulative or high-risk AI practices. These developments demonstrate the growing global emphasis on responsible AI implementation and ethical digital governance within organizations (Anderson et al., 2025).

Furthermore, organizations must establish clear boundaries for behavioral manipulation within AI-mediated workplaces. Behavioral-by-Design systems should support employee empowerment rather than exploit cognitive vulnerabilities or intensify productivity pressure. Ethical governance frameworks increasingly advocate principles such as fairness, accountability, human oversight, privacy protection, and psychological well-being as foundational standards for organizational AI systems. Ethics-by-design approaches, therefore, emphasize continuous ethical assessment, stakeholder participation, and governance integration throughout system development processes. By incorporating ethical AI governance into organizational information systems, firms can create adaptive digital environments that balance productivity objectives with employee autonomy, trust, and sustainable well-being (Nussbaumer et al., 2023).

3. Technology-Driven Productivity vs. Employee Well-Being

Technology-driven productivity has become a dominant organizational objective in the era of generative artificial intelligence, algorithmic mediation, and digitally integrated work systems. Organizations increasingly rely on artificial intelligence, automation platforms, predictive analytics, and digital collaboration technologies to optimize operational efficiency, accelerate decision-making, and improve organizational performance. While these technologies provide substantial productivity advantages, they also create complex behavioral and psychological tensions that significantly affect employee well-being. The relationship between technology-driven productivity and employee welfare, therefore, represents a central paradox in contemporary organizational information systems, where efficiency gains frequently coexist with cognitive strain, emotional exhaustion, and declining psychological resilience.

One of the most critical issues within digital workplaces is the efficiency paradox. Although advanced organizational technologies are designed to reduce workload and improve efficiency, employees often experience intensified work demands and increased performance pressure following digital transformation initiatives. AI-assisted workflows, automated reporting systems, and continuous communication platforms frequently accelerate work expectations and create cultures of perpetual responsiveness (Suhud et al., 2025). As organizations pursue productivity optimization through digital infrastructures, employees are increasingly expected to multitask, maintain constant availability, and rapidly adapt to evolving technological demands. Consequently, technologies intended to simplify work processes may unintentionally increase cognitive burden and diminish sustainable work engagement (Rahmi et al., 2025).

Hyperconnectivity further intensifies these behavioral tensions within digitally mediated organizations. Digital communication systems, cloud-based collaboration tools, and mobile work technologies have blurred traditional boundaries between professional and personal life. Employees frequently remain connected to organizational systems beyond formal working hours, creating continuous exposure to notifications, work requests, and performance expectations. Such conditions contribute to emotional fatigue, work-life imbalance, and reduced psychological recovery. This phenomenon increasingly reflects what scholars describe as the "burnout economy," where digital productivity cultures prioritize continuous efficiency and accelerated performance while neglecting long-term employee well-being and psychological sustainability (Ter Hoeven et al., 2016).

These developments reveal a substantial theoretical tension between organizational efficiency objectives and human-centered workplace sustainability. Technology-driven productivity models often emphasize measurable outputs, operational visibility, and algorithmic optimization, whereas employee well-being depends on autonomy, manageable workloads, psychological safety, and cognitive balance. Consequently, organizations face significant trade-offs between maximizing short-term productivity and maintaining sustainable workforce resilience. Excessive dependence on algorithmic productivity systems may undermine creativity, weaken engagement, and contribute to organizational fatigue over time. From an organizational sustainability perspective, digital transformation strategies that neglect employee well-being may ultimately reduce innovation capacity, increase turnover intentions, and weaken long-term organizational adaptability (Dhand & Dhand, 2025).

Despite these challenges, technology-driven productivity and employee well-being do not necessarily represent incompatible organizational goals. Human-centered digital workplace strategies emphasize adaptive technologies, ethical AI governance, workload management, and psychologically supportive organizational cultures to balance productivity enhancement with employee welfare. Organizations that integrate behavioral insights and digital well-being principles into organizational information systems are more likely to achieve sustainable productivity, workforce resilience, and long-term organizational performance in increasingly AI-mediated work environments (Pezzolo & Gupta, 2026).

SOLUTIONS AND RECOMMENDATIONS

1. Behavioral-by-Design Framework for Organizational Information Systems

The Behavioral-by-Design framework offers an integrative, human-centered approach to developing organizational information systems that simultaneously enhance productivity and employee well-being in digitally mediated workplaces. As organizations increasingly adopt artificial intelligence, algorithmic management systems, and adaptive digital infrastructures, traditional technology-centered implementation models have become insufficient for addressing the behavioral and psychological consequences of digital transformation. Behavioral-by-Design extends beyond technical system optimization by integrating behavioral science, digital psychology, organizational behavior, and human-centered design into a unified conceptual framework. This framework contributes theoretically by bridging behavioral psychology and organizational information systems, while providing practical pathways to develop sustainable and ethically governed digital workplaces.

The Behavioral-by-Design framework conceptualizes organizational information systems as adaptive behavioral ecosystems that continuously influence employee cognition, motivation, emotional responses, and workplace interactions. Rather than treating employees as passive users of technology, the framework positions human behavior as a central component of organizational system design. The framework incorporates five interconnected dimensions: Behavioral Input, Psychological Mechanism, Adaptive System, Organizational Outcome, and Well-being Output. Behavioral Input refers to employee behaviors, cognitive patterns, digital interactions, and organizational communication processes. Psychological Mechanisms involve motivational dynamics, cognitive load, emotional responses, and behavioral adaptation processes influenced by digital systems. Adaptive Systems represent AI-driven technologies, behavioral analytics, feedback systems, and human-centered interfaces that dynamically respond to employee needs and organizational conditions. Organizational Outcomes include productivity, collaboration quality, innovation capacity, and operational efficiency, while Well-being Outputs encompass psychological safety, reduced technostress, resilience, and sustainable employee engagement (Hevner et al., 2004).

Figure 2. shows the conceptual structure of the Behavioral-by-Design framework for organizational information systems.

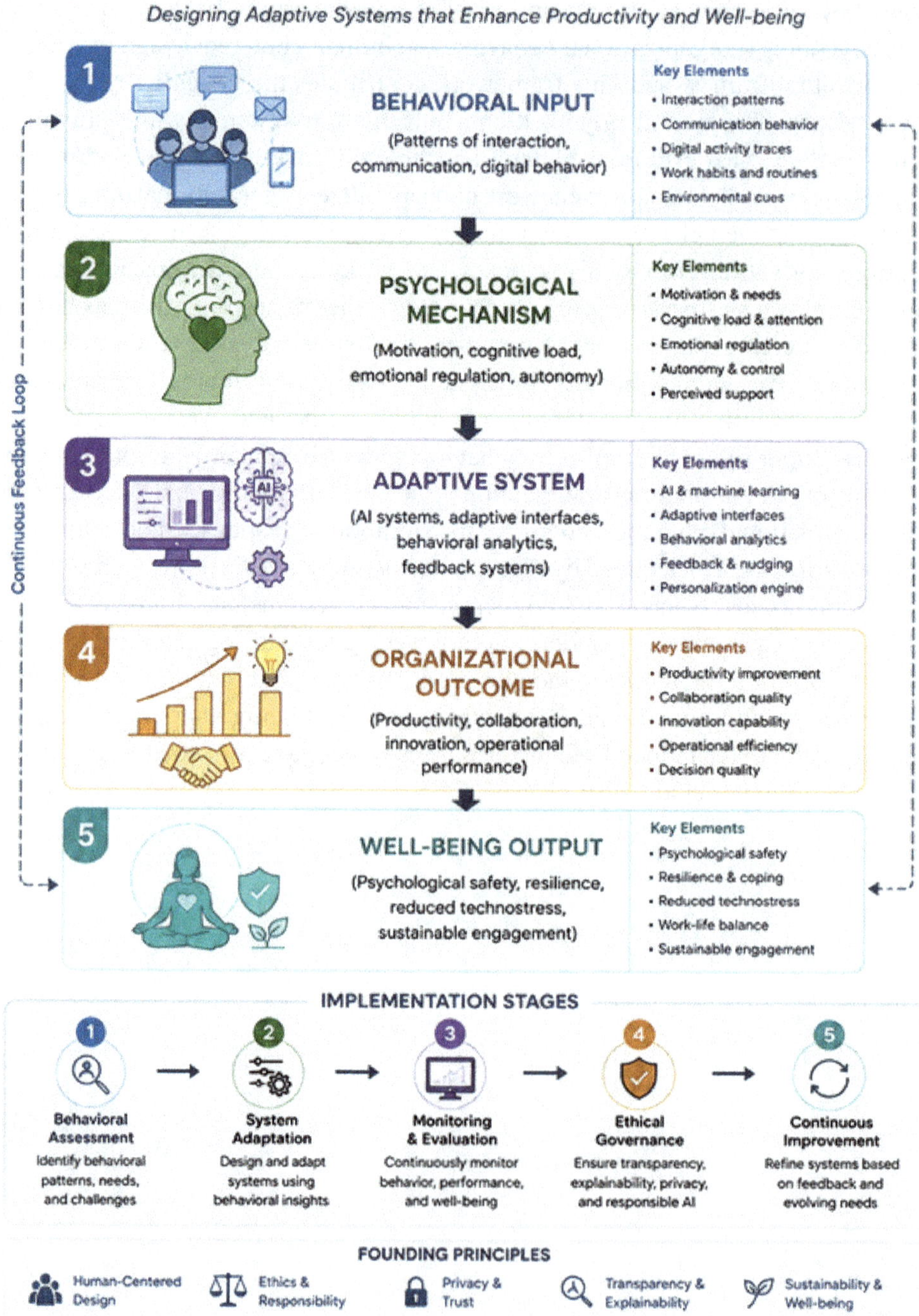

The framework also proposes several implementation stages to support organizational adoption and sustainable digital transformation. The first stage involves behavioral assessment, where organizations identify employee behavioral patterns, cognitive challenges, and digital workplace stressors. The second stage focuses on system adaptation through the integration of human-centered design principles, adaptive technologies, and behaviorally informed interfaces. The third stage emphasizes continuous monitoring using behavioral analytics and organizational performance indicators to evaluate system effectiveness and employee experiences. The fourth stage concerns ethical governance, including transparency, explainability, privacy protection, and responsible AI implementation to ensure organizational trust and accountability. Finally, the fifth stage involves continuous improvement, where organizations iteratively refine digital systems in response to behavioral feedback, technological changes, and evolving organizational needs (Caschera & Guzzo, 2026).

Furthermore, the Behavioral-by-Design framework integrates systems thinking and design thinking perspectives to address complex organizational challenges associated with digital transformation. Systems thinking enables organizations to understand the interdependencies among technological infrastructure, employee behavior, and organizational culture, while design thinking promotes empathy, collaboration, and iterative innovation. By integrating these perspectives, Behavioral-by-Design provides both a conceptual contribution and a practical organizational strategy for creating adaptive, ethical, and sustainable digital workplaces that balance technological efficiency with employee well-being and long-term organizational resilience (Gholami, 2025; Abraham et al., 2004).

2. Designing Productivity-Oriented and Well-Being-Focused Systems

Designing productivity-oriented and well-being-focused organizational systems has become increasingly important in the era of artificial intelligence, algorithmic management, and digitally mediated workplaces. Contemporary organizations face growing pressure to enhance operational efficiency while simultaneously maintaining employee well-being, psychological resilience, and sustainable engagement. Traditional organizational information systems have primarily emphasized productivity optimization, workflow automation, and performance measurement, often overlooking the behavioral and psychological consequences of digitally intensive work environments. Consequently, organizations require more actionable and human-centered implementation strategies that integrate behavioral insights, adaptive technologies, and ethical governance into digital workplace systems.

One of the most important implementation strategies involves adopting AI-assisted personalization within organizational information systems. AI-driven personalization technologies can adapt interfaces, workflows, communication patterns, and digital recommendations based on employee behaviors, cognitive preferences, and work contexts. Personalized systems may help employees manage workloads more effectively, reduce unnecessary interruptions, and improve task prioritization. For example, intelligent workflow systems can recommend optimal task sequences, automatically adjust notification frequency, and identify periods of excessive digital overload. Such adaptive mechanisms may reduce cognitive fatigue and improve employee productivity while supporting healthier digital work experiences. However, organizations must ensure that personalization systems remain transparent, ethical, and supportive rather than behaviorally manipulative or excessively intrusive (Casalino et al., 2021).

Adaptive interface design also represents a critical component of well-being-focused organizational systems. Human-centered interface structures should prioritize usability, clarity, and cognitive simplicity to minimize digital fatigue and fragmented attention. Excessive notifications, complex interfaces, and constant multitasking requirements frequently contribute to technostress and declining employee engagement. Therefore, organizations should implement adaptive communication structures, simplified dashboard systems, and customizable interface environments that support employee autonomy and psychological comfort. In hybrid and remote work environments, adaptive interfaces can also facilitate healthier communication rhythms and reduce hyperconnectivity by enabling employees to manage digital availability and collaboration intensity more effectively (Asha & Kumar, 2025).

Another essential strategy involves implementing cognitive load management systems within organizational information infrastructures. Cognitive load management refers to organizational mechanisms designed to minimize information overload, excessive multitasking, and continuous digital interruptions. Organizations can adopt practices such as structured communication policies, scheduled focus periods, intelligent notification filtering, and workload balancing systems to support sustainable employee productivity. For instance, some organizations have introduced "digital quiet hours," asynchronous communication policies, and AI-assisted workload monitoring systems to reduce burnout and improve psychological recovery. These practices demonstrate how organizational digital policies can directly influence employee well-being and the sustainability of long-term performance (Rahmi et al., 2025).

Organizations must also establish governance-oriented digital workplace policies that align technological implementation with ethical and behavioral objectives. Effective organizational practices include transparent AI use policies, employee participation in digital transformation, privacy protection protocols, and responsible monitoring guidelines. Ethical AI governance frameworks should clearly define acceptable boundaries regarding behavioral analytics, employee monitoring, and algorithmic decision-making. Furthermore, organizations should provide digital literacy training, well-being support programs, and leadership initiatives that promote psychologically safe digital environments. These organizational practices reinforce trust, employee autonomy, and sustainable engagement within AI-mediated workplaces (Nussbaumer et al., 2023).

Ultimately, productivity-oriented and well-being-focused systems require organizations to move beyond purely efficiency-driven technological implementation toward adaptive, behaviorally informed, and ethically governed digital ecosystems. Integrating AI-assisted personalization, adaptive interface design, and cognitive load management into organizational information systems enables organizations to balance operational productivity with employee well-being, resilience, and sustainable organizational performance in increasingly digital work environments (Pezzolo & Gupta, 2026).

3. Organizational Strategies for Digital Well-Being Implementation

The successful implementation of digital well-being initiatives requires organizations to adopt comprehensive strategic approaches that integrate governance structures, leadership commitment, human resource policies, and digital culture transformation into organizational information systems. As organizations increasingly depend on artificial intelligence, digital collaboration technologies, and algorithmic infrastructures, employee well-being can no longer be treated as an isolated human resource concern. However, it must instead become a strategic organizational priority. Digital well-being implementation, therefore, requires coordinated organizational strategies that balance technological efficiency with psychological sustainability, ethical governance, and long-term workforce resilience.

One of the most critical organizational strategies involves establishing governance models for digital well-being and responsible AI implementation. Governance-oriented approaches enable organizations to define ethical standards, behavioral boundaries, and accountability mechanisms related to digital workplace systems. Effective governance frameworks should include policies on algorithmic transparency, employee privacy protection, the use of behavioral analytics, and AI-assisted decision-making processes. Organizations should also establish interdisciplinary governance teams involving information technology departments, human resource management, organizational leaders, and employee representatives to ensure that digital transformation initiatives align with employee well-being objectives. Such governance models are essential for maintaining organizational trust, ethical accountability, and sustainable digital workplace practices (Nussbaumer et al., 2023).

Leadership also plays a central role in fostering digital well-being within organizational environments. Organizational leaders significantly influence how employees perceive digital transformation, technological adaptation, and workplace expectations. Supportive leadership practices can reduce employee anxiety, strengthen psychological safety, and encourage healthier digital work behaviors. Leaders must therefore promote balanced productivity expectations, encourage sustainable communication practices, and model responsible digital engagement. In hybrid and remote work environments, leadership behaviors that emphasize empathy, flexibility, and awareness of well-being are increasingly important for preventing burnout and excessive hyperconnectivity. Furthermore, organizational leaders should actively communicate the purpose, benefits, and ethical safeguards associated with AI-assisted systems to strengthen employee trust and organizational transparency (Asha & Kumar, 2025).

Human resource management policies also represent essential mechanisms for implementing digital well-being strategies. HR departments should integrate digital well-being principles into workload management, employee development, performance evaluation, and workplace support systems. Practical HR initiatives may include flexible work arrangements, digital fatigue prevention policies, mental health support programs, and digital literacy training. Organizations may also implement communication policies such as “right to disconnect” initiatives, structured asynchronous collaboration practices, and scheduled digital recovery periods to reduce cognitive overload and emotional exhaustion. These policies support sustainable employee engagement while reinforcing organizational commitment to psychological well-being and workforce resilience (Rahmi et al., 2025).

Digital culture transformation is another essential requirement for the successful implementation of well-being. Organizational culture increasingly shapes employees' behavioral norms regarding technology use, productivity expectations, and digital responsiveness. In many organizations, productivity-oriented digital cultures encourage constant availability and accelerated performance, contributing to technostress and burnout. Therefore, organizations must cultivate human-centered digital cultures that value psychological safety, sustainable productivity, ethical use of technology, and collaborative well-being practices. Table 2 presents practical organizational strategies to address digital workplace challenges through behavioral and governance-oriented solutions.

Table 2. Organizational Strategies for Digital Well-Being Implementation

Organizational Problem	Behavioral Solution	Expected Outcome
Technostress and cognitive overload	Cognitive load management systems and digital quiet hours	Reduced fatigue and improved concentration
Hyperconnectivity and burnout	Right-to-disconnect policies and workload balancing	Better work-life balance and resilience
AI distrust and surveillance concerns	Transparent AI governance and employee participation	Increased trust and psychological safety
Fragmented communication	Adaptive collaboration systems and asynchronous communication	Improved collaboration and reduced interruptions
Low digital adaptability	Digital literacy training and behavioral coaching	Higher engagement and sustainable productivity

Organizations that integrate governance models, supportive leadership, strategic HR policies, and human-centered digital cultures into organizational information systems are more likely to achieve sustainable digital transformation and long-term employee well-being in AI-mediated workplaces (Casalino et al., 2021).

FUTURE RESEARCH DIRECTIONS

1. AI-Driven Behavioral Adaptive Systems

AI-driven behavioral adaptive systems signify a nascent domain within corporate information systems, in which artificial intelligence dynamically responds to user behavior, environmental factors, and organizational goals. Future research must investigate how adaptive systems might improve productivity while protecting employee well-being in the era of generative AI and algorithmic mediation. These systems employ behavioral analytics, machine learning, and real-time feedback mechanisms to continually modify digital environments, thereby establishing personalized and adaptive work systems. As enterprises increasingly rely on data, AI-driven behavioral adaptive systems present opportunities to enhance corporate efficiency, decision-making, and employee experience.

A primary focus for future research is the creation of adaptive AI frameworks that incorporate behavioral insights into organizational processes. AI-driven systems can assess employee behavior, workload patterns, and engagement levels to enhance task allocation and communication tactics. These adaptive frameworks enable firms to adjust dynamically to evolving work environments, thereby improving resilience and operational efficiency. Research indicates that incorporating AI into organizational behavior will profoundly impact future job design, necessitating systems that can learn from human interactions and adapt to changing organizational requirements (Çitli, 2025).

A further significant research avenue is to multi-agent behavioral modeling and distributed intelligence. AI-driven adaptive systems may employ multi-agent architectures to replicate and orchestrate intricate organizational behaviors. Multi-agent systems enable autonomous entities to engage, cooperate, and enhance workflows in real time. These models are especially beneficial in collaborative settings when teams function across digital platforms and geographic borders. Subsequent research should investigate how multi-agent behavioral systems might improve collaboration, knowledge dissemination, and decision-making in adaptive organizational contexts (Gorodetsky et al., 2015).

Explainable and ethical AI is a vital research goal in AI-driven behavioral adaptive systems. As AI systems increasingly impact employee conduct, openness and trust are paramount. Explainable AI methodologies seek to render algorithmic conclusions comprehensible and accountable, thereby alleviating apprehensions about bias, surveillance, and privacy. Studies on AI-augmented organizational frameworks underscore the importance of ethical governance and responsible AI implementation in preserving employee trust and organizational legitimacy. Future research should focus on developing explainable behavioral models that harmonize customization with ethical responsibility (Mishra & Jadeja, 2025).

Furthermore, subsequent research ought to explore AI-facilitated optimization and adaptive resource allocation. Adaptive AI systems can enhance workload allocation, workforce management, and operational efficiency through reinforcement learning and predictive analytics. These technologies enable firms to enhance agility, performance, and employee well-being concurrently. AI-driven optimization models can adapt workflows in real time based on performance metrics, ensuring sustainable productivity in complex digital environments (Luo, 2025).

2. Neuroadaptive Organizational Information Systems

Neuroadaptive Organizational Information Systems (NOIS) constitute a nascent research domain that amalgamates neuroscience, artificial intelligence, and organizational information systems to improve productivity and employee welfare. In the era of generative artificial intelligence and algorithmic mediation, forthcoming research should investigate how neuroadaptive systems might adaptively respond to users' cognitive and emotional conditions. These systems seek to enhance human-technology interaction by modifying digital environments according to brain feedback, cognitive load, and emotional states. As organizations increasingly rely on digital technologies for decision-making and collaboration, neuroadaptive organizational information systems have considerable potential to foster intelligent, human-centered workplaces.

A significant avenue for future study entails enhancing neuroadaptive system design via real-time personalization and adaptive feedback systems. Neuroadaptive systems use brain signals, cognitive metrics, and behavioral data to modify user interfaces and workflows dynamically. These solutions can streamline task complexity, alleviate cognitive burden, and improve user engagement. Investigations into neuroadaptive technologies underscore the significance of adaptive interfaces that respond to mental workload and attention levels, thereby facilitating enhanced and sustainable organizational performance. Future research should investigate the potential of real-time neuroadaptive feedback to enhance productivity and promote employee well-being in intricate digital settings (Fafrowicz et al., 2012).

A vital research avenue involves integrating neuroscience techniques into organizational information systems. Technologies such as electroencephalography (EEG), eye-tracking, and biometric sensors provide insights into cognitive and emotional processes during digital interactions. These instruments help businesses better understand decision-making behavior, stress responses, and engagement levels. NeuroIS research indicates that integrating cognitive neuroscience into information systems can markedly improve system usability and user experience. Subsequent research ought to explore scalable and ethical approaches for incorporating these technologies into routine organizational processes (Zhao & Siau, 2018).

Subsequent studies ought to investigate cognitive and emotional processes in organizational decision-making. Cognitive and emotional states affect employees' interpretation of information, strategic decision-making, and collaboration with digital systems. Neuroadaptive systems facilitate decision-making by detecting cognitive exhaustion, emotional stress, and attention patterns. Studies on cognition and emotion in decision-making reveal that both emotional and cognitive elements profoundly influence organizational results. Neuroadaptive systems that consider these characteristics may enhance leadership efficacy, team collaboration, and organizational intelligence (Kim et al., 2006).

Furthermore, the multidisciplinary amalgamation of neuroscience, artificial intelligence, and intelligent organizational systems signifies a promising avenue for research. Neuroadaptive systems can improve human–AI collaboration by offering context-sensitive decision support and adaptive learning settings. Intelligent organizational systems using neuroadaptive insights may enhance workforce resilience and adaptive performance. Subsequent studies ought to investigate the role of neuroadaptive systems in enhancing intelligent organizational ecosystems and facilitating sustainable digital transformation (Methuku & Kamatala, 2025).

3. Digital Well-Being Metrics and Measurement Models

The increasing incorporation of artificial intelligence and algorithmic systems inside organizational settings has heightened the demand for comprehensive digital well-being measures and assessment frameworks. As digital technologies increasingly influence employee conduct, productivity, and mental health, future research should focus on developing comprehensive frameworks for assessing digital well-being within organizational information systems. These assessment models are crucial for comprehending the impact of digital environments on cognitive burden, emotional states, and employee engagement in the era of generative artificial intelligence and algorithmic mediation.

A significant avenue for future research is the development of multidimensional digital well-being indicators. Digital well-being is intrinsically multifaceted and necessitates assessment across psychological, social, and professional spheres. Recent studies highlight the need for comprehensive indices to assess employee well-being across both professional and personal digital environments. Multifaceted assessment instruments, such as comprehensive workplace well-being indices, enable firms to evaluate employee experiences and identify risk factors associated with digital overload and stress. These models offer significant insights into behavioral patterns and facilitate the development of productivity-centered and well-being-oriented organizational structures (Floridou et al., 2025).

A promising research avenue is the creation of context-specific digital well-being assessment instruments. Diverse organizational contexts, sectors, and labor demographics necessitate customized measuring frameworks. Digital well-being metrics used in business settings must account for factors such as remote employment, digital collaboration, and algorithmic surveillance. Psychometric validation studies emphasize the need to develop reliable, contextually relevant digital well-being tools that accurately reflect employees' perceptions and behavioral responses to digital technologies. Subsequent studies ought to investigate the adaptation of these tools across various organizational environments and cultural contexts (Cruz et al., 2025).

Subsequent research should investigate the incorporation of sophisticated technologies and real-time measuring methodologies. Artificial intelligence, machine learning, and behavioral analytics provide avenues for dynamic monitoring of digital well-being. Ecological momentary assessment and computational phenotyping methodologies enable researchers to document real-time behavioral and psychological alterations associated with digital technology use. These strategies enable organizations to detect early signs of digital weariness, stress, and diminished engagement, thereby permitting proactive treatments. Real-time assessment methods can increase organizational decision-making and facilitate adaptive digital workplace initiatives (Zhan & Wang, 2026).

Moreover, cohesive frameworks for assessing digital well-being constitute a vital research imperative. Human-centered artificial intelligence frameworks underscore the need to incorporate digital well-being indicators into organizational systems and decision-making processes. Interdisciplinary collaboration among researchers in psychology, information systems, and organizational behavior can enhance comprehensive measurement models that integrate productivity and employee well-being. Subsequent research ought to concentrate on establishing standardized digital well-being frameworks that facilitate sustainable digital transformation and the appropriate implementation of AI (Shin, 2025).

CONCLUSION

The rapid evolution of organizational information systems, artificial intelligence, and digitally mediated work environments has fundamentally transformed how organizations manage productivity, employee behavior, and workplace interactions. This chapter demonstrates that digital transformation should no longer be understood solely as a technological process but rather as a behavioral and psychological transformation that significantly influences employee well-being, organizational culture, and long-term sustainability. By integrating perspectives from digital psychology, behavioral design, organizational information systems, and human-centered AI, this chapter contributes to the growing discourse on how organizations can balance technological efficiency with sustainable employee well-being in increasingly algorithmic workplaces.

The primary intellectual contribution of this chapter lies in the development of the Behavioral-by-Design framework as an integrative conceptual perspective for organizational information systems. Unlike traditional approaches to organizational information systems that primarily emphasize technological adoption and operational performance, this chapter positions behavioral and psychological dimensions as central components of digital workplace design. The framework contributes to the existing literature by synthesizing concepts from behavioral psychology, persuasive technology, human-centered AI, cognitive load theory, and organizational behavior into a unified model that explains how digital systems shape employees' cognition, motivation, emotional regulation, and workplace behavior. Consequently, this chapter extends the behavioral information systems perspective beyond technology acceptance and usability toward broader issues of digital well-being, ethical governance, and sustainable organizational performance (Hevner et al., 2004).

This chapter also provides several important theoretical implications. First, it advances the integration of digital psychology and organizational information systems by conceptualizing organizational technologies as adaptive behavioral ecosystems rather than passive operational infrastructures. Second, it contributes to theoretical debates concerning technostress, hyperconnectivity, algorithmic dependency, and digital surveillance by emphasizing the paradoxical relationship between productivity optimization and employee well-being. Third, the chapter highlights the importance of ethical AI governance, transparency, explainability, and human-centered system design within AI-mediated organizational environments. These contributions support the development of more interdisciplinary and behaviorally informed approaches to digital transformation research (Walter, 2024).

From a practical perspective, the chapter provides actionable implications for managers, human resource professionals, digital leaders, and organizational policy-makers. Organizations are encouraged to adopt governance-oriented digital transformation strategies that integrate behavioral assessment, adaptive system design, cognitive load management, ethical AI implementation, and employee well-being initiatives into organizational information systems. Human resource departments should incorporate digital well-being policies, flexible communication practices, and digital literacy programs to reduce burnout and strengthen workforce resilience. Organizational leaders must also foster psychologically safe digital cultures that support sustainable productivity and responsible technology use in hybrid and AI-driven workplaces (Rahmi et al., 2025).

Strategically, this chapter emphasizes that the future of digital workplaces depends on organizations' ability to develop human-centered AI systems that align technological innovation with employee psychological needs and organizational sustainability objectives. Sustainable digital transformation requires organizations to move beyond efficiency-driven automation toward adaptive, ethically governed digital ecosystems that support both productivity and well-being. Ultimately, Behavioral-by-Design offers a strategic foundation for future organizational information systems by demonstrating that technological advancement and human well-being should not be treated as competing priorities but as interconnected dimensions of sustainable organizational success in the age of artificial intelligence (Casalino et al., 2021).

ACKNOWLEDGMENT

The authors acknowledge financial support from the Indonesian Ministry of Higher Education, Science, and Technology (Kemendiktisaintek) through the PMDSU (Pendidikan Magister menuju Doktor untuk Sarjana Unggul) program under Grant Numbers 0419/C3/DT.05.00/2025 and 083/C3/DT.05.00/PL/2025.

REFERENCES

Åberg, P., Arenö, E., & Alvinius, A. (2021). Organizational challenges in the public sector: A qualitative study of the Swedish Armed Forces and elderly care. *Qualitative Sociology Review, 17*(3), 34–54. DOI: 10.18778/1733-8077.17.3.02

Aboshi, S., Thomas, D. R., & Moshfeghi, Y. (2025). The ethics of psychological manipulation in adversarial conversational AI: Confronting the recognition-behaviour gap. In *Proceedings of the 7th ACM Conference on Conversational User Interfaces* (pp. 1–6). DOI: 10.1145/3719160.3737616

Abraham, D., Leon, L., Nakatsu, R., Przasnyski, Z., & Seal, K. (2004). The alignment of organizational incentives with organizational goals across IT adoption stages. In *Proceedings of the Americas Conference on Information Systems.*

Anderson, J., Frank, L. E., & Spahn, A. (Eds.). (2025). *The ethics of behaviour change technologies: Beyond nudging and persuasion.* Bloomsbury Publishing. DOI: 10.5040/9798881847432

Asha, M., & Kumar, A. (2025). Interface design and employee well-being in the digital workplace: The role of basic psychological need satisfaction. *Asian Journal of Interdisciplinary Research, 8*(3), 29–40.

Bala, H., & Bhagwatwar, A. (2018). Employee dispositions to job and organization as antecedents and consequences of information systems use. *Information Systems Journal, 28*(4), 650–683. DOI: 10.1111/isj.12152

Borsato, M., Lattanzio, S., & Newnes, L. (2025). Leveraging motivational theories to enhance engagement and productivity in manufacturing digitalisation projects. In *Transdisciplinarity for a better world* (pp. 409–418). IOS Press. DOI: 10.3233/ATDE251113

Casalino, N., Armenia, S., & Di Nauta, P. (2021). Inspiring the organizational change and accelerating the digital transition in public sector by systems thinking and system dynamics approaches. In *International KES Conference on Smart Education and Smart E-Learning* (pp. 197–214). Springer. DOI: 10.1007/978-981-16-2834-4_17

Caschera, M. C., & Guzzo, T. (2026). User-centred interaction design for enhancing professional well-being in healthcare environments. *Health Care*, *14*(5), 637. PMID: 41827591

Çitli, I. (2025). AI and the employee: Emerging organizational behavior trends for the future of work. In *The future of work and work design*.

Cruz, G. V., Liberacka-Dwojak, M., Wiłkość-Dębczyńska, M., Terzioğlu, M. A., Farchione, T., Lecomte, T., & Khazaal, Y. (2025). Perceived digital well-being scale in the United States and United Kingdom: Psychometric validation study. *JMIR Mental Health*, *12*(1), e78334. DOI: 10.2196/78334 PMID: 41166607

Dhand, S. (2025). Human-centric digital workplace: Designing for employee well-being and productivity. In *Human-centric, sustainable, and resilient organizations in the digital age* (pp. 125–146). IGI Global Scientific Publishing.

Diniz, P., Marques, I. C. P., & Pereira, Â. M. (2025). Leadership, human-centred management and organisational culture: Pathways to well-being and innovative work based on a systematic review. *Sustainability (Basel)*, *17*(24), 11181. DOI: 10.3390/su172411181

Fafrowicz, M., Marek, T., Karwowski, W., & Schmorrow, D. (Eds.). (2012). *Neuroadaptive systems: Theory and applications*. CRC Press. DOI: 10.1201/b13019

Faryabi, M., & Tajvidi, M. (2012). Investigation the effect of investment in information technology on organization productivity. *Iranian Journal of Information Processing and Management*, *27*(1), 340–352.

Floridou, G. A., Katre, F., & Jeuken, E. (2025). A digital tool for assessing well-being at the workplace and in personal life: Development and validation of the Quan Well-Being Index. *JMIR Formative Research*, *9*, e73713. DOI: 10.2196/73713 PMID: 40779765

Gephart, R. P.Jr. (2002). Introduction to the brave new workplace: Organizational behavior in the electronic age. *Journal of Organizational Behavior*, *23*(4), 327–344. DOI: 10.1002/job.143

Gholami, B. (2025). Pathways to innovation: Empowering change with systems and design thinking. In *Mastering innovation in business* (pp. 21–46). IGI Global.

Gorodetsky, V. I., Samoylov, V. V., & Trotskii, D. V. (2015). The reference ontology of collective behavior of autonomous agents and its extensions. *Journal of Computer and Systems Sciences International*, *54*(5), 765–782. DOI: 10.1134/S1064230715030089

Gram-Hansen, S. B. (2021). Defining features of behavior design: Considering context. In *International Conference on Persuasive Technology* (pp. 308–319). Springer International Publishing. DOI: 10.1007/978-3-030-79460-6_24

Han, Z., Song, G., Zhang, Y., & Yan, L. (2025). Enhancing employees' workplace well-being through workplace digitization: Exploring the mediating roles of job demands and digital anxiety. *Frontiers in Psychology*, *16*, 1642489. DOI: 10.3389/fpsyg.2025.1642489 PMID: 40787118

Hevner, A. R., March, S. T., Park, J., & Ram, S. (2004). Design science in information systems research. *Management Information Systems Quarterly*, *28*(1), 75–105. DOI: 10.2307/25148625

Illgen, K. M., & Thomas, O. (2025). Towards the operationalization of digital well-being in the world of new work: Development of a taxonomy. In *INFORMATIK 2025* (p. 843). Gesellschaft für Informatik.

Kim, K. H., Payne, G. T., & Tan, J. A. (2006). An examination of cognition and affect in strategic decision-making. *The International Journal of Organizational Analysis*, *14*(4), 277–294. DOI: 10.1108/19348830610849709

Li, Q., Abdul Ghani Azmi, I., & Norman, A. A. (2025). Enhancing sustainable innovation through workplace well-being and digital capability: A systematic literature review toward responsible and cleaner consumption. *Cleaner and Responsible Consumption*, *18*, 100305. DOI: 10.1016/j.clrc.2025.100305

Luo, J. (2025). AI empowers enterprise agility and performance: Research trends and implications for future research. *Business Information Review*, *42*(4), 238–257. DOI: 10.1177/02663821251384881

Mago, B., Ishaq Almaazmi, K., Jafar Almaazmi, A., Mohammed Falaha, K., & Dahi Almidfaa, E. (2022). Modeling situational IT ethics in UAE. *International Journal for Global Academic & Scientific Research*, *1*(2), 21–35. DOI: 10.55938/ijgasr.v1i2.10

Marsh, E., Perez Vallejos, E., & Spence, A. (2024). Overloaded by information or worried about missing out on it: A quantitative study of stress, burnout, and mental health implications in the digital workplace. *SAGE Open*, *14*(3), 21582440241268830. DOI: 10.1177/21582440241268830

Meske, C. (2019). Digital workplace transformation: On the role of self-determination in the context of transforming work environments.

Methuku, V., & Kamatala, S. (2025). Intelligent systems and organizational intelligence: A literature review and conceptual framework. In *2025 6th International Conference on Data Intelligence and Cognitive Informatics (ICDICI)* (pp. 1–8). IEEE. DOI: 10.1109/ICDICI66477.2025.11135342

Mishra, R., & Jadeja, D. (2025). A literature review on the impact of AI-enhanced HRIS on employee retention and engagement. In *Intersecting natural language processing and FinTech innovations in service marketing* (pp. 11–20). DOI: 10.4018/979-8-3693-9944-6.ch002

Morato, O., & Nunes, D. J. C. (2023). The use of behavioral design on technological platforms and their regulatory initiatives: A study of the Hook model. *Revista Justiça e Direito*, *37*, 207.

Nussbaumer, A., Pope, A., & Neville, K. (2023). A framework for applying ethics-by-design to decision support systems for emergency management. *Information Systems Journal*, *33*(1), 34–55. DOI: 10.1111/isj.12350

Pacheco, P. O., & Coello-Montecel, D. (2023). Does psychological empowerment mediate the relationship between digital competencies and job performance? *Computers in Human Behavior*, *140*, 107575. DOI: 10.1016/j.chb.2022.107575

Shin, Y. (2025). Toward human-centered artificial intelligence for users' digital well-being: Systematic review, synthesis, and future directions. *JMIR Human Factors*, *12*(1), e69533. DOI: 10.2196/69533 PMID: 40928842

Sihotang, D. S. (2026). Digital Twins as an Enabler of Cognitive Enterprise Architecture: Reconfiguring Organizational Systems and Decision Intelligence. In *Transforming Physical Assets to Cognitive Enterprises With Digital Twins* (pp. 289–320). IGI Global Scientific Publishing. DOI: 10.4018/979-8-3373-9998-0.ch010

Stock, O., Guerini, M., & Pianesi, F. (2016). Ethical dilemmas for adaptive persuasion systems. *Proceedings of the AAAI Conference on Artificial Intelligence*, *30*(1), •••. DOI: 10.1609/aaai.v30i1.9803

Suhud, U., Allan, M., Hoo, W., Azinuddin, M., Madhavedi, S., Mukhibad, H., & Sihotang, D. (2026). Digitally literate, habitually engaged: Unpacking sustainable urge to travel in coffee tourism. *International Journal of Data and Network Science*, *10*(2), 925–938. DOI: 10.5267/j.ijdns.2025.11.006

Suhud, U., Boonkaew, S., Sihotang, D. S., Azinuddin, M., & Aujirapongpan, S. (2025). Bridging Social Responsibility and Sustainability: A Case Study of Modelling Tourist Citizenship Behaviour in Indonesia. *International Journal of Sustainable Development and Planning*, *20*(12), 5381–5393. DOI: 10.18280/ijsdp.201229

Supriyadi, T., Sulistiasih, S., Rahmi, K. H., Pramono, B., & Fahrudin, A. (2025). The impact of digital fatigue on employee productivity and well-being: A scoping literature review. *Environment and Social Psychology*, *10*(2), 1–13. DOI: 10.59429/esp.v10i2.3420

Sylqa, D. A. (2025). Enhancing organizational performance through quality information systems in internationally engaged enterprises. *Journal of Risk Analysis and Crisis Response*, *15*(1), 11–11. DOI: 10.54560/jracr.v15i1.568

Ter Hoeven, C. L., van Zoonen, W., & Fonner, K. L. (2016). The practical paradox of technology: The influence of communication technology use on employee burnout and engagement. *Communication Monographs*, *83*(2), 239–263. DOI: 10.1080/03637751.2015.1133920 PMID: 27226694

Tudose, A. (2025). Understanding organizational stress in the era of digital transformation. In *European Conference on Innovation and Entrepreneurship* (pp. 865–871). Academic Conferences International Limited. DOI: 10.34190/ecie.20.1.3849

Vargas-Hernandez, J. G., & Vargas-González, O. C. (2025). Digital organizational culture: A literature review and analysis. In *Knowledge sharing and fostering collaborative business culture* (pp. 277–296). DOI: 10.4018/979-8-3373-0710-7.ch015

Walenta, D. C., & Koppe, T. (2025). Exploring sociotechnical alignment and productivity: Post-pandemic insights. In *Proceedings of the Pacific Asia Conference on Information Systems*.

Walter, Y. (2024). Digital psychology: Introducing a conceptual impact model and the future of work. *Trends in Psychology*, •••, 1–37. DOI: 10.1007/s43076-024-00408-w

Warkentin, M., & Mutchler, L. (2014). Behavioral information security management. In *Computing handbook: Information systems and information technology*. DOI: 10.1201/b16768-62

Whitney, P., Thompson, S., Wolf, K., & Brothers, A. (2009). Bayesian assessments of likelihood, consequence and risk for comparing scenarios. In *Behavior Representation in Modeling and Simulation Conference*.

Zhan, Y., & Wang, Y. (2025). Network dynamics between digital media use and depressive symptomatology: A computational phenotyping approach using ecological momentary assessment. *Psychiatry Research*, •••, 116896. PMID: 41411707

Zhang, M. J. (2005). An empirical assessment of the performance impacts of IS support for knowledge management. In *International Conference on Electronic Business Proceedings*.

Zhao, Y., & Siau, K. (2018). Cognitive neuroscience in information systems research. In *Applications of neuroscience: Breakthroughs in research and practice* (pp. 158–175). DOI: 10.4018/978-1-5225-5478-3.ch009

Chapter 5

Cognitive Sustainability and Algorithmic Ergonomics:

Re-Architecting Organizational Information Systems for Human-Centered Productivity

Ravikumar Natarajan
http://orcid.org/0009-0009-3705-1681
Marwadi University, Rajkot, India

Aarthi Selvakumar
http://orcid.org/0009-0006-9064-2091
Marwadi University, Rajkot, India

Pardaev Anvar
Termez University of Economics and Service, Termez, Uzbekistan

Mirzayev Bobur
Alfraganus University, Tashkent, Uzbekistan

Nilufar Aminova
Tashkent State University of Economics, Tashkent, Uzbekistan

Nasiba Jumaniyazova
Mamun University, Khiva, Uzbekistan

ABSTRACT

Organizational Information Systems that are powered by Artificial Intelligence have become more efficient but also cause more cognitive workload by making people constantly connected and always monitored by algorithms and overloaded with information. In this chapter, the author presents the concept of Cognitive Sustainability as the design idea that helps safeguard long-term attention, decision-making, and emotional stability at digital workplaces. It offers Algorithmic Ergonomics to make intelligent systems conform to human mental capacity through minimizing interruptions, workload adaptation, and privacy-by-design protection. The idea

DOI: 10.4018/979-8-2600-0111-0.ch005

of a conceptual architecture and dual-outcome measurement model illustrate how productivity and digital well-being may be maximized at the same time. Case-based observations indicate that sustainable performance arises when AI frameworks stabilize the attention as opposed to increasing the speed of digital intensity.

1. INTRODUCTION

The current organizational landscape is characterized by the ability to stay connected, algorithmic decision support, predictive dashboards, and automation and the implementation of AI embedded in Organizational Information Systems (OIS). Though these developments have made things efficient, quick and data driven coordination, they have also created some cognitive strain among the employees. The 24/7 digital work architecture is likely to dishearten the attention, increase the number of notifications, and promote multi-tasking, thereby redesigning the experience and experience of work. The traditional paradigms of productivity are based on the throughput, acceleration and the measurable output but such measures do not always pay attention to the long-term mental health, the persistent attention and mental health. Human cognitive system is increasingly becoming a valuable but overloaded resource as AI systems and algorithms are applied to do more and more work, track as well as analyze performance (González-Reyes et al., 2026). The chapter introduces the need to rebrand OIS design to emphasize the cognitive sustainability i.e. long-term attention, emotional regulation, and performance sustainability instead of short-term improvement in output. It makes human-centered principles of re-architecting OIS not only a technological requirement but also a strategic one in terms of the long-term organizational stability and the well-being of its workforce.

1.1 Digital Intensification and Cognitive Strain

The term digital intensification can be explained as the increasing exchange of technologies, messages, real-time analytics, and automated decision messages at everyday workplaces. Communication tools, task trackers, AI assistants, monitoring dashboards, and predictive alerts are combined into one ecosystem as enterprise platforms. Though it enhances coordination and visibility, these systems in the same breath, dispense attention and reduce the mental recovery process. The cumulative cognitive switching costs accumulated during the working day is due to the frequent context switching between the applications, chat threads, dashboards, and automated suggestions. Employees are more mentally exhausted; they lose the power to work in depth and become weak-willed. On top of that, the performance surveillance algorithms have the potential of establishing implicit pressure on the psyche, which reinforces the principle of responsiveness over critical thinking (Ravikumar, 2025a). This may result in the reduction of creativity in the long run, memory visualization and an even surging stress by such digitally mediated stress. Digital intensifying is thereby transforming work into an order of tasks into series of micro-interruptions, and is at this point necessitating a redesign of OIS consciously acting upon the cognitive load, as opposed to simply aggregating it.

1.2 From Throughput to Sustainable Productivity

In the traditional productivity models, the volume of output, processing speed, and throughput that can be measured are the key parameters of organizational performance. Automation saves even more time in AI-enhanced businesses, allowing completing the tasks quickly and tracking the performance in real-time. Nevertheless, throughput-based measures tend to overlook the sustainability of the human cognitive ability in the long-term perspective. Sustainable productivity ensures that there is a shift towards short-term acceleration to a sustained level of clarity, focus continuity, emotional balance, and consistency of performance over a long period of time. Instead of prioritizing busy time, sustainable productivity espoused rhythmed work patterns, safeguarded deep-work periods, and formal rest periods (Aarthi, et al., 2025). This paradigm acknowledges that high acceleration may reduce the quality of decision, raise the rate of errors and cause burnout. Incorporating cognitive sustainability into the performance evaluation systems allows the organizations to synchronous technology efficiency and human constraints. Thus, productivity is a constructed balance: where smart systems assist in the prioritization, lessen the needless cognitive drag, and allow lasting interaction instead of sustaining a sense of constant urgency and discontinuous attention.

1.3 Need for Human-Centered OIS Redesign

The default architecture of most Organizational Information Systems is focused on functionality, automation and data visibility without systematically taking into consideration the human cognitive constraints. With the increase in the role of AI systems in routing tasks, monitoring, analytics, and communication management, the interaction design of OIS can greatly shape the patterns of attention and stress levels. A redesign that is human friendly demands cognitive ergonomics within the architecture of the system so that the algorithms are in favor of the user and not overpowering. These include the suppression of non-essential notifications, attention aware communication flows, simplifying the interface complexity, and adaptive workload management (A. Farid, 2024). Transparency, explainability and consent-based analytics should also be included in human-centered OIS to avoid the sense of intrusive surveillance. Organizations are able to create trust and sustainable performance by matching the behavior of the system to the psychological safety level and the cognitive load level (Shreha et al., 2025). Re-designing OIS on human principles turns intelligent systems into productivity accelerators instead of cognitive stabilizers to make sure that digital innovation augments and not displaces human steady-state capacity.

2. BACKGROUND TO THE STUDY

Information Systems in organizations have been developed to be more of an integration-based ecosystem, featuring AI, and managing communication, analytics, workflow automation, and strategic decision support. Older systems were less concerned with machine learning and predictive analytics and more involved in record-keeping and operational efficiency, but modern architectures incorporate machine learning algorithms, predictive analytics and adaptive interfaces into work processes. This has completely changed the way employees interact using digital tools (Ravikumar, 2025). The priorities of tasks and their execution are now determined by AI-based dashboards, real-time performance indicators, and automatic notifications. Although these developments increase the level of data transparency and responsiveness, the level of information density and the speed of work rhythms also increase. Combination of AI, behavioral analytics and ubiquitous connectivity has led to situations where attention is actively sought. With the growing pressure of cognitive overload, it is important to comprehend the socio-technical consequences of the work systems mediated by AI. The history of this paper hence places cognitive sustainability in the larger context of OIS evolution and AI-based enterprise change.

2.1 Evolution of Organizational Information Systems

The first Information Systems in organizations developed as transaction-processing systems which were meant to automate accounting, inventory management and administration. With time, the features of the Enterprise Resource Planning (ERP), Customer Relationship Management (CRM) and business intelligence platforms were extended to enable integration of data across functions to aid in making managerial decisions. The further inclusion of cloud computing and mobile access helped to have real-time cooperation and coordinate the work remotely. At the new stage, AI and machine learning algorithms are directly integrated into OIS, which allow predictive forecasting, automated distribution of various tasks, anomaly detection, and behavioral analytics (Brunyé et al., 2026). This development has transformed systems into passive storage of information to dynamic agents of decisions. Modern OIS affect the workflow ordering, assign priorities to tasks with the help of algorithmic recommendations and produce performance data on its own. With smarter and smarter systems, the design of these systems no longer just aids work, but provides the organization of the cognitive activity. This change demands the redefinition of the role of system architectures on human attention, freedom, and mental health (Shreha et al., 2026). Table 1 The comparison of the conventional OIS, ERP-based systems, and AI-enabled OIS is based on functionality, decision support, and cognitive impact.

Table 1: Evolution of Organizational Information Systems

Dimension	Traditional OIS	ERP/Integrated Systems	AI-Enabled OIS
Primary Function	Transaction processing	Cross-functional integration	Predictive and adaptive decision support
Automation Level	Rule-based	Process integration	Machine learning-driven
User Role	Data entry & reporting	Monitoring & coordination	Human–AI collaboration
Decision Support	Historical reporting	Real-time dashboards	Predictive analytics & automation
Cognitive Impact	Structured workload	Increased visibility	High information density & interruption risk

2.2 AI-Driven Work Environments

The qualities of AIs within workplaces rely on the nature of algorithmic mediator in working, communication and performance feedback. It has intelligent assistants who suggest priorities, predictive dashboards, and monitoring systems to monitor the productivity measures in real-time. They are technologies that aid an organization to respond in a timely manner to the emerging situations and attain efficiency in operations. However, algorithmic orchestration also changes agency of employees and distribution of attention. It may be overtaken by automated notifications and predictive suggestions rather than the intuitive prioritization, which is inclined in decision directions. Constant performance view can institute and create a constant assessment burden on the individual whereby they are always provoked to act rather than to think (El Arab et al., 2025). The pace of the AI-based systems tend to be greater than the natural cognitive pace, which consequently fractionates the deliberation and overloads the brain. In spite of the fact that these environments introduce a lot of efficiency, they are also hazardous in the sense of normalizing constant acceleration. The inclusion of the cognitive sustainability in the AI-based ecosystems also contributes to the fact that automation will increase the reasoning of the human beings not by congesting attention loops and lowering the level of psychological safety in digitally vast working environments.

2.3 Cognitive Overload in Digital Enterprises

Cognitive overload is experienced when the amount and speed of information is more than the processing of a person. Employees in digital businesses often have to juggle concurrent communication devices, real-time display boards, automated notifications, and work team applications. Extensive micro-interruptions add up to discontinuous concentration and diminishes deep-work ability. As studies in digital psychology suggest, continuous context switching causes cognitive fatigue, decision accuracy, and impairs the working memory. In addition, predictive surveillances, and data visibility devices can also aggravate perceived surveillance, which is added to stress and diminished autonomy. The quantity of information is not the only form of overload but also the shape of design, inefficiently tuned notification systems, and a complicated interface contribute to the mental load (Lima, 2024). Unless the ergonomics are achieved intentionally, AI-based systems can incidentally promote burnout and disengagement. The solution to cognitive overload should be to redesign the architecture in a structured manner that incorporates workload modeling, adaptive prioritization, and attention-sensitive communication protocols in the Organizational Information Systems to guarantee cognitive resilience in the long run. Table 2 The important sources of digital intensification (notifications, dashboards, monitoring, multitasking) and their effect on cognition are listed.

Table 2: Cognitive Strain Factors in AI-Driven Work Environments

Digital Factor	Description	Cognitive Impact
Notification Density	Frequent alerts & messages	Attention fragmentation
Real-Time Dashboards	Continuous data visibility	Decision fatigue
Performance Monitoring	Algorithmic tracking	Psychological pressure
Multitasking Platforms	Multiple simultaneous tools	Context switching overload
Predictive Prompts	AI-based suggestions	Reduced deliberation time

3. RESEARCH OBJECTIVES

The faster automation that is aided by AI, the predictive analytics and real-time monitoring enter the Organizational Information Systems (OIS) in a manner that the research agenda ought to be structured under the influence of research that lacks the perspective of assessing productivity. The design of OIS that is capable of supporting human thinking and at the same time, does not compromise its functions will be given a theoretical and architectural background in this paper. These objectives are conceptual exposition, architectural delineation, resultant quantification and governance condensation to render intelligent systems more fruitful and digitally sound.

- To conceptualize and formally define Cognitive Sustainability within AI-enabled Organizational Information Systems, emphasizing durable attention, emotional regulation, and long-term decision quality.
- To develop an Algorithmic Ergonomics framework that integrates cognitive load modeling, attention-aware communication, adaptive workload distribution, and interface simplification into OIS architecture.
- To design a dual-outcome measurement model linking operational productivity indicators (efficiency, accuracy, throughput stability) with digital well-being metrics (focus continuity, recovery time, stress patterns).
- To establish governance principles for cognitively sustainable systems, incorporating transparency, explainability, privacy-by-design, and consent-based analytics to prevent surveillance creep.
- To propose a re-architected human-centered OIS model that systematically reduces cognitive friction, supports deep work cycles, and enables sustainable AI-augmented performance.

4. CONCEPTUAL MODEL

Cognitive Sustainability and Algorithmic Ergonomics are merged in a single Organizational Information Systems (OIS) architecture as they are being drawn in the conceptual model that is put forward in this chapter. Instead of viewing productivity and well-being as two distinct outputs, the model puts them as mutually supporting consequences of smart system design. The model is based on socio-technical system theory, Human-Computer Interactions, digital psychology, and responsible AI governance. It also describes OIS as a dynamic cognitive system that is constantly engaged in reactions to the attention cycles of employees, workload patterns, and behavior reacting (SGH & Brodowicz, 2025). The model operates on the three interconnected subunits: a Cognitive Sustainability Architecture that equilibrates the focus and workload allocation; Algorithmic Ergonomics Design Layers that incorporate human-centered principles into the functions of AI; a Dual-Outcome Measurement Model that assesses the operational and psychological performance metrics. Combined with these elements, it re-architectures OIS of throughput maximising systems to cognitively consistent ecosystems that maintain continuity of focus, friction reduction and sustainable human-AI cooperation in digitally intensive firms. The integration of cognitive sustainability architecture, algorithmic ergonomics and dual-outcome measurement model into a human-centered Organizational Information System as shown in Figure 1.

Figure 1. Integrated OIS Architecture for Cognitive Sustainability

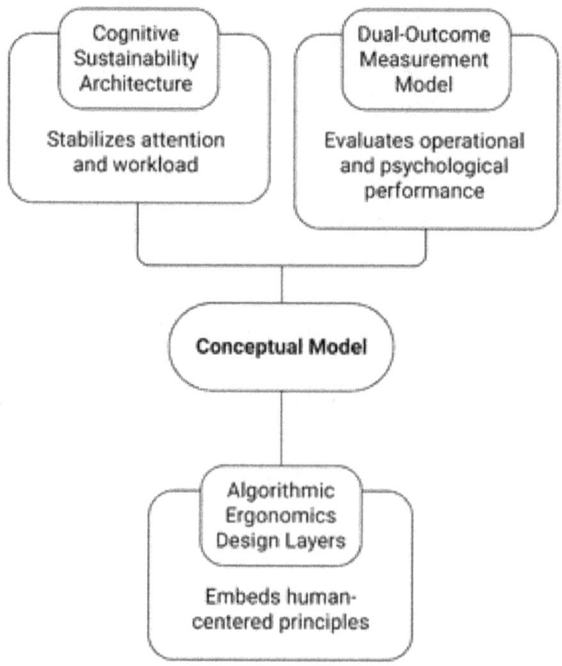

4.1 Cognitive Sustainability Architecture

The Cognitive Sustainability Architecture establishes the setup of the structural planning of OIS that defends and empowers their human mental capability. It possesses the workload adaptive modeling, notification filtering and attention, deep-work-supportive scheduling and the cognitive load monitoring mechanisms. It has controlled topology, which is also based on the observability of real time task intensity, density and frequency of interaction and uses them to dynamically tune system prompts and alerts (Ravikumar et al., 2026). The mechanism of the inhibition of the non-essential notifications and recombination of task queues in case of cognitive strain messages release is presented in figure 8 (non-essential notifications during high-focus periods) and paper 9 respectively. Recovery cycle planning is also incorporated in the architecture to allow the sequencing tasks to be deviated and halted in order to prevent brain overworking. The transparency modules will also be able to update the user about the creation of the decisions of prioritization and filtering, and this will not destroy the trust and agency (Eilouti, 2023). The resulting architecture that contributes to such mechanisms being inherent in the balance of the system design makes OIS cognitive stabilizers rather than interruption amplifiers because of the fact that digital infrastructure has been placed at a concord with sustainable human rhythms of performance. Table 3 explains some important conceptual points (adaptive workload modeling, attention filtering, recovery cycles, transparency modules) and their primary functions.

Table 3: Cognitive Sustainability Architecture Components

Component	Function	Expected Benefit
Adaptive Workload Modeling	Dynamically adjusts task flow	Reduced overload
Attention-Aware Filtering	Suppresses low-priority alerts	Improved focus continuity
Deep-Work Scheduling	Protects uninterrupted intervals	Enhanced cognitive stability
Recovery Cycle Integration	Encourages structured breaks	Fatigue reduction
Transparency Module	Explains algorithmic decisions	Increased trust

4.2 Algorithmic Ergonomics Design Layers

Algorithms The field of Algorithmic Ergonomics applies the ergonomic principles of the past to the algorithms of the enterprise systems operating AI algorithms, and is especially concerned with the effects of algorithms on the patterns of attention, behavior, and stress. The design layers are defined on interface, workflow, analytics and governance layers. The adaptive dashboards at the interface layer simplify the visualization and present context-related information following the requirements of tasks. Intelligent routing and AI-assisted prioritization on the workflow layer help to minimize the unneeded context switching. The analytics layer also offers behavioral feedback loops and they monitor the stability of engagement and signal overload. Finally, the governance layer is also ensuring that it can ensure it is explainable, consent-based analytics as well as privacy-by-design (Sadeghi & Hoseinpour Jajarm, 2025). These layers are working in combination with each other to bring in clarity and reduction of mental friction. Algorithms ergonomics modulates system responsiveness to the point of view of human mental capacity, instead of augmenting the amount of interaction. By introducing the element of ergonomical-aware algorithms, the organizations will be capable of ensuring that the smart systems are used to ensure deep focus, mitigating digital fatigue, and developing a psychologically safe workplace. Table 4 Maps interface, workflow, analytics and governance layer to cognitive complexities and expected ergonomic outcome.

Table 4: Algorithmic Ergonomics Design Layers

Design Layer	System Feature	Cognitive Outcome
Interface Layer	Simplified dashboards	Reduced visual complexity
Workflow Layer	AI-based prioritization	Lower context switching
Analytics Layer	Behavioral feedback loops	Early overload detection
Governance Layer	Privacy-by-design & explainability	Psychological safety
Communication Layer	Intelligent notification timing	Stabilized attention cycles

4.3 Dual-Outcome Measurement Model

The Dual-Outcome Measurement Model is a model of measuring the efficiency of cognitive sustainability OIS through the combination of productivity measures and digital well-being indices. Conventional operational measures like rate of throughput, time of completion of a task, precision and minimization of errors are maintained but put into context of cognitive performance stability. The additional well-being predictors consist of the continuity of focus, recovery duration between intensive work, stability of engagement, cognitive load index, and stress fluctuation patterns. The model considers third wave optimization, which means that productivity gains would not be accompanied by an increase in mental strain (Alassaf, 2025). Statistics on these indicators could be obtained based on the logs of interaction with a system, the analytics of workloads and voluntary well-being tests, which are conducted under strict privacy protection. Through matching the operational performance with the cognitive sustainability metrics, organizations are able to determine the sustainable performance ratios which depicts the long-term viability as opposed to short term acceleration. This combined assessment system allows making strategic choices that meet AI-intensified efficiency with long-term human capacity and resilience of the organization (Ravikumar, 2025b). The figure 2 which shows the manner in which productivity measures and digital well-being measures are combined with sources of data to facilitate sustainable strategic decision-making within AI-enabled organizational systems.

Figure 2. Dual-Outcome Measurement Model for Cognitively Sustainable OIS

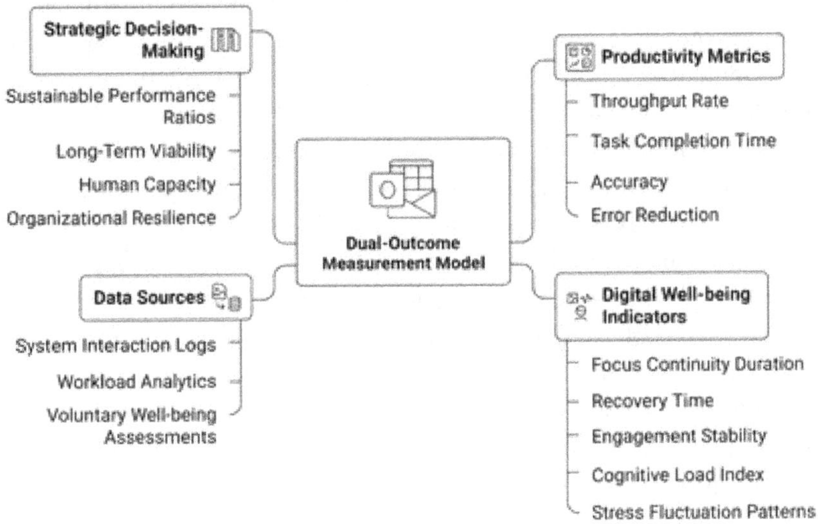

5. RESEARCH METHODOLOGY

The approach to the research chosen in this chapter should build an idea structure of Cognitive Sustainability and Algorithmic Ergonomics in Organizational Information Systems (OIS) and prove it. As the topic is interdisciplinary, the methodology combines the theoretical synthesis, systematic literature alignment, and qualitative analysis based on the case. The model is built through the use of socio-technical systems theory, Human-Computer Interaction studies, digital psychology, and responsible AI governance theories to come up with an architecturally based model. The research, instead of basing itself on empirical experimentation alone, uses the design-based research approach with emphasis on conceptual clarity, architectural integration as well as evaluative logic (Akintola et al., 2025). Two current contexts of enterprise level cases are included to demonstrate feasibility in the field and topicality. Analytical analysis is concerned with how the system design elements reflect on the two outputs of productivity and digital well-being. The methodology is rigorous in theory and applies practically, which allows it to arrive at a structured and practicable human-centered OIS model.

5.1 Conceptual and Theoretical Synthesis

This research has a conceptual foundation that is acquired through a systematic synthesis of various theoretical streams. The socio-technical systems theory has provided the macro level view of the interaction between technological systems and human actions. Interfaces are designed using design principles of Human-Computer Interaction, usability is taken into account and cognitive load managed. Some knowledge of the attention cycles, stress pattern and behavioral response of digital mediated environments can be found in the body of literature concerning digital psychology. To this, responsible AI models offer aspects of governance such as transparency, explainability and privacy-by-design. These areas of theory were synthesized in line with observation of challenges in the AI-enabled OIS environments, especially cognitive overload and attention fragmentation (Islam, 2025). Identification of overlapping constructs and integration into one architectural model were done through conceptual mapping techniques. Such conceptual integration allows defining Cognitive Sustainability as an organized design concept not an abstract notion of well-being and anchoring it squarely in the research of organizational information systems.

5.2 Case Study Selection Criteria

To demonstrate the relevance of the proposed framework, two new enterprise situations were chosen. The use of purposive sampling criteria as criteria of selecting the cases was based on the factors of the intensity of AI integration, quantifiable productivity indicators, and the possibility of observing digital work patterns. The organizations that work in the knowledge-intensive or digitally mediated settings were considered to be a priority since such settings are usually characterized by increased cognitive pressure. Other requirements were the availability of automated workflow management, real-time analytics report, communication tools with notification systems, and measures of well-being or performance recorded. The selection of cases was done to capture diversity in the sectoral application and also to keep a level of comparability in terms of technological sophistication (Arigbabu et al., 2024). The reliability of contextual information was ensured by publically available reports, enterprise documentation and proven secondary sources. The goal of the selection was not to statistically generalize but to offer analytically rich examples of how the principle of algorithmic ergonomics and cognitive sustainability can be translated into the modern system of AI-based organizational functionality.

5.3 Analytical and Evaluation Approach

Analytical approach subjects the architectural design elements to a systematic assessment grid in comparison with the dual-outcome performance indicators. Every case scenario was compared with the defined dimensions, which were adaptive workload modeling, attention-aware communication, density management in notifications, simplification of the interface, and transparency in governance. The indicators of productivity, e.g. throughput efficiency, error reduction, and process stability were examined along with the digital well-being indicators that included focus continuity, recovery intervals, and engagement stability. The convergences between the cognitively aligned system design and sustainable performance outcomes were identified through comparative pattern analysis (Abdulgafar et al., 2025). The test is focused on causal plausibility as opposed to statistical inference with the aim being to assess the logical consistency of system properties and actual results. To make sure that governance is present, ethical and privacy concerns were included in the assessment. This integrative assessment method can validate the conceptual framework and can show how re-architected OIS can be used to improve both the operational productivity and ensure cognitive sustainability over the long-term.

6. LITERATURE REVIEW

The literature on the AI-enabled Organizational Information Systems (OIS) sparks more and more controversy of the conflict between technological pace and human intellectual capacity. Although the old research on the information systems focused on efficiency, integration and decision support, the modern research widens the scope to human-centered design, digital well-being, sustainable performance. Cognitive Sustainability and Algorithmic Ergonomics can be conceptualized on the multidisciplinary platform of convergence of digital psychology, Human-Computer Interaction (HCI), ergonomics, and ethical AI governance. The domains all look into the impact of the digital setting on attention distribution, mental load, patterns of behavior, trust, and psychological security (Björck et al., 2025). Instead of considering productivity as operation-related, new visions are beginning to view attention as a limited organizational resource that needs to be defended with strategy. The intelligent systems are also supposed to automatize activities, on top of which the flow of information, complexity of interfaces and the degree of notifications are to be regulated according to the literature. The framework proposed enables OIS to be a dynamic cognitive space that can address performance efficiency and sustainable human capacity and well-being by integrating the knowledge of these interrelated fields.

6.1 Digital Psychology and Attention Theory

Digital psychology refers to the constant technological interaction that is shaping the manner of thoughts, feelings and actions of people. The attention theory and the selective attention and the cost of cognitive-switching theory in particular demonstrates that the repetitive interruptions hurts the working memory and reduces the ability of deep focusing. The research on the multitasking demonstrates that a rapid change of tasks increases the degree of mental fatigue and decreases the quality of the decisions even though the productivity rates might appear to be stationary at the beginning. The concept of attentional residue explains that the unfinished tasks remain in the mind and thus decrease the concentration of other tasks. The studies on the digital stress also reveal the psychological outcomes of the ever-present nature, the multiplicity of notifications, and the costliness of performance (Sousa, 2025). The shortening of the recovery time is associated with the cognitive resilience, and the exposure of high information density conditions is related to the prolonged exposure. These results confirm the thesis that productivity cannot be optimized sustainably in terms of ignoring the cycles of attention and restoring mental energy. Incorporating the digital psychology into OIS design thus means having ways to filter the stimuli that do not need to be spent on, the deep-work time protection, and system prompts in sync with the natural cognitive rhythms.

6.2 Human–Computer Interaction and Ergonomics

The research on Human-Computer Interactions offers design guidelines on maximizing usability, easing the complexity of the interface, and streamlining interactions. Ergonomics used to be concerned with physical workplace occupational compatibility, but nowadays, it is considered to be regarded as cognitive ergonomics, i. e. mental load and clarity of decision. The HCI literature focuses on the idea of the minimalist interface design, contextual relevance, and adaptive information presentation as the measures to alleviate cognitive load. User-centered design theories support the idea of an iterative assessment according to human feedback instead of technical performance (Rathinavel et al., 2025). Adaptive interfaces, which dynamically regulate the number of elements on screen and visual complexity, have been proven to enhance task understanding and decrease the amount of error in systems that are driven by AI. Workflow ergonomics also recommends that the system architecture reduce the needless navigation clicks and data exposure. Using ergonomic principles in algorithmic processes, intelligent systems are able to tune the frequency of the notifications, rank the tasks intelligently and refine the flow of communications. This alignment makes OIS favorable cognitive structures instead of the factors of digital friction and overload.

6.3 Ethical AI, Privacy, and Psychological Safety

The spread of AI-based surveillance and analytics in companies has heightened the issue of privacy, disclosure, and emotional security. The concept of explainability, consent-based analytics and accountability in ensuring the trust of employees is emphasized in ethical AI scholarship (Universitas, 2025). Unless done in a transparent way, constant monitoring of performance may project an image of surveillance and undermine independence. According to psychological safety literature, employees will work better when they are not afraid of punitive surveillance and secretive algorithmic decision-making. The principles of privacy-by-design believe that data minimization, clear consent guidelines and governance controls need to be built directly into system structure. The responsible AIs also focus on fairness, reduction of bias, and accountable algorithmic reasoning. These aspects of governance are part of Cognitive Sustainability, in that cognitive strain is increased in a situation of uncertainty or sense of helplessness. When the ethical use of AI is aligned with the ergonomics of the system design, the productivity improvement will be enhanced without interfering with the dignity, trust, and long-term engagement.

7. CASE STUDIES

This section brings out three of the most recent, practice-based case scenarios on how Cognitive Sustainability and Algorithmic Ergonomics can be executed in the modern Organizational Information Systems (OIS). The cases will be selected in terms of (i) AI-based optimization of workflow in core business processes, (ii) emphasis continuity through attention-sensitive collaboration and communication design, and (iii) privacy-minded analytics that will enable the researcher to keep employees as agents at work but deliver insights comparable to governance. Each of the cases is addressed as a socio-technical intervention, rather than the implementation of technology per se - the unification of the algorithms configuration, the choice of interface, and analytics administration in a combination to predetermine the cognitive load, interruption, and sustainable performance (Ma et al., 2025). The reported results are concerned with quantifiable gains (percentage-based) to evaluate the comparability in the evaluative setting between settings. The assembly of the cases hints at the fact that in the case of intelligent systems, it is feasible to match productivity acceleration and digital well-being that are arranged in such a manner, that cognitive friction is reduced, deep-work intervals are secured, and privacy-by-design solutions are provided.

7.1 AI-Enabled Workflow Optimization in Enterprises

One of the recent examples of workflow optimization in an enterprise is traced to the case of Canon USA whose finance processes were optimized through the use of intelligent automation in processing invoices. Within nine months of automation implementation, the organization had to process an average of 40,000 invoices and had a straight-through processing (STP) rate of about 90%, i.e. most of the invoices were processed automatically. This was a higher performance than the original target of 75% STP meaning that orchestration of workflows, match-based rules and exception reasoning logic was well developed to support high automation reliability (Bedmutha, 2025). According to the cognitive sustainability view, the value of such a case is not in the improved throughput but also in the lessened weight of manual checks and interruption-prone circles of repetitive and rework (Sang et al., 2025). The greater STP redirects human effort toward the resolution of exceptions and supervision of them, instead of the micro-decisions (validation, routing, data entry) involved in it, and it is generally characterized by fewer context switches and more immediate delimiting of tasks. The case consequently illustrates algorithmic ergonomics at the workflow layer: automation takes over standard thinking, and humans are left in control over the ambiguous or risky exceptions. This division helps in maintaining a sustainable productivity by balancing the attention cycles and minimizing the fatigue levels related to discontinuous administrative tasks. Figure 3 on the initial straight-through processing objective (75) and the obtained rate (90) after the implementation of automation.

Figure 3. AI-Enabled Workflow Optimization Performance

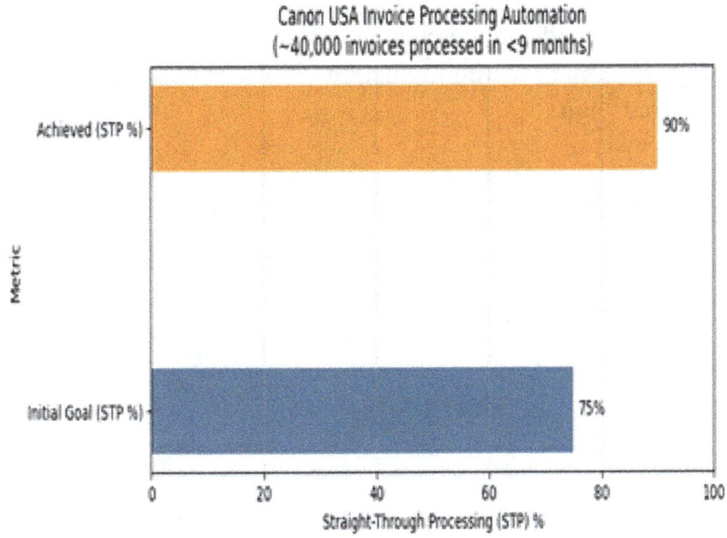

7.2 Attention-Aware Communication Platforms

An example of an attention-sensitive collaboration scenario is the recent case of Microsoft deploying Workplace Analytics (since part of the Viva Insights ecosystem) to re-architecture collaboration, meetings and spatial proximity effects on focus. In a massive in-house situation of 1,900 engineers, analytics-based planning saved 46% of the time traveling to meetings, which amounted to a significant amount of time saved to transition and continuous work. The results obtained were also nearly 10% greater focus duration, approximately 15% greater unofficial cooperation (facilitated by being next to each other) and a consequent near 20% less formal meeting time. The case itself is of immediate interest to cognitive sustainability since the problem of attention fragmentation is often caused by back-to-back meetings, lack of clearing time, and high coordination overhead (Daassi et al., 2006). The intervention illustrates an algorithmic design of ergonomics collaboration: based on aggregation of data on work patterns, the redesign of the interaction opportunities, the elimination of unnecessary meeting load, and the preservation of focus continuity without a decrease in collaboration quality. The reduction of the formal meetings, more opportunistic problem-solving, and more time on focus are the sign of a transition between interruption-based coordination and more balanced attention rhythms (Pega et al., 2024). It is also demonstrated by the case that analytics may be utilized to streamline the attention infrastructure (meeting structures, collaboration timing, and workspace decisions) and not merely measure output, thus making OIS-supported coordination patterns consistent with sustainable human performance patterns. Figure 4 that indicate percentage changes in travel time, focus time, and collaboration growth and meeting reduction duration resulted of analytics-driven communication redesign.

Figure 4. Attention-Aware Communication Performance Outcomes

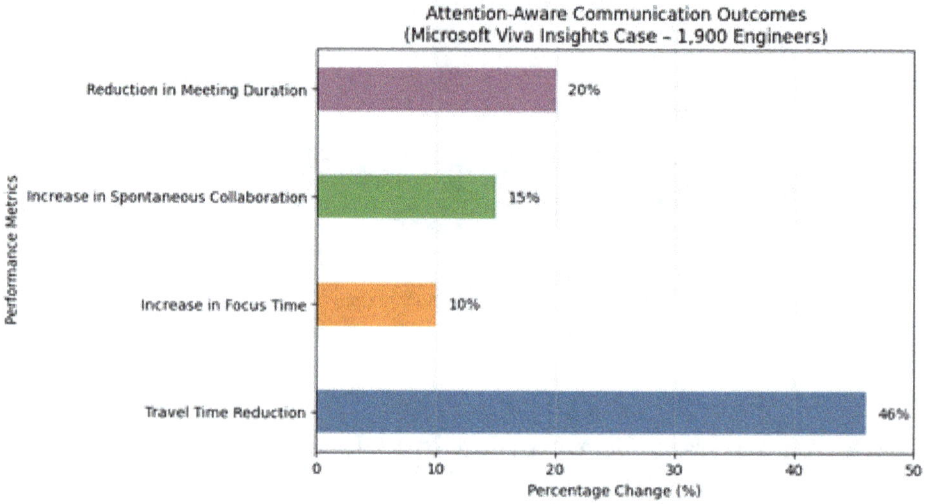

7.3 Privacy-Centric Analytics in Knowledge Work

A recent case of analytics and governance that focuses on privacy is described by the deployment results of Microsoft Purview in the form of a summary that represents the findings of a Forrester Total Economic Impact (TEI). The documented findings encompass a 30% decrease in the chances of data breaches, which is explained by the refined Data Loss Prevention (DLP) policy and increased transparency of the sensitive information across settings. Privacy-focused analytics enhances cognitive sustainability in the knowledge work by lowering the potential risk of surveillance creep, and enforcing psychological safety by ensuring sensitive data are handled in a controlled and policy-based manner (Aarthi, Ravikumar, Sapayev Odilbek Uglu, et al., 2025). Governance analytics does not necessarily involve increasing the intrusion monitoring but rather protects the boundaries of data, reduces avoidable exposure, and facilitates compliant collaboration. As OIS analytics layers include privacy safeguards, the quality of trust and perceived autonomy would likewise enhance, which would facilitate stable engagement and performance sustainability in the long-term.

Table 5 is a summary of the percentage improvements in the three case studies; the productivity measures are correlated with the focus and governance measures.

Table 5: Case Study Performance Outcomes

Case	Key Intervention	Productivity Outcome	Cognitive/Trust Outcome
AI Workflow Optimization	Intelligent automation	90% straight-through processing	Reduced repetitive cognitive load
Attention-Aware Collaboration	Meeting redesign analytics	46% less travel time; 20% shorter meetings	~10% more focus time
Privacy-Centric Analytics	Data governance optimization	30% reduced breach likelihood	Improved trust & safety perception

8. RESULTS AND DISCUSSION

The analyses of the cases all prove that Cognitive Sustainability and Algorithmic Ergonomics are able to produce measurably performance gains and balance attention dynamics and strengthen trust. In the workflow automation, attention-aware collaboration design, and privacy-focused analytics, productivity gains were found not only to arise due to acceleration but also through an organized process of alleviating cognitive friction. The AI-powered workflow case demonstrated the high straight-through processing rates minimizing repetitive decision-making processes and human interventions. In the attention-aware communication case, it was found that the focus time increased significantly and the meeting time was cut as well, which shows the continuity of attention restored (Rakhra & Mann, 2018). The privacy-focused analytics case showed that the probability of breaches is lower, which enhances governance reliability and perceived system security. These findings indicate that intelligent systems can absorb routine load, filter unimportant stimuli and integrate transparent governance controls leading to sustainable productivity. The results confirm the dual-outcome assumption of the conceptual model: the operational efficiency and digital well-being are not mutually exclusive goals but can mutually support each other under the condition of ergonomic functionality of OIS architecture and the cognitive capacity.

8.1 Productivity and Focus Stability Outcomes

The case of workflow optimization had nearly 90% straight-through processing which had greatly cut short on manual intervention and exception handling. This change relocated mental workload no longer away on repetitive micro-observations but instead on more specific analytical supervision. Because of it, the fragmentation of the tasks and the continuity of the workflow increased. In the case of attention-conscious communication, the travel time of meetings reduced by 46% and the duration of formal meetings by 20% helped to earn about 10% more time on concentration (Zhao & Yim, 2025). These measures serve as signs of improved concentration and decreased concentration. Instead of raising the level of activity, productivity improvements were realized by better structuring of the attention cycles and less switching of cognitive functions. Sustainable productivity was also manifested in not only through efficiency in throughputs, but also stabilized engagement patterns (Oluwafemi et al., 2021). The data proves the thesis that attention-conscious system design enhances the performance and concentration sustainability. Reduced unnecessary coordination overhead and routine processing loads resulted in balanced improvements in output consistency and deep-work capacity in organizations. Table 6 shows both the operational productivity indicators and digital well-being indicators with quantifiable variables.

Table 6: Dual-Outcome Measurement Framework

Productivity Metric	Digital Well-Being Indicator	Measurement Variable
Throughput Rate	Focus Continuity	Duration of uninterrupted work
Error Reduction	Cognitive Load Index	Task-switching frequency
Process Stability	Recovery Time	Interval between intensive tasks
Automation Rate	Engagement Stability	Sustained interaction patterns
SLA Compliance	Stress Fluctuation	Alert/notification density trends

8.2 Cognitive Load and Recovery Metrics

There was cognitive load decrease in cases in the form of automation of routine activities and optimization of communication systems. In the workflow scenario, high automation levels have reduced the frequency of repeated validation requests leading to reduced mental burden in the manual processing procedures. The communication redesign example showed that the shortened meeting time and enhanced spatial coordination provide the space with better transition opportunities between activities, which indirectly enhances recovery opportunities. Longer attention periods imply more stable mental processes, and low numbers of fatigue peaks caused by interruptions (Forcellini & Gracikova, 2025). Though the direct physiological measures were not provided, the proxy indicators, including the achievement of compression, and time gains of focus, and exception reduction were used to indicate less cognitive load. The digitally intensive environments that have a limited recovery time are simpler to control when task sequencing and notification intensity are tuned. These findings are congruent with the notion that the density of interaction during a particular interaction must be regulated by algorithmic ergonomics to secure cognitive resilience. The central focus of AI-mediated business burnout prevention and preserving the mental sharpness of a worker, therefore, lie in organizing the working workload and intelligent filtering systems.

8.3 Governance and Trust Implications

The case on privacy-focused analytics showed a 30% reduction of the probability of breaches, which indicates the strengthening of the governance and the reliability of data protection. These implications are applicable directly to psychological safety because transparent and policy-based analytics decrease the vision of inquisitive surveillance. Trust of the digital infrastructure becomes stronger when the employees feel that the intelligent systems are built to ensure privacy and accountability mechanisms (Tabatabaei & Khalili, 2025). Trust, by its turn, allows maintaining a stable engagement and decreases stress related to the opaque algorithmic assessment. Governance transparency is also a complement to cognitive sustainability because it reduces the degree of uncertainty regarding the collection and interpretation of performance data. By applying privacy-by-design principles to OIS architecture, the analytics improves security without increasing the lack of autonomy. Taken together, the examples suggest that productivity improvements can only be maintained with trust-enhancing systems of governance. Harmonised ethical configuration, consent-via analytics and explainable algorithmic logic are thus pillars to support in re-architecturalizing OIS to long-term human-centred productivity.

9. FUTURE RESEARCH

The proposed Cognitive Sustainability and Algorithmic Ergonomics framework makes a few opportunities available into the research in the future. Though the given conceptual model and analysis based on a case demonstrates the feasibility of the topic in its practical implementation, the area requires further empirical validation and technological enhancement to be made. Recent developments in adaptive AI, behavioral sensing and intelligent interface personalization give perspectives of designing systems that would be able to adjust dynamically to the human cognitive rhythms. The longitudinal problem that should also be researched is the long-term impact of AI mediated workplaces on the stability of attention, emotional regulation, and long-term productivity (Palaniappan, 2025). The existing measures of organizational performance mostly fall under the short-term efficiency measures, yet further research ought to examine the trends of multi-year cognitive resilience. In addition, the situational factors that might influence the designing and adoption of the cognitively sustainable systems would encompass cultural prerequisites, sector necessities and the regulatory necessities. Studies in numerous industries and areas will contribute to the generalizability of theory and strength of practice. All these directions are aimed at the Cognitive Sustainability achievement as not a design philosophy but a quantifiable and scalable organizational strategy.

9.1 Adaptive AI and Cognitive Modeling

The future research should center on adoption of adaptive AI system which has the ability to model real-time cognitive real time models. The evolution of machine learning, emotion computing, and behavioral analytics allows foretelling the workload load, attention shift and engagement variability in terms of the interaction patterns. One of the greatest challenges is the development of models that can be capable of detecting cognitive strain without having to intrusively observe. Research may as well be directed to the creation of privacy-saving computations that may infer the cognitive load in non-sensitive indicators of behavioral states such as task switching frequency, typewriter speed or reaction response time. The adaptive systems could then react to the strain levels by adding and removing the notification density, interface complexity, and task sequencing (Boztas et al., 2025). The experimental work could be carried out in the form of comparison of the OIS architectures of the type of static and adaptive to evaluate the differences in focus continuity and performance stability. In order to enable transparency and user trust, explainable AI mechanisms need to be incorporated into adaptive models. With the further evolution of the cognitive modeling techniques, the networks of the future can be moved to the status of truly responsive digital environments supporting the human attention facility.

9.2 Longitudinal Well-Being Measurement

The majority of the existing assessments of AI-powered productivity are based on performance assessments in the short run. The future studies should be based on longitudinal designs to assess cognitive sustainability in the long run. The multi-year studies may determine the ways attention stability, recovery periods and engagement patterns undergo improvement or decline under AI-mediated systems. Integrating the system log data with the voluntary well-being surveys, indicators of stress, and metrics of productivity could offer the comprehensive understanding of sustainable performance curves. Other delayed outcomes of digital intensification that can be determined in longitudinal research include cumulative fatigue or gradual disengagement (Trstenjak et al., 2025). There are high-level statistical modeling tools such as time-series analysis and mixed-effects modeling that can be used to establish dynamic aspects of system design and cognitive resilience. The establishment of common sustainability standards would make it easier to compare across organizations. This type of research is one that ensures that increment of productivity is not a transient high but a long term high productivity with respect to mental health and overall organizational performance in the long term.

9.3 Cross-Cultural and Sectoral Extensions

There are possibilities of cognitive sustainability to be expressed in different ways in different societies and industries. The future research should establish how the cultural orientations to authority, monitoring, collaboration, and work intensity influence the acceptance of algorithmic ergonomics. More often in the heavily-regulated fields of healthcare and finance, governance and privacy regulations can contribute more to the formation of psychological safety. Or alternatively, it could be that the creative industries are flexi-friendly and autonomous than the workflow optimization. The contextual adaptation requirements of OIS architecture can be identified in comparison with the cross-sector studies. Besides, cultural differences may affect communication norms and computer etiquette that may affect attention patterns and toleration of interruptions (Hou et al., 2011). The frameworks will be improved in terms of their universal applicability and flexibility as a result of the increased empirical research in a wide range of organizational settings. Such extensions ensure that the principles of cognitive sustainability are both adaptable and responsive to the variety of circumstances and, at the same time, are not deprived of their original aim that is to achieve intelligent systems that are in line with the performance of humanity that is sustainable.

10. MANAGERIAL IMPLICATIONS

The move towards AI as the basis of Organizational Information Systems requires managerial policies that would balance technology and cognitive sustainability. Leaders must realize that attention, thinking capacity and psychological safety is not an incidental result of work, but a strategic asset of an organization. There is evidence in the case that maximum productivity improvement occurs when the intelligent systems are placed well in relation to the human cognitive rhythms. Therefore, this managerial activity must not be reduced to the procedure of the system procurement but also include the architectural calibration, governance supervision, and cultural transformation (Pasupuleti, 2024). The key pillars of implementation include design thinking, introduction of ethical algorithmic controls and the development of the culture that values sustainable productivity. In order to ensure that automation does not intensify the friction rate and does not promote the number of interruptions, managers will have to liaise with IT officers, human resource managers, and data governance officials. The operational measures and digital health indicators should also be reviewed by the strategic monitoring on a regular basis. In the redefinition of productivity as a balanced practice, the organizations will be able to shift cognitively sustainable practices that are institutionalized and that can lead to success in workforce and performance in the long run.

10.1 Designing Attention-Sensitive Systems

To safeguard deep-work intervals and minimize unwarranted cognitive disruptions, the managers must be concerned about the structure of Organizational Information Systems. Attention sensitive design involves the calibration of notification thresholds, reduction of unnecessary alerts, and making smart prioritization policies that are consistent with the workload. Information shown in workflow dashboards ought to be contextual as opposed to a flood of real-time streams of information (Bouchon-Meunier, 2021). With the help of analytics, structured meeting policies will help to reduce the coordination load and preserve the continuity of focus. Managers can also implement system-wide quiet time or adaptive focus which will automatically silence low priority communication when executing high demand tasks. Notably, performance evaluation systems must encourage the long-term quality and accuracy as opposed to continual responsiveness. Iterative changes should be made based on continuous feedback provided by the employees on digital fatigue and usability of the systems. Organizations might turn OIS into favorable infrastructures that stabilize focus, decrease the stress level, and promote sustainable production by incorporating attention conscious principles into system design and management.

10.2 Implementing Ethical Algorithmic Controls

When AI is deployed, ethical governance has to be introduced to ensure trust and psychological safety. Managers ought to make sure that monitoring, prioritization, and performance analytics algorithms are easily comprehensible, clear, and reasonable. System architecture should have consent-based data collection and privacy-by-design. Easy explanation of how information is utilized and how automatic judgments are made will alleviate ambiguity and prevent the sense of being spied on. Biases, unintended pressure of the behavior, or extreme high intensity of the monitoring can be detected through periodic algorithmic audits (Veldurthi, 2025). It is through the creation of cross-functional oversight committees that include IT, HR, and compliance units that develop accountability. Other ethical control measures involve a limitation on data retention, restriction of access to the data, and provision of a means through which the employees can humanly view automated appraisals. Employees will be more inclined to believe AI-enabled systems when the governance safeguards are seen to be institutionalized. Ethical algorithmic controls thus serve as compliance systems as well as cognitive stabilizers that decrease the anxiety and enforce sustainable interaction.

10.3 Building Cognitive Sustainability Culture

Cultural congruence is not achievable without overhauling technology. Managers are obliged to create corporate cultures, which embody focused working, low working pace, and balanced digital communications. The way the leader behaves is also a significant dimension; neither does the leader expect to be so much available to act as an example to set standards of organized communication. The training programs would be able to enlighten the employees about cognitive load management, attention cycles, and healthy digital habits. The fact that the organizational well-being is introduced into organizational dashboards through the digital well-being measures is a sign that the institution takes the idea of cognitive sustainability seriously. It is possible to apply recognition to stimulate quality outcomes and smart problem solving rather than action (Shah, 2025). By means of cross-functional communication between the employees and the leadership on computer strain, transparency and collective refinement of systems becomes possible. With the incorporation of the concept of cognitive sustainability in strategic planning, performance reviews and talent development activities, it is ensured that it becomes institutionalized in the long term. The institutions are resilient due to the system design which is not only ergonomically correct but also consistent in its ability to remain innovative and be able to maintain high outcomes due to culture.

11. CONCLUSION

The revolution of Artificial Intelligence in Organizational Information System has transformed the way that the concept of measuring, controlling, and experiencing productivity has been reshaped. However, as the digital infrastructures are worsened, and the orchestration of the algorithm becomes the center of the enterprise operations, the productive potential can no longer be narrowed to the acceleration, throughput, or the permanent connection. The chapter has substantiated the point that productivity has to be redefined in a strategic manner which recognizes cognitive sustainability as one of the key goals of the organization. Incorporating Cognitive Sustainability Architecture and Algorithmic Ergonomics in the system design, organizations will be capable of reducing cognitive friction, regularizing attention cycles, and scaling automation to human capacity. The case studies indicated that majority of the performance gains such as higher levels of automation, lower cost of coordination, and better governance mechanisms can be sustainable when the smart systems acquire normal workloads and remain transparent and psychologically secure. The concept of human attention turns out to be a form of organizational capital: it is a limited resource, and only with the help of organized rest, it can be restored, as well as directly related to long-distance innovation and the quality of the decisions. This capital entails the security of vital capital and it can be secured only with the help of attention-conscious communication systems, adaptive workload modeling, plain analytics, and privacy-by-design. Sustainable AI-driven work is therefore not founded on replacing the human thought process with the automation process but presupposes the development of the systems that will increase the capabilities of the human resource and regulate the degrees of digital intensity. When the productivity indicators are balanced with sustainability of concentration, revitalization period and sustainability of the engagement, the organizations shift to a healthy model of performance. The competitive edge in the digital era will rather depend on the ability to create cognitively sustainable ecosystem where intelligent technologies can contribute to, and not drain the human resource of permanent superlative.

REFERENCES

Aarthi, S. Ravikumar, Sapayev Odilbek Uglu, V., Sottarov, A., & Singh, A. (2025). The privacy paradox. In *User-Centric Cybersecurity Implications for Sustainable Digital Transformation* (pp. 223–256). IGI Global Scientific Publishing. DOI: 10.4018/979-8-3373-3171-3.ch007

Aarthi, S., Ravikumar, R. N., Sobirova, K., & Mamadiyarov, Z. (2025). Empowering a sustainable future through digital learning and the SDGs. In *Harnessing E-Learning to Create a Sustainable Future* (pp. 145–172). IGI Global Scientific Publishing., DOI: 10.4018/979-8-3373-0112-9.ch006

Abdulgafar, A. A., Michael Oluwaseyi, A., Popoola, R., Anuoluwapo Rachael, A., & Chinonyerem, C. A. (2025). Human Factors Engineering and AI for optimizing human-machine interaction in industrial systems. *Asian Journal of Advanced Research and Reports*, *19*(10), 1–15. DOI: 10.9734/ajarr/2025/v19i101164

Akintola, A. S. O., Fawehinmi, Y., Aiyenitaju, O., Chinemerem, B., & Emmanuella, O. (2025). Digital transformation in telehealth: A systematic review of user trust, privacy, and regulatory governance in AI-powered remote monitoring systems. *Journal of Scientific Research and Reports*, *31*(11), 163–182. DOI: 10.9734/jsrr/2025/v31i113658

Alassaf, N. (2025). From abstraction to realization: A diagrammatic BIM framework for conceptual design in architectural education. *Sustainability (Basel)*, *17*(19), 8853. DOI: 10.3390/su17198853

Arigbabu, A. T., Olaniyi, O. O., Adigwe, C. S., Adebiyi, O. O., & Ajayi, S. A. (2024). Data governance in AI - enabled healthcare systems: A case of the Project Nightingale. *Asian Journal of Research in Computer Science*, *17*(5), 85–107. DOI: 10.9734/ajrcos/2024/v17i5441

Bedmutha, A. S.Akangsha Sunil Bedmutha. (2025). Adaptive Cognitive Reality: AI-driven personalized reality for optimized human potential. *International Journal of Computational and Experimental Science and Engineering*, *11*(4). Advance online publication. DOI: 10.22399/ijcesen.4496

Björck, A., Vogel, B., Pugnetti, C., & Lopez, M. (2025). Advancing cyber crisis readiness: Context, microfoundations and the role of leadership. *Journal of Communication Management (London)*, •••, 1–20. DOI: 10.1108/JCOM-01-2025-0006

Bouchon-Meunier, B. (2021). Ethics, diversity and consciousness in AI [president's message]. *IEEE Computational Intelligence Magazine*, *16*(3), 3–4. DOI: 10.1109/MCI.2021.3084388

Boztas, C., Ghadafi, E., & Ibrahim, R. (2025). Metaverse architectures: A comprehensive systematic review of definitions and frameworks. *Future Internet*, *17*(7), 283. DOI: 10.3390/fi17070283

Brodowicz, D. P.SGH Warsaw School of Economics. (2025). From smart to agentic environments: AI and innovative technologies transforming learning, work and urban living. *E-Mentor*, *111*(4), 54–61. DOI: 10.15219/em111.1720

Brunyé, T. T., Mitroff, S. R., & Elmore, J. G. (2026). Artificial intelligence and computer-aided diagnosis in diagnostic decisions: 5 questions for medical informatics and human-computer interface research. *Journal of the American Medical Informatics Association : JAMIA*, *33*(2), 543–550. DOI: 10.1093/jamia/ocaf123 PMID: 41101774

Daassi, M., Daassi, C., & Favier, M. (2006). Integration visualization techniques in groupware interfaces. In *Encyclopedia of Virtual Communities and Technologies* (pp. 279–284). IGI Global., DOI: 10.4018/978-1-59140-563-4.ch053

Eilouti, B. (2023). A framework for integrating ergonomics into architectural design. *Ergonomics in Design*, *31*(1), 4–12. DOI: 10.1177/1064804620983672

El Arab, R. A., Al Moosa, O. A., Sagbakken, M., Ghannam, A., Abuadas, F. H., Somerville, J., & Al Mutair, A. (2025). Integrative review of artificial intelligence applications in nursing: Education, clinical practice, workload management, and professional perceptions. *Frontiers in Public Health*, *13*(1619378), 1619378. DOI: 10.3389/fpubh.2025.1619378 PMID: 40823249

Farid, A., A. (. (2024). An approach for enhancing architectural performance-based design assessment in terms of sustainability. *Engineering Research Journal (Shoubra)*, *53*(1), 170–180. DOI: 10.21608/erjsh.2023.243056.1235

Forcellini, M., & Gracikova, E. (2025). From cognitive bias to algorithmic influence: Theoretical shifts in behavioral finance. *Journal of Behavioral Economics and Policy*, *1*(1), 20–27. DOI: 10.55121/jbep.v1i1.766

González-Reyes, C., Ficapal-Cusí, P., & Torrent-Sellens, J. (2026). AI and organizational leadership: Bibliometric review and future trends. *Journal of Organizational Change Management*, •••, 1–35. DOI: 10.1108/JOCM-03-2025-0291

Hou, M., Zhu, H., Zhou, M., & Arrabito, G. R. (2011). Optimizing operator–agent interaction in intelligent adaptive interface design: A conceptual framework. *IEEE Transactions on Systems, Man, and Cybernetics. Part C, Applications and Reviews*, *41*(2), 161–178. DOI: 10.1109/TSMCC.2010.2052041

Islam, F. A. S. (2025). Artificial intelligence-powered carbon market intelligence and blockchain-enabled governance for climate-responsive urban infrastructure in the Global South. *Journal of Engineering Research and Reports*, *27*(7), 440–472. DOI: 10.9734/jerr/2025/v27i71585

Lima, S. A.Sungida Akther Lima. (2024). Algorithmic fairness in HRM balancing AI-driven decision making with inclusive workforce practices. *Journal of Information Systems Engineering & Management*, *9*(4s), 2760–2769. DOI: 10.52783/jisem.v9i4s.13251

Ma, Y., Li, X., Hu, S., Liu, S., & Cheong, K. H. (2025). Trustworthy AI in education: Framework, cases, and governance strategies. *Innovation and Emerging Technologies*, *12*(2550026), 2550026. Advance online publication. DOI: 10.1142/S2737599425500264

Oluwafemi, I. O., Clement, T., Adanigbo, O. S., Gbenle, T. P., & Adekunle, B. I. (2021). A review of ethical considerations in AI-driven marketing analytics: Privacy, transparency, and consumer trust. *International Journal of Multidisciplinary Research and Growth Evaluation*, *2*(2), 428–435. DOI: 10.54660/.IJMRGE.2021.2.2.428-435

Palaniappan, K. (2025). The future of enterprise software: Enabling human-AI collaboration in the age of trillion-scale data. *European Modern Studies Journal*, *9*(5), 190–196. DOI: 10.59573/emsj.9(5).2025.18

Pasupuleti, M. K. (2024). *Human Factors and Ergonomics*. National Education Services., DOI: 10.62311/nesx/rb978-81-974226-6-9

Rakhra, A. K., & Mann, D. D. (2018). Design and evaluation of individual elements of the interface for an agricultural machine. *Journal of Agricultural Safety and Health*, *24*(1), 27–42. DOI: 10.13031/jash.12410 PMID: 29528604

Rathinavel, P., Ravikumar, R. N., Aarthi, S., Habib, M., Salaeva, N., & Pardaev, J. (2025). Augmenting human capabilities. In *Advances in Computational Intelligence and Robotics* (pp. 1–30). IGI Global Scientific Publishing. DOI: 10.4018/979-8-3373-2372-5.ch001

Ravikumar, R. N., & Aarthi, S. (2025b). Augmented decision-making. In *Advances in Computational Intelligence and Robotics* (pp. 227–258). IGI Global Scientific Publishing. DOI: 10.4018/979-8-3373-7416-1.ch009

Ravikumar, R. N., Aarthi, S., & Mamadiyarov, Z. (2026). Building the foundations of augmented organizations through AI empowerment. In *Advances in Computational Intelligence and Robotics* (pp. 101–130). IGI Global Scientific Publishing. DOI: 10.4018/979-8-3373-8607-2.ch006

Ravikumar, & Aarthi, S. (2025a). Cognitive collaboration. In *Advances in Computational Intelligence and Robotics* (pp. 125–158). IGI Global Scientific Publishing. DOI: 10.4018/979-8-3373-7416-1.ch006

Sadeghi, S., & Hoseinpour Jajarm, M. (2025). Evaluating the performance of architectural structures using NLP-enhanced fuzzy logic. *Engineering, Construction, and Architectural Management*, •••, 1–18. DOI: 10.1108/ECAM-07-2025-1214

Sang, L. T., Ravikumar, R. N., Aarthi, S., & Ben, T. L. (2025). Optimizing sales and inventory performance using AI and business intelligence in POS environments. In *Advances in Computational Intelligence and Robotics* (pp. 259–290). IGI Global Scientific Publishing. DOI: 10.4018/979-8-3373-4392-1.ch011

Shah, I. (2025). AI-driven price discrimination: Strategic applications, ethical challenges, and regulatory implications. *International Science Journal of Management. Economics & Finance*, *4*(5), 33–50. DOI: 10.46299/j.isjmef.20250405.04

Shreha, S. A., Ravikumar, R. N., & Aarthi, S. (2025). Neuro-symbolic AI and Behavioral Intelligence. In *Advances in Computational Intelligence and Robotics* (pp. 121–152). IGI Global Scientific Publishing. DOI: 10.4018/979-8-3373-5012-7.ch005

Shreha, S. A., Ravikumar, R. N., & Aarthi, S. (2026). Precision medicine, genomics, and health equity challenges and opportunities. In *Advancing Equity in Global Healthcare Systems* (pp. 321–354). IGI Global Scientific Publishing., DOI: 10.4018/979-8-3373-1330-6.ch012

Sousa, N. M. T. (2025). Integration of artificial intelligence in the digital preservation of academic repositories and scientific data in higher education libraries. *Digital Library Perspectives*, •••, 1–21. DOI: 10.1108/DLP-06-2025-0074

Tabatabaei, E. M., & Khalili, S. (2025). Cognitive hybridization: Redefining human identity at the interface of neuroscience and artificial intelligence: A narrative review. *Journal of Advanced Biomedical Sciences*. DOI: 10.18502/jabs.v16i1.20125

Trstenjak, M., Benešova, A., Opetuk, T., & Cajner, H. (2025). Human factors and ergonomics in Industry 5.0—A systematic literature review. *Applied Sciences (Basel, Switzerland)*, *15*(4), 2123. DOI: 10.3390/app15042123

Veldurthi, A. K. (2025). Ethical considerations in AI-driven financial decision-making. *European Journal of Computer Science and Information Technology*, *13*(31), 49–64. DOI: 10.37745/ejcsit.2013/vol13n314964

Zhao, G., & Yim, J. (2025). Towards usability-driven optimization: A human-in-the-loop approach to interface evaluation. *Edelweiss Applied Science and Technology*, *9*(12), 630–643. DOI: 10.55214/2576-8484.v9i12.11407

KEY TERMS AND DEFINITIONS

Adaptive Workload Modeling: AI-based adjustment of task distribution according to workload intensity and cognitive capacity.

Algorithmic Ergonomics: The design approach that aligns AI systems, notifications, dashboards, and workflows with human cognitive limits to reduce overload and stress.

Attention Stability: The capacity to concentrate on tasks without frequent interruptions or excessive context switching.

Attention-Aware Communication: Communication systems that manage notification timing and priority to protect focus time.

Cognitive Load: The amount of mental effort required to process information and complete tasks.

Cognitive Sustainability: The ability of employees to maintain focus, mental clarity, decision quality, and emotional balance over long periods in digitally intensive work environments.

Deep Work Cycles: Focused periods of uninterrupted work that enable high-quality thinking and problem-solving.

Dual-Outcome Measurement Model: A framework that evaluates both productivity performance and digital well-being indicators together.

Organizational Information Systems (OIS): Integrated digital platforms used by organizations to manage workflows, communication, analytics, and decision-making processes.

Privacy-by-Design: A governance approach where data protection and consent mechanisms are built directly into system architecture.

Psychological Safety: A work environment where employees feel secure, trusted, and free from excessive surveillance or punitive monitoring.

Sustainable Productivity: A balanced form of productivity that maintains long-term performance without causing cognitive fatigue or burnout.

Chapter 6
Designing Smarter Systems for Better Work: Reducing Cognitive Load in Digital Workplaces

K. Premkumar
St. Joseph College of Engineering, India

M. Navaneethakrishnan
St. Joseph College of Engineering, India

A. Sunitha
St. Joseph College of Engineering, India

J. Tharun
http://orcid.org/0009-0004-8433-9315
KCG College of Technology, India

P. Preethi
St. Joseph College of Engineering, India

N. G. Harine
http://orcid.org/0009-0006-0250-7309
KCG College of Technology, India

ABSTRACT

This chapter examines the impact of modern Information Systems on cognitive performance in digitally intensive work environments. It identifies key challenges such as the toggle tax, attentional residue, cognitive overload, and decision fatigue, which collectively reduce productivity and increase mental strain. Drawing on cognitive ergonomics and behavioral research, the chapter proposes a human-centered design approach that aligns system architecture with the limitations of human cognition. It explores solutions including unified digital hubs, intelligent notification management, focus shielding, and automation of routine tasks. The chapter further introduces concepts such as strategic friction, adaptive interfaces, and the right to disconnect

DOI: 10.4018/979-8-2600-0111-0.ch006

as mechanisms to support sustained attention and well-being. It concludes by proposing new metrics for sustainable productivity that prioritize cognitive health, task quality, and long-term performance over superficial activity measures.

1. INTRODUCTION

The contemporary workplace has undergone a significant transformation, shifting from traditional office-based environments to highly dynamic and digitally interconnected systems. While these advancements have enabled faster communication and seamless global collaboration, they have also introduced serious cognitive challenges for knowledge workers. One of the most prominent issues is the toggle tax, which refers to the mental cost incurred when individuals frequently switch between multiple applications and tasks. Research shows that the average knowledge worker switches between applications nearly 1,200 times per day, leading to a substantial loss of productivity amounting to nearly five working weeks annually (Henderson, 2021) (Mark et al., 2012) (Gonzalez & Mark, 2004).

Frequent task switching disrupts cognitive continuity and creates a phenomenon known as attentional residue, where a portion of the user's attention remains tied to the previous task even after moving on to a new one. This reduces the efficiency and quality of work performed on the current task and significantly affects overall productivity (Leroy, 2009) (Rubinstein et al., 2001) (Monsell, 2003). Over time, this fragmentation of attention contributes to increased mental fatigue, higher error rates, and reduced ability to engage in deep, meaningful work (Pashler, 1994) (Newport, 2016).

Modern Information Systems (IS) are often designed with an emphasis on speed, connectivity, and data processing capabilities, while overlooking the biological limitations of human cognition. According to Kirsh (2000), when individuals are exposed to overly complex information environments, their cognitive processing efficiency declines sharply, resulting in overload and reduced decision-making quality (Sweller, 2011) (Sweller et al., 2011). This mismatch between system design and human capability creates a scenario where managing the system becomes more demanding than the actual task being performed.

Another critical issue is the emergence of a culture of perpetual urgency, driven by continuous notifications, alerts, and real-time communication tools. These features force users into a constant state of responsiveness, preventing them from achieving sustained concentration. Studies indicate that interruptions not only disrupt workflow but also significantly increase stress levels and reduce job satisfaction, as it takes considerable time for individuals to regain their original focus after being interrupted (Mark et al., 2008) (Altmann & Trafton, 2002) (Baethge & Rigotti, 2013) (Kushlev & Dunn, 2015).

To address these challenges, it is essential to rethink the design philosophy of Information Systems by recognizing human attention as a limited and valuable resource. Instead of treating users as passive data processors, future systems must actively support cognitive well-being by reducing unnecessary interruptions and minimizing context switching. The integration of Artificial Intelligence (AI) offers promising opportunities in this regard, as it can be used to filter, prioritize, and manage information based on user context. However, improper implementation of AI may introduce an automation tax, where users spend excessive time verifying or correcting automated outputs, thereby negating its benefits (Parasuraman & Riley, 1997) (Endsley, 1995) (Dzindolet et al., 2002).

In conclusion, the future of productivity lies not in increasing the volume of tasks performed but in preserving and enhancing cognitive capacity. By designing systems that align with human cognitive limitations and promote deep focus, organizations can achieve a balance between efficiency and well-being, ultimately leading to sustainable performance and innovation (Cal Newport, 2016) (Kahneman, 2011).

Figure 1: Impact of Toggle Tax and Context Switching on Cognitive Load

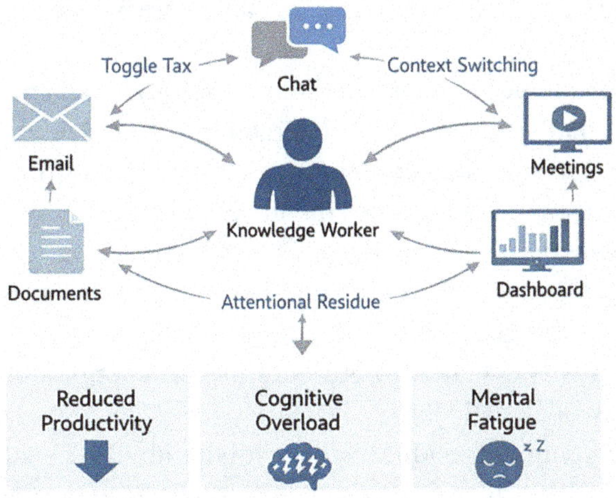

Illustrates how frequent switching between multiple applications leads to attentional residue, cognitive overload, and reduced productivity in knowledge work environments.

2. THE COGNITIVE ERGONOMICS OF THE INFORMATION SYSTEMS

Cognitive ergonomics focuses on designing systems that align with the natural capabilities and limitations of the human brain. In the modern digital workplace, the primary source of strain has shifted from physical effort to cognitive demand, as individuals are required to process large volumes of information continuously. As Information Systems (IS) become more complex and pervasive, they often exceed the brain's processing capacity, leading to cognitive overload, reduced efficiency, and increased stress. Cognitive load theory clearly establishes that working memory is inherently limited, and when systems impose excessive or poorly structured demands, both learning and task performance deteriorate significantly (Sweller, 2011) (Sweller et al., 2011) (Paas et al., 2004).

A major challenge in poorly designed systems is the high noise-to-signal ratio, where users are exposed to excessive and often irrelevant notifications. Each interruption forces the brain to shift attention, disrupting concentration and reducing productivity. Empirical research demonstrates that interruptions carry a measurable cognitive penalty, requiring substantial time for individuals to re-establish focus and resume task continuity (Mark et al., 2008) (Altmann & Trafton, 2002). Observational studies further show that frequent digital interruptions fragment work into short bursts, preventing sustained engagement and increasing error rates (Gonzalez & Mark, 2004).

Another important issue is decision fatigue, which arises when users are required to make numerous small decisions while interacting with a system. These decisions, such as navigating interfaces, adjusting settings, or managing notifications, gradually consume cognitive resources and reduce mental efficiency over time. As the volume of micro-decisions increases, the quality of subsequent decisions declines, leading to suboptimal outcomes and increased mental exhaustion (Baumeister et al., 2007) (Vohs et al., 2008). From a cognitive ergonomics perspective, minimizing unnecessary decision points is essential to preserve mental energy and improve overall system usability (Sweller, 2011).

The concept of attentional residue further explains how task switching negatively affects productivity. When individuals switch from one task to another, part of their attention remains focused on the previous task, reducing their ability to fully engage with the new one. This residual cognitive load interferes with working memory and slows down task execution, particularly in complex knowledge work environments (Leroy, 2009) (Rubinstein et al., 2001). Additional research on task-switching behavior indicates that these switching costs are not merely momentary disruptions but accumulate over time, significantly reducing overall efficiency (Monsell, 2003).

To mitigate these challenges, cognitive ergonomics emphasizes the importance of designing systems that support deep, uninterrupted work. One effective strategy is the use of peripheral awareness, where non-critical information is presented in a subtle and non-intrusive manner. Instead of demanding immediate attention, systems provide background cues that allow users to remain focused while still being aware of important updates. This approach reflects how human perception naturally prioritizes salient stimuli while filtering out low-priority information, thereby enabling efficient processing without overwhelming cognitive resources (Weiser & Brown, 1997) (Endsley, 1995).

In addition, poorly designed feedback systems often lead to psychological effects such as hyper-vigilance and phantom notifications, where users feel compelled to repeatedly check for updates even in the absence of new information. This persistent state of alertness increases cognitive strain and contributes to stress-related outcomes. Research shows that even the anticipation of interruptions can degrade performance, as individuals allocate part of their attention to monitoring potential disruptions rather than focusing fully on the task (Mark et al., 2008). Over time, this anticipatory behavior reinforces compulsive interaction patterns with digital systems, further reducing well-being (Kushlev & Dunn, 2015).

In conclusion, cognitive ergonomics plays a critical role in the design of effective Information Systems. By recognizing the limitations of human cognition and minimizing unnecessary mental effort, systems can enhance both productivity and user well-being. Designing environments that support sustained focus, reduce unnecessary interruptions, and structure information in cognitively efficient ways is essential for enabling individuals to perform effectively without experiencing mental exhaustion (Sweller, 2011) (Kahneman, 2011).

3. MINIMIZING THE "TOGGLE TAX": THE RISE OF UNIFIED DIGITAL HUBS

The cognitive architecture of the modern knowledge worker is increasingly strained by the fragmentation of digital tools, a condition primarily driven by what is known as the toggle tax. This term refers to the measurable loss in productivity and mental clarity that occurs whenever users switch between multiple, disconnected applications to complete a single workflow. In contemporary work environments, professionals often move between email platforms, messaging applications, cloud storage systems, and project management tools in rapid succession. Henderson (2021) reports that the average worker toggles between applications nearly 1,200 times per day, resulting in a significant cognitive burden and consuming up to 40% of productive capacity (Mark et al., 2012) (Gonzalez & Mark, 2004). This continuous switching forces the brain to repeatedly reorient itself, disrupting focus and increasing the likelihood of errors (Monsell, 2003) (Rubinstein et al., 2001).

From a cognitive perspective, each transition between applications requires the brain to unload one set of rules and goals while simultaneously loading another. This process is neither instantaneous nor efficient, as it introduces attentional residue, where a portion of cognitive resources remains tied to the previous task (Leroy, 2009) (Pashler, 1994). Over time, this leads to fragmented thinking and diminished performance. When individuals are required to manage complex external information environments, their internal cognitive processing efficiency declines, making it more difficult to perform high-level analytical tasks (Kirsh, 2000) (Sweller et al., 2011). As a result, the fragmented nature of modern Information Systems directly conflicts with the biological limitations of human cognition.

Unified digital hubs have emerged as a strategic response to this challenge by consolidating multiple tools and workflows into a single, cohesive interface. These hubs are designed around the principle of contextual proximity, where all resources required for a specific task are accessible within one environment. In a fragmented system, completing a simple task may require navigating through several applications, each with its own interface, notification system, and interaction logic. This not only increases the time required to complete tasks but also raises the risk of digital distraction, as users may encounter irrelevant notifications or information during each transition (Mark et al., 2008). By contrast, unified hubs minimize these disruptions by allowing users to access all relevant data without leaving the primary workspace, thereby preserving cognitive continuity (Weiser & Brown, 1997).

An important advancement within unified digital hubs is the development of composable interfaces, which allow users to customize their workspace based on their specific needs and workflows. Unlike traditional systems that enforce rigid structures, composable interfaces enable users to arrange tools, data, and functionalities in a way that reduces visual clutter and enhances usability. Reducing extraneous cognitive load, defined as the mental effort spent navigating systems rather than solving problems, is essential for improving performance and user efficiency (Sweller, 2011) (Paas et al., 2004). By presenting only relevant information and hiding unnecessary complexity, composable interfaces support deeper concentration and more efficient task execution (Norman, 2013).

Another critical feature of unified digital hubs is the integration of global search and universal indexing, which addresses the widespread issue of information scavenging. Knowledge workers often spend a significant portion of their time searching for information across multiple platforms. Studies estimate that a substantial portion of the workweek is consumed by locating and retrieving fragmented data, representing a major inefficiency in digital work environments (Hacker et al., 2019) (Davenport & Prusak, 1998). Fragmented systems exacerbate this problem by isolating information within separate applications, each requiring independent searches. Unified hubs solve this issue by creating a centralized data layer, allowing users to retrieve information from multiple sources through a single query. This not only improves efficiency but also reduces the cognitive strain associated with searching and switching between platforms (Pirolli & Card, 2005).

Despite their advantages, unified digital hubs introduce a trade-off between feature depth and integration breadth. Specialized applications often offer advanced functionalities that may not be fully replicated within a unified system. However, for most knowledge work, the cognitive benefits of reduced context switching outweigh the loss of highly specialized features. Modern approaches to system design aim to balance this trade-off through deep integration, where specialized tools are incorporated into the hub using APIs while maintaining a consistent interface and workflow (Davenport & Ronanki, 2018). This approach ensures that users can access advanced functionalities without leaving the unified environment, thereby minimizing disruption.

Furthermore, unified digital hubs contribute to reducing techno-stress, a condition caused by the excessive use of complex technologies. Continuous exposure to multiple systems, each with its own set of rules and interactions, increases mental fatigue and reduces overall job satisfaction (Tarafdar et al., 2007) (Ayyagari et al., 2011). By simplifying the digital environment and reducing the number of interfaces users must navigate, unified hubs create a more manageable and less stressful work experience. Simplifying external information structures can significantly improve internal cognitive efficiency, reinforcing the importance of integrated system design (Kirsh, 2000).

Ultimately, the goal of minimizing the toggle tax through unified digital hubs is to create an environment where the interface becomes nearly invisible, allowing users to focus entirely on their work. By aligning system design with human cognitive capabilities, organizations can enhance productivity, reduce mental strain, and support sustained concentration (Kahneman, 2011) (Newport, 2016). As digital work continues to evolve, the shift toward unified, integrated systems represents a critical step in building workplaces that prioritize both efficiency and cognitive well-being.

Figure 2: Transition from Fragmented Systems to Unified Digital Hub Architecture

Compares traditional fragmented digital tools with unified digital hubs, highlighting reduced context switching, improved workflow continuity, and enhanced productivity.

4. DESIGNING FOR ASYNCHRONOUS EXCELLENCE

The integration of Artificial Intelligence (AI) into Information Systems (IS) represents a transformative shift in how digital environments are structured and experienced. Unlike traditional systems that rely heavily on manual input and user-driven navigation, AI-driven systems introduce adaptive capabilities that can learn from user behavior, predict needs, and automate routine tasks. This evolution offers significant potential for reducing cognitive load, improving efficiency, and enhancing decision-making. However, it also introduces new challenges that must be carefully managed to avoid unintended cognitive and operational consequences (Davenport & Ronanki, 2018) (Brynjolfsson & McAfee, 2014).

One of the primary advantages of AI in Information Systems is its ability to filter and prioritize information. In environments characterized by information overload, users are often exposed to large volumes of data, much of which may be irrelevant to their immediate tasks. AI algorithms can analyze user behavior, context, and historical patterns to deliver only the most relevant information at the right time. This reduces the noise-to-signal ratio and allows users to focus on meaningful activities. Systems that effectively augment human decision-making can significantly enhance productivity by minimizing unnecessary cognitive effort (Davenport & Ronanki, 2018) (Wilson & Daugherty, 2018).

Another important contribution of AI is the automation of repetitive and routine tasks, which are often a major source of cognitive fatigue. Tasks such as scheduling meetings, sorting emails, generating reports, and managing workflows can be handled by AI systems, allowing users to allocate their cognitive resources to higher-level thinking and creative problem-solving. Automation, when properly implemented, can improve efficiency and reduce workload, particularly in knowledge-intensive environments where routine operations consume a significant portion of time (Parasuraman & Riley, 1997) (Endsley, 1995). However, this benefit is conditional and depends heavily on system reliability and user trust.

This introduces the concept of the automation tax, which refers to the additional cognitive effort required to oversee and validate AI-generated outputs. While AI systems can perform tasks quickly, they are not always perfectly accurate or transparent. As a result, users may need to spend time checking the reliability of AI decisions, which can offset the intended productivity gains. Poorly designed automation can create additional layers of work, particularly when systems fail unpredictably or require constant monitoring (Parasuraman & Riley, 1997) (Dzindolet et al., 2002). This highlights the importance of designing AI systems that reduce, rather than redistribute, cognitive effort.

Another significant challenge associated with AI-driven systems is the issue of algorithmic opacity, often referred to as the black box problem. Many AI models, especially those based on complex machine learning techniques, operate in ways that are not easily interpretable by users. This lack of transparency can reduce trust and make it difficult for individuals to understand how decisions are made. Successful AI adoption depends not only on technical performance but also on user trust and acceptance, which are strongly influenced by system transparency and explainability (Davenport & Ronanki, 2018) (Rai, 2020). Systems that provide clear explanations and maintain interpretability are more likely to be trusted and effectively utilized.

AI also plays a crucial role in enabling context-aware systems, which can adapt their behavior based on the user's current task, environment, and preferences. For example, an AI-driven system can suppress non-essential notifications during periods of deep work or prioritize urgent messages based on contextual relevance. This aligns closely with the principles of cognitive ergonomics, as it reduces interruptions and supports sustained concentration. Minimizing unnecessary interruptions is essential for maintaining productivity and reducing stress in digital work environments (Mark et al., 2008).

Despite these advantages, the implementation of AI must be approached with caution to avoid reinforcing negative patterns such as over-dependence and reduced critical thinking. When users rely too heavily on AI systems, they may become less engaged in decision-making processes, leading to a decline in analytical skills over time. This phenomenon, often described as automation complacency, can be particularly problematic in high-stakes environments where human oversight is critical (Parasuraman & Riley, 1997) (Lee & See, 2004). Maintaining an appropriate balance between automation and human control is therefore essential.

Furthermore, ethical considerations play a vital role in the design and deployment of AI-driven Information Systems. Issues such as data privacy, bias in algorithms, and fairness in decision-making must be addressed to ensure that AI systems operate responsibly. Biased training data can lead to discriminatory outcomes, while excessive data collection raises legitimate concerns about user privacy and surveillance. Organizations must establish clear governance frameworks to ensure that AI systems are both effective and ethically aligned with societal expectations (Davenport & Ronanki, 2018) (Floridi et al., 2018).

In conclusion, AI-driven Information Systems offer powerful tools for enhancing productivity and reducing cognitive load, but their success depends on careful design and implementation. By balancing automation with human control, ensuring transparency, and addressing ethical concerns, organizations can harness the benefits of AI while minimizing its risks. The goal is not to replace human intelligence but to augment it in a way that supports both efficiency and cognitive well-being (Kahneman, 2011) (Cal Newport, 2016).

Figure 3: Role of AI in Enhancing and Challenging Information Systems

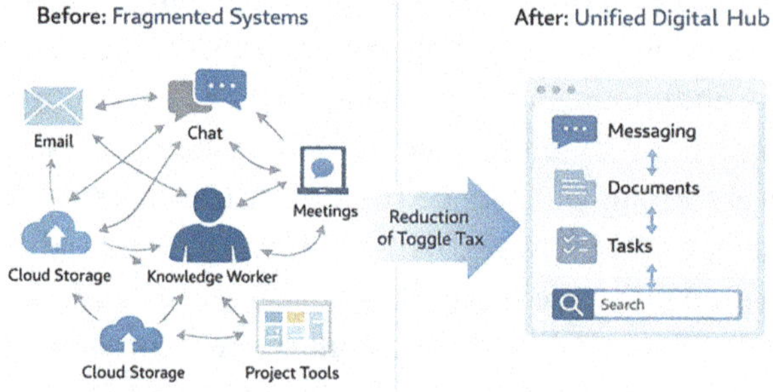

Depicts how AI-driven systems support task automation, context awareness, and decision-making while also introducing challenges such as automation tax and algorithmic opacity.

5. INTELLIGENT NOTIFICATION MANAGEMENT AND "FOCUS SHEILDING"

In modern digital environments, notifications have become one of the most significant sources of cognitive disruption. While they are designed to facilitate communication and ensure timely access to information, their excessive and poorly managed use has led to a constant state of interruption. This phenomenon contributes directly to attentional fragmentation, reduced productivity, and increased stress levels. As Information Systems (IS) continue to evolve, there is a growing need to rethink how notifications are designed and delivered, giving rise to the concept of intelligent notification management and focus shielding (Mark et al., 2012) (Kushlev & Dunn, 2015).

Notifications inherently demand attention, often triggering an immediate cognitive response regardless of their importance. Each alert, whether it is an email, message, or system update, interrupts the user's current task and forces a shift in attention. Such interruptions significantly disrupt workflow, and it can take considerable time for individuals to regain their original level of focus after being interrupted (Mark et al., 2008) (Altmann & Trafton, 2002). This repeated cycle of disruption not only reduces efficiency but also increases cognitive fatigue over time (Monsell, 2003).

The concept of focus shielding addresses this issue by protecting the user's attention from unnecessary interruptions during periods of deep work. Focus shielding involves the strategic suppression or deferral of non-essential notifications, allowing users to maintain sustained concentration on their primary tasks. This approach aligns with the principles of cognitive ergonomics, which emphasize minimizing external disruptions to support optimal mental performance (Sweller, 2011) (Sweller et al., 2011). By creating uninterrupted work intervals, focus shielding enables individuals to engage more effectively in complex and cognitively demanding activities (Newport, 2016).

Intelligent notification management builds upon this concept by leveraging Artificial Intelligence (AI) to determine the relevance and timing of notifications. Instead of delivering all alerts immediately, AI-driven systems analyze contextual factors such as user activity, task priority, and historical behavior to decide when and how notifications should be presented. For example, a system may delay non-urgent messages while a user is engaged in deep work or prioritize critical alerts based on their importance. AI systems capable of context-aware decision-making can significantly improve productivity by reducing unnecessary cognitive interruptions (Davenport & Ronanki, 2018).

Another important aspect of intelligent notification systems is the ability to categorize and prioritize information. Not all notifications carry the same level of importance, yet traditional systems often treat them equally, leading to information overload. By classifying notifications into categories such as urgent, important, and low-priority, systems can ensure that only the most critical information reaches the user immediately, while less important updates are grouped or delivered at appropriate times. This structured prioritization reduces the noise-to-signal ratio and supports more efficient information processing (Eppler & Mengis, 2004) (Pirolli & Card, 2005).

Furthermore, intelligent systems can incorporate adaptive learning mechanisms that evolve based on user preferences and behavior. Over time, the system learns which types of notifications are frequently ignored or acted upon, refining its delivery strategy accordingly. This personalization enhances user experience and ensures that the system aligns with individual work patterns. However, excessive automation must be carefully managed to avoid overdependence and to ensure that users retain control over critical decisions (Parasuraman & Riley, 1997) (Lee & See, 2004).

The psychological impact of poorly managed notifications is another critical consideration. Continuous exposure to alerts can create a sense of urgency and anxiety, even when the information is not immediately relevant. This leads to hyper-vigilance, where users feel compelled to constantly monitor their devices for updates. Over time, this behavior can contribute to stress and reduced well-being (Kushlev & Dunn, 2015) (Ayyagari et al., 2011). The anticipation of interruptions can be as disruptive as the interruptions themselves, further highlighting the need for controlled and predictable notification systems (Mark et al., 2008).

Focus shielding also involves giving users greater control and autonomy over their notification settings. While AI can assist in managing notifications, it is essential that users have the ability to customize their preferences based on their needs. This includes setting priorities, defining focus periods, and choosing which types of notifications should be suppressed or delivered. Providing such control enhances usability and strengthens trust in the system, as users remain active participants rather than passive recipients of automated decisions (Norman, 2013).

In addition, the concept of batching notifications has emerged as an effective strategy for reducing cognitive disruption. Instead of delivering notifications individually in real time, systems can group them and present them at scheduled intervals. This reduces the frequency of interruptions and allows users to process information more efficiently. Structured information delivery is less disruptive than random interruptions, as it aligns more closely with the brain's natural processing patterns and reduces cognitive switching costs (Sweller, 2011) (Baethge & Rigotti, 2013).

Ultimately, intelligent notification management and focus shielding aim to transform notifications from a source of disruption into a tool for enhancing productivity and well-being. By aligning notification systems with human cognitive processes, organizations can create digital environments that support sustained attention and reduce mental strain (Kahneman, 2011) (Newport, 2016). The challenge lies in achieving the right balance between accessibility and interruption, ensuring that users remain informed without being overwhelmed.

In conclusion, the future of effective Information Systems depends on the ability to protect and manage user attention. Intelligent notification systems, combined with focus shielding strategies, provide a powerful framework for achieving this goal. By minimizing unnecessary interruptions, prioritizing relevant information, and supporting deep work, these systems can significantly improve both productivity and cognitive well-being in the digital workplace (Davenport & Ronanki, 2018) (Sweller, 2011).

Figure 4: Intelligent Notification Management and Focus Shielding Model

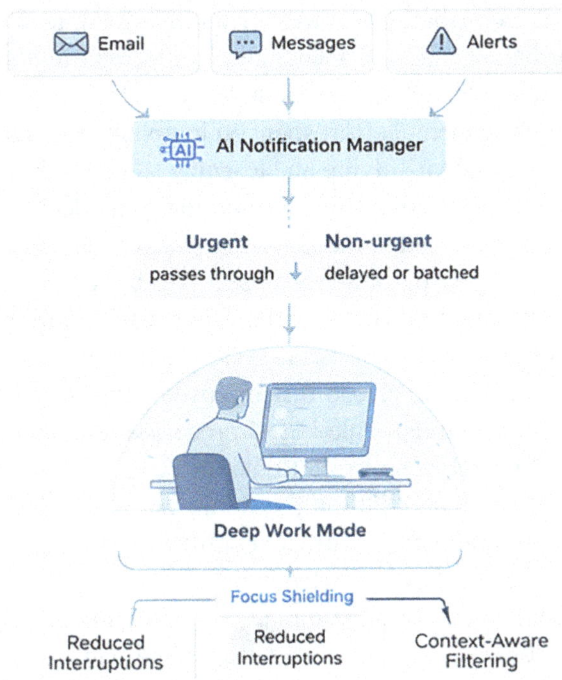

Shows how AI-based notification filtering prioritizes critical alerts while suppressing non-essential interruptions to support deep work and sustained attention.

6. AUTOMATION OF "DIGITAL BUSYWORK": RECLAIMING HUMAN AGENCY

In the modern digital workplace, a substantial portion of time is consumed not by meaningful, high-value work but by what can be described as digital busywork. This includes routine, repetitive, and low-impact tasks such as sorting emails, updating records, formatting documents, scheduling meetings, and navigating between systems. Although individually trivial, these tasks collectively impose a significant cognitive burden and consume valuable time that could otherwise be devoted to creative, analytical, and strategic activities. The automation of such tasks represents a critical opportunity to enhance productivity while restoring human agency in digital work environments (Davenport & Ronanki, 2018) (Brynjolfsson & McAfee, 2014).

Digital busywork contributes heavily to cognitive load, as it requires constant attention, decision-making, and task switching. Even simple actions, when repeated frequently, accumulate into substantial mental effort. Human cognitive capacity is limited, and unnecessary mental effort spent on low-value tasks reduces the ability to engage in complex problem-solving and learning (Sweller, 2011) (Sweller et al., 2011). This misallocation of cognitive resources not only decreases efficiency but also leads to mental fatigue and reduced job satisfaction (Kahneman, 2011).

Automation technologies, particularly those driven by Artificial Intelligence (AI) and robotic process automation (RPA), offer a powerful solution to this problem. By delegating repetitive tasks to automated systems, organizations can significantly reduce the cognitive demands placed on employees. AI systems are particularly effective in handling structured, rule-based processes, enabling faster and more accurate task execution (Davenport & Ronanki, 2018) (Willcocks et al., 2015). For example, automated email filtering systems can categorize messages based on priority, while scheduling assistants can coordinate meetings without requiring manual input (Lacity & Willcocks, 2016).

However, the benefits of automation extend beyond efficiency gains. One of the most important outcomes is the restoration of human agency, defined as the ability of individuals to exercise control over their work and focus on meaningful activities. When employees are relieved of repetitive tasks, they can allocate more time to creative thinking, innovation, and decision-making. This shift not only enhances productivity but also improves motivation and engagement, as individuals are able to contribute more meaningfully to organizational goals (Deci & Ryan, 2000) (Hackman & Oldham, 1976).

Despite these advantages, the implementation of automation must be approached carefully to avoid unintended consequences. One such issue is the automation paradox, where increased automation can lead to greater complexity and oversight requirements. While automation reduces direct workload, it can increase the need for monitoring and intervention, particularly when systems fail or produce unexpected results (Parasuraman & Riley, 1997) (Endsley, 1995). This creates a situation where users must remain vigilant, potentially introducing a new form of cognitive burden (Dzindolet et al., 2002).

Another important concern is the risk of deskilling, where excessive reliance on automation reduces the development and maintenance of human skills. When tasks are fully automated, users may lose the opportunity to practice critical thinking and problem-solving abilities. Over time, this can lead to decreased competence and confidence, particularly in situations where human intervention is required (Carr, 2010) (Autor, 2015). To address this, it is essential to design automation systems that support human-in-the-loop interaction, where users remain actively engaged in decision-making processes (Lee & See, 2004).

Transparency and explainability are also crucial in ensuring the effectiveness of automated systems. Users must be able to understand how and why decisions are made, particularly in complex or high-stakes scenarios. Lack of transparency can lead to distrust and reluctance to rely on automated systems. Successful AI adoption depends on building systems that are not only accurate but also interpretable and user-friendly (Davenport & Ronanki, 2018) (Rai, 2020).

Furthermore, the automation of digital busywork can significantly reduce context switching, which is a major contributor to the toggle tax. By handling routine transitions and background tasks, automated systems allow users to maintain focus on their primary activities. Reducing task switching minimizes attentional residue, thereby improving cognitive performance and efficiency (Leroy, 2009) (Rubinstein et al., 2001). This reinforces the importance of integrating automation into workflows in a way that supports continuous and uninterrupted work (Mark et al., 2012).

Another key aspect of reclaiming human agency is providing users with control over automation. While automation can enhance efficiency, it should not override user preferences or decision-making authority. Systems should allow users to customize automation levels, override automated decisions, and intervene when necessary. This balance between automation and control ensures that users remain empowered rather than constrained by technology (Norman, 2013).

In addition, ethical considerations must be addressed when implementing automation in Information Systems. Issues such as job displacement, fairness, and accountability require careful attention. While automation can improve efficiency, organizations must ensure that it is implemented in a way that supports employees rather than replacing them entirely. The goal of automation should be to augment human capabilities rather than eliminate them (Parasuraman & Riley, 1997) (Floridi et al., 2018).

Ultimately, the automation of digital busywork represents a shift toward more meaningful and human-centered work. By reducing the time and effort spent on repetitive tasks, organizations can unlock the full potential of their workforce. This not only enhances productivity but also promotes a more satisfying and engaging work experience (Kahneman, 2011) (Newport, 2016).

In conclusion, reclaiming human agency in the digital workplace requires a thoughtful approach to automation. By focusing on augmenting human capabilities, maintaining transparency, and ensuring user control, Information Systems can transform from sources of cognitive burden into tools that empower individuals. The future of work lies in creating a balance where machines handle routine tasks, allowing humans to focus on creativity, critical thinking, and innovation (Davenport & Ronanki, 2018) (Brynjolfsson & McAfee, 2014).

7. ALGORITHMIC TRANSPARENCY AND THE "SURVEILLANCE STRESS" FACTOR

As Information Systems increasingly integrate Artificial Intelligence (AI) and algorithmic decision-making, concerns surrounding transparency, trust, and psychological well-being have become more prominent. While AI-driven systems offer efficiency and automation, they also introduce a layer of invisibility in decision processes, often referred to as algorithmic opacity. This lack of clarity can significantly affect how users interact with systems and how they perceive control over their work environment. Consequently, the need for algorithmic transparency has emerged as a critical factor in the design of modern Information Systems (Davenport & Ronanki, 2018) (Rai, 2020).

Algorithmic transparency refers to the extent to which users can understand how decisions are made within a system. In many AI-driven environments, decisions such as task prioritization, performance evaluation, and information filtering are handled by complex models that are not easily interpretable. User trust in AI systems is strongly influenced by the degree of transparency provided, and when users cannot understand or predict system behavior, they are more likely to question its reliability and resist its adoption (Davenport & Ronanki, 2018) (Lee & See, 2004).

A major consequence of low transparency is the emergence of what can be described as the surveillance stress factor. This phenomenon arises when users feel that their actions are constantly being monitored, analyzed, and evaluated by digital systems. In workplaces where performance metrics, activity tracking, and behavioral analytics are heavily utilized, employees may develop a heightened sense of being observed. Digital monitoring can lead to increased anxiety, reduced autonomy, and a decline in job satisfaction, particularly when individuals perceive the monitoring as intrusive or unfair (Ravid et al., 2020) (Ball, 2010) (Moore et al., 2018).

The psychological impact of surveillance stress is closely linked to the concept of perceived control. When users feel that they have little or no control over how their data is collected or used, it can lead to feelings of helplessness and stress. Cognitive efficiency is strongly influenced by the structure of the external environment, and environments that create uncertainty or lack of control can significantly impair mental performance (Kirsh, 2000) (Karasek, 1979). In this context, opaque algorithmic systems not only affect productivity but also have broader implications for mental well-being (Kahneman, 2011).

Another critical issue associated with algorithmic systems is the potential for bias and unfair decision-making. AI models are trained on historical data, which may contain inherent biases. If these biases are not identified and addressed, they can be perpetuated and even amplified by automated systems. This raises ethical concerns, particularly in areas such as performance evaluation, hiring, and resource allocation (Barocas & Selbst, 2016) (O'Neil, 2016). Organizations must implement rigorous validation and auditing mechanisms to ensure fairness and accountability in AI-driven decisions (Davenport & Ronanki, 2018) (Floridi et al., 2018).

To mitigate these challenges, the implementation of explainable AI has gained significant attention. Explainable AI focuses on developing models that provide clear and understandable explanations for their decisions. By offering insights into how outcomes are generated, these systems enhance transparency and build user trust (Rai, 2020) (Doshi-Velez & Kim, 2017). Trust in automated systems is essential for effective human-machine collaboration, and transparency plays a key role in achieving this trust (Parasuraman & Riley, 1997) (Lee & See, 2004).

In addition to technical solutions, organizational policies and governance frameworks are essential in addressing surveillance stress. Clear communication about what data is collected, how it is used, and for what purpose can significantly reduce uncertainty and anxiety among users. Providing users with access to their own data and allowing them to control privacy settings further enhances trust and autonomy (Ravid et al., 2020) (Dinev & Hart, 2006). Perceived fairness and transparency in monitoring practices are crucial for maintaining positive employee attitudes and well-being (Colquitt et al., 2001).

Moreover, balancing the benefits of data-driven insights with the need for privacy is a critical challenge in modern Information Systems. While data collection can improve system performance and personalization, excessive monitoring can undermine user trust and create a hostile work environment. Striking this balance requires a human-centered approach, where technological capabilities are aligned with ethical considerations and user expectations (Zuboff, 2019) (Floridi et al., 2018).

Algorithmic transparency also plays a vital role in reducing cognitive load. When users understand how a system operates, they can interact with it more efficiently and with greater confidence. Conversely, opaque systems require users to spend additional cognitive effort trying to interpret system behavior, which contributes to mental fatigue. Reducing unnecessary cognitive effort is essential for improving performance and maintaining user efficiency (Sweller, 2011) (Sweller et al., 2011).

Ultimately, addressing the surveillance stress factor requires a combination of transparent design, ethical practices, and user empowerment. By making algorithmic processes visible and understandable, organizations can create environments where users feel supported rather than monitored. This shift is essential for fostering trust, enhancing productivity, and ensuring the long-term sustainability of AI-driven Information Systems (Kahneman, 2011) (Newport, 2016).

In conclusion, algorithmic transparency is not merely a technical requirement but a fundamental component of human-centered system design. By reducing opacity, addressing bias, and managing surveillance-related stress, Information Systems can create a more balanced and trustworthy digital environment. The future of AI integration depends on the ability to align technological innovation with human values, ensuring that systems enhance rather than undermine user well-being (Davenport & Ronanki, 2018) (Parasuraman & Riley, 1997).

8. FRICTION BY DESIGN: INTENTIONAL PAUSES FOR QUALITY CONTROL

The prevailing emphasis on speed in digital environments often overlooks the critical role of strategic friction in ensuring high-quality decision-making. Modern Information Systems (IS) are typically optimized for seamless and rapid interactions, promoting efficiency and minimizing delays. However, in high-stakes scenarios, excessive speed can become detrimental, leading to impulsive decisions and increased error rates. Strategic friction introduces intentional pauses such as multi-stage confirmations, verification prompts, or enforced cooling-off periods designed to slow down user actions when necessary. Under conditions of urgency, individuals tend to rely on fast, intuitive cognitive processing that is efficient but prone to systematic biases, whereas slower, analytical processing is required for complex and critical decisions (Kahneman, 2011) (Stanovich & West, 2000). By embedding deliberate pauses, Information Systems can shift users toward more reflective reasoning, thereby reducing the likelihood of costly mistakes (Thaler & Sunstein, 2008).

The concept of forced reflection further extends the application of strategic friction within organizational workflows. In high-pressure environments, individuals and teams often fall victim to cognitive biases such as the sunk cost fallacy and action bias, where decisions are driven by past investments or the urgency to act rather than rational evaluation. Strategic friction can be embedded into project management systems at key decision points, requiring users to engage in structured reflection before proceeding. For instance, systems can mandate the completion of a pre-mortem analysis, where potential risks and failure scenarios are identified in advance. Reflective practices such as pre-mortem analysis improve decision accuracy by encouraging critical evaluation and reducing overconfidence, particularly in uncertain and dynamic contexts (Klein, 2007) (Lovallo & Kahneman, 2011).

In addition to decision-making, strategic friction plays a vital role in maintaining data integrity within complex Information Systems. In frictionless environments, users may input incorrect or inconsistent data without sufficient verification, leading to the well-known problem of poor data quality and downstream errors. Systems that incorporate contextual friction can detect anomalies and prompt users to verify their inputs before acceptance. When entered data deviates significantly from expected patterns, verification prompts encourage users to reassess their inputs, transforming routine data entry into a more deliberate cognitive process. This approach aligns with principles of human error prevention, where system design actively anticipates and mitigates potential mistakes (Reason, 1990) (Norman, 2013).

The introduction of intentional pauses also has important implications for managing decision fatigue. When users are required to process a continuous stream of tasks at high speed, their cognitive resources become depleted, reducing their ability to make effective decisions over time. Strategic friction functions as a triage mechanism, differentiating between routine and critical tasks by selectively slowing down interactions where greater attention is required. This selective pacing helps preserve mental energy and improves decision quality across extended periods of work (Baumeister et al., 2007) (Vohs et al., 2008). Situational awareness, defined as the ability to perceive, understand, and anticipate elements within an environment, is fundamental to effective decision-making in complex systems, and friction can enhance this awareness by signaling the importance of specific actions (Endsley, 1995).

Furthermore, strategic friction contributes to the development of a more mindful and deliberate work culture. In contrast to environments that prioritize speed above all else, systems designed with intentional pauses encourage users to reflect, verify, and evaluate their actions before proceeding. This shift reduces the likelihood of errors that arise from rushed decisions and supports more consistent and reliable outcomes. By embedding friction at critical points, Information Systems act as safeguards that balance efficiency with accuracy, ensuring that rapid execution does not compromise decision quality (Thaler & Sunstein, 2008).

In conclusion, friction by design represents a fundamental shift in how Information Systems are conceptualized and developed. Rather than eliminating all barriers to speed, strategic friction introduces carefully designed constraints that enhance cognitive processing, improve data integrity, and reduce the risks associated with impulsive decision-making. The objective is not to slow systems unnecessarily but to apply targeted interventions that support thoughtful action. In high-stakes environments, such friction is not a limitation but a necessary mechanism for achieving sustainable, reliable, and human-centered performance (Kahneman, 2011) (Norman, 2013).

9. ADAPTIVE INTERFACES AND AFFECTIVE COMPUTING

The next frontier of cognitive ergonomics lies in the development of adaptive interfaces and affective computing, where information systems evolve from static tools into responsive, context-aware partners. Affective computing involves the use of sensors and machine learning algorithms to detect a user's physiological and psychological state, including stress levels, cognitive load, or fatigue, through signals such as typing cadence, pupillary response, or facial micro-expressions (Picard, 1997) (D'Mello & Kory, 2015). When a system detects that a user is entering a state of heightened stress or mental exhaustion, it can dynamically adjust its interface to create a more supportive interaction environment. This bio-adaptive feedback loop allows systems to modulate complexity, reduce information density, and minimize interruptions during high-pressure periods, thereby acting as a buffer against cognitive overload rather than amplifying it (Sweller, 2011) (Kahneman, 2011).

The integration of linguistic affective analysis further extends these capabilities by enabling systems to interpret the emotional tone of digital communication in real time. By analyzing patterns in language use, such as sentiment intensity, word choice, and syntactic structure, systems can detect early signs of frustration, stress, or hostility. When such patterns emerge, the interface can introduce subtle interventions, such as suggesting a pause, prompting message revision, or offering alternative phrasing. Real-time emotional scaffolding has been shown to reduce the escalation of negative interactions and support more constructive communication in digital environments (D'Mello & Graesser, 2012). By functioning as a reflective layer, the system supports self-regulation and helps prevent transient emotional states from resulting in long-term professional consequences.

Affective computing also plays a critical role in addressing circadian disruption associated with prolonged digital engagement. Continuous exposure to high-intensity screens and information-rich environments can interfere with natural biological rhythms, particularly in knowledge workers who operate across extended hours. Adaptive interfaces can align system behavior with the user's circadian cycle by adjusting visual parameters such as brightness and color temperature, while also modulating interface complexity as cognitive capacity declines throughout the day. Exposure to blue light during evening hours has been shown to suppress melatonin production and negatively affect sleep quality, which in turn impacts next-day cognitive performance (Chang et al., 2015) (Cajochen et al., 2011). By gradually transitioning to lower-stimulation interface modes, systems can support recovery and maintain long-term cognitive sustainability.

Despite these advantages, the implementation of affective computing raises significant concerns related to privacy, data ownership, and ethical use. For such systems to be viable, users must have clear assurance that sensitive emotional and behavioral data is handled responsibly. A privacy-first architecture, where affective data is processed locally and not transmitted to centralized systems, is essential for maintaining trust. The unchecked use of behavioral data for monitoring or performance evaluation can lead to misuse and reinforce asymmetries of power within organizations (Zuboff, 2019) (Floridi et al., 2018). Ensuring data sovereignty and transparent governance mechanisms is therefore critical for ethical adoption.

Furthermore, the effectiveness of adaptive interfaces depends on maintaining an appropriate balance between automation and user control. While systems can provide intelligent adjustments, users must retain the ability to override, customize, or disable these features based on their preferences. Over-automation may reduce user agency and lead to overdependence, particularly if users become disengaged from managing their own cognitive states (Parasuraman & Riley, 1997) (Lee & See, 2004). Designing for human-in-the-loop interaction ensures that adaptive systems remain supportive rather than prescriptive.

Ultimately, the goal of adaptive interfaces is to create a functional synergy between human cognition and digital systems. By sensing and responding to fluctuations in attention, emotion, and fatigue, these systems enable a model of productivity that is aligned with biological constraints rather than in conflict with them. This represents a shift from tool-centered design toward a more integrated human-centered partnership, where systems actively contribute to cognitive balance, emotional regulation, and sustained performance (Norman, 2013) (Kahneman, 2011). Such an approach reframes productivity not as continuous output, but as the effective management of cognitive resources over time.

10. TECHNICAL IMPLEMENTATION OF THE "RIGHT TO DISCONNECT"

The right to disconnect represents a critical transition from policy-level recommendations to enforceable system-level design within Information Systems. In continuously connected digital environments, employees often experience implicit pressure to remain responsive beyond formal working hours, blurring the boundary between professional and personal life. Behavioral guidelines alone are insufficient to address this structural issue. Embedding boundaries directly into system architecture enables consistent enforcement of disconnection, reducing reliance on individual self-regulation. Protocol-based rest mechanisms, where non-urgent communications are automatically deferred until the next work cycle, provide a practical solution to this challenge. Structural interventions of this nature have been shown to reduce technostress and emotional exhaustion more effectively than voluntary behavioral adjustments (De Bloom et al., 2020) (Tarafdar et al., 2007).

Another significant issue addressed by system-level disconnection is re-entry anxiety, where employees experience stress due to the anticipated accumulation of unread messages and pending tasks after a break. This anticipation can undermine the restorative value of non-work periods, reducing overall recovery. Information Systems can mitigate this problem through task rerouting and intelligent summarization. During periods of absence, critical tasks can be dynamically reassigned to colleagues or managed through automated systems, while non-essential information is aggregated into concise summaries. This reduces the cognitive burden associated with returning to work and supports continuity without overwhelming the user. Reducing information overload has been consistently linked to improvements in both well-being and task performance (Mark et al., 2008) (Eppler & Mengis, 2004).

Traditional vacation mode features are often limited in functionality, typically providing only automated responses. More advanced implementations introduce an availability shield, where synchronization between work systems and user devices is temporarily suspended. This creates a genuine disconnection from digital work environments. In exceptional circumstances, a controlled override mechanism can be introduced, requiring justification before interrupting the user. This intentional friction ensures that only critical situations bypass the system. Clear boundaries between work and personal life have been associated with improved sleep quality, reduced stress, and higher life satisfaction, reinforcing the importance of enforceable disconnection mechanisms (Arlinghaus & Nachreiner, 2014) (Sonnentag & Fritz, 2015).

In conclusion, implementing the right to disconnect through technical systems ensures consistent enforcement of boundaries that are otherwise difficult to maintain. By reducing after-hours interruptions, managing workload continuity, and supporting recovery periods, organizations can create environments that sustain both productivity and employee well-being. The effectiveness of such systems lies in their ability to shift responsibility from individuals to infrastructure, ensuring that disconnection is not optional but embedded within the logic of digital work environments (Kahneman, 2011) (De Bloom et al., 2020).

11. MEASURING "SUSTAINABLE PRODUCTIVITY": NEW KPIs FOR IS SUCCESS

Traditional metrics used to evaluate Information Systems, such as active usage time or message volume, often fail to capture meaningful productivity. In many cases, increased activity reflects fragmentation, distraction, and inefficient workflows rather than high-value output. This disconnect has led to the emergence of sustainable productivity metrics that emphasize cognitive health, quality of work, and long-term performance. The productivity paradox highlights how digital technologies can increase activity while simultaneously reducing deep, focused thinking, underscoring the need for more meaningful evaluation frameworks (Brynjolfsson & McAfee, 2014) (Kahneman, 2011).

One important metric is Time-to-Focus, which measures how quickly a user transitions from task initiation to a state of sustained concentration. A high Time-to-Focus indicates the presence of distractions, poor interface design, or fragmented workflows, whereas a low value suggests that the system effectively supports cognitive immersion. The ability to rapidly enter a deep work state is increasingly recognized as a critical determinant of productivity in knowledge-intensive environments (Newport, 2016) (Mark et al., 2012).

Another key metric is Interruption Recovery Time, which measures the duration required to regain focus following a disruption. Frequent interruptions introduce attentional residue and significantly reduce cognitive efficiency. Empirical research shows that recovering from interruptions can take substantial time, with cumulative effects on performance and error rates (Mark et al., 2008) (Altmann & Trafton, 2002). Monitoring this metric enables organizations to identify system features or communication patterns that contribute to unnecessary disruptions.

A more advanced metric is System-Generated Stress, which evaluates the physiological and psychological impact of digital systems on users. This can be measured through indicators such as heart rate variability, interaction patterns, or self-reported stress levels. Elevated stress associated with specific tools or workflows may signal poor system design or excessive cognitive demands. Reducing stress is strongly associated with improved long-term productivity, better decision-making, and increased employee retention (Ayyagari et al., 2011) (Kushlev & Dunn, 2015).

Another important measure is Social Connectivity Health, which shifts the focus from the quantity of communication to its quality and effectiveness. Instead of measuring message volume, this metric evaluates whether interactions are purposeful, structured, and aligned with task requirements. Systems that facilitate clear and meaningful communication reduce ambiguity, minimize redundant exchanges, and improve collaboration outcomes (Daft & Lengel, 1986) (Mazmanian et al., 2013).

Overall, these new KPIs redefine productivity as a human-centered construct rather than a measure of system activity. By focusing on attention, recovery, stress, and communication quality, organizations can design and evaluate Information Systems in ways that support sustainable performance. This approach ensures that productivity gains are not achieved at the expense of cognitive well-being but are aligned with the long-term capabilities of the human workforce (Kahneman, 2011) (Brynjolfsson & McAfee, 2014).

12. CONCLUSION

The future of Information Systems lies in designing technologies that support human cognition rather than overwhelm it. As digital tools become more advanced, it is essential to view them as biological scaffolds that extend and enhance human intelligence rather than replace it. The integration of Artificial Intelligence, adaptive interfaces, and affective computing introduces powerful capabilities for improving efficiency and decision-making, yet these advancements must be carefully aligned with human cognitive limits to avoid unintended consequences such as overload, fatigue, and reduced autonomy (Davenport & Ronanki, 2018) (Picard, 1997). A system that is technically advanced but cognitively misaligned ultimately undermines its own purpose.

Key concepts such as strategic friction, focus shielding, and the right to disconnect highlight a necessary shift in design philosophy toward protecting attention as a finite resource. In environments dominated by constant connectivity and real-time communication, uninterrupted focus has become increasingly rare, yet it remains essential for high-quality work. Systems that deliberately reduce interruptions, introduce reflective pauses, and enforce boundaries between work and personal life create conditions that support sustained cognitive engagement and recovery (Sweller, 2011) (Sonnentag & Fritz, 2015). A well-rested and focused mind consistently produces better decisions, more creative outputs, and more reliable long-term performance (Kahneman, 2011) (Newport, 2016).

Moreover, the shift toward sustainable productivity metrics reinforces the need to evaluate Information Systems based on cognitive outcomes rather than superficial activity levels. Traditional measures such as time spent online or volume of communication fail to capture meaningful performance and often reward fragmented work patterns. Metrics that assess focus, recovery, stress, and communication quality provide a more accurate representation of productivity in knowledge-intensive environments (Brynjolfsson & McAfee, 2014) (Mark et al., 2008). By aligning evaluation systems with human cognitive dynamics, organizations can avoid the trap of equating busyness with effectiveness.

In conclusion, the goal of modern Information Systems should be to establish a balanced and mutually reinforcing relationship between humans and technology. Systems must be designed not only for efficiency but also for clarity, transparency, and psychological safety. By integrating intelligent automation with human-centered design principles, organizations can foster innovation while safeguarding the well-being of their workforce (Norman, 2013) (Floridi et al., 2018). The future of digital work will not be defined solely by technological capability, but by the ability to design systems that respect, support, and enhance human potential over time.

REFERENCES

Altmann, E. M., & Trafton, J. G. (2002). Memory for goals: An activation-based model. *Cognitive Science*, *26*(1), 39–83.

Arlinghaus, A., & Nachreiner, F. (2014). Health effects of supplemental work from home in the European Union. *Chronobiology International*, *31*(10), 1100–1107. DOI: 10.3109/07420528.2014.957297 PMID: 25229274

Ayyagari, R., Grover, V., & Purvis, R. (2011). Technostress: Technological antecedents and implications. *Management Information Systems Quarterly*, *35*(4), 831–858. DOI: 10.2307/41409963

Baethge, A., & Rigotti, T. (2013). Interruptions to workflow: Their relationship with irritation and satisfaction. *Journal of Organizational Behavior*, *34*(6), 855–875.

Barocas, S., & Selbst, A. D. (2016). Big data's disparate impact. *California Law Review*, *104*(3), 671–732.

Baumeister, R. F., Vohs, K. D., & Tice, D. M. (2007). The strength model of self-control. *Current Directions in Psychological Science*, *16*(6), 351–355. DOI: 10.1111/j.1467-8721.2007.00534.x

Brynjolfsson, E., & McAfee, A. (2014). *The second machine age*. W. W. Norton & Company.

Cajochen, C., Frey, S., & Anders, D.. (2011). Evening exposure to LED-backlit screens affects circadian rhythms. *Journal of Applied Physiology*, *110*(5), 1432–1438. DOI: 10.1152/japplphysiol.00165.2011 PMID: 21415172

Chang, A. M., Aeschbach, D., Duffy, J. F., & Czeisler, C. A. (2015). Evening use of light-emitting devices negatively affects sleep. *Proceedings of the National Academy of Sciences of the United States of America*, *112*(4), 1232–1237. DOI: 10.1073/pnas.1418490112 PMID: 25535358

Colquitt, J. A., Conlon, D. E., Wesson, M. J., Porter, C. O. L. H., & Ng, K. Y. (2001). Justice at the millennium. *The Journal of Applied Psychology*, *86*(3), 425–445. DOI: 10.1037/0021-9010.86.3.425 PMID: 11419803

Daft, R. L., & Lengel, R. H. (1986). Organizational information requirements and media richness. *Management Science*, *32*(5), 554–571. DOI: 10.1287/mnsc.32.5.554

Davenport, T. H., & Prusak, L. (1998). *Working knowledge: How organizations manage what they know*. Harvard Business Press.

Davenport, T. H., & Ronanki, R. (2018). Artificial intelligence for the real world. *Harvard Business Review, 96*(1), 108–116.

De Bloom, J., Vaziri, H., Tay, L., Kujanpää, M., & Kinnunen, U. (2020). Effects of vacation and recovery. *Journal of Occupational Health Psychology, 25*(5), 1–14.

Dinev, T., & Hart, P. (2006). Privacy concerns and trust in information systems. *Management Information Systems Quarterly, 30*(1), 61–88.

) Doshi-Velez, F., & Kim, B. (2017). Towards a rigorous science of interpretable machine learning.

Dzindolet, M. T., Pierce, L. G., Beck, H. P., & Dawe, L. A. (2002). The perceived utility of human and automated aids in a visual detection task. *Human Factors, 44*(1), 79–94. DOI: 10.1518/0018720024494856 PMID: 12118875

Endsley, M. R. (1995). Toward a theory of situation awareness. *Human Factors, 37*(1), 32–64. DOI: 10.1518/001872095779049543

Eppler, M. J., & Mengis, J. (2004). The concept of information overload. *The Information Society, 20*(5), 325–344. DOI: 10.1080/01972240490507974

Floridi, L., Cowls, J., & Beltrametti, M.. (2018). AI4People—An ethical framework for artificial intelligence. *Minds and Machines, 28*(4), 689–707. DOI: 10.1007/s11023-018-9482-5 PMID: 30930541

Gonzalez, V. M., & Mark, G. (2004). Constant, constant, multi-tasking craziness. CHI Proceedings. DOI: 10.1145/985692.985707

Hacker, J., vom Brocke, J., Handali, J., Otto, M., & Schneider, J. (2019). Virtually in this together. *Information Systems Journal, 29*(1), 3–45.

Kahneman, D. (2011). *Thinking, fast and slow*. Farrar, Straus and Giroux.

Karasek, R. (1979). Job demands, job decision latitude, and mental strain. *Administrative Science Quarterly, 24*(2), 285–308. DOI: 10.2307/2392498

Kirsh, D. (2000). A few thoughts on cognitive overload. *Intellectica, 30*(1), 19–51. DOI: 10.3406/intel.2000.1592

Klein, G. (2007). Performing a premortem. *Harvard Business Review, 85*(9), 18–19.

Kushlev, K., & Dunn, E. W. (2015). Checking email less frequently reduces stress. *Computers in Human Behavior, 43*, 220–228. DOI: 10.1016/j.chb.2014.11.005

Lee, J. D., & See, K. A. (2004). Trust in automation. *Human Factors, 46*(1), 50–80. DOI: 10.1518/hfes.46.1.50.30392 PMID: 15151155

Leroy, S. (2009). Why is it so hard to do my work? *Organizational Behavior and Human Decision Processes*, *109*(2), 168–181. DOI: 10.1016/j.obhdp.2009.04.002

Mark, G., Gudith, D., & Klocke, U. (2008). The cost of interrupted work. CHI Proceedings, 107–110. DOI: 10.1145/1357054.1357072

Mark, G., Voida, S., & Cardello, A. (2012). A pace not dictated by electrons. CHI Proceedings. DOI: 10.1145/2207676.2207754

Monsell, S. (2003). Task switching. *Trends in Cognitive Sciences*, *7*(3), 134–140. DOI: 10.1016/S1364-6613(03)00028-7 PMID: 12639695

Newport, C. (2016). *Deep work: Rules for focused success in a distracted world.* Grand Central Publishing.

Norman, D. A. (2013). *The design of everyday things.* Basic Books.

O'Neil, C. (2016). *Weapons of math destruction.* Crown Publishing.

Paas, F., Renkl, A., & Sweller, J. (2004). Cognitive load theory: Instructional implications of the interaction between information structures and cognitive architecture. *Instructional Science*, *32*(1/2), 1–8. DOI: 10.1023/B:TRUC.0000021806.17516.d0

Parasuraman, R., & Riley, V. (1997). Humans and automation. *Human Factors*, *39*(2), 230–253. DOI: 10.1518/001872097778543886 PMID: 18689061

Picard, R. W. (1997). *Affective computing.* MIT Press. DOI: 10.7551/mit-press/1140.001.0001

Rai, A. (2020). Explainable AI: From black box to glass box. *Journal of the Academy of Marketing Science*, *48*(1), 137–141. DOI: 10.1007/s11747-019-00710-5

Ravid, D. M., Tomczak, D. L., White, J. C., & Behrend, T. S. (2020). EPM is not for everyone. *The Journal of Applied Psychology*, *105*(6), 585–606.

Rubinstein, J. S., Meyer, D. E., & Evans, J. E. (2001). Executive control of cognitive processes. *Journal of Experimental Psychology*, *27*(4), 763–797. PMID: 11518143

Sonnentag, S., & Fritz, C. (2015). Recovery from job stress. *Annual Review of Organizational Psychology*, *2*, 1–26.

Stanovich, K. E., & West, R. F. (2000). Individual differences in reasoning. *Behavioral and Brain Sciences*, *23*(5), 645–665. DOI: 10.1017/S0140525X00003435 PMID: 11301544

Sweller, J. (2011). Cognitive load theory. *Psychology of Learning and Motivation*, *55*, 37–76. DOI: 10.1016/B978-0-12-387691-1.00002-8

Sweller, J., Ayres, P., & Kalyuga, S. (2011). *Cognitive load theory*. Springer. DOI: 10.1007/978-1-4419-8126-4

Tarafdar, M., Tu, Q., Ragu-Nathan, T., & Ragu-Nathan, B. (2007). The impact of technostress. *Journal of Management Information Systems*, *31*(2), 301–328. DOI: 10.2753/MIS0742-1222240109

Thaler, R. H., & Sunstein, C. R. (2008). *Nudge*. Yale University Press.

Vohs, K. D., & Baumeister, R. F.. (2008). Decision fatigue. *Journal of Personality and Social Psychology*, *94*(5), 883–898. DOI: 10.1037/0022-3514.94.5.883 PMID: 18444745

) Weiser, M., & Brown, J. S. (1997). The coming age of calm technology.

Zuboff, S. (2019). *The age of surveillance capitalism*. PublicAffairs.

Chapter 7
Designing the Attention-Resilient Enterprise: A Socio-Technical Framework for Productivity and Digital Well-Being in AI-Enabled Organizational Systems

Aarthi Selvakumar
http://orcid.org/0009-0006-9064-2091
Marwadi University, Rajkot, India

Ravikumar Natarajan
http://orcid.org/0009-0009-3705-1681
Marwadi University, Rajkot, India

Eshniyozov Asadbek
Termez University of Economics and Service, Termez, Uzbekistan

Nazirjon Rajabov
http://orcid.org/0000-0002-8155-5790
Alfraganus University, Tashkent, Uzbekistan

Nilufar Aminova
Tashkent State University of Economics, Tashkent, Uzbekistan

Nasiba Jumaniyazova
Mamun University, Khiva, Uzbekistan

ABSTRACT

The rapid implementation of Artificial Intelligence, predictive analytics, and always-on collaborative platforms have added cognitive burdens to the modern organizations. The chapter suggests a socio-technical model named Attention-Resilient Enterprise in which the strategic asset of the organization is attention. The framework integrates the emphasis on technology development, ethical AI regulation, and behavioral orientation to demonstrate that sustainable productivity does not conflict with digital health. Using the existing evidence in the cases, the chapter provides the particular

DOI: 10.4018/979-8-2600-0111-0.ch007

quantifiable metrics of attention and architecture to ensure that the AI-based systems can help in creating continuity of the focus, decreasing overload, and increasing the sustainability of the stability within an organization.

1. INTRODUCTION

The contemporary organization is in the world of algorithmic decision support, smart automation, predictive analytics, and the all-networked collaboration platforms. These technologies also make cognitive tasks more efficient and scalable; they also disrupt the attention of employees and create continuous waves of digital stimuli. Productivity is not limited by the lack of information anymore but the ability of human beings to handle and assign real meaning to information. With the advent of the AI integrated into the organizational information systems, the problem does not lie in the faster processing of information but rather in the maintenance of the cognitive state in which the high quality of thinking is to happen. In this chapter, attention is established as a strategic organizational asset and not a personal constraint (Pasupuleti, 2024). It states that the ability to work sustainably relies on the creation of the socio-technical systems that safeguard the continuity of attention, control the digital disturbances, and coping with the rhythm of human cognition. The introduction creates the precondition of creating the Attention-Resilient Enterprise as a systematic reaction to digital acceleration by redefining digital well-being as an infrastructural issue.

1.1 Digital Acceleration and Cognitive Fragmentation

It has led to acceleration in the digital world that has shortened communication cycles, opened up data flows and accelerated organizational decision-making. Employees are operating within a forest of emails, messaging apps, dashboard, automated alerts and AI generated suggestions and they are not typically prioritized in an organized manner. Despite the fact that these systems are expected to be effective, they frequently lead to cognitive fragmentation which is a successive rotation of tasks, superficial processing and reductions in the periods of deep work. Human mind though operates more effectively in systematic concentration time and not continual attention. (Bobrytska et al., 2025). Constant distractions destroy working memory, raise errors and heighten cognitive exhaustion. When developed with no awareness of attention, AI systems may increase this overload, the systems will create more notifications or performance prompts. Digital acceleration therefore has to be supported by conscious architectural measures to filter, cluster and contextualize streams of information. Were such design principles lacking, technological development caters counterproductively to strategic thinking and innovation ability.

1.2 Productivity-Well-Being Paradox

Companies tend to think that productivity and digital health are two opposing aspects: increased productivity seems to require unlimited connectivity and quick reaction. There is however a growing evidence to support the idea that long term performance sustainability is decreased by extreme digital intensity. Constant access generates algorithmic performance, which promotes responsive behaviour over reflective analysis. When measurement of output takes the centre stage in attention management practices, burnout, cognitive fatigue and reduced creativity will arise. The productivity-well-being paradox occurs as a result of short-term rises in responsiveness possible at the cost of long-term organizational strength. Sustainable productivity involves a balance between taking the initiative and cognitive rest (Aarthi et al., 2025). AI systems can become used to tightening the monitoring and metric fixation or assist in adjusting the workload and recovery intervals in an adaptive manner. Organizations can make well-being a priority instead of an addition to productivity by restructuring performance models to reward depth of work, good decisions, and strategic creativity, and so on.

1.3 Emergence of Attention as Infrastructure

or time management methods. Attention, when focused in digitally intensive environments, however, should be conceived as an organizational infrastructure which is designed through technological and managerial design. The allocation of attention is determined by interface structures, notification systems, model of algorithmic prioritization, and communication norms. The misalignment of these elements leads to systemic and not personal fragmentation. The idea of considering attention as infrastructure resettles the responsibility on the individual employee to the enterprise architecture. Smart systems have the capabilities to sequence tasks in real time, group communications, suggest focus, and change dashboards according to contextual interest (Independent USA et al., 2025). There can be leadership practices that strengthen the demarcation of deep work and recovery time. With the incorporation of attention awareness into socio-technical systems, organizations will shift to reactive connectivity optimization to conscious cognition coherence management. Table 1 Matches the most important digital acceleration variables (AI alerts, collaboration tools, dashboards) with the risks of cognitive fragmentation and the results of attention.

Table 1. Digital Acceleration and Cognitive Impact Mapping

Digital Acceleration Factor	System Feature	Cognitive Risk	Attention Impact	Organizational Outcome
Real-time Notifications	Continuous alerts	Task switching	Fragmented focus	Reduced deep work
AI Performance Dashboards	Live metrics display	Performance pressure	Cognitive overload	Short-term reactivity
Always-On Collaboration Tools	Instant messaging	Interruption clustering	Reduced recovery time	Decision fatigue
Predictive Analytics Prompts	Automated recommendations	Alert dependency	Reduced autonomy	Efficiency with strain
Multi-Platform Integration	Parallel tool usage	Context switching	Load variability	Error probability increase

2. BACKGROUND TO THE STUDY

The development of organizational information systems indicates the wider changes in technology and theory of work organization and its control. Initial systems were data processing focused, and then evolved to enterprise integration and analytics. The adoption of artificial intelligence brings about the adaptive and predictive functions that change information systems to the decision-support ecosystems. At the same time, organizational behavior studies, as well as digital psychology, point to the intellectual implications of constant digital communication. The problem of attention is, in fact, the problem of scarcity that defines the modern productivity (Ravikumar, Aarthi, Sapayev, et al., 2026). The paper is based on the socio-technical systems theory in which it is held that technology and human behaviour should be optimized together. It also takes into consideration the results of the human/computer interaction and attention economics that dwells on the contribution of interface design and filtering of algorithms on cognitive effort distribution. Having these theoretical underpinnings, it can be realized that it offers conceptual underpinnings of the design of organizational systems that will enhance performance, without causing any deleterious effects to the psychological sustainability.

2.1 Socio-Technical Systems Foundations

The socio-technical systems theory proposes that, optimization of the social and the technical sub system results in the organizational performance. The theory brings out two-way communication between human behavior, managerial structures and technological design rather than viewing technology as a bias tool. Absence of correspondence of these factors can lead to inefficiencies, stress or reduced flexibility. The fragmentation of attention is easy to take into capture the socio-technical imbalance (thus the technical systems maximize speed and volume and the social systems lack the protective norms) in the digital intensive spaces (Thao and Mai Dr, 2025). The application of AI-based systems through the principles of socio-technology would require the introduction of the possibilities of algorithms and human mental rhythms. This is added by the character of governance, participatory design and open decision logic. The foundation stresses that, sole use of automation cannot achieve sustainable productivity but a balanced blend of technological intelligence and human welfare.

2.2 AI-Enabled Organizational Information Systems

The combination of Machine Learning, predictive analytics and adaptive automation means that AI-enabled information systems of organizations get more than the more traditional enterprise resource planning. The systems analyze the behavior information and project the trends of the workload and generate real-time recommendations. As much as these features are useful in terms of operational efficiencies, it also affects the distribution of attention in giving alerts, performance metrics, and automatic rankings. The AI can create more conspicuous data by worsening the overload or minimize the data by decreasing the scope of irrelevant and noisy inputs, and intelligently organize the work (Ravikumar, Aarthi, and Mamadiyarov, 2026). How AI will become an issue of pressure or a stabilizing mechanism will then depend on the design orientation. It has a balanced interaction supported by explainability, circumstantial prioritization and customization control by the user into AI systems. When placed in the right line with the concepts of socio-technology, AI transforms not into the enhancer of productivity but into the cognitive regulator of organizational environments.

2.3 Digital Psychology and Attention Economics

Digital psychology is a study of the effect of constant communication with digital technologies on cognition, emotion, and behavior. The literature shows that multitasking lowers productivity, constant notifications increase stress responses, and performance dashboard determines the motivation trends. Attention economics also understands attention as a limited resource in which platforms and communication systems are competing. In organizations internal digital tools tend to recreate attention-extractive processes in consumer media. The identification of attention as an economic asset causes an emphasis on its distribution as opposed to the exposure of the data. The design imperatives become intelligent filtering, recovery cycles, as well as, contextual relevance (Hutsaliuk & Shainovskyi, 2025). Through the combination of the knowledge of digital psychology and attention economics, the organizational systems can be redesigned to safeguard cognitive bandwidth, decrease decision fatigue, and maintain long-term interest in the workplaces that are augmented with AI (Ravikumar & Aarthi, 2025b). Table 2 Overview The socio-technical systems theory, digital psychology, AI governance, and work design principles fit the framework.

Table 2. Theoretical Foundations Supporting Attention Resilience

Theoretical Domain	Core Principle	Relevance to Attention Resilience	Application in Chapter
Socio-Technical Systems	Joint optimization	Align tech & human systems	3-layer conceptual model
Digital Psychology	Cognitive load limits	Protect working memory	Focus continuity metrics
Work Design Theory	Autonomy & recovery	Sustainable performance	Deep-work structures
AI Governance	Transparency & oversight	Trust & safety	Ethical guardrails
Attention Economics	Scarcity of attention	Strategic resource framing	Attention as infrastructure

3. RESEARCH OBJECTIVES

In the information systems that are based on AI, this chapter seeks to reposition attention as a strategic organizational resource. The research integrates the two areas, productivity and digital well-being, into the other in a socio-technical design methodology. Its objectives are the clarity of concepts, the principles of architectural design, concordance of governance and empirical measurability. To provide a systematic ground on how the organizational systems can be restructured to achieve cognitive sustainability and performance-based systems, the study will design the Attention-Resilient Enterprise on theory and operational levels.

- To conceptualize Attention Resilience as an organizational capability that stabilizes focus continuity, cognitive recovery, and workload adaptability in AI-enabled environments.
- To develop a socio-technical framework that aligns technological infrastructure, algorithmic decision systems, managerial practices, and employee behavioral dynamics.

- To design AI-aligned productivity systems that integrate intelligent task sequencing, contextual notification filtering, and adaptive workload distribution.
- To establish measurable attention metrics including focus continuity indices, cognitive load variability, recovery time measures, and sustainable productivity ratios.
- To propose ethical governance mechanisms that ensure transparency, explainability, privacy-by-design, and participatory system design to protect autonomy and psychological safety.

4. CONCEPTUAL MODEL

Attention Resilient Enterprise Conceptual model brings together technological intelligence, organizational governance and human cognitive dynamics into one socio-technical building. The model does not divide the productivity tools and their links with well-being as the attention is the most important coordinating variable between the system layers. It is observed that the behavior of the employees, the management structures and AI systems depend on each other and they are together optimized (Pandit et al., 2025). In the model, three overlapping layers will be proposed, including an Attention-Conscious Technology Layer, which regulates the flows of the digital stimuli and task; Organizational Governance Layer, which establishes the ethical guardrails and performance norms; and Behavioral and Cognitive Alignment Layer, which helps to make the focus and psychological safety stable. The layers are not hierarchically structured but rather dynamically organized and do not contradict each other to prevent digital overload and algorithmic pressure (Ravikumar & Aarthi, 2025c). The model moves the information systems within the organizations towards an optimized responsiveness to information connectivity in reaction to the environment, towards premeditated cognitive consistency and long-term productivity through structural insertion of the attention management information system into the organization enterprise architecture. In Figure 1, the dynamic interaction between the technology of attention-consciousness and the organizational governance, and behavioral alignment to introduce cognitive coherence and sustainable productivity is dynamic.

Figure 1. Attention-Resilient Enterprise Conceptual Model

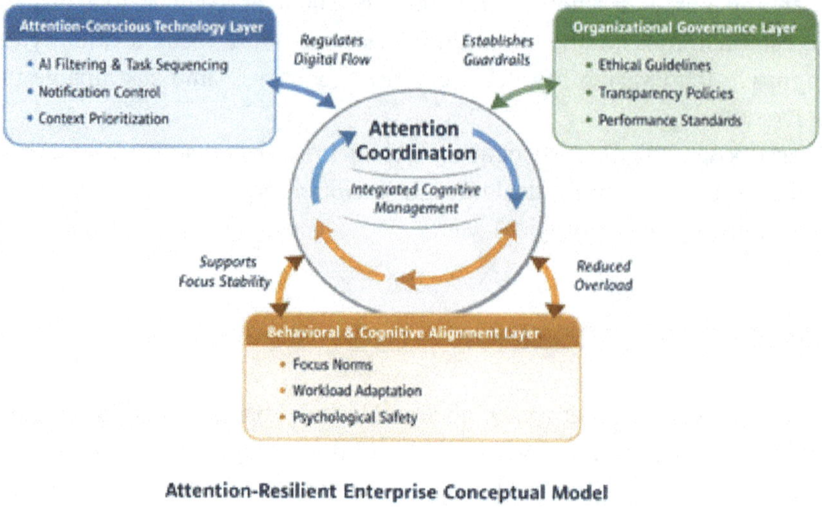

4.1 Attention-Conscious Technology Layer

The model is based on the Attention-Conscious Technology Layer. It is also AI-enabled, which regulates flow of information, prioritises activities and reduces any distraction that is unproductive. Alerts can be clustered using smart filters on the urgency of the alerts and assignment can be matched with attention cycles and cognitive load patterns using task sequencing. Dashboards are also customizable and only present the metrics that are needed at any given time instead of overwhelming the user with more data points than necessary. The situation of overload can be predicted by predictive analytics based on the density of the workload and the frequency of communication. It is important to note that explainable AI is prioritized in the system to ensure the clarity of logic in priorities and the possibility to control its functioning by the user (E. and S. I. «Dnipro M. I. of the U. S. U. of S. and Technology et al., 2026). This layer is continuity-oriented and cognitively efficient instead of making it visible as much as possible and responsive. The attention awareness in the system architecture will cause technology to become a stabilizing factor which will enable the long term held attention and quality decision making. The digital flow may be controlled to keep flow continuity with the continuity in focus and cognitive efficiencies by using the Figure 2 plot of how AI filtering, sequencing of context tasks, adaptive dashboards and predictive overload detection can be employed to control digital flow.

Figure 2. Attention-Conscious Technology Layer Architecture

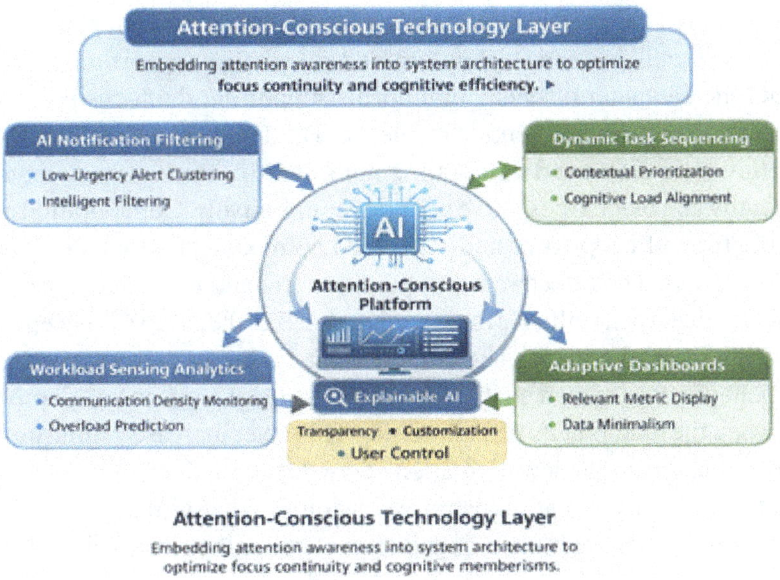

4.2 Organizational Governance Layer

The Organizational Governance Layer provides normative and ethical security by means of which work of AI systems in the business is governed. The governance systems stipulate transparency levels, boundaries to data privacy and tolerable surveillance to prevent the excessive spread of algorithms. The measures of performance are such that they are based on the depth of work, quality of decisions and innovation over the long run instead of on the availability or high-response rates. The participatory system design ensures the employees are part of the process of configuring digital workflow and this makes them trustful and responsible to themselves. The autonomy and the interpretive authority are the key human control aspects that ensure that the algorithmic recommendations are under clear escalation paths (Zhu, 2025). There are policy frameworks as well, which detail the recovery periods and workload restriction to prevent chronic overworking. The fact that technological efficiency has no impact on the psychological safety can be addressed by taking care of by institutionalizing the protection of attention within the governance systems on the part of the organizations. This layer balances the ethical accountability with the functioning of the operations and makes it more robust in the long term.

4.3 Behavioral and Cognitive Alignment Layer

Behavioral and Cognitive Alignment Layer is focused to align patterns of interaction between employees and technology and governance organization. The system design and the character of behavioral norms supporting the focus protection and recovery also determine the attention resilience. The development of digital literacy is achieved through training and it helps the employees to perceive the AI recommendations critically and react to cognitive boundaries effectively. Collaboration protocols identify the time of deep-work and scheduled communication windows to reduce the fragmentation. The effective assessment criteria and the reduced performance anxiety related to the surveillance measurements makes the safe working environment stronger (Shreha et al., 2025). The cognitive load awareness is internalized in the management practice, which enables the distribution of work in an adaptive way at the time when the load is at its peak intensity. This layer increases uniformity within the enterprise by meeting the anticipation of conduct with the requirements of focus sensitive technologies and administrative customs. What will come out is a place of work that will improve human cognitive patterns rather than being distorted by digital systems. Table 3 Three-layer model (Technology, Governance, Behavioral) and essential functions and outcomes are provided.

Table 3. Attention-Resilient Enterprise Conceptual Model Components

Model Layer	Core Components	Design Mechanisms	Expected Outcomes
Attention-Conscious Technology	AI filtering, task sequencing	Context prioritization	Reduced overload
Organizational Governance	Transparency, privacy-by-design	Ethical monitoring	Trust & legitimacy
Behavioral Alignment	Focus norms, workload adaptation	Recovery intervals	Cognitive stability
Integrated Architecture	Cross-layer coordination	Dynamic recalibration	Sustainable productivity

5. RESEARCH METHODOLOGY

The study design assumes a systematic conceptual-development model that is complemented by the analysis of cases and the design of metrics. Since attention resilience implies interdisciplinary approach, the research combines the knowledge of socio-technical systems theory, human-computer interaction, organizational behavior, digital psychology, and AI governance. The approach will be structured in a manner that will help in harmonizing the theoretical synthesis with applicability. The chapter is based not on empirical experimentation only but on creating a framework that is based on existing literature and confirmed by the modern examples of organizations functioning in the sphere of AI-enabled conditions (Ravikumar & Aarthi, 2025a). The conceptual architecture is informed by a systematic review of the related scholarship and operational feasibility is shown by recent examples of enterprises. Another suggestion is the use of measurable indicators so that future studies are able to empirically validate it. This methodological design shall have conceptual rigour, contextual relevance and practical transferability. The synthesis, case-based example and metric operationalization of the study permits a logical foundation of the examination of the redesigned organizational information systems in the consequences both of productivity and digital well-being.

5.1 Conceptual Synthesis Approach

This synthesis methodology of conceptual synthesis is an integration of a number of streams of thought so as to develop the Attention-Resilient Enterprise model. First of all, the socio-technical systems theory introduces the structural logic of joint optimization of technological subsystem and human subsystem. Second, information about cognitive loads, switching costs, and recovery time can be obtained under digital psychology. Third, the concepts of transparency, explainability and interface design rely on the AI governance and human-computer interaction literature. These perceptions are critically reviewed and analysed to establish typical constructs in respect to attention stability and sustainable productivity (Udupa et al., 2024). The methods used during the match up of technological characteristics to behavioral and governance systems are conceptual mapping. The process of synthesis is also coherent rather than fragmented so that attention is considered as a unifying variable across disciplines. The research adds clarity to the theory by not only incorporating multiple strands of research in a single integrative model but also laying the foundation on which an activity of the research in an organizational context could be operationalized.

5.2 Case Selection and Criteria

One of the case selections is connected with the contemporary organizations engaged in the AI-powered or digitally saturated environment. The selection of the cases is made based on three primary criteria, such as intelligent systems are integrated in the workflow management, specific productivity outcomes are measurable, and the focus on the welfare of employees or management of workloads. The hybrid workplaces, knowledge work platforms which are AI-enabled and digitally intensive service organizations are prioritized due to their highly cognitive exposure. Secondary criteria include the openness of the reporting of the measures of performance and the existence of the mechanism of governance that controls the action of algorithms (Bastiaansen and Wilderom, 2022). The selected cases are compared to ascertain the preferences of socio-technical alignment and attention stabilization practices. These are exemplary validation of the conceptual model as opposed to statistical generalizations. They demonstrate the working of the design concepts into the working environments and provide useful details about the implementation problems and strategies of adaptation.

5.3 Attention-Resilience Evaluation Metrics

To conceptualize the concept of attention resilience, the study hypothesizes a multidimensional assessment instrument of performance and well-being measures. Continuity in focus is assessed by continuous working time and frequency of switching tasks. The variability of cognitive load is measured through the density of work, the amount of communication as well as the rate of error. Measurements of recovery time compare the sufficiency of recovery periods between work-intensive activities. Sustainable productivity ratios combine the terms of output quality with the indicators of well-being like the risk of burnout and the stability of engagement. Also, indices of transparency and autonomy determine perceptions of fairness and explainability in AI decision systems (Chauhan et al., 2025). These metrics are meant to go beyond the conventional output-based appraisals by introducing cognitive variables of sustainability. Connecting the aspects of infrastructural design to the quantifiable results, the evaluation framework makes it possible to test the Attention-Resilient Enterprise model empirically in the upcoming studies of organizations. Table 4 Lists associates continuity, variability of cognitive load, recovery time, productivity ratio, and trust indices with measurement indicators.

Table 4. Attention-Resilience Evaluation Metrics Framework

Metric Category	Indicator	Measurement Approach	Strategic Purpose
Focus Continuity	Uninterrupted work intervals	Time-tracking analytics	Deep work stability
Cognitive Load Variability	Task-switch frequency	Interaction logs	Load balance
Recovery Time	Break interval adequacy	Calendar density analysis	Burnout prevention

continued on following page

Table 4. Continued

Metric Category	Indicator	Measurement Approach	Strategic Purpose
Sustainable Productivity Ratio	Output ÷ overload index	Combined KPI model	Long-term efficiency
Trust Index	Perceived AI transparency	Survey + system audit	Governance validation

6. LITERATURE REVIEW

The surrounding of literature on AI-enabled organizational systems shows an emerging conflict between the hastening of technology and cognitive sustainability. The first researches conducted on information systems were more efficiency oriented, automation and maximization of performance. However, recent studies show the cognitive/psychological implications of the persistence of the online activity. The research of organizational behavior, human-computer interaction, and digital psychology is gradually shifting towards the fact that attention is a scarce resource in the knowledge-intensive environments. As AI is a part of workflow management, decision support, and performance analytics, division of attention is no longer an incidental factor, but a predetermined structure of the system design (Haque, 2025). The literature reviewed aligns with the objectives of the chapter, as it talks about three out of three major strands: the relationship between AI and cognitive load, incorporating digital well-being into work design, and the mechanisms of governance that need to be in place to prevent the cases of algorithmic overreach. All these projections of literature together provide the conceptual foundation on which attention resilience is to be imagined as a strategic organizational competency.

6.1 AI, Productivity, and Cognitive Load

The works on AI and productivity demonstrate the positive effect on the efficiency, prediction ability and optimization of the processes. The automation with intelligence reduces workload of the monotonous, and machine learning systems enhance fore-thinking and quality of decisions. However, the similar analysis of cognitive load shows that the advantages of the performance are dependent on the integration of the AI systems into the working processes (Economics et al., 2025). Recurring notifications, real-time dashboarding and suggestions can positively impact the percentage of task-switching and attention fragmentation unless they are carefully considered. The cognitive load theory demonstrates that high information stimuli negatively affect the working memory and reduce the level of deep analysis. Knowledge workplace studies have shown that the level of productivity flattens or drops at the stage of excessive indulgence of digital interruptions (E. and S. I. «Ukrainian E. and P. A. of V. N. K. K. N. University & Vasyliev, 2025). According to new methods, AI does not only have the ability to work faster, but it also manages information flow. The context relevance systems, cluster notification system as well as support focused interval system are connected with better cognitive stability. The current literature favors the need to come up with AI systems that would prove efficient and sensitive to sustainability.

6.2 Digital Well-Being and Work Design

The literature of digital well-being changes toward the quality of experience of work rather than output metrics. The studies emphasize the dangers of burnout, exhaustion of decision-making, and psychological burden related to the at-all-time connectedness. The design theories of work are focused more and more on autonomy, meaningful engagement, and recovery cycles as key elements of sustainable performance (Aldhafeeri, 2025). The findings of studies focused on hybrid and remote work also indicate that the uncertainty of professional and personal time increases cognitive load. According to scholars, digital systems need to be deliberately designed with deep work in mind, less density of unnecessary communications, and periodic disengagement. There has been a positive outcome of design interventions like planned quiet time, focused focus blocks, and workload redistribution to support teamwork, as a result of which engagement and innovation are enhanced (Ravikumar, 2026). Incorporating the ideas of digital well-being into organizational management redefines the nature of attention management as a shared responsibility and not a personal coping mechanism. This literature facilitates the goal of harmonizing productivity with cognitive wellness by designing a system.

6.3 Algorithmic Governance and Ethical Safeguards

As the use of AI systems to mediate the performance evaluation and task prioritization continues to increase, the problem of surveillance, bias and autonomy has been brought up. The three safeguards that are featured in algorithms governance literature are transparency, explainability, and human oversight. Without the existence of clear accountability structures, automated monitoring systems can cause performance anxiety and kill trust. As it has been discovered, the employees are more likely to accept AI-related recommendations in situations where the reasoning behind the decision-making is comprehensible and has an option to escalate (Aisyah and Dp, 2025). The ideas of privacy-by-design or participatory system development, which are the foundations of the ethical design, render the work more legitimate and psychologically safe. The model of governance that can balance data-driven optimization and protection against autonomy reduces the opposition and enhances sustainability in the adoption. This literature points out that not only is attention resilience a technical problem but also it is an ethical problem. The institutions will be necessary to maintain the cognitive coherence such that the pressure of the algorithm does not weaken dignity and long-term involvement.

7. CASE STUDIES

To demonstrate the practical feasibility of the Attention-Resilient Enterprise, the following section provides three recent and metrics-based examples that demonstrate how socio-technical alignment can result in the decrease of the interruption density, enhancement of the state of focus and retention of performance in the AI-assisted workplaces. The selection of the cases was based on (i) the hybrid workspace organization where attention relies on space, meeting patterns, and flow of collaboration; (ii) the AI-enhanced knowledge work where the cognitive load is predetermined by the complexity of tasks and the assistance of the tools; and (iii) the service operations that are digital-heavy and can be under the acute load (Ravikumar, Aarthi, Kurbanova, et al., 2026). All the cases are presented as an attention engineering intervention that consists of a set of technology configuration, workflow redesign and behavioral norms with measured results. It is not directed toward statistical generalization, but operational representation: how can quantifiably declines in the attention friction (travel, meetings, repeat contacts, time-to-completion) be transformed into productivity gains, as well as higher measures of digital well-being.

7.1 Hybrid Workplace Attention Engineering

An example of hybrid-work attention engineering is the use of workplace analytics, internally at Microsoft (since it is now part of the Viva Insights suite) to restructure the spatial proximity and meeting patterns in which focus conditions are dictated. Access to work had also been designed in such a way that it would minimize to the greatest extent possible an excess of transitions, as part of an enormous engineering relocation, and to learn the time that would be met with collaboration, calendar metadata had been researched to learn about the time that would be met with collaboration and the between-meeting recovery (Naqshbandi et al., 2024). The outcome in regards to the reported outcome indicated that it saved the traveling time to and out of the meetings by 46% which was approximated to be about 100 hours per week saved in the population under consideration. Other changes that are reported following the same nature of intervention include spontaneous chat increasing by 15% and formal meeting reducing by 20%. According to attention-resilience perspective, time saved is not the only effects that can be quantified, but there are also less transition load and less interruption cost: there are fewer micro-slices between back-to-back meetings, the foci of attention are also longer and the cognitive pacing of hybrid schedules is more appropriate. As demonstrated in the case, the power of attention can be enhanced through reforming the logistics of meetings, the proximity of working in partnership, and rhythms in the place of work using data instead of personal coping prescriptions. The outcomes of meetings optimization indicated in figure 3 with the help of analytics and spatial planning decrease the transition time, the time of meeting, and focus blocks that are sustained.

Figure 3. Hybrid Workplace Attention Engineering Model

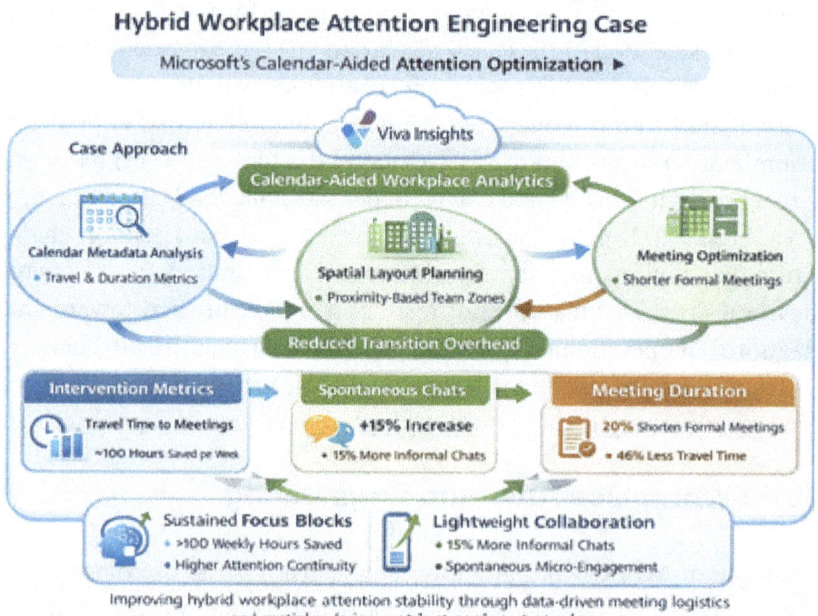

7.2 AI-Assisted Knowledge Work Systems

A very recent example of a knowledge-work with high quantified evidence is controlled study of AI pair-programming with GitHub Copilot. In a controlled experiment, Copilot access developers completed a standardized coding task 55.8%

faster than the control group, which means that AI assistance can help to alleviate friction in the execution process and accelerate the completion of problems in the workflow, given a reasonably appropriate integration. In addition to speed, experience and engagement outcomes, which are directly related to cognitive sustainability in the context of enterprise-oriented reporting, are detailed by 90% and 95% of developers, respectively, stating that they feel more fulfilled when using Copilot and that their enjoyment of coding has increased, which is an indicator of reduced mental load and higher quality of motivation in knowledge work (Okuboye, 2021). Explained in the Attention-Resilient Enterprise model, the attention mechanism is called cognitive offloading, and micro-decision reduction: the AI produces less low-level syntactic search and boilerplate generation, thus leaving attention to higher-order reasoning. Another important design indicator in the case is that AI must be a focus-saving assistant (in aid of flow), rather than a notification-inducing supervisor (more interruptions). Fig. 4 that shows how AI pair-programming leads to a cognitive load reduction, faster task completion, and development engagements and focus sustainability.

Figure 4. AI-Assisted Knowledge Work Attention Optimization Model

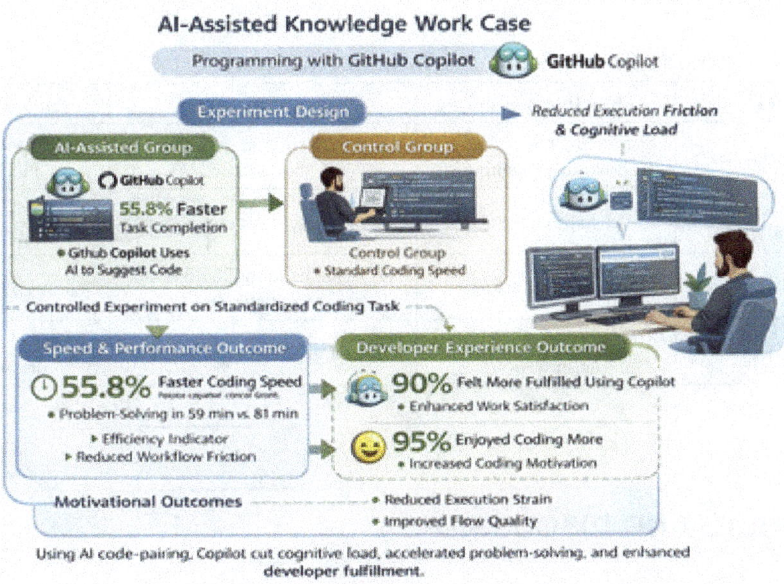

7.3 Digitally Intensive Service Operations

An example of a case of high-volume service operations is the customer service AI assistant of Klarna, which has been implemented in various markets. The reported outcomes indicate that the assistant was able to cover two-thirds of customer service conversation and do the same amount of work as 700 full-time worker, which is to demonstrate that the assistant absorbed the workload in a message-saturated environment significantly. The indicators of quality and rework were also measured: the number of repeat inquiries reduced by 25%, and customer issues were addressed within less than 2 minutes, as compared to 11 minutes before. Relevance to attention-resilience: the used number of repeats and the time used in resolution cycles are shorter, which decreases pressure in the backlog, agent context switching, and escalation loads (Narayan et al., 2025). Meanwhile, subsequent reporting indicates that organizations might have to juggle the level of automation with safety-nets on the quality of the service, which supports the necessity of governance and human control in digitally-heavy operations. Table 5 The cases with hybrid workplace, AI-assisted knowledge work, and service operations are compared to the percentage of the performance outcome.

Table 5. Case Study Comparative Performance Outcomes

Case Context	Key Intervention	Quantified Result	Attention Impact
Hybrid Workplace	Meeting redesign & proximity planning	46% reduction in travel time; 20% shorter meetings	Increased focus blocks
AI-Assisted Knowledge Work	AI coding assistant	55.8% faster task completion	Reduced cognitive switching
Service Operations	AI chat automation	66% chat handling; 25% fewer repeat queries	Stabilized workload
Service Efficiency	Resolution time optimization	2 min vs 11 min resolution	Reduced backlog pressure

8. RESULTS AND DISCUSSION

The evidence presented in the case proves the fact that attention-sensitive socio-technical design has quantifiable positive results in the context of productivity, cognitive stability and trust. Instead of considering efficiency as the output-based one, the cases under analysis reveal that the decrease in interruption density, workload fragmentation, and response pressure are associated with enhanced quality of performance and engagement. The redesign of hybrid workplaces eased transition load and meeting compression, knowledge labor with AI support decreased micro-decision fatigue and shorter completion time, and automation of services relieved the communication load of high volume and decreased repetitive interactions. In various contexts, the same trend is increasing, which is that productivity increases when there is a drop in attention friction (Minkkinen & Mäntymäki, 2023). The findings imply that the resilience to attention is an enabling factor: stabilizing the cognitive states results in the rapidity of performance, the reduction of errors, and long-term activity. Nevertheless, governance balance is also presented in the discussion. At the point of increased automation in the absence of transparency or oversight, dependency or over-automation risks occur. Environmentally friendly results hence necessitate concurrent optimization of technology and morality.

8.1 Focus Continuity and Load Stabilization

The structural redesign case involving the hybrid workplace has shown direct stability of attention by structural redesign. The transition overhead was also reduced by 46% in meeting travel time and 20% in formal meeting time, and interruption clustering. These modifications widened continuous concentration spans, and lessened micro-divisions amid teamwork incidences. Equally, AI-assisted knowledge work indicated that developers were able to do their tasks 55.8% faster with intelligent assistance in the form of code assistance. This enhancement is not only speed-related but also less thinking, switching between search, syntax recall, and implementation. Automation of two-thirds of chat traffic in digitally intensive service setting decreased the number of repetitive cycles of interaction and repeat queries by 25%, stabilizing workload on agents (Thota, 2025). In all the cases, load stabilization was achieved when systems were filtered, sequenced or absorbed of unwanted digital stimuli. The results support the idea that focus continuity is not an individual ability but a structural design that is being produced by clustering tasks, controlling interruptions, and redistributing workloads with AI instead of by personal will.

8.2 Sustainable Productivity Ratios

According to the findings of the case, the greatest productivity gains are observed when the efficiency gains are facilitated by a decrease in cognitive strain. The reclaimed time and the compression of meetings in the hybrid workplace case became the enhancement of the allocation of deep-work periods without compromising the collaboration. In AI-aided development, the higher rate of completion was reported, and the engagement and fulfillment were reported to have increased, which may indicate that productivity gains were gained without mentally straining the participants. In service work, a customer problem that was solved within two minutes, as opposed to eleven minutes earlier, caused a substantial decrease in the number of backlogs and the growth of strain. Balanced performance is thus reflected by sustainable productivity ratios higher throughput with lower repetition, less overload, and quality decisions being sustained (Rausch et al., 2024). The findings indicate that the output durability is enhanced with the time of attention resilience and reduces the risk of burnout without hindering the continuance of the service provision. It is possible to make productivity sustainable by adding cognitive recovery and focus stability to the list of operational metrics.

8.3 Trust, Autonomy, and Psychological Safety

Although performance indicators were also getting better in all cases, long-term success relies on trust and maintenance of autonomy. The AI-assisted development environments were received positively when they were presented as collaborative tools, as opposed to being supervisory monitors. The degree of user satisfaction is very high, which means that cognitive offloading promoted agency, not substituting it. Although the automation of the services has led to absorption of high workload, it has unveiled new challenges in terms of the degree of automation and it has signified the need to have human element and elucidate governance. They tolerated the use of hybrid workplace analytics when offered in the context of collaboration optimization, but not surveillance (Khavandi et al., 2023). These findings demonstrate that attention resilience requires data use transparency, explainability of priority logic and configuration of participatory systems. The psychological safety will be enhanced provided that the interpretive control has been maintained among the employees and the upward escalation routes are available. The discussion confirms that attention design must be morally driven otherwise the performance would be jeopardized by mistrust or coercion using an algorithm.

9. FUTURE RESEARCH

The Attention-Resilient Enterprise model leaves numerous possibilities to empirical validation and theoretical development. Although the conceptual model and case examples show that it is practically feasible in real-world situations, longitudinal studies (systematic and in contexts and time) need to be conducted to understand durability. Further research must take into account the inquiry of long-term improvement in productivity rather than the short-term advancement of attention stabilization and the impact on innovation capability, employee retention, and organizational flexibility. Moreover, the development of AI-based analytics gives an opportunity to address cognitive patterns more accurately and comply with ethical limitations. Boundary condition, such as cultural difference, industry variation, and remote-hybrid work structure, should also be researched. The inclusion of the metrics of attention into the enterprise dashboards must be verified to make sure that they are not turned into new surveillance tools (Fawzy Eid, 2024). Finally, the future research can examine a hypothesis that attention resilience is a predictive variable of sustainable performance and resilience of an organization. Increasing empirical evidence may help scholars to improve measurement models and advance the theoretical basis of socio-technical attention design.

9.1 Attention Analytics and AI Adaptation

The research concerning the matter of how enhanced analytics can detect the instability of attention in real-time and update AI systems needs further research. The opportunities to identify the indicators of clusters of interruptions, analysis of the patterns of interaction and workload density allow the use of the behavioral telemetry development, which allows revealing the signs of the interaction and cognitive overload. Smart AI systems can re-organize the labor process automatically, switch off non-urgent notifications or propose a rest period based on the prediction analytics (Dhand et al., 2025). However, the technical possibility must be weighed against ethical protection to prevent the intrusive watching. The optimal intervention thresholds, user customization and transparency, which can be relevant to adaptive attention systems, should be researched. They can also be demonstrated through experimental research of the inference of performance and well-being of the workflow as a fixed or adaptive AI. This can be enhanced by developing reactive notification management towards activity detection to proactive cognitive stabilization by creating responsible attention analytics and future systems.

9.2 Longitudinal Attention Metrics

There is a need to engage in long-term studies that would confirm the existence of long-term organizational benefits associated with the use of attention-resilience indicators. Cumulative cognitive fatigue or changing behavioral norms may not be reflected by short-term increases in the speed of task completion or compression. The longitudinal studies must monitor the continuity of focus, variability of workload, variability of recovery as well as level of engagement and turnover rates over the course of multiple quarters or years. Measures of psychological safety of the workplace that are assessed qualitatively should be supplemented with quantitative measures of performance in order to enhance measurement reliability. Researchers can also examine relations between measures of stable attention and innovation performance, the quality of strategic decisions or crisis resilience (Bhushan, 2025). Also, studies should assess the unintentional outcomes, including over-optimisation of attention that will result in the lack of spontaneity in collaboration. It will be possible to create validated longitudinal standards so that organizations can distinguish short-term efficiency bursts and long-term cognitive sustainability.

9.3 Cross-Industry Validation Studies

Different organizational settings should attend to attention resilience to establish the generalizability. The thinking habits of knowledge-based industries such as software creation, finance, and research may not be similar to those of the manufacturing industry, health sector, or government (Sang et al., 2025). The effect of task difficulty, the strength of the regulations, and the number of communication can be determined by comparing across industries to identify the impact of task complexity on the process of attention stabilization. Another aspect, cultural and geographic backgrounds of the hybrid and remote work model should be compared to explore the diversity of digital norms and practices of recovery. Multi-case and multi-country studies may contribute to the conceptual framework to make it stronger. Moreover, the details of the industry regulation may place some restrictions on the governing e.g., data privacy policies or decision-making strategies that are crucial to safety; thus, the attention-conscious technologies may be not structured in the same way in this case. Attention-Resilient Enterprise model scalability and flexibility will also be reduced by additional empirical validation in industries.

10. MANAGERIAL IMPLICATIONS

The conclusions of the Attention-Resilient Enterprise model suggest that the productivity gains with artificial intelligence-based environment are not as technologically-oriented but rather socio-technical-oriented. Managers play a major role in the translation of the theoretical concepts into practice. Rather than merely focusing on speed, responsiveness, or digital presence, the organizations ought to restructure performance apparatus, models of governance, and practices of leadership in ways that protect cognitive coherence. The attention should be considered an organizational strategic resource that may be incorporated into the infrastructure, workflow design, and evaluation systems (Ebojoh & Högberg, 2024). As the evidence in the case demonstrates, the objective benefits are achieved, including a reduction in the density of interruptions, shorter completion cycles, and a lower number of repeat workloads in the case of managerial interventions aimed at managing digital flow but not improving it. The leadership ought to therefore balance the algorithmic optimization and human sustainability. Sustained productivity can be achieved in enterprises through formalizing attention-sensitive metrics, ethical AI management, and cultural-based criteria on attention and rest without negatively influencing psychological security and prolonged engagement.

10.1 Redesigning Performance Metrics

Conventional performance indicators tend to encourage fast reaction, twenty-four seven accessibility, and obvious online movement. Nevertheless, the results of the case have shown that sustained performance increases with the metrics that are focused on depth, quality, and cognitive persistence. The indicators that should be combined by managers include continuous focus periods, the quality of completion of the tasks, the decrease in the number of repeats, and efficient collaboration as opposed to measuring the frequency of communication or the responsiveness in the real time. The productivity gains in the form of shorter meetings and lower transition time can be identified in hybrid environments instead of low engagement. The AI-aided workflows are to assess benefits and error reduction of cognitive offloading instead of speed (O. N. U. of Technology et al., 2025). Companies can utmost align performance assessment and preservation of attention by modifying their approach to activity-based measurement to these outcome-based and sustainability-focused measurements. The redesign eliminates the ability of algorithmic pressure to designate reactive behaviour as rewarded and promotes organised deep work, creativity and long-term strategic thinking.

10.2 Ethical AI Governance Frameworks

The productivity systems enabled by AI should be guided by well-established ethical guardrails to ensure that they are trusted and legitimate. Algorithms The governance systems should inculcate a sense of transparency in algorithmic prioritization, should be clear about the limit of data use, and should be explicable on automated suggestions. Managers ought to make a difference between attention supportive analytics and intrusive surveillance systems. The participatory configuration processes allow them to influence the notification settings, workload and dashboard customization to an improved sense of ownership and acceptance. Avoiding AI outputs is that clear human control channels must be available to dispute or interpret AI outputs (Uriasiev & Voloschuk, 2026). Moreover, privacy-by-design theories should be integrated into the data collection procedures to prevent over-observation of the behavioral patterns. Organizations can avoid the impairment of autonomy or psychological safety by mechanisms to ensure that the performance optimization aligns with the goals of cognitive sustainability. Ethical governance is thereby enabled as strategic to bring forth attention resilience and not a mandatory requirement. The alignment of AI productivity systems with trust, autonomy, and cognitive sustainability is shown in Figure 5 using transparency, privacy protection, configuration to participation, and human-mechanism to ensure control.

Figure 5. Ethical AI Governance Framework for Attention Resilience

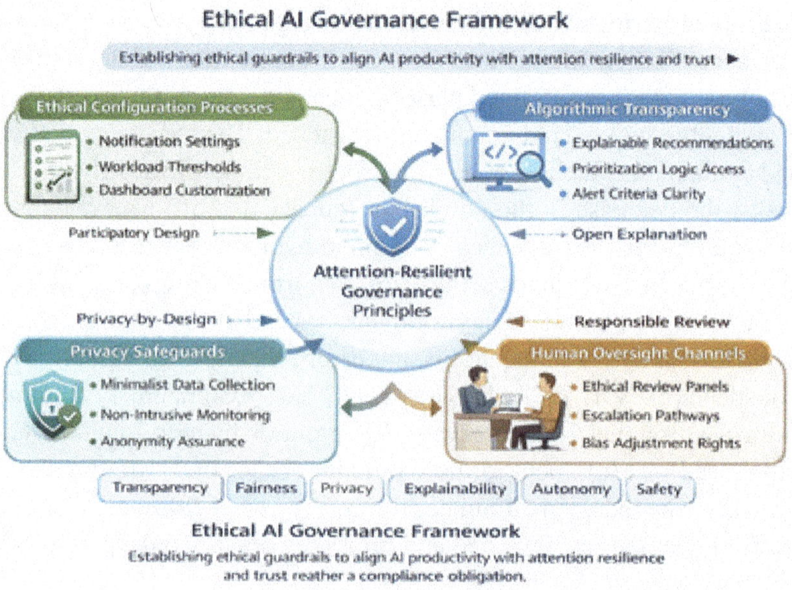

10.3 Leadership for Attention Stewardship

The culture of organizational attention is heavily influenced by the behavior of leadership. Protecting deep-work periods, limiting unnecessary messages and communicating without performance signaling based on round-the-clock availability are attention conscious practices that executives and managers have to model. Attention stewardship entails establishing norms which bring about collaboration and balance with stability of focus. Leaders must be keen to observe the trend of overloads and redistribute the workload when the intensity is at its peaks. Digital literacy can be improved through training programs that allow employees to become more critical of AI recommendations instead of responding accordingly. Honest communication regarding the use of analytics supports the psychological safety and fear of secret assessment (L. N. T. University & Topalov, 2025). Moreover, the leaders should acknowledge that innovation does not rely on constant Internet connectivity but rather on continuous thinking processes. Integrating attention stewardship in the leadership philosophy provides organizations with an environment wherein technological intelligence supplements and not divides human capacity. Sustainable competitive advantage therefore results as an outcome of cognitive coherence that is aided by responsible managerial practice. Tables 6 Matches performance redesign, governance safeguards and leadership actions with quantifiable organizational benefits.

Table 6. Managerial Action Framework for Attention Stewardship

Managerial Domain	Key Action	Attention Benefit	Organizational Gain
Performance Redesign	Measure depth over speed	Focus preservation	Quality outcomes
AI Governance	Ensure explainability	Autonomy protection	Trust sustainability
Workload Management	Adaptive task allocation	Load stabilization	Reduced burnout
Leadership Norms	Protect deep-work intervals	Reduced fragmentation	Innovation growth
Cultural Reinforcement	Encourage recovery cycles	Cognitive resilience	Long-term engagement

11. CONCLUSION

It is the shift to digitally that demands a paradigm shift of connectivity optimization to the formation of cognitive coherence that every enterprise has become an attention strong enterprise. The above discussion in this chapter indicates that AI-enabled systems in organizations are not only effective depending on the strength of automation or access to data, but based on the functionality of socio-technical systems to manage the flow of attention. The hybrid workplace, knowledge work with the help of AI, and digital intensity of operations are what can be redesigned to demonstrate that the quantifiable benefits are obtained in case the interruption density is reduced and focus continuity is more predictable. It is therefore the attention as a strategic infrastructure but not as a personal limitation. Protective layers of technology that intelligently filter and sequence data incorporate transparency and protection of autonomy and leadership models enhance the depth rather than necessarily being responsive, productivity, and digital well-being are convergent rather than competitive. Attention infrastructure is strategically important because it enables AI to be converted into a performance pressure to a cognitive support mechanism. Basic enterprise design should be subjected to ethical guardrails, dynamic work load allocation, and quantifiable metrics of attention as a key to sustainable AI-based enterprise design. By making attention stewardship an institutional practice not only do businesses get more efficient in their operations but also more innovative in their capabilities, they also survive the pace of the accelerated digital environment and have a sustainable workforce in the long run. The competitive nature among the landscape of the algorithmic administration and the entirety of analytics will increase as the ability to coordinate the technological intelligence and human cognitive stability.

REFERENCES

Aarthi, S. Ravikumar, Sapayev Odilbek Uglu, V., Sottarov, A., & Singh, A. (2025). The privacy paradox. In *User-Centric Cybersecurity Implications for Sustainable Digital Transformation* (pp. 223–256). IGI Global Scientific Publishing. DOI: 10.4018/979-8-3373-3171-3.ch007

Aisyah, P. N., & Dp, R. T. (2025). Artificial Intelligence and Cloud-Based Accounting Information Systems: Enhancing financial reporting reliability and cybersecurity in the digital era. *Jurnal Ekonomi Dan Bisnis Digital*, *4*(3), 203–222. DOI: 10.55927/ministal.v4i3.14519

Aldhafeeri, F. M. (2025). Governing artificial intelligence in radiology: A systematic review of ethical, legal, and regulatory frameworks. *Diagnostics (Basel)*, *15*(18), 2300. DOI: 10.3390/diagnostics15182300 PMID: 41008671

Bastiaansen, C. A. J., & Wilderom, C. P. M. (2022). Agile and generic work values of British vs Indian IT workers: A culture-clash case. *Journal of Strategy and Management*, *15*(3), 353–376. DOI: 10.1108/JSMA-03-2021-0071

Bhushan, N. (2025). Artificial intelligence (AI) and its role in enhancing the well-being of employees in the public sector: A systematic review. *International Journal of Scientific Research and Modern Technology*, *13*, 13. Advance online publication. DOI: 10.38124/ijsrmt.v4i12.1060

Bobrytska, V. I., Krasylnykova, H. V., Protska, S. M., Skyrda, T. S., Krasylnykov, S. R., & Chkhalo, O. M. (2025). Digitalisation in higher education: A systematic review of its impact on health, cognition, and social interaction. *International Journal of Learning Teaching and Educational Research*, *24*(5), 339–359. DOI: 10.26803/ijlter.24.5.18

Chauhan, A., Sarkar, D., Verma, G. S., Rastogi, H., Adapa, K., & Duggal, M. (2025). Evaluating trustworthiness in AI-Based diabetic retinopathy screening: Addressing transparency, consent, and privacy challenges. *BMC Medical Ethics*, *26*(1), 140. DOI: 10.1186/s12910-025-01265-7 PMID: 41107928

Dhand, S., Pandey, A., Mishra, S., Sharma, K., Kadanga, A., Rawat, A., Kumari, V., Yadav, M., & Chand, B.-U.-N. (2025). Role of Artificial Intelligence in enhancing employee well-being at the workplace. In *Advances in Computational Intelligence and Robotics* (pp. 25–46). IGI Global Scientific Publishing. DOI: 10.4018/979-8-3373-1270-5.ch002

Ebojoh, S., & Högberg, K. (2024). Exploring leadership in the hybrid workplace. [IJAC]. *International Journal of Advanced Corporate Learning*, *17*(4), 16–41. DOI: 10.3991/ijac.v17i4.50857

Economics, S. K. K. N. U. (2025). of, Grynevych, L., Kniazieva, O., University, O. S. A., Pedorenko, D., & University, P. S. T. (2025). Analysis of the impact of marketing strategy on the formation of the components of the information and logistics system of a trading enterprise. *Ukrainian Journal of Applied Economics and Technology*, *2025*(3), 12–15. DOI: 10.36887/2415-8453-2025-3-1

Fawzy Eid, M. (2024). Using artificial intelligence in electronic health record systems to mitigate physician burnout: A roadmap. *Journal of Healthcare Management*, *69*(4), 244–254. DOI: 10.1097/JHM-D-24-00094 PMID: 38976785

Haque, A. (2025). Responsible artificial intelligence (AI) in healthcare: A paradigm shift in leadership and strategic management. *Leadership in Health Services (Bradford, England)*, *38*(4), 644–656. DOI: 10.1108/LHS-01-2025-0018 PMID: 40911384

Hutsaliuk, O., & Shainovskyi, R. (2025). Decision-making in selecting information and analytical systems for corporate IT cluster enterprises. *Herald of the Economic Sciences of Ukraine*, (2(49)), 152. DOI: 10.37405/1729-7206.2025.2(49).152-165

Independent researcher New Haven CT 06511 USA, B. I. at A. A., Mokashi, S. P., Naik, S., & Solutions Consultant San Francisco CA 94103 USA, S. (2025). Cognitive-aware shift scheduling in smart manufacturing: An AI framework for reducing burnout and fatigue and investigating the impact of. *Frontiers in Emerging Artificial Intelligence and Machine Learning*, *02*(08), 16–29. DOI: 10.37547/feaiml/Volume02Issue08-03

Khavandi, S., Zaghloul, F., Higham, A., Lim, E., de Pennington, N., & Celi, L. A. (2023). Investigating the impact of automation on the health care workforce through autonomous telemedicine in the cataract pathway: Protocol for a multicenter study. *JMIR Research Protocols*, *12*, e49374. DOI: 10.2196/49374 PMID: 38051569

Minkkinen, M., & Mäntymäki, M. (2023). Discerning between the "easy" and "hard" problems of AI governance. *IEEE Transactions on Technology and Society*, *4*(2), 188–194. DOI: 10.1109/TTS.2023.3267382

Naqshbandi, M. M., Kabir, I., Ishak, N. A., & Islam, M. Z. (2024). The future of work: Work engagement and job performance in the hybrid workplace. *The Learning Organization*, *31*(1), 5–26. DOI: 10.1108/TLO-08-2022-0097

Narayan, P., Kedia, G., & Tiwari, S. (2025). Digital Sustainability and it's implications in the era of 5.O. In *Integrating Management Principles with Business Analytics Concepts and Applications* (pp. 82–91). QTanalytics India. DOI: 10.48001/978-81-980647-9-0-7

Okuboye, A. (2021). Cross-cultural variability in workforce optimization: A bpm perspective on remote and hybrid teams. *International Journal of Multidisciplinary Futuristic Development*, *2*(1), 15–24. DOI: 10.54660/IJMFD.2021.2.1.15-24

Pandit, S., Ravikumar, R. N., Joshi, N., Pandit, S., Kishore, S., & Aarthi, S. (2025). Retrieval-Augmented Generation (RAG) for enterprise intelligence. In *Leveraging LLMs for Business Innovation* (pp. 69–106). IGI Global Scientific Publishing. DOI: 10.4018/979-8-3373-3912-2.ch003

Pasupuleti, M. K. (2024). *AI-driven leadership: Crisis management and virtual organizations in the digital age*. National Education Services., DOI: 10.62311/nesx/rb978-81-981179-1-5

Rausch, L., Burtscher, J., Ruedl, G., Schindelwig, K., Steidl-Müller, L., & Mohr, M. (2024). How to embrace interdisciplinarity in sport science – An approach at the ÖSG Congress Innsbruck 2024. *Current Issues in Sport Science (CISS), 9*(4), 001. DOI: 10.36950/2024.4ciss001

Ravikumar, A. S., Kurbanova, N., Sevdim, K. E., Zaynitdinovna, B. D., & Jumaniyazova, N. (2026). Bridging knowledge and policy. In *Advances in Computational Intelligence and Robotics* (pp. 119–150). IGI Global Scientific Publishing. DOI: 10.4018/979-8-3373-7620-2.ch005

Ravikumar, R. N., & Aarthi, S. (2025b). Augmented decision-making. In *Advances in Computational Intelligence and Robotics* (pp. 227–258). IGI Global Scientific Publishing. DOI: 10.4018/979-8-3373-7416-1.ch009

Ravikumar, R. N., & Aarthi, S. (2025c). Human-AI synergy for organizational resilience. In *Advances in Computational Intelligence and Robotics* (pp. 287–322). IGI Global Scientific Publishing. DOI: 10.4018/979-8-3373-7416-1.ch011

Ravikumar, R. N., Aarthi, S., & Mamadiyarov, Z. (2026). Building the foundations of augmented organizations through AI empowerment. In *Advances in Computational Intelligence and Robotics* (pp. 101–130). IGI Global Scientific Publishing. DOI: 10.4018/979-8-3373-8607-2.ch006

Ravikumar, R. N., Aarthi, S., Sapayev, V., & Esanov, A. (2026). Generative artificial intelligence for visual branding and creative automation in modern marketing ecosystems. In *Advances in Computational Intelligence and Robotics* (pp. 1–32). IGI Global Scientific Publishing. DOI: 10.4018/979-8-3373-4506-2.ch001

Ravikumar, & Aarthi, S. (2025a). AI-driven climate resilience. In *Advances in Computational Intelligence and Robotics* (pp. 207–238). IGI Global Scientific Publishing. DOI: 10.4018/979-8-3373-5540-5.ch007

Ravikumar, & Aarthi, S. (2026). Synergizing innovation. In *Advances in Computational Intelligence and Robotics* (pp. 59–90). IGI Global Scientific Publishing. DOI: 10.4018/979-8-3373-7620-2.ch003

Sang, L. T., Ravikumar, R. N., Aarthi, S., & Ben, T. L. (2025). Optimizing sales and inventory performance using AI and business intelligence in POS environments. In *Advances in Computational Intelligence and Robotics* (pp. 259–290). IGI Global Scientific Publishing. DOI: 10.4018/979-8-3373-4392-1.ch011

Shreha, S. A., Ravikumar, R. N., & Aarthi, S. (2025). Neuro-symbolic AI and Behavioral Intelligence. In *Advances in Computational Intelligence and Robotics* (pp. 121–152). IGI Global Scientific Publishing. DOI: 10.4018/979-8-3373-5012-7.ch005

Technology, E. (2026). Digital technologies as the basis of a constructive business environment in large industrial enterprises. *Problemi Ekonomìki*, *4*(66), 230–238. DOI: 10.32983/2222-0712-2025-4-230-238

Technology, O. N. U. (2025). The role of the marketing complex in the formed logistics system of enterprise. *Economic Herald of the Donbas*, (2 (80)), 50–55. DOI: 10.12958/1817-3772-2025-2(80)-50-55

Thao, N. V. H., & Mai Dr, L. T. T. (2025). Optimizing employee motivation in the era of artificial intelligence: Evidence from MH Raroma, a digital creative enterprise in Vietnam. *International Journal of Innovative Science and Research Technology*, (IJISRT25OCT658), 1196–1206. DOI: 10.38124/ijisrt/25oct658

Thota, S. (2025). A scalable microservices-based architecture for AI-driven Salesforce Cloud applications. *American International Journal of Computer Science and Technology*, *7*, 92–103. DOI: 10.63282/3117-5481/AIJCST-V7I6P110

Udupa, A. N., Majmudar, A. A., & Tran, L. (2024). A systematic review of neurological airway respiratory cardiovascular other-surgical severity (NARCO-SS) score as a pediatric perioperative scoring system. *Paediatric Anaesthesia*, *34*(5), 396–404. DOI: 10.1111/pan.14846 PMID: 38300020

University, E. (2025). The algorithm for integrating digital technologies into enterprise management system. *Biznes Inform*, *3*(566), 67–75. DOI: 10.32983/2222-4459-2025-3-67-75

University, L. N. T., & Topalov, V. (2025). Development of the information security system for small business entities. *Business Navigator*, (4(81)). Advance online publication. DOI: 10.32782/business-navigator.81-34

Uriasiev, M., & Voloschuk, L. (2026). Digital transformation of information support for enterprise financial flow management. *Economic Scope*, (209), 319–329. DOI: 10.30838/EP.209.319-329

Zhu, Z. Y. (2025). Ethical AI governance in urban governance: Normative, descriptive and prescriptive challenges and opportunities of autonomous vehicles. *Transforming Government*, *19*(4), 914–932. DOI: 10.1108/TG-06-2025-0191

KEY TERMS AND DEFINITIONS

Algorithmic Governance: Organizational policies and controls that regulate how AI systems operate, ensuring transparency, fairness, and accountability.

Attention Infrastructure: The technological and managerial systems that shape how information is filtered, prioritized, and delivered within an organization.

Attention Resilience: The organizational ability to protect focus continuity, regulate digital interruptions, and sustain cognitive stability in AI-enabled work environments.

Attention-Conscious Design: Interface and system design principles that minimize overload and support structured focus intervals.

Cognitive Fragmentation: The disruption of sustained focus caused by frequent task-switching, notifications, and digital interruptions.

Cognitive Load: The mental effort required to process information and complete tasks.

Digital Well-Being: The state of maintaining psychological health and balanced engagement in digitally intensive work environments.

Explainable AI (XAI): AI systems that provide clear reasoning behind their recommendations or decisions.

Focus Continuity: The ability to maintain uninterrupted work periods that support deep thinking and high-quality output.

Psychological Safety: A workplace condition where employees feel secure to express concerns, question systems, and retain autonomy without fear of negative consequences.

Sustainable Productivity Ratio: A performance measure that balances output efficiency with employee well-being and cognitive recovery.

Workload Adaptability: The ability of systems to dynamically adjust task allocation based on intensity and cognitive capacity.

Chapter 8

Algocracy, Ethical Residue, and the Quest for Meaningful Work in the Age of Algorithmic Management

Deniz Dirik
http://orcid.org/0000-0002-7652-5079
Manisa Celal Bayar University, Turkey

ABSTRACT

This chapter explores the human and ethical implications of algorithmic management and the possibility for meaningful work in an age of algocracy. Algocracy refers to organizational environments where algorithms function as central regulatory mechanisms. The growing reliance on algorithmic decision-making introduces challenges related to agency, transparency, responsibility, and autonomy. The reign of algocracy also leads to "ethical residue", referring to the gap between quantified organizational performance metrics and the lived experience of value produced through everyday collegial acts of support. Contemporary organizations privilege outputs and performance indicators as primary indicators of success. Yet, organizational functioning depends equally on forms of contribution that resist measurement such as informal mentoring, discretionary judgment, and relational care. Recognizing this residue is essential for sustaining organizations that are efficient, morally responsible, and capable of supporting meaningful collective work in the algorithmic age.

DOI: 10.4018/979-8-2600-0111-0.ch008

INTRODUCTION

We created the Machine, to do our will, but we cannot make it do our will now. It has robbed us of the sense of space and of the sense of touch, it has blurred every human relation and narrowed down love to a carnal act, it has paralysed our bodies and our wills, and now it compels us to worship it. The Machine develops — but not on our lines. The Machine proceeds — but not to our goal.
E.M. Forster, from "The Machine Stops"

E.M. Forster articulated these concerns as early as 1909. It resonates with many people by the second quarter of the 21st century.

The history of organized work is fundamentally a history of the struggle between human discretion and the quest for calculable control. Since the early days of the Industrial Revolution, organizations have sought ways to make human labor more predictable and more efficient for those in power. This trajectory reached a definitive peak in the early twentieth century with the birth of scientific management, where the stopwatch and the time-and-motion study were used to reduce complex human activity into mechanical movements (Singh & Gupta, 2025). For decades, the primary concern was how to better manage the body. Later, however, we have entered a new era where technology sought to manage the mind and the moral character of the individual through algorithmic decision-making systems and data-driven choice architectures. The emergence of new technologies has been accompanied by concerns regarding individuals' experience of social and labor relations as well as acts of resistance.

Today, algorithms, the so-called "supercarriers of formal rationality" (Lindebaum et al., 2020) are taking over control in organizations. Organizations increasingly rely on algorithmic systems to inform decisions about hiring, evaluation, promotion, reward, punishment, and retention (Kellogg et al., 2020). Algorithmic management systems monitor, track, and analyze employee behaviors through digitalized and coded data structures. These systems promise consistency and efficiency. They also promise a form of neutrality that human judgment is often accused of lacking. While algorithms are praised for efficiency and objectivity on the one hand, lack of human discretion and contextual sensitivity are criticized aspects of algorithmic management (Fousiani et al., 2026). AI-supported decision-making mechanisms that are rising in numbers in contexts such as medical diagnostics, finance, autonomous vehicles, digital platforms, criminal justice, traditional workplaces, etc., are provoking debates about moral agency, accountability, transparency, intentionality, biases, human oversight, as well as value alignment (Boos, 2024; Ilie, 2026). Much of the current debate revolves around improving these systems, making them less biased, more transparent, or more accountable. These are important concerns. Still, they tend to assume that the main problem lies in how algorithms process information rather than in what they are able to recognize as meaningful in the first place. On a parallel trajectory, research focusing on the evolving nature of digitalized work ecosystems and the role of algorithmic management on employees' perceptions are increasingly emphasizing the negative repercussions such as feelings of privacy invasion, stress, disengagement, non-compliant and unethical behavior (Gao et al., 2025) and everyday acts of resistance or "infrapolitics" (Miszczynski, 2026). Algorithmic management is presenting a duality whereby greater efficiency, consistency and data-driven insights are being bargained in exchange for less transparency and fairness, as well as greater quantification and mechanization of human experience. At this conjuncture, new forms of concern, uncertainty, and workplace anxiety continue to emerge.

The anxiety regarding automatization and the rise of machines is not a new phenomenon. In fact, it has been remarkably persistent and widespread throughout modern history (Rifkin, 1995). During the Industrial Revolution, technological resistance movements emerged, driven by workers who feared losing their livelihoods. These groups came to be later known as the Luddites and they organized protests and attacks by destroying machinery perceived as a threat to employment. In response, the British Parliament passed legislation in 1812 that made machine-breaking punishable by death, a penalty later replaced with transportation to Australia. Much as this anxiety, concerns about technological unemployment have resurfaced repeatedly across generations. A New York Times article published in the 1940s described technological unemployment as an "obsolete debate." Yet, as of 2026, it is evident that the debate has hardly become obsolete. President John F. Kennedy warned of automation as a "dark menace" capable of displacing workers. Albert Einstein similarly suggested that machines designed to liberate humanity might ultimately undermine their own creators. John Maynard Keynes, writing in the 1930s, famously predicted that within a century technological progress would advance to such an extent that people would work only three hours a day, or roughly fifteen hours a week. He envisioned what he called an "Age of Leisure." However, with only a few years remaining until Keynes's forecast horizon, history may prove him partially mistaken. Rather than entering an era of leisure, we appear to remain firmly within an age structured around labor. Nevertheless, Keynes was profoundly correct in one respect. According to OECD data, working hours in developed economies have been systematically declining on an annual basis for at least the past fifty years. In this sense, we may conclude that for more than a century, societies have continuously lived with the recurring claim and accompanying anxiety that technology will take people's jobs and leave them unemployed. Yet, we have new and emerging concerns thanks to our new digitized world of work. As technological developments have a pervasive nature, they are changing the overall context where work takes place. This comes with a price tag on labor, relations of control, organizational power, human agency, and moral structures.

At the intersection of the rise of algorithmic management systems and the evolving landscape of work, organizational relations of power, control, agency, and team dynamics are being reshaped. This chapter is focusing on the consequences of translating human activity into measurable indicators. Within organizations, acts of care, ethical judgment, and quiet generosity are essential for collective functioning, yet these qualities rarely appear in the data structures that inform algorithmic decision-making. To name this gap, I use the concept of ethical residue. Ethical residue describes the important qualities left behind when evaluation is reduced to quantifiable metrics. By examining the rise of algorithmic management and its evolution into algocracy, it becomes possible to identify structural barriers that prevent organizations from recognizing the full spectrum of human contribution. These debates necessitate engagement with both emerging concepts and longstanding discussions on morality, ethics, human agency, and intentionality. Furthermore, algorithmic management systems are fostering digitally supported systems of "augmented despotism", prompting at least some to engage in what Scott (1990) terms "infrapolitics", or micro acts of resistance within coercive systems, such as gossiping, foot-dragging, or using coded language to protect themselves from external control and restrictive norms. Although such acts of resistance (in digitalized contexts as well) may not fundamentally alter the (algorithmic) power relations, they serve as subtle forms of retaliation, providing momentary relief against disciplinary powers and agents of control within organizational context. The following discussion attempts to synthesize emergent ideas from these relevant streams of research to construct a coherent narrative on algorithmic management of work.

THE ARCHITECTURE OF ALGOCRACY

At the heart of the modern workplace is a model of governance that has moved beyond the traditional hierarchy of people. This system is known as algocracy or algorithm-mediated management (Aneesh, 2009; Neves et al., 2021), a term used to describe an automated or semi-automated model of organization where algorithms replace human supervision and intervention. Unlike older forms of bureaucracy that relied on human managers to interpret rules, an algocracy embeds authority directly into the code and software interfaces that workers interact with every day. Algocracy refers to a new logic of governance based on programming code that helps us understand the global organization of labor today. This new form of governance goes beyond the limits of traditional hierarchical bureaucracy and market exchange model. The endless possibilities of programming, like a new language of communication or an all-purpose exchange system like money, points to an emergent new organizational form, based on online labor and transformation of work into coded flows (Aneesh, 2009).

This model is built on the process of datafication, where every human action is treated as raw material to be captured, quantified, and processed. In an algocratic environment, the system itself collects data, compares it against performance benchmarks, and communicates directions to the worker without a human intermediary. By eliminating the need for human intervention, algocracy creates a state of silent management where control is omnipresent but accountability is often obscured. For example, in platform-based work, the algorithm might autonomously assign tasks, set prices, and even deactivate a worker's access based on opaque metrics. Everyday examples of algocracies and algocratic management are already embedded in many forms of work and organizational life. Although algorithmic management is often discussed in relation to gig or platform economy firms such as Uber, Amazon, or TaskRabbit, organizations across different sectors, scales, and national contexts increasingly rely on algorithmic systems to improve operational efficiency. It takes place in both geographically tettered work on demand by app (such as food delivery) and in cloudwork that is possible to be completed anywhere across the globe as long as there is a computer and connection. Recommendation systems used by Netflix and Spotify, for instance, or the just-in-time production models of Zara and Walmart, companies in grocery retailing, delivery and packaging, hospitality and many other industries are relying on algorithms to shape both consumer experiences and organizational decision-making processes (Mateescu & Nguyen, 2019). As such, management in companies today is no longer only done by managers as it is increasingly embedded into software, apps, ratings, dashboards, sensors, and automated decision systems, with some inevitably negative consequences. The Chinese tech company TikTok, for example, as a digital platform governs the reach of user-generated content through algorithmic or regulatory means, usually unbeknownst to the users and creators (Zeng, & Kaye, 2022). Amazon has been accused of weaponizing algorithms through monitoring and manipulation to direct and discipline warehouse workers, and to discourage them from unionizing by distributing anti-union messages (Wiggin, 2025). The carsharing company Uber has been shown to engage in algorithmic surveillance and to use asymmetric information, automated dispatching, and blind rating systems to dictate gig workers' behavior (Rosenblat & Stark, 2016). From a financial algocracy perspective, fintech companies are increasingly turning to algorithms and the predictive power of AI-generated alternative data to identify borrower creditworthiness and for loan decision-making (Di Maggio et al., 2021; Langenbucher & Corcoran, 2021). A media studies lens has emphasized the significant role of private global companies in enabling platformization and algorithmic construction of reality in most of the contemporary information societies, and the increasing threat of algorithmic reality construction that create and shape collective perceptions and behavior to the detriment of social equality and accountability (Just & Latzer, 2016). A large-scale OECD survey spanning six countries and investigating attitudes towards algoritmic management showed that employers voice concerns about unclear accountability, inability to easily follow the tools' logic, and inadequate protection of workers' health (Milanez et al., 2025). As these examples show, the idea of algocracy winces at the sociology of work literature and relations of control and power, focusing on the dark side of digitization in the neoliberal context such as surveillance capitalism, Foucauldian theories of panopticon surveillance, big data capitalism, platform economy and similar others (Kellogg et al., 2020; Konjen, 2025; Zuboff, 2019).

THE TYRANNY OF THE APP: QUANTIFICATION, COMMENSURATION, AND METRIC BLINDNESS

An algocracy is basically a system of control where management power is embedded into digital systems rather than traditional bureaucratic power hierarchies. The rise of algocracy is often legitimized by the discourse of the flexible and autonomous worker. However, this flexibility is frequently a camouflage for a deeper power asymmetry. While workers may choose when to log on, they are subject to a triangular visibility where the platform and the customer monitor their performance through rating systems. In the meantime, the logic of the algorithm remains a black box to the worker. This environment restricts human agency by mediating relationships through metrics rather than dialogue. Ultimately, algocracy represents a technified system of domination that operates at a magnitude unimaginable in previous eras. Moreover, the technological solutionism and naturalized functionalism of the digitalized organization obscures practices of disempowerment, exploitation, surveillance, and manipulation (Neves et al., 2021). Research has highlighted the mechanisms of control intrinsic to algocracy as follows (Kellogg et al., 2020): restrictions and recommendations for guiding and directing behavior, registration and classification for evaluating and assessing performance, and replacement and reward for disciplinary purposes. Lehdonvirta (2018) quips about the algorithmic management as the replacement of the industrial era "tyranny of the clock" with the digital era "tyranny of the app". Supposedly, these previously human-enacted practices become less error-prone, more systematic and reliable, and more objective when operationalized in real-time by an algorithmic decision architecture. This is the dominant narrative for the contemporary organization of labor and workforce.

A useful point for better understanding algocracy is the literature on quantification. Work in sociology has shown that measurement does more than describe reality.

Indeed, figures create and shape reality. The idea of commensuration, which is defined as "*the expression or measurement of characteristics normally represented by different units according to a common metric*" (Espeland & Stevens, 1998) describe the process through which different qualities are transformed into a common medium of quantifying such as price, number of votes, view counts, cost-benefit ratio, etc. This process allows comparison and calculation. It also flattens distinctions that resist standardization, even at the risk of exclusion, and invisibility of relevant and valuable aspects of life. Algorithmic management upholds measurement and quantification as central features of creating and describing objective reality. However, too much emphasis on measurability might lead to a trap called *McNamara Fallacy*, which is the tendency to assume that if something cannot be quantified, it either does not exist or is not of significance (this reminds me of Shakespeare's famous quote from Romeo and Juliet Act II Scene II, "*A rose by any other name would smell as sweet").* This in turn leads to metric blindness, a condition where an organization's formal dashboards display high efficiency while the underlying operational reality is crumbling because unmeasured risks are ignored.

This creates a subtle shift as employees learn what is visible to the system and what is not over time and adapt their attitudes accordingly. Activities that align with measurable outputs are reinforced. Others become secondary, even if they are essential for collective functioning. The issue is not simply that measurement is imperfect. It is that measurement sets the terms of what counts. In this architecture, statistical correlations override moral reasoning and ethical contemplation in decision-making. The overreliance on training data raises concerns over the unbiased or objective stance of algorithm-generated choices, which also create problems for agentic responsibility and democratic accountability. A system that has been associated with greater impartiality might end up promoting the exact opposite at a much larger scale.

MAPPING THE ALGOCRATIC TOPOLOGY

According to an actor-network theory (ANT) perspective which situates technological agents as active participants in decision-making, algorithms are actors that participate in power relations, mediate communication, and influence outcomes (Latour, 2005). From a sociotechnical perspective, there is an interdependence between social arrangements and technological designs, and that the latter is never a neutral technical artefact. Through the facilitation of algorithms, for instance, previously human-controlled organizational and human resource tasks are passed on to automated assessments and quantifiable metrics. The identification, assessment and evaluation of knowledge, skills and abilities, key performance indicators and human analytics systems operate through similar logics. They require that diverse forms of contribution be translated into comparable units. This translation however reduces employees to read-only excel sheet figures. What cannot be translated tends to disappear from formal evaluation. This is not necessarily because organizations deny the existence of such contributions. It is because their decision infrastructures are not designed to accommodate them. A related point is made by Porter (1995) who shows how numbers gain authority via an appearance of impersonality and objectivity, especially in contexts where trust is fragile.

It is hard to grasp the full-scale repercussions of this structural invisibility unless we give up on viewing algorithmic management as a localized tool for employee surveillance or control. To support this contention, Stark and Vanden Broeck (2024) offers a substantially different theoretical argument. Accordingly, algorithmic management should not simply be understood as Digital Taylorism or a technologically upgraded version of scientific management. This would be a mistakenly narrow and underestimating perspective. Algorithmic management, strongly tied to the rise of platforms and boundaryless organizations, represents a fundamentally different organizational logic. Rather, it is about coordinating and co-opting broad ecosystems of users, assets, activities, and data flows which usually exist outside traditional organizational boundaries. From an ecosystem shift perspective, for instance, Uber does not simply manage drivers. It manages riders, maps, pricing behavior, traffic flows, ratings, and demand patterns simultaneously. On a similar line of logic, Amazon coordinates, through interconnected algorithms, consumers, sellers, warehouse workers, logistics infrastructures, and recommendation systems. YouTube manages creators through recommendation algorithms, monetization incentives, demonetization risks, and visibility metrics. TikTok shapes behavior not through direct commands but through algorithmic visibility, virality incentives, and engagement optimization.

By extending management beyond organizational boundaries, these systems substantially transform the context and content of work. By their structural configurations, algorithmic management systems risk narrowing the contextual dimensions of work (Konjen, 2025). This narrowing operates through structured and multi-layered mechanisms of control which include directing, evaluating, and disciplining to effectively automate or restrict traditional human interaction (Kellogg et al., 2020; Neves et al., 2021). As these decision infrastructures expand, they change the very topology of the organization, turning public streets, private homes, and digital interfaces into a distributed, continuous factory floor, leading to a "*complex entanglement of information flows, practices and users*" (Stark & Vanden Broeck, 2024).

This macro-structural shift reconfigures the daily experienced lives of individuals in these distributed spaces. From a micro-organizational perspective, research examining the effects on employees has emphasized the implications of classical job stress models such as job-demand-control-support and effort-reward imbalance. These frameworks explain the psychological mechanisms through which algorithmic management creates consequences (*i.e.* degrades) for individual wellbeing and work quality dimensions, including workload, income insecurity, task significance, schedule stability, socioemotional rewards, interpersonal rewards, decision authority, and organizational trust (Vignola et al., 2023).

This psychological strain is tied to a broader loss of worker sovereignty over their own labor. When human labor is stripped of its qualitative context only to be viewed through automated metrics, it triggers a form of epistemic degradation whereby workers lose the capacity to meaningfully contest or participate in workplace governance (Turner, 2025). Such an algorithmic drive for quantified efficiency fundamentally collides with the core prerequisites for meaningful work as it creates profound power asymmetries and diminishes employee autonomy, socioemotional rewards, and institutional trust (García-Ruiz & Rocchi, 2026; Vignola et al., 2023).

Ethical Residue: Managing the Gap Between Metrics and Care

Algorithms are defined as an automated set of rules for sorting data, and algorithmic decision-making refers to automated decision-making based on predefined rules and/or goals (Lindebaum et al., 2020). This practical definition might conceal the sociopolitical implications of the rise of algorithms across life domains. As technologies are not neutral and purely objective innovations, there is always an ethical downside that reveals in short, medium, and long run. Ethics of algorithms is a multidimensional problem area. Algorithms and their widespread use are associated with various ethical concerns, including normative and epistemic aspects. Among them are the emergence of inconclusive evidence (seeing patterns where there are none), inscrutable evidence (related with a lack of transparency), misguided evidence (due to algorithmic bias), unfair outcomes, transformative effects that are creating challenges for autonomy and privacy, and traceability concerns (Tsamados et al., 2022).

From a historical perspective, algorithmic management might be said to have its antecedents in Frederick Taylor's scientific management (Singh & Gupta, 2025). During the late 19th and early 20th century when management science was being institutionalized, Taylor used physical tools to regulate and optimize manual labor. Today, we are living through an ecosystemic shift where algorithms are using data to measure labor. While some researchers view algocracy as Digital Taylorism 2.0, others claim algocracies cannot be reduced to localized surveillance only (Stark & Vanden Broeck, 2024). These debates aside, what remains the same is the pursuit for maximum efficiency through the reduction of worker discretion. The early scientific management practices created ethical problems related with regulating the physical bodies and movements of workers whereas the modern management ideology raise ethical concerns related with governing the minds, psychological states, emotions, and identities of workers. Taylor's model relied on a human foreman to control others. Today's algorithmic models utilize software and AI agents that operate without empathy or the ability to grant exceptions in order to exercise control. This evolution from early scientific management period to late algorithmic management era is reminiscent of the rationalization process in Western society as described by the sociologist Max Weber. Within this vast architecture, acknowledging ethical residue makes it structurally harder to defer systemic failures to an objective machine, returning human accountability to view.

Max Weber famously warned of the iron cage of bureaucracy where human beings are trapped in a calculable world and reduced to 'specialty without spirit, sensualism without heart' (Mokoagow et al., 2026). This iron cage is an experience that has also been carried onto the digital sphere today. The algorithm is the new filing clerk, only without any regard for the people on both ends of the transaction. The Weberian ideal-typical bureaucracy, which is characterized by rationality, demand for efficiency, formal hierarchy, functional specialization, impersonality, and technical competence remains relevant for today's organizations, with modifications dictated by digitalization. A university professor for example, may be committed to fostering intellectual curiosity as a core educational value, yet the algorithmic performance system may prioritize student satisfaction scores and completion rates over meaningful engagement. A judge committed to justice as a moral ideal might be intimidated by the newly adopted algorithmic risk assessment tool that might be subverting individualized judicial judgment in favor of statistical prediction. A physician might treat the welfare of a patient as a supreme value, yet algorithms in protocol form could place priorities in billing episodes versus clinical judgment. This tension between a person's calling and the organization's metrics leads to a disenchantment of professional work, where the intrinsic meaning of a vocation is hollowed-out by the demand for auditable data (García-Ruiz & Rocchi, 2026). Similar challenges are becoming everyday experience across sectors to create quandaries for decision-makers and feelings of disappointment, disillusionment and alienation for workers.

Combined, the increasingly digitalized pressure for efficiency, quantification, close monitoring and surveillance, metric-dependence, emphasis on numbers rather than meaning result in a remainder that I would like to name "ethical residue". Ethical residue highlights where numbers fail us. Algorithms ingest massive data streams far beyond human capability, acting with cold efficiency. Balancing such mechanical strength against nuanced human insight creates a friction that defies simple resolution. Previously, Epstein and Hamric (2009) defined moral residue as "*the accumulation of persisting moral distress from repeated exposure to morally stressful situations*". Following their footsteps, I wanted to conceptualize ethical residue as unrecognized labor, including the acts of kindness that stabilize a team, moments of integrity when someone chooses the hard right over the easy wrong, forms of relational support that make collective work possible and informal acts of support that humanizes the work atmosphere. These qualities are situational and context-dependent, and their meaning cannot be predetermined without losing what makes them valuable. From this perspective, ethical residue is the gap between rigid metrics and the lived experience of value. The ethical residue also includes all the quiet helping moments that enable another person's work to continue. They penetrate the informal organization and affects the working atmosphere, which is otherwise radically competitive. On occasions, managers consider them for their discretionary decisions. They rarely feature in structured data, however. Attempts to capture them in the form of simplified indicators are fraught with the risk of turning them into something else. Attempting to rank the kindness of people on a numerical scale can open up the entire system to outlying influences, performative behavior and unkind people trying to game the system. When organizations ignore this residue, they risk creating a culture where care and judgment are discouraged because these aspects are invisible to the system. Viewed from this perspective, ethical residue is less a problem to be dispelled than a condition to be recognized.

Traditional ethics of care remind us that moral existence stays rooted in relationships (Tronto, 1993; Held, 2005). Responsiveness requires situational awareness rather than static rules. Situations demand judgment. Actually, organizational life often forces workers to suppress real empathy. Hochschild (1983) identified emotional labor decades ago, noting how feeling remains a quiet, often invisible job requirement. Modern algorithmic management shifts this burden further, favoring data points over the subtle, human labor that keeps systems functioning. Kellogg and colleagues (2020) argue these systems prioritize what is easily tracked, sidelining anything that defies convenient categorization. Ethical residue sits directly at the intersection where quantification meets genuine care. It occupies the quiet space where moral considerations persist, even when they lack formal representation in a spreadsheet. Dismissing this gap does not erase its weight. Unrecognized values continue to crawl under the surface, quietly molding organizational culture from within. When workplaces fail to support ethical judgment, they risk draining the empathy required for long-term health. These ignored fragments of labor do not vanish simply because they remain unmeasured. They linger, creating an uneven distribution of burden that ultimately impacts everyone involved. It is difficult to navigate this tension, but acknowledging the residue remains a vital step toward building a more honest, human-centered framework for our everyday working lives.

Managing ethical residue remains difficult because adding more variables rarely solves the actual problem. Relying solely on cold data strips away the human context needed for complex decisions. Organizations consistently attempt to quantify all facets of labor, but that approach ignores significant gaps in logic. Treating algorithmic outputs as inputs for broader human judgment creates necessary space for qualitative feedback. Narrative evaluations, peer reflections, and case-based discussions act as vital supplements to standard numerical indicators. Instead of blindly assuming fairness exists within a system, teams should actively question what the data lacks. Efficiency is important, sure, but it is not the only metric for success. Recognizing that complexity exists prevents us from blindly trusting automated logic. To top it all, there is the question of accountability. When decisions are heavily shaped by algorithms, it can become unclear who is responsible for what. Acknowledging ethical residue makes it harder to defer responsibility to the system. It brings human judgment back into view, not as a source of bias to be eliminated, but as a necessary component of organizational life. That is why we need to talk about responsibility.

THE ACCOUNTABILITY DEFICIT AND RESPONSIBILITY GAP

Management practices are undergoing a radical shift due to the growing presence of intelligence systems in organizations. As a result of this emergent organizational experience, the negative effects of algorithmic management in work contexts is a growing topic of interest to researchers and there is a lot of work in progress regarding the impact of algorithmic monitoring on individual and organizational outcomes.

One of the most pressing ethical challenges of algorithmic systems is the so-called responsibility gap or whether there is responsibility for harmful outcomes involving AI systems (Kasar, 2025). This occurs when a system causes harm, such as a biased hiring decision or an accident involving an autonomous vehicle, but no single human agent appears to meet the conditions of knowledge and control required for accountability. Some scholars argue that we should not view this as a total gap but as a modifier of responsibility whereby designers and users of those systems should bear a normative residue. This means that agents or institutions who design such systems have an ongoing duty to offer explanations, apologies, or compensation when a system they deployed causes unintended harm and accept blame. However, our social and organizational theories, legal systems and social contracts are not ready for this technological revolution, and we are in the midst of a cultural lag.

Organizations often try to address the responsibility gap challenges by providing more transparency (Coron & Porcher, 2026). There are instances when more transparency is the only or the best way to address the gap. To make these systems more acceptable and aligned with expectations of justice, organizations sometimes anthropomorphize them by giving them human names, gendered voices, or avatars (Fousiani et al., 2026). While this can make an algorithmic manager seem less rigid and more relatable, it also raises ethical concerns about potential for deception. If a worker believes a system has empathy or discretion when it is actually just following a script, they may develop unrealistic expectations that undermine accountability. Whereas anthropomorphizing helps alleviate the negative effects of algorithmic rigidity, there is also the risk of excessive amounts of it obscuring the boundaries between organic versus synthetic experiences. That is why there is a need for legal and ethical arrangements for ensuring that individuals are fully informed about the nature of their algorithmic interlocutors. However, it is not a magical formula as the next argument demonstrates.

Indeed, algorithmic governance literature has championed transparency as a dominant paradigm, as if more transparency will automatically translate into better decisions, greater overall well-being and more humane outcomes, overlooking users' experience of a transparency overload. Contrary to this perspective, technical explanations can paradoxically erode trust and create consent fatigue when they are too complex for a person to process (Čvokić, 2025). Excessive disclosure can actually reduce a person's ability to know when they should override an algorithm's advice. This is because of violation of certain cognitive thresholds and the resulting overload. Instead of absolute transparency, researchers propose context-dependent transparency, where information is layered and simplified to support a person's genuine understanding rather than overwhelming them with data.

The responsibility gap comes with moral implications. According to moral disengagement theory (Bandura et al., 1996; Barsky, 2011), morality is not a fixed trait. Individuals change their moral stance and criteria based on circumstances, and external stimuli trigger different attitudes. Moreover, individuals need to morally justify their actions by laying responsibility for their unethical or morally ambiguous behavior elsewhere. This ensures a sense of disengagement from one's actions and eliminates feelings of guilt. Cognitive mechanisms such as moral justification, euphemistic labeling, advantageous comparisons, diffusion and displacement of responsibility, dehumanization, disregard for outcomes, and attribution of blame help people deny and reconstruct their behavior from a self-righteous perspective (Gao et al., 2025). Algorithmic management systems enable moral disengagement when and if the outcomes of data-driven decisions cause harm, perpetuate inequality, promote biased selection, objectified discrimination, or violation of individual rights such as privacy. From an employee perspective, research has found that gig workers might find it more convenient and justified to engage in unethical behaviors when they are monitored through algorithmic management systems and especially so when they perceive these systems to be inducing unfair pressure, negative feelings, and stress. As such, algorithmic management might act as an external stimulus triggering negative attitudes which is morally justified through displacement of responsibility back at algorithms. At this conjuncture, there is an unethical behavior and violation of social norms on the table, while there is no feelings of guilt, responsibility, and moral sanctions. At the intersection of algocracy, ethical residue and responsibility gap, one of the biggest casualties might be the experience of meaningful work.

ALGORITHMIC MEANINGFULNESS AND POSSIBILITY OF MEANINGFUL WORK IN A WORLD OF ALGOCRACY

Let us first take a look at what meaningful work means. Meaningful work has been a topic of interest for scholars and philosophers for decades (Alderfer, 1972; Maslow, 1965) as meaningfulness is a fundamental human need. Its absence has been associated with detrimental outcomes such as suicidal ideation, and alienation (Allan et al., 2019). Despite contentions about its conceptualization, meaningfulness is generally accepted to be a multidimensional construct and a positive subjective experience, incorporating both the self (in the form of self-actualization) and others (in the form of serving others' needs) (Lepisto & Pratt, 2016; Lips-Wiersma & Wright, 2012). Meaningfulness has been considered a positive construct, in direct opposition to alienation. In a similar line of reasoning, meaningful work has been defined as work that is personally enriching and that makes a positive contribution. Everyone attaches a different "meaning" to their work, be it a means of making ends meet, status, game, career, calling, etc. However, meaningfulness of one's work implies an evaluative judgment about how significant the experience of work is for someone, with an emotional as well as a cognitive component (Martela & Pessi, 2018). Meaningful work is commonly defined as work experienced as personally significant, purposeful, and contributing to the greater good (Rosso et al., 2010; Steger et al., 2012). The idea of meaningful work captures the existential alignment between one's self-concept and one's occupational role (Pratt & Ashforth, 2003). A multidimensional conceptualization of meaningful work implies that there are multiple sources of meaningfulness instead of a single or few causes.

There has been a substantial interest from management scholars in meaningful work as it has been linked to employee well-being, motivation, and organizational functioning, and positive work-related outcomes at individual and organizational levels (Lips-Wiersma & Wright, 2012). Theorists have identified several dimensions of meaningful work, including positive meaning, meaning-making through work, and the motivation to contribute beyond the self as well as broader thematic pathways such as authenticity, unity, and service (Lips-Wiersma & Morris, 2009) and self-connection, contribution, unification, and individuation (Rosso et al., 2010). A comprehensive measure of meaningful work identified four subdimensions, including "unity with others," "developing the inner self," "serving others," and "expressing full potential" (Lips-Wiersma & Wright, 2012). A comprehensive review of the literature looking for a definitive meaning of "work meaningfulness" (Martela & Pessi, 2018) identified three common elements that have been emphasized in 36 separate definitions of work meaningfulness: significance, broader purpose, and self-realization. Significance refers to the intrinsic value embedded in one's work-related activities, and the degree of significance assigned to one's work contributes to answering the existential question of "why" one continues engage in such work, beyond instrumental necessity. Broader purpose is connected to the idea of doing something larger than those serving one's individual benefits and contributing to the society. Last but not the least, self-realization is the feeling of connectedness between oneself and work, which is the opposite of feelings of alienation from work that arises when individuals cannot express themselves or exert control on aspects of their work. A meaningful work provides opportunities for growth and facilitate individuals to realize their full potential (Martela & Pessi, 2018).

Empirical evidence demonstrates that meaningful work is positively associated with life satisfaction, work engagement, organizational commitment, and ethical behavior, while it is negatively associated with burnout and turnover intention (Allan et al., 2019). Several outcome variables have also been associated with meaningful work, including work-related, performance-related, and individual outcomes that include but are not limited to higher levels of engagement, job satisfaction, life satisfaction, commitment, creativity, knowledge sharing, and lower intentions to quit (Allan et al, 2015; Allan et al, 2019). Additionally, the experience of meaningful work has been theoretically grounded in several foundational frameworks that explain why individuals perceive their work as purposeful and significant. Researchers have utilized i) job characteristics theory as a framework to conceptualize the effects of meaningful work on work-related outcomes as well as ii) self-determination theory to explain that people perceive their work to be significant and valuable when it provides them with enhanced autonomy, competence, and relatedness (Bailey et al., 2018). Work has also been associated with greater meaningfulness from an identity theory perspective, particularly when it aligned with one's self concept (Pratt & Ashforth, 2003). A variety of factors including job design and management style as well as factors such as autonomy and task significance, leadership styles and organizational justice climate have been identified as key antecedents of meaningful job experiences (Rosso et al., 2010). Job characteristics such as work-role fit and job enrichment have been found to contribute to enhanced meaningfulness; leadership styles such as transformational leadership and leader-member exchange have been found to correlate with higher perceived meaningfulness; organizational and workplace related factors such as a supportive culture and positive workplace climate have also been found to increase employees' sense of meaningfulness (Lozovetska et al., 2024). Algorithms have been transforming many of the factors shaping meaningfulness perceptions.

The sociological imagination has always recognized that work is not merely an economic transaction but a site of identity formation, moral development, and social belonging. Despite the constraints of the digitized iron cage, workers are not passive cogs in the system. Algorithmic management does not abolish human dimensions of organizational life. It displaces them into the informal, the invisible, and the contested. Yet, the need for meaningful work experiences persists. Meaningful work is not only a desirable individual experience but also a strategic organizational asset that enhances both human sustainability and long-term organizational performance. From a *MacIntyrean perspective*, work achieves meaningfulness when it is structured as a cooperative human activity that allows for the pursuit of internal goods and standards of excellence (García-Ruiz & Rocchi, 2026). Algorithmic systems threaten these practices by causing "deskilling" and "fragmentation", leading workers to care more about their ratings and rankings than the actual quality of their craft. In response, employees often engage in strategies of resistance to reclaim their autonomy. Platform drivers, for instance, play "work games" to circumvent algorithmic control, selectively accepting tasks or manipulating data to ensure financial stability. Middle managers also play a critical role as algorithmic middlemen. As documented in empirical assessments of highly surveilled fulfillment centers, these managers often engage in infrapolitical acts, such as data bending or reinterpreting metrics to protect their teams from the most punitive dimensions of the algorithmic architecture (Miszczynski et al., 2026). These managers provide affective buffering, softening the impact of cold algorithmic decisions to maintain the well-being of their workforce.

These acts of resistance show that human agency persists even in the most automated environments. Workers who have lost formal authority over how their work is structured have not, as a rule, lost the desire for meaning. They pursue it through the informal relationships, private negotiations, and small acts of creative refusal that infrapolitics describes. The platform driver who maintains a conversation with a passenger in defiance of the algorithmic script that would have him silent. The warehouse worker who assists a struggling colleague in ways that do not appear in any performance record. The middle manager who writes a narrative note alongside a numeric rating to ensure that the algorithm's output is interpreted in context. These acts do not dismantle algorithmic power. But they maintain, at the margins, the human dimensions of work that make it bearable and, occasionally, meaningful. The loss of craft autonomy is further compounded by the loss of epistemic agency or the capacity to actively participate in and deliberate over values and beliefs that govern labor (Turner, 2025). When algorithms systematically curb this agency through opaque and hard-coded feedback loops, the workplace is stripped of the capacity to function as a moral community and environment that is amenable for human flourishment. Yet, we do not know if and how it will be possible to sustain meaningful work experiences in an age of algocracy and under conditions of algorithmic management. The challenge for the modern organization is to design infrastructures that support, rather than constrain moral engagement.

CONCLUSION: TOWARD HUMAN-CENTERED DECISION INFRASTRUCTURES

Uruguay's late former president Pepe Mujica once reportedly said, "There is no guarantee that an ambulance will be at your door in 30 minutes, but your pizza will arrive.", a saying that reflects the pathologies of contemporary (digital) bureaucracies.

Algorithmic decision-making research has been flourishing across different streams of research, including organizational management and theory, psychology, ethics theories as well as computational decision theory, and research on individual and organizational levels of analysis are on a rise (Wang, 2026). Considering this interest and given the fragmented nature of existing research, there is a need to set some ground rules before proceeding to discuss its nomological network in organizational or any other context. To begin with, algorithmic decision making is a not a unidimensional concept, rather it encompasses descriptive (historical narratives of what it is, how it developed, etc.), predictive (extrapolative inferences about future outcomes, behaviors, etc.), and prescriptive forms (autonomous selections, recommendations, etc.) in practice. As such, algorithms could be better understood as sociotechnical processes that emerge from the interaction of users and systems. Second, algorithmic decision-making systems have a huge potential for more robust, less biased, and smarter decision-making, albeit only in case of proper auditing. However, these systems also risk creating an autonomy paradox by simultaneously providing greater spatial flexibility to individuals on one hand and subjecting them to stricter monitoring and control on the other. Additionally, they bring back a new form of Taylorist exploitation to the table by deskilling, standardizing, quantifying, and measuring the contextual and previously unquantifiable aspects of individual or organizational behavior. Further into organizational algorithmic decision-making research, it becomes evident that algorithmic management has implications for organizational learning, human resource management practice and theory, established theories such as role theory, self-determination theory, actor-network theory, technology acceptance models, organizational trust, and organizational justice, as well as distribution of power, among others. These experiences lead to individual level outcomes such as an algorithm aversion, some newly emerging symptoms like AI derangement or feelings of a double bind between the extremes of dehumanization versus overt anthropomorphism (Burton et al., 2020).

The omnipresence of algorithmic decision systems and AI technologies are creating a huge potential for organizational contexts. In human resources, practices, and benefits such as automation, accuracy, real-time experience, personalization, computing power, storage capacity, etc. are enabling time and cost savings. Algorithmic decision making is also facilitating performance evaluation, resource allocation, strategic planning, and a more agile human resource management (Nawaz et al., 2024). The algorithmic management of work represents the most recent and most technically sophisticated iteration of an impulse that Frederick Taylor expressed with a stopwatch. That this impulse continues to generate resistance, ethical complexity, and organizational dysfunction is evidence that human beings are not, in the end, the kind of thing that can be fully managed.

Table 1 presents a summary configuration of the effects of transitioning from traditional human bureaucracy to an algocracy. Collectively, the emergent characteristics of algocracies destroy the capacity of the organization to function as a democratic moral community and eliminates opportunities for meaningful work experiences.

Table 1. What Does Algocracy Do to Work Meaningfulness

Core Meaningfulness Dimension	Algocratic Mechanism of Disruption	Lived Consequences for the Individual
Significance (The intrinsic value of activities answering "why" one works)	**Deskilling and Fragmentation**: Systems prioritize surface-level metrics, automated benchmarks, and throughput speeds	Driven to care more about their ratings, rankings, and dashboards than the actual quality of their craft
Self-Realization (Connectedness between self and work; opposite of alienation)	**The Autonomy Paradox**: Stricter monitoring and algorithmic surveillance under the camouflage of spatial flexibility	Experience feelings of privacy invasion, stress, disengagement, and an overall degradation of individual well-being
Broader Purpose & Unity with Others (Contributing to the greater good and social belonging)	**Commensuration and Datafication**: The translation of diverse forms of human contribution into quantifiable metrics	Informal acts of care, quiet generosity, and moments of integrity disappearing from formal evaluation, becoming "Ethical Residue"
Decision Authority & Expressing Potential (The capacity to express oneself and exercise control)	**Opaque & Hard-Coded Feedback Loops**: Authority is embedded directly into code and software interfaces, acting as a black box	Lose the capacity to meaningfully contest or participate in workplace governance, stripping the workplace of its status as a moral community

The concept of ethical residue argues that not everything important about human contribution is measurable. Whatever a given system measures, something morally significant will remain outside its frame, and that organizations will be healthier and more just to the extent that they acknowledge this remainder rather than proceeding as though it does not exist. The responsibility gap generated by algorithmic decision-making, the moral disengagement it enables, the transparency paradoxes it creates, and the infrapolitical resistance it provokes are all downstream consequences of institutions that have mistaken the map for the territory.

To address the ethical residue of quantification, we must move beyond the idea that algorithms can replace human judgment. There have been various attempts to integrate AI methodologies to enhance decision making across various settings. For one, the Hybrid Ethical Decision Model (HEDM) proposes that algorithms should be treated as epistemic instruments, tools for gathering facts and probabilities while normative authority must remain with human beings (Ilie, 2026). This ensures that decisions affecting human rights and dignity are always subject to deliberative checkpoints and context-sensitive review. In the highly sensitive clinical decision-making settings, there has been various attempts like the Bioethics Artificial Intelligence Advisory (BAIA) framework (Dutta Roy, 2025), which suggests using mattering maps and narrative ethics to integrate an individual's story and perspective into the decision-making process. This allows organizations to supplement data-driven decisions with the human context required to assess social and moral implications. Ultimately, the goal is to build moral communities where technology enhances human capacity rather than substituting it. In organizational settings, ethical leadership remains the most critical lever in this transition (Caldeira & Infante-Moro, 2025), as leaders who embody integrity and fairness foster the commitment necessary to maintain a human-centered workplace.

Algorithmic decision-making will continue to expand across organizational contexts. Its potential for more robust decision-making is genuine. Its risks, including the autonomy paradox, the new forms of exploitation, organizational justice, moral agency, and accountability are equally real. I would like to conclude this chapter by posing a question that has become personally significant to me as a researcher working in an algorithmic age in which the very experience of meaningfulness appears increasingly fragile: What would it mean to take ethical residue seriously as an organizational problem rather than dismissing it as a measurement gap to be eventually closed by better technology? It would mean, first of all, acknowledging that the legitimacy of algorithmic governance depends not on the creation of moral machines but on the maintenance of institutional arrangements in which human beings remain accountable for the outcomes of the systems they deploy. That also means maintaining the human oversight that algorithmic systems cannot supply for themselves, and creating institutional conditions in which meaningful work remains possible even as the forms it takes continue to change. And it means taking seriously, as both an ethical and an organizational matter, the dimensions of human contribution that will always exceed the reach of any system designed to count them. By recognizing the limits of quantification and valuing the unmeasurable, we can ensure that the digitized workplace remains a space for dignity and meaningful contribution. The management of workplace ethics in the age of algorithms requires a sophisticated balance between technological precision and human moral imagination. That is the reason why we must design decision infrastructures that remain sensitive to what they cannot capture.

REFERENCES

Alderfer, C. (1972). *Existence, relatedness and growth: Human needs in organizational settings*. Free Press.

Allan, B.A., Batz-Barbarich, C., Sterling, H. M., & Tay, L. (2019). Outcomes of Meaningful Work: A Meta-Analysis. Journal of Management Studies, Special Issue: Meaningful Work: Prospects for the 21st Century, 56(3), 500-528. https://doi.org/ DOI: 10.1111/joms.12406

Allan, B. A., Duffy, R. D., & Douglass, R. (2015). Meaning in life and work: A developmental perspective. *The Journal of Positive Psychology*, *10*(4), 323–331. DOI: 10.1080/17439760.2014.950180

Aneesh, A. (2009). Global Labor: Algocratic Modes of Organization. *Sociological Theory*, *27*(4), 347–370. DOI: 10.1111/j.1467-9558.2009.01352.x

Bailey, C., Yeoman, R., Madden, A., Thompson, M., & Kerridge, G. (2018). A Review of the Empirical Literature on Meaningful Work: Progress and Research Agenda. Human Resource Development Review, 18(1), 83-113. (Original work published 2019)DOI: 10.1177/1534484318804653

Bandura, A., Barbaranelli, C., Caprara, G. V., & Pastorelli, C. (1996). Mechanisms of moral disengagement in the exercise of moral agency. *Journal of Personality and Social Psychology*, *71*(2), 364–374. DOI: 10.1037/0022-3514.71.2.364

Barsky, A. (2011). Investigating the effects of moral disengagement and participation on unethical work behavior. *Journal of Business Ethics*, *104*(1), 59–75. DOI: 10.1007/s10551-011-0889-7

Boos, A. K. (2024). Conceptualizing automated decision-making in organizational contexts. *Philosophy & Technology*, *37*(3), 1–30. DOI: 10.1007/s13347-024-00773-5 PMID: 39027378

Caldeira, R., & Infante-Moro, A. (2025). The importance of ethics in organisations, their leaders, and sustainability. *Administrative Sciences*, *15*(9), 372. DOI: 10.3390/admsci15090372

Coron, C., & Porcher, S. (2026). Ethical considerations in algorithm construction: Evidence from two human-resources algorithms. M@n@gement,, 29(1), 7-20. DOI: 10.37725/mgmt.2025.9830

Čvokić, D. D. (2025). The unintended consequences of algorithmic transparency on trust: A multi-disciplinary analysis. *Acta Scientifica Balcanica*, *6*(1), 22–40. DOI: 10.63356/asb.2025.002

Di Maggio, M., Ratnadiwakara, D., & Carmichael, D. (2021). Invisible Primes: Fintech Lending with Alternative Data. Harvard Business School Working Paper, No. 22-024.

Dutta Roy, T. P. (2025). Bioethics artificial intelligence advisory (BAIA): An agentic artificial intelligence (AI) framework for bioethical clinical decision support. *Cureus*, *17*(3), e80494. DOI: 10.7759/cureus.80494 PMID: 40083589

Epstein, E. G., & Hamric, A. B. (2009). Moral distress, moral residue, and the crescendo effect. *The Journal of Clinical Ethics*, *20*(4), 330–342. DOI: 10.1086/JCE200920406 PMID: 20120853

Espeland, W. N., & Stevens, M. L. (1998). Commensuration as a social process. *Annual Review of Sociology*, *24*(1), 313–343. DOI: 10.1146/annurev.soc.24.1.313

Forster, E. M. (1909). The Machine Stops. In The Eternal Moment and Other Stories. Sidgwick & Jackson. Available at chrome-extension://efaidnbmnnnibpcajpcglclefindmkaj/https://www.cs.ucdavis.edu/~koehl/Teaching/ECS188/PDF_files/Machine_stops.pdf

Fousiani, K., Cremer, L. R., Çetin, M., & Raeder, S. (2026). When algorithmic managers fail to fulfill their promises: The role of anthropomorphism in shaping justice perceptions. *PLoS One*, *21*(2), e0340860. DOI: 10.1371/journal.pone.0340860 PMID: 41719274

Gao, S., Jia, Y., Liu, B., & Mu, W. (2025). Algorithmic monitoring increases unethical behavior in gig workers: The mediating role of moral disengagement. *Information Technology & People*, *38*(6), 2506–2530. DOI: 10.1108/ITP-07-2023-0693

García-Ruiz, P., & Rocchi, M. (2026). Can work be meaningful under algorithmic management? A MacIntyrean perspective. *Business Ethics Quarterly*, *36*(1), 3–30. DOI: 10.1017/beq.2025.5

Held, V. (2005). *The ethics of care: Personal, political, and global.* Oxford University Press. DOI: 10.1093/0195180992.001.0001

Hochschild, A. R. (1983). *The managed heart: Commercialization of human feeling.* University of California Press.

Ilie, A.-C. (2026). Human ethics vs. algorithmic ethics: The limits of automating moral decision-making. *Theoretical and Applied Economics*, *33*(1), 219–240.

Just, N., & Latzer, M. (2016). Governance by Algorithms: Reality Construction by Algorithmic Selection on the Internet (2017). Media, Culture & Society, 39(2), 238-258; , Available at *SSRN*: https://ssrn.com/abstract=3871903DOI: 10.1177/0163443716643157

Kasar, P. (2025). There is a problem, but not a responsibility gap. *Ethics and Information Technology*, *27*(4), 1–11. DOI: 10.1007/s10676-025-09851-4

Kellogg, K. C., Valentine, M. A., & Christin, A. (2020). Algorithms at work: The new contested terrain of control. *The Academy of Management Annals*, *14*(1), 366–410. DOI: 10.5465/annals.2018.0174

Konjen, H. (2025). Algorithmic management and the future of human work: Implications for autonomy, collaboration, and innovation (No. arXiv:2511.14231v1). arXiv.

Langenbucher, K., & Corcoran, P. (2021). Responsible AI Credit Scoring – A Lesson from Upstart.com. In Avgouleas, E., & Marjosola, H. (Eds.), *Digital Finance in Europe: Law, Regulation, and Governance*. De Gruyter., DOI: 10.1515/9783110749472-006

Latour, B. (2005). *Reassembling the Social: An Introduction to Actor-Network-Theory*. Oxford University Press. DOI: 10.1093/oso/9780199256044.001.0001

Lehdonvirta, V. (2018). Flexibility in the gig economy: Managing time on three online piecework platforms. *New Technology, Work and Employment*, *33*(1), 13–29. DOI: 10.1111/ntwe.12102

Lepisto, D. A., & Pratt, M. G. (2016). Meaningful work as realization and justification: Toward a dual conceptualization. Organizational Psychology Review, 7(2), 99-121. (Original work published 2017).DOI: 10.1177/2041386616630039

Lindebaum, D., Vesa, M., & Courpasson, D. (2020). Insights from 'the machine stops' to better understand rational assumptions in algorithmic decision-making and its implications for organizations. *Academy of Management Review*, *45*(1), 247–260. DOI: 10.5465/amr.2018.0181

Lips-Wiersma, M., & Morris, L. (2009). Discriminating between 'meaningful work' and the 'management of meaning'. *Journal of Business Ethics*, *88*(3), 491–511. DOI: 10.1007/s10551-009-0118-9

Lips-Wiersma, M., & Wright, S. (2012). Measuring the meaning of meaningful work: Development and validation of the Comprehensive Meaningful Work Scale (CMWS). *Group & Organization Management*, *37*(5), 655–685. DOI: 10.1177/1059601112461578

Lozovetska, V., Pavlov, Y., & Fedorenko, L. (2024). Meaningful work literature meta-review. Multidisciplinary Science Journal, 6, 2024ss0740. DOI: 10.31893/multiscience.2024ss0740

Martela, F., & Pessi, A. B. (2018). Significant work is about self-realization and broader purpose: Defining the key dimensions of meaningful work. *Frontiers in Psychology*, *9*, 363. Advance online publication. DOI: 10.3389/fpsyg.2018.00363 PMID: 29632502

Maslow, A. H. (1965). Humanistic science and transcendent experiences. *Journal of Humanistic Psychology*, *5*(2), 219–227. DOI: 10.1177/002216786500500211

Mateescu, A., & Nguyen, A. (2019). Explainer: Algorithmic management in the workplace. Data & Society Research Institute. Available at https://datasociety.net/wp-content/uploads/2019/02/DS_Algorithmic_Management_Explainer.pdf?utm_source=chatgpt.com

Milanez, A., Lemmens, A., & Ruggiu, C. (2025). Algorithmic management in the workplace: New evidence from an OECD employer survey. OECD ARTIFICIAL INTELLIGENCE PAPERS February 2025 No. 31. Available at https://www.oecd.org/content/dam/oecd/en/publications/reports/2025/02/algorithmic-management-in-the-workplace_3c84ed6d/287c13c4-en.pdf

Miszczynski, M., Pieczka, A., & Klimek, J. (2026). The algorithm's middlemen: Resistance, compliance and managerial contradictions in Amazon's warehouses in Poland. Critical Perspectives on International Business, ahead-of-print. DOI: 10.1108/cpoib-05-2025-0109

Mokoagow, M. S., Sukmana, O., & Yumitro, G., & Nurudin. (2026). Max Weber's social action and rationality: An analysis of bureaucracy and rationalization processes in modern organizations. International Journal of Economics. *Management and Social Science*, *9*(1), 1–20.

Neves, I. B. S., Vianna, F. R. P. M., & Sutil, B. N. (2021). Algocracy: A critical analysis on management mediated by algorithms. Contextus - Revista Contemporânea de Economia e Gestão, 19, 246-256. DOI: 10.19094/contextus.2021.67949

Porter, T. M. (1995). *Trust in numbers: The pursuit of objectivity in science and public life*. Princeton University Press.

Pratt, M. G., & Ashforth, B. E. (2003). Fostering Meaningfulness in Working and at Work. In Cameron, K. S., Dutton, J. E., & Quinn, R. E. (Eds.), *Positive Organizational Scholarship: Foundations of a New Discipline* (pp. 309–327). Berret-Koehler.

Rifkin, J. (1995). *The End of Work: The Decline of the Global Labor Force and the Dawn of the Post-Market Era*. G. P. Putnam's Sons.

Rosenblat, A., & Stark, L. (2016) Algorithmic Labor and Information Asymmetries: A Case Study of Uber's Drivers International Journal of Communication, 10, 27. Available at *SSRN*: https://ssrn.com/abstract=2686227 or DOI: 10.2139/ssrn.2686227

Rosso, B. D., Dekas, K. H., & Wrzesniewski, A. (2010). On the Meaning of Work: A Theoretical Integration and Review. *Research in Organizational Behavior*, *30*, 91–127. DOI: 10.1016/j.riob.2010.09.001

Singh, V. K., & Gupta, R. (2025). From Taylorism to algorithmic management: How technological evolution reshapes foundational management principles. International Journal of Latest Technology in Engineering, Management &. *Applied Sciences (Basel, Switzerland)*, *14*(8), 1–15. DOI: 10.51583/IJLTEMAS.2025.1408000206

Stark, D., & Vanden Broeck, P. (2024). Principles of algorithmic management. *Organization Theory*, *5*(2), 1–24. DOI: 10.1177/26317877241257213

Steger, M. F., Dik, B. J., & Duffy, R. D. (2012). Measuring Meaningful Work: The Work and Meaning Inventory (WAMI). *Journal of Career Assessment*, *20*(3), 322–337. DOI: 10.1177/1069072711436160

Tronto, J. C. (1993). *Moral boundaries: A political argument for an ethic of care*. Routledge.

Tsamados, A., Aggarwal, N., Cowls, J., Morley, J., Roberts, H., Taddeo, M., & Floridi, L. (2022). The ethics of algorithms: Key problems and solutions. *AI & Society*, *37*(1), 215–230. DOI: 10.1007/s00146-021-01154-8

Turner, B. (2025). Workplace democracy, algorithmic management, and epistemic agency. *Critical Review of International Social and Political Philosophy*, •••, 1–25. DOI: 10.1080/13698230.2025.2588074

Vignola, E. F., Baron, S., Abreu Plasencia, E., Hussein, M., & Cohen, N. (2023). Workers' Health under Algorithmic Management: Emerging Findings and Urgent Research Questions. *International Journal of Environmental Research and Public Health*, *20*(2), 1239. DOI: 10.3390/ijerph20021239 PMID: 36673989

Wang, Y. (2026). Algorithmic decision-making in organizations: A systematic review toward an integrated tension alignment framework. *Organizational Management Journal*, *23*(1), 115–131. DOI: 10.1108/OMJ-11-2024-2342

Wiggin, T. (2025). Weaponizing the Workplace: How Algorithmic Management Shaped Amazon's Antiunion Campaign in Bessemer, Alabama. *Socius: Sociological Research for a Dynamic World*, *11*, 11. DOI: 10.1177/23780231251318389

Zeng, J., & Kaye, D. B. V. (2022). From content moderation to visibility moderation: A case study of platform governance on TikTok. *Policy and Internet*, *14*(1), 79–95. DOI: 10.1002/poi3.287

Zuboff, S. (2019). *The age of surveillance capitalism: the fight for a human future at the new frontier of power*. PublicAffairs.

Chapter 9
Ethics, Privacy, and Governance in AI-Enabled Information Systems:
Measuring Productivity

Gautam Shivaraj
http://orcid.org/0009-0000-5184-8448
Adarsh Institute of Management and Information Technology, Chamarajpet, India

ABSTRACT

The integration of artificial intelligence (AI) into organizational information systems (IS) has fundamentally altered the landscape of workplace productivity, decision-making, and data governance. While AI-enabled IS offer unprecedented capabilities for automating complex tasks, augmenting human cognition, and accelerating information flows, they simultaneously introduce profound ethical, privacy, and governance challenges that cannot be resolved through purely technical solutions. This chapter explores the confluence of these dimensions, arguing that sustainable productivity in AI-enabled environments must be defined and measured through an ethical lens. It develops a comprehensive framework for understanding how ethical principles, privacy regulations, and governance architectures interact with productivity outcomes in modern organizations.

DOI: 10.4018/979-8-2600-0111-0.ch009

1. INTRODUCTION

It is not only the kind of technology the organization embraces, but more the values it instills in that technology that define the twenty-first century organization. The last ten years have seen artificial intelligence coming out of the periphery of organizational life and taking the center stage of organizational life. Nowadays machine learning models help in the process of hiring, customer segmentation, financial risk scoring, medical diagnosis, and even evaluation of the employee performance. Once seen as passive passive repositories of organized information, organizational information systems today have been redefined as dynamic, intelligent, entities that monitor, predict, recommend and in most cases, make decisions. There is an imperative that follows as a result of this transformation: how do we make sure that AI-enabled IS are used to the benefit of humankind instead of causing harm?(Zhang et al., 2026)

The productivity of AI-enhanced organizations is a question that is closely interwoven with this imperative. Historically, productivity has been a ratio of productivity in inputs and outputs of a product or organization - units of products produced per hour, decisions made per analyst, customer inquiries closed per agent. When AI is introduced in this calculus it seems that immediate benefits can be achieved: the calculus is faster, there is less error, it is always available and can be scaled. In fact, multiple empirical investigations in any industry will willingly indicate how much higher productivity will be in case of a well-considered implementation of the AI tools. But the mindless search of these benefits, freed of any moral argument, produces an alternative sort of loss, loss which is now being counted not in terms of hours of work done but in terms of trust, fair play, privacy and the human dignity. (Monteiro & Singh, 2025)

It is the thesis of this chapter that the productivity of AI application in the context of information systems is measured incompletely - and ultimately misinformed - through its consideration without reference to the ethical, privacy, and governance aspects of AI application. We hypothesize that organizations need to embrace an extended conception of productivity: one considering the caliber of decision making, the honesty of algorithmic outputs, security of personal data, security of employee wellbeing and fairness of governance frameworks. Not an idealistic trade off efficiency, this broadened perception which we call Ethical Productivity. Contrarily, through our demonstration we prove that organizations with solid ethics and governance systems are in a better place to enjoy long-lasting, scalable and stakeholder-supported productivity returns.(Saghafi & Angelopoulos, 2025)

This chapter has the following structure. Section 2 has a conceptual backing, revising the overlapping literature on AI ethics, privacy governance, and organizational productivity. Part 3 will discuss the main ethical dilemmas which are considered to be a result of embedding AI in information systems. Section 4 examines the idea of privacy as a governance requirement, tracing the regulatory environment, and how this impacts the design of ISs. Section 5, builds a typology of AI governance models suitable in the context of various organizations. Section 6 suggests an overall scheme of gauging the issue of productivity through an ethical perspective, such as the Ethical Productivity Index. The section 7 talks about the role of stakeholders, and organizational enablers. In Section 8, a roadmap on implementation is outlined. Section 9 ends by synthesizing what has been observed and to provide suggestions as to where to go next.(Tunca, 2026)

2. THEORETICAL UNDERPINNING: AI, ETHICS, PRIVACY AND PRODUCTIVITY.

2.1 The History of Information Systems in the Organization.

Organizational information systems have developed as a series of waves of technological advancement which have increased the scope of what is meant by managing, processing and acting on information. Transaction processing systems and management information systems were the first generation of IS to automate simple clerical tasks, and to generate well-structured reports to be used by middle management. The second-generation information processing systems (decision support systems, executive information systems and enterprise resource planning platforms) brought information processing down to, and including, strategic thinking. The third generation, which is currently underway, is marked by intelligent systems: platforms, which learn with data, adapt with circumstances and simulate, with the help of machine learning, natural language processing, computer vision, and reinforcement learning.(Autili et al., 2025)

The third generation radically changes the bond between people and the information systems. The nature of prior systems was a tool: they did what they were told to do and said what they were told to say. Agents Intelligent systems make consequential decisions; in automated pipelines, these decisions are made automatically, and the decisions are not reviewed by a human at each step. It is this, the agentic nature, which inherently makes them potent productivity instruments - and which makes them at the same time ethically consequential.

In productivity literature, tradition has been to gauge the effectiveness of IS using models like those of DeLone and McLean, where the models measure IS effectiveness based on factors such as system quality, information quality, use and net benefit. Not that these frameworks lack value, they are based on a world of passive systems and served the purpose of human decision-makers. With the new age of AI-savvy IS, the success measurement would need to incorporate the following new dimensions of quality fairness, explainability, keeping privacy intact, and accountability. A system which makes the best throughput and generates systematically biased results or infringes upon people's rights to privacy is not in any meaningful sense of the term successful.(Agbabiaka et al., 2025)

2.2 Ethics of the Artificial Intelligence.

The field of AI ethics has increased exponentially in response to high-visibility failures of AI systems: recruitment algorithms that prioritized women and racial minorities over other social groups, facial recognition algorithms with varying levels of discriminate between races, predictive policing algorithms that increased the likelihood of selected social groups experiencing over-policing, and social media recommendation systems that fostered extremist politics. The resulting uproar of ethical systems both academic and institutional, - from the four principles of AI ethics (beneficence, non-maleficence, autonomy, and justice) offered by Floridi, to the European Commission, and its reliable AI policy guidelines (human agency, robustness, privacy, transparency, diversity, societal wellbeing, and accountability) - has been followed by the NIST AI Risk Management Framework.(Evangelista & Salman Bukhari, 2026)

These frameworks have some points of divergence in regard to their use of emphasis and vocabulary but they overlap at a point that reflects a universal set of ethical dimensions that directly apply to design and measurement of AI-enabled IS. Fairness demands that AI systems be able to generate fair recommendations across a variety of people, and not solely aim at maximizing their overall output, without regard to the negative impacts on disadvantaged subgroups. Transparency requires that the reasoning behind the AI decisions be intelligible at least to individuals who have more than curiosity in the decision-making. Introduction Accountability requires identifiable human actors assume responsibility of the AI results and there should be remedial mechanisms in case of harms. Human control stipulates that the consequential decisions should not be beyond their human review and intervention. Non-maleficence requires designers and operators to predict and avoid harms, such as subtle harms like degradation of digital wellbeing and loss of cognitive autonomy. (Nayak & Jagadeeswari, 2026)

These principles find their reflection in the real design and governance needs in the context of organizational IS. The algorithm of hiring has to be demographically par with the algorithm on a regular basis. A performance monitoring system should have the ability to give a reason to the employees, on how their scores are calculated. A credit scoring provision by customer credit should be subject to revocation by a designated principal who could be in turn, paid so as to ensure compliance with the law. The clinical decision support system should also allow the physician to override its recommendations since it might interfere with the doctor. These requirements do not constitute some optional decorations of the IS design, but rather in the jurisdiction where AI regulation has reached maturity, they are legally enforceable requirements thereof.(Mehdi & Naz, 2025)

2.3 As a Foundational Value, Privacy.

Privacy takes a notably central role in the ethics of the AI-enabled IS, due to two aspects that are intertwined. To start with, AI systems are inherently data greedy: their performance tends to be proportional to the quantity and the type of training data, which in an organizational context is always related to or contains personal information about employees as well as customers, patients or citizens. Second, AI outputs, such as predictions, recommendations, classifications and decisions, often impact individuals in ways that are privacy-invasive despite the underlying carving of data processing as nominally legal. A predictive model of the probability of an employee to resign, e.g., may take the form of an entirely unaware employee receiving outputs which influence decisions impacting the career of the unaware employee.(Pesqueira et al., 2024)

The statutory framework that regulates data privacy in AI-enabled IS has evolved immensely hence becoming intricate worldwide regulatory or legislative setting. A groundbreaking rights-based approach to the processing of personal data, with its particular rules applicable in the case of automated decision-making, was established under the General Data Protection Regulation of the European Union which came into force in 2018. The Digital Personal Data Protection Act (2023) of India presented along with the consent and purpose limitation principles of consumer privacy laws, a duty of data fiduciaries that aligns with the commonly accepted principles of the Article 2 Directive of the European Union. Most of the sectors have added new levels of complexity through the introduction of their specific Personal Information Protection Law (2021) in China, the Consumer Privacy Act in California, the Lei Geral de Protecao dos Dados in Brazil, and an increasing number of industry-specific laws in health, finances, and education.(Díaz-Rodríguez et al., 2023)

This regulatory environment is a limitation and an opportunity to IS designers and governance professionals. The limitation is self-evident: in case of non-compliance, there is a great risk of legal and reputational damage. The less obvious, but equally significant resource is conformance to strong privacy models which are likely to lead to an IS that is more credible, more accepting and, as a result, more effective as productivity tools. Users with confidence in the ethicalness of their data handling tend to be more interested in using AI-driven tools, providing the correct data and adopting the suggestions provided by processors.(Jafarinezhad et al., 2026)

2.4 Governance being the Enabling architecture.

The form of government, the structures, processes, and norms that organizations use to exercise authority, make decisions and manage accountability is the form of government in which ethics and privacy are translated into operational practice. Good AI governance is not a sure way of ethical AI to emerge but lack of AI governance structures are virtually guaranteed to lead to ethical failures. A long history of AI implementation in organizations abounds with accounts of systemically harmful effects being realized through the work of individuals who are well intentioned, but tend to work in the margins of current organizational frameworks and structures.

The AI governance in the organizational IS covers a set of dimensions: strategic governance (board-level monitoring of AI strategy and risk), operational governance (procedures to follow to develop AI, to test it, to deploy it, and to monitor it), data governance (policies to follow to enhance AI quality, to establish its lineages, to control its access, and to retain it), model governance (version control, auditing bias, document explainability, monitoring performance), and stakeholder governance (mechanisms to follow in an effort to enhance user feedback, complaints, and remediation). The very process of uniting these dimensions into a consistent governance structure is in itself a substantial organizational asset - one that has to be nourished on a long-term basis, involves cross-functional cooperation, and is committed to throughout.(Rouzky et al., 2025)

3. ETHICAL ISS IN AI-POWERED INFORMATION SYSTEMS.

3.1 Fairness and Algorithmic bias.

Perhaps the most widely-reported ethical issue in AI-powered IS is algorithmic bias, or the systematic generation of unfair or inequitable results by the AI models. Prejudice may be introduced to AI systems in various steps in the machine learning signal-path. Historical bias: A biased model of recruitment that is trained to learn good sequences of recruitment actions will learn to reproduce historical preferences, including preferences that themselves are discriminatory. Representation bias occurs when the training set is biased against one or more subsets of the population, causing the model to make bad predictions on the subset(s). Measurement bias will occur when measurement that is used to train or test a model is imperfect proxy of the construct of interest: using arrest records as a proxy of criminal tendency, such as examples, confounds police behavior with individual behavior.(Omotayo et al., 2025)

There are straightforward and significant implications on the measurement of productivity. An online performance management system based on AI to score the productivity of employees may be systematically underestimating the contributions of the remote worker (or the older employee or the employee in a non-dominant cultural background etc.), not because he is a less productive worker, but because the model has learned to associate proxies to productivity (such as online presence times or frequency of communication) with attributes that are systematically distributed across demographic groups. The warning signs in an HR analytics system that identifies employees as flight risk can also be disproportate between employees in minority groups who are subjected to additional structural pressures, provoking the raising of flight risk flags which in fact mask the underlying inequity.(Murikah et al., 2024)

Algorithms bias can only be addressed through both technical and organizational measures. In practice, bias in the model outputs can be minimized with fairness-aware machine learning algorithms, such as pre-processing methods of equalizing the training data, in-processing methods of imposing fairness constraints on model training, and post-processing methods of adjusting the outputs to achieve demographic parity. Organizationally, periodic bias audits, and diverse development teams, inclusive stakeholder involvement in the design of systems, clear pathways of escalation of bias reports are necessary complements to technical solutions.(Ji et al., 2023)

3.2 Transparency and Explainability Decompositionality.

It is inherent in the nature of modern machine learning models - especially deep neural networks - that they are susceptible to a fundamental conflict with the demands of transparency in ethical governance. Under circumstances where an AI model declines a loan application, prescribes a treatment procedure or evaluates a performance rating, the stakeholders have a genuine interest in understanding why. This is not just an epistemic interest; it is one of practice (understanding makes us able to appeal and correct) and of law (Article 22 of the GDPR establishes a single right to know: we have the right to know why we receive specific automated decisions).

However, the explanations that can be given by the modern AI systems are often partial, a circumstance depending on the situation, or are technically complex in a way that cannot be comprehended by the affected individuals or parties. Post-hoc approximations of model behavior can be provided by model-agnostic methods of explanation, such as LIME (Locally Interpretable Model-Agnostic Explanations) and SHAP (Shapley Additive explanations). More fundamentally, those explanation techniques that are based on the importance of features need not be based on the causes of action of a model in a particular instance.(Chigbu & Makapela, 2025)

The designers of organizational IS have to cope with this tension between the model performance and model interpretability. In other applications, such as credit scoring, employee evaluation and clinical decision support, the ethical and regulatory imperative of transparency is so strikingly that a compromise based on some performance degradation to obtain inherently interpretable model (such as decision trees or logistic regression) should be accepted. In other situations, one would respond by investing in more elaborate explanation infrastructure and more elaborate models, and, to create translation capacities that can translate technical explanations into meaningful explanations to the affected stakeholders.(Zaidan et al., 2026)

3.3 Surveillance, Monitoring and employee's privacy.

The introduction of AI-powered monitoring tools in organizational IS attracts avert acuity in the privacy issues, especially when it comes to the field of workforce management. The present-day systems of employee monitoring have the capacity to record keystrokes, movements of the mouse, application use, content of communications, facial expression through camera feeds and location through building access system and wearables. When such flows of data are inputted into the chip of artificial intelligence, organizations can see more than they ever could regarding the finer workings of employee behavior - workings that bring significant potential in the realms of productivity improvement and privacy invasion.(Socorro Márquez et al., 2026)

The privacy issues deplored by the AI-powered surveillance of workers are manifold. Constant monitoring of the workforce produces a panopticon effect - the realization that one is being monitored changes behaviour in such a way as to produce a superficially desirable effect on measurable productivity whilst inhibiting creativity, teamwork and the sort of conscious intellectual rest that enables the fundamental art of problem-solving. Data about surveillance used to achieve a specific purpose (e.g., physical security) may be reused to achieve a different purpose (e.g., performance evaluation) without the knowledge and consent of the employee, which is in violation of the principles of data protection. The data collected in the form of behavioral data which is individually innocuous may be privacy-invasive when aggregating over time -revealing personal health conditions, religious beliefs, relationship statuses, or political affiliations.

The policy governing AI-enabled employee surveillance, should have clear policies on what data is collected, what purposes it will serve, how long that data will be retained, who can access that data, and how that data will impact consequential decisions. Practices of monitoring the employees have to be communicated in a straightforward comprehensible manner to the employees before the employment is commenced or the monitoring system is changed. Strong labor protections, such as most of the European Union and some Indian states, further restrict what should be the scope and use of monitoring data.(Liao et al., 2025)

3.4 Automation Bias and Human Deskilling.

Another, more nuanced, but equally significant ethical issue in AI-enabled IS is the so-called automation bias phenomenon: the current propensity of human decision-makers to over-depend on automated suggestions instead of applying their own experience or situational knowledge and make a more appropriate decision. Automation bias has been widely reported in medical practices - where clinicians occasionally overlook the possibility of questioning AI diagnosis suggestions even those suggestions that are clearly inconsistent with patient presentation - and there is a growing body of evidence on the prevalence of automation bias in organizational IS contexts, including legal document review, financial risk assessment, and HR screening.(Eastwood et al., 2026)

Automation bias has far-reaching implications in governance. In case AI-enabled IS systematically lower the exercise of human judgment, they churn down the organizational capacity to detect and rectify AI mistakes. This also calls into question questions of moral responsibility: when a recommendation by an AI system leads to a truly bad decision; and when the human decision-maker is conditioned to the point of reflexivity by the system to make a bad decision.(Hodzic et al., 2026)

The approach to eliminating automation bias involves purposeful, conscious choices of design of ISs - such as incorporation of explanation requirements that require active involvement with AI reasoning, design of points of friction that will slow the processing rate of automated processes to enable consequential decisions to be made, and maintenance of human knowledge through regular practice and training that does not solely rely on AI-assisted judgment. It also demands that governance structures be put in place that hold humans accountable in regards to the decisions being made by artificially intelligent means way that will not serve to rubber-stamp a decision.(Sebastian, 2026)

4. GOVERNANCE AS A GOVERNANCE IMPERATIVE.

4.1 The Regulatory Landscape

The international regulatory environment on data privacy in AI-based IS is intricate, as well as changing swiftly. AI-based organizations processing personal information have to navigate a multi-layered regulatory framework that consists of international, regional, national, sectoral, and organizational regulatory frameworks. This landscape is an understanding which precedes a design of legally and ethically sound IS.

Table 1. Comparative Analysis of Major Privacy Regulatory Frameworks

Framework	Core Principles	Scope	Penalty Structure	Compliance Mechanism
GDPR (EU)	Data minimization, consent, right to erasure	Broad (all sectors)	Fines up to 4% global turnover	DPIAs, data registers, DPO appointment
CCPA (USA-CA)	Opt-out rights, disclosure, non-discrimination	Commercial entities	Civil penalties up to $7,500/violation	Privacy notices, opt-out mechanisms
DPDP (India)	Consent, purpose limitation, data fiduciary	Digital personal data	Penalties up to INR 250 crore	Notice-consent-purpose framework
PIPL (China)	Sensitive data protection, cross-border rules	Personal information processing	Fines, suspension of services	Prior impact assessments
ISO/IEC 27701	Privacy information management system	Cross-sector	Certification-based	PIMS integration, audit trails

Such differences in these frameworks pose great challenges in complying to the laws of the organizations, which operate and function across a number of jurisdictions. A multinational implementing an unified AI-enabled IS platform must, at the same time, comply with the consent regulations of GDPR, data fiduciary regulations of DPDP, cross-border transfer limitations of PIPL, and opt-out mechanisms of CCPA, not to mention regulations in finance (e.g. Basel IV, MiFID II), in medical care (e.g. HIPAA, Clinical Trials Regulation), and in education (e.g. FERPA). This compliance burden is, but is best seen not simply as a cost that needs to be minimized but as organizational discipline that when incorporated into IS design at the very beginning in terms of privacy-by-design principles actually costs less in terms of compliance over the long term and improves the quality of the system.(Bokhari, 2026)

4.3 Data Subject rights and IS Architecture.

The contemporary privacy laws provide data subjects, or the individuals whose personal data are being processed with a set of rights that entail major consequences concerning IS architecture. Right of access gives rights to the subjects to access a copy of their personal data and information on how it is utilized. The right of rectification gives them the right to rectify the erroneous data. The right of erasure (the 'right to be forgotten') is an erasure right that demands the deletion of personal information under certain circumstances. The data portability rights allows data subjects to be provided their data in machine readable form and transfer this data to a second controller. The right to object enables the data subjects to challenge the processing of their data on mentioned purposes. The data subject is safeguarded by the right not to be subjected to purely automated decision-making (GDPR Article 22) to avoid being victim of consequential decisions made solely by artificial intelligence systems without human intervention.

All these rights introduce some requirements to the IS architecture, which should be expected at the design level. With a right-of-access request, all the personal data about a particular individual can be accurately identified, extracted, and formatted - again, something that is simple to do when the data is well-structured as in a well-organized relational database but extremely difficult to accomplish when dealing with the disorganized data environments that AI systems create and rely on. A right-of-erasure request is any request that requires not only deletion of the primary data stores but also of the backup systems, model training data and any derived data (including model embeddings) that contains information about the individual. A right to appeal automated decisions offers the availability and power of a human reviewer, to make an independent judgment.(Bokhari, 2026)

5. AI GOVERNANCE OIS MODELS OF ORGANIZATIONAL INFORMATION SYSTEMS.

5.1 A Typology of AI Governance Styles.

Successful AI governance in organizational IS necessitates commensurate structures of an organization in its size, sector, AI maturity and risk profile. No one particular governance model can be deemed as universally best and therefore organizations need to choose and make some adaptations to the environment of their organization by applying what is best suited to them. The following table comprises a typology of AI governance models, as well as analyses all of them by structure, strengths, limitations and contextual fit:

Table 2. Typology of AI Governance Models

Governance Model	Structure	Strengths	Limitations	Best Fit
Centralized AI Ethics Board	Single authority for all AI decisions	Consistent policy; clear accountability	Bottlenecks; limited domain expertise	Large enterprises, regulated industries
Distributed Governance	Embedded ethics across business units	Agility; domain-specific nuance	Inconsistency; coordination costs	Decentralized multinationals
Hybrid Model	Central policy + local implementation	Balance of control and flexibility	Complexity in role demarcation	Most recommended for large IS environments

continued on following page

Table 2. Continued

Governance Model	Structure	Strengths	Limitations	Best Fit
Algorithmic Auditing	External/independent audit of AI systems	Objectivity; public trust	Access limitations; audit fatigue	High-risk sectors (finance, health, HR)
Participatory Governance	Stakeholder co-creation of AI norms	Inclusivity; legitimacy	Time-intensive; conflicting interests	Public sector; community-facing systems

In particular, the hybrid governance model (a combination of the centralized policy-making and the distributed implementation) suits well large organizations implementing AI-enabled IS in multiple business units and across geographies. In this model, the structure of the overall policy framework concerning AI, the fairness criteria, and approval of the high-risk AI application can be established by an AI Ethics Board (or equivalent) that is central to the organization. It is then the responsibility of the business units to commit these standards in their specifics of operations with bridges in between central governance functions and operational teams.(Bokhari, 2026)

5.2 AI Ethics Board.

Increasingly accepted as a requisite element of adult AI regulation, the AI Ethics Board (AEB), sometimes known simply as AI Advisory Committee, Responsible AI Council or Technology Ethics Committee in other organizations, can also be referred to as AI Advisory Committee (AIAC), Responsible AI Council (RAIC), or Technology Ethics Committee (TEC). The main characteristics of an effective AEB include its make-up (which should include representatives with a legal, compliance, technology, HR, operations, communications and other external stakeholders, as well as domain experts in AI ethics and affected community representatives), its mandate (which needs to include both prospective review of high-risk AI applications and the retrospective review of AI-related incidents), and its authority (which must be sufficient to pause, amend, or terminate AI deployments that represent unacceptable ethical risks).(Bokhari, 2026)

The association of the AEB to the productivity measurement is direct. The AEB should evaluate the risks related to ethics, rather than the productivity issues of ethical protection, when AEB reviews a proposed AI application. In this evaluation, there is a need to develop common metrics, which can be used to express the trade-offs between productivity gains and ethical risks in commensurable terms - a challenge that can motivate the Ethical Productivity framework created in Section 6. The retrospective review functionality of the AEB is equally pertinent: by comparing the actual outcomes of deployment, projected productivity and ethical impact, organizations are able to tune the risk model, to identify the unforeseen ethical repercussions, and keep the governance process optimized.(Madanchian & Taherdoost, 2025)

5.3 Algorithmic Auditing

The most important form of governance regarding high-stakes AI applications is taking shape in the form of algorithmic auditing which refers to a systematic, independent examination of AI systems with the aim of gauging their behavior, fairness, accuracy and adherence to legal and ethical requirements. Evidence of credibility, objectivity and, most importantly, regulatory acceptability comes not only out of internal quality assurance processes but also of algorithmic audits, conducted by independent parties. In the EU, the 2024 EU AI Act explicitly mandates conformity assessments (a type of algorithmic audit) of high-risk AI systems, such as the ones used in employment, education, credit, law enforcement, and essential services.

The typical elements of an algorithmic audit of an AI-enabled IS include documentation review (examining specifications, design options, training data provenance, and governance procedures), technical testing (how well the model performs across demographic subgroups, how well the model identifies adversarial examples, the quality of model explanations), process review (examining deployment procedures, incident response procedures, how humans checked the deployed model), and stakeholder consultation (gathering the views of users, affected communities, and domain experts). An algorithmic audit would give its findings the most value when it is incorporated into governance improvement processes in addition to it being stored away in regulatory compliance purposes.(Zaidan et al., 2026)

6. ETHICAL MEASUREMENT OF PRODUCTIVITY.

6.1 The shortcomings of traditional measures of productivity.

Traditional productivity metrics in organizational IS are input-output relations that can be measured, e.g., the number of tasks performed per unit of time, the cost of each transaction, the throughput per server hour, the accuracy of a decision made by a specific analyst. These measures do have real value: They offer objective, comparable and actionable measures of operational performance. Nonetheless, when applied to AI-enabled IS, they are systematically nondecomposable ways, which can give rise to perverse incentives and damaging effects.

An example of a customer service AI which serves 85 per cent of customer requests without a human being escalation, as compared to 60 per cent prior to the implementation of AI. On the traditional productivity measure of resolution rate this is a 42 percent improvement - a really persuasive gain. But, take the case where the 15% halo has not been finalized, and, disproportionately, consists of queries by elderly customers less at ease with the computer interface, by customers with non-standard linguistic structure, or by rural customers with low internet connectivity. Suppose in addition that the resolved queries are resolved faster yet customer satisfaction with resolved queries is lower than in the pre-AI baseline. The standard productivity measure focuses on a fairness issue (reduced service quality in a disparate situation) and a quality issue (reduced level of satisfaction) as it glorifies an efficiency improvement.

The example highlights a larger point that traditional productivity measures are optimized in respect to dimensions that are the most easily measured, and may not necessarily be the most important dimensions as far as contribution to organizational values is concerned, or whether ethical legitimacy prevails. A broader productivity measurement system of AI-enabled IS should include matters of equity across user groups, quality of outputs and not just quantity of outputs as a component of sustainable productivity, a sustainable size of AI computation, employee wellbeing as a metric of sustainable productivity, environmental sustainability of AI computation and trust and reputational value created by ethical AI practice.(Chigbu & Makapela, 2025)

6.2 The Ethical Aspects of AI Enabled Productivity.

We suggest that the ethical aspects of AI based productivity should be structured around six major constructs that are measurable by combining a collection of quantitative indicators and/or are quantifiable by utilizing the collection of qualitative assessments:

Table 3. Ethical Dimensions of AI-Enabled Productivity — Components and Measurement

Ethical Dimension	Key Components	Example Metrics	Measurement Approach
Algorithmic Fairness	Bias detection, equitable outputs, non-discrimination audits	Disparate impact ratio, false positive parity, equal opportunity difference	Statistical parity testing; third-party audits; fairness-aware ML libraries
Transparency & Explainability	Interpretable models, audit trails, user-facing explanations	Explanation satisfaction score, decision traceability index	SHAP/LIME scores; user comprehension surveys; XAI benchmarks
Data Privacy Compliance	GDPR/DPDP adherence, anonymization, consent management	Compliance rate (%), data breach incidents, PIA completion rate	Regulatory checklists; automated compliance monitoring tools
Human Oversight	Human-in-the-loop, override mechanisms, escalation protocols	Override rate, escalation frequency, human intervention accuracy	Workflow audits; role-based access logs; escalation dashboards
Accountability & Governance	Responsibility assignment, policy enforcement, ethical review boards	Policy violation rate, governance maturity score	ISO 38500 assessments; COBIT audits; ethics committee reviews
Societal Impact	Stakeholder wellbeing, job displacement mitigation, inclusivity	Net social value score, employment retention index	Stakeholder surveys; longitudinal impact studies

These dimensions do not stand on their own: they are in a mutual interaction with each other and reinforcing each other in intricate ways. The fairness of an algorithm, such as algorithmic fairness, is a condition necessary to achieve true transparency an account of the decision of a biased model is a technically transparent explanation that is a substantively misleading account. Transparency is then a requirement towards meaningful human oversight - humans cannot exercise genuine oversight of processes they cannot understand. Human oversight would be a precondition to accountability - accountability would require recognizable human actors who would actual have an understanding of the reasons and can defend the actions that are attributed to them. The interdependencies created by this implies that the ethical aspects of AI enabled productivity cannot be tackled in bits but rather in totality.(Ji et al., 2023)

6.3 Productivity Index Ethical.

We use the Ethical Productivity Index (EPI) as a composite measure of productivity which combines more traditional measures of productivity with ethical measures of quality. The EPI aims to give organizational leaders, AI governance boards, and regulators one, interpretable, measure of the ethical quality of productivity gains in AI-enabled IS settings.

The EPI can be calculated in such a way that EPI = (Σ Wi, times, Pi) x E where Pi means individual conventional productivity measures (scaled 0-1) and Wi is the weight of an individual conventional productivity measure based on the organization priorities and regulatory requirements. The Ethics Multiplier also has a range of 0 (complete ethical failure at all levels) to 1 (full compliance with all ethical standards), and is an in turn weighted composite of dimension-level scores. The low EPI of an organization with a high-AI-enabled IS, would show the real value-adjusted productivity of AI implementation in the organization. On the other hand, a successful organization which attains moderate traditional productivity gains on a basis of strong ethical governance (E close to 1) may be able to achieve similar or higher EPI than did its less ethical competitor.

Table 4. Conventional vs. Ethics-Adjusted Productivity Metrics

Productivity Metric	Standard Definition	Ethical Considerations	Ethics-Adjusted Formula/ Approach
Task Completion Rate	% of tasks completed per unit time	Ensure AI assistance does not disadvantage protected groups	Fairness-adjusted TCR = TCR × Equity Weight
Decision Throughput	Number of decisions processed per hour	Monitor for speed-accuracy tradeoffs; avoid automation bias	Quality-weighted DT = Volume × Decision Quality Score
Error Rate Reduction	Decrease in errors attributable to AI	Audit error distributions across demographic lines	Bias-corrected ERR with demographic parity checks
Employee Cognitive Load	Perceived mental demand (NASA-TLX scale)	Ensure AI augments rather than creates stress	Composite cognitive load index with wellbeing thresholds
Process Cycle Time	Time elapsed from initiation to completion	Identify disparate impact of time savings on work equity	Ethically adjusted cycle time = Mean CT × Inclusion Factor
Return on AI Investment	Financial and non-financial value generated by AI	Include social ROI (trust, equity, reputation)	Extended ROI = Economic Gains + ESG Value + Risk Mitigation
Knowledge Worker Output	Quality and volume of knowledge-based deliverables	Protect against algorithmic performance scoring bias	Transparent KPI design with human oversight validation

The EPI is not designed to substitute traditional measures of productivity but seeks to put them into a framework of assessment that is richer than conventional productivity measures. It may be helpful to organizations to monitor EPI alongside traditional measures in their AI governance dashboards, to allow them to quickly identify which cases are being optimized by focusing on improving their productivity, at the cost of ethical quality - or where ethical constraints are unnecessarily limiting opportunities to optimize the productivity to cases.(Chigbu & Makapela, 2025)

6.4 Ethical Productive Measurement Cycle.

To successfully implement the EPI, a continuous measurement cycle is needed, which integrates productivity measurement, ethical measurement, and governance measurement, as well as continuous improvement. The figure below shows the Ethical Productivity Measurement Cycle of six stages:

Figure 1. The Ethical Productivity Measurement Cycle

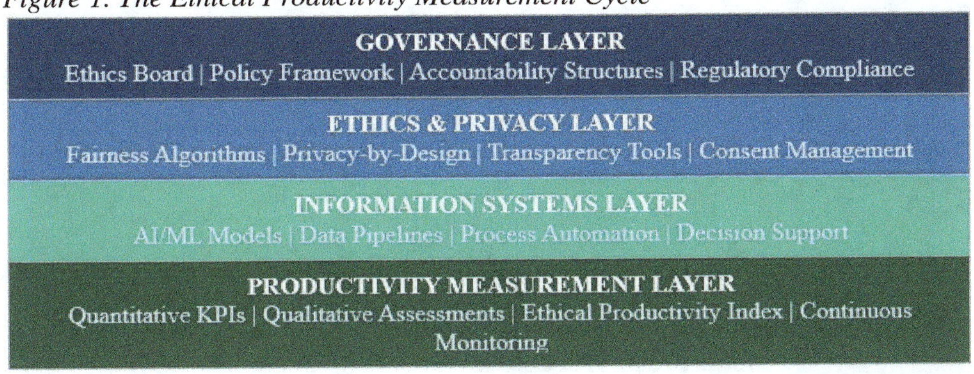

The proposed Ethical Productivity Measurement Cycle is operational integrable with the current processes in the organization (as a manager) to manage the performance of its employees and the management process using AI technologies. At Stage 1 (Define), the AI governance boards and operation teams worked with the setting of ethical parameters within which productivity would be measured, including fairness limits, privacy constraints, and transparency requirements, which would constrain the design space. During stage 2 (Measure), traditional and ethics-adjusted productivity indicators are gathered by using a set of automated tracking, periodic surveys and audit procedures. During Stage 3 (Analyze), the analysis of the collected data includes the fairness analysis, bias detection, and impact assessment of privacy, creating a comprehensive image of AI system functioning in both productivity and ethical aspects. At the Stage 4 (Intervene), the analysis results lead to deliberate interventions on identified gaps in the productivity, or ethical quality: between model retraining and process redesign, policy revision and personnel training. In Stage 5 (Monitor), continuous automated monitoring is supervising the key indicators in between formal measurement cycles or identifying any ethical risk. In Stage 6 (Report), the results of the measurement cycle are reported smoothly to the relevant parties, including employees, customers, regulators and the public, and by using the forms, which are distinct to each audience.(Zaidan et al., 2026)

6.5 Architecture with Ethical Productivity Governance.

The ethical productivity can be operationalized in four interdependent layers in the architectural framework of the AI-enabled IS illustrated in the following figure:

Figure 2. Four-Layer Architecture for Ethical Productivity Governance

1. DEFINE	Establish ethical boundaries, privacy requirements, and fairness criteria for each AI-enabled process.
2. MEASURE	Collect productivity data using ethics-adjusted metrics aligned with organizational values and legal mandates.
3. ANALYZE	Apply fairness analysis, bias detection algorithms, and privacy impact assessments to measured data.
4. INTERVENE	Implement corrections: model retraining, process redesign, policy updates, or human override activation.
5. MONITOR	Continuously track KPIs, governance compliance, and stakeholder sentiment through automated dashboards.
6. REPORT	Publish transparent reports to internal boards, regulators, and stakeholders with full audit trails.

The Governance Layer provides the strategic and policy backbone: ethics board, compliance framework, control structures, and organizational values that define the ethical envelope that AI-enabled IS operate in. The Ethics and Privacy Layer expresses governance principles in technical and operational specifications: fairness algorithms that are implemented as trains of data model training, privacy-by-design requirements that restrict data architecture, transparency tools that produce explanations of AI decisions, and consent management platforms that implement data subject rights. The operational core; the AI models, data pipelines, process automation tools and decision support systems that create a productivity value within the ethical limits that are defined by the upper layers. The feedback mechanism, the quantitative and qualitative metrics, dashboards and reporting systems that measures performance in both conventional and ethical aspects, are provided by the Productivity Measurement Layer.(Autili et al., 2025)

This four-layered architecture is both a reflection of a major design principle: ethical governance is not imposed outside and restrictive to IS productivity, but rather an innate part of IS architecture that facilitates, shapes and sustains productivity over time. Organization's that put in place solid layers of governance and ethics tend to develop more resilient to change-in-regulation, more trusted by consumers, more competent to attract quality employees who find ethics values inspirational and to compete in markets where competitive ethical AI practice is quickly becoming a distinguishing feature.(Agbabiaka et al., 2025)

7. STAKEHOLDER ROLE AND ORGANIZING ENABLERS.

7.1 The Stakeholder Ecosystem

Successful AI-powered IS ethical governance is a multi-stakeholder affair. The roles and interests of the various groups of stakeholders need to be well understood, coordinated and adjusted so as to produce effective and legitimate systems of governance. The next figure locates the main stakeholder groups with the corresponding roles highlighted:

Figure 3. Stakeholder Ecosystem for Ethical AI Governance

Stakeholder Group	Role in Ethical AI Governance & Productivity
Senior Leadership	Mandate ethical AI strategy; allocate resources; sign off on governance charters
IT & Data Teams	Implement privacy-by-design; manage AI model fairness; maintain audit logs
Legal & Compliance	Ensure regulatory adherence; manage DPIA; interpret policy requirements
HR & People Teams	Monitor workforce impact; handle bias complaints; design ethical performance frameworks
Ethics & AI Board	Review high-risk decisions; develop ethical guidelines; oversee external audits
End Users / Employees	Provide feedback; exercise override rights; participate in ethics training
External Regulators	Set legal boundaries; conduct inspections; enforce penalties for non-compliance
Customers / Clients	Data subjects; consent holders; stakeholders in AI-driven service delivery

These issues of coordination between these groups of stakeholders are critical. Top-level management may be more focused on the outcomes of increased productivity and competitive advantage; law firms may be more focused on minimizing the risks of noncompliance; IT firms may be more focused on the technical feasibility and system performance; human resources may be more focused on the experience of the employee and labor relations; ethical boards may advocate a more cautious and deliberate approach; end users may be interested in subjective ease of use and system functionality; and external regulators in consumer protection and competitive integrity. Best AI governance models should create deliberation spaces in which these potentially divergent priorities can be articulated, negotiated and resolved, not by prioritizing one priority over the other, but by developing context-sensitive judgement processes that should in a limited secondary way weigh competing values. (Nayak & Jagadeeswari, 2026)

7.2 Develop Organizational Capabilities to build ethical AI.

The ethical application of AI governance in organizational IS is not a mere policy undertaking; it needs the establishment of specific organizational abilities that need to be nurtured over time by deliberate investment in people, processes and tools.

The entry-level capability is AI ethics literacy: All employees working with AI-enabled IS (not only AI specialists) should be able to understand the foundational principles of the algorithmic fairness, data privacy, and AI accountability in the context of their work. This will necessitate continual training processes which will vary according to the audience with the top level board members requiring to understand the conceptual knowledge and the lowest level data scientists who may require to understand the technical knowledge.

The maturity of data governance is a crucial enabler: well-developed data governance capabilities, such as clear data ownership, documented data lineage, effective data quality management and effective access control have significantly better chances of realizing the principle of privacy-by-design and conducting meaningful bias audits than organizations with a disjointed, undocumented data environment. Ethical AI governance, thus, is not a particular corporate action, but a prerequisite to ethical AI governance.

Cross-functional teamwork is an imperative organizational design: ethical AI governance necessitates sustained, systematic collaboration among the functions, including legal, IT, HR, operations, communications and finance that tend to be operated within silos in an organization. Better governance structures to provide formal roles and processes of cross-functional deliberation regarding AI issues are more effective than those that create coordination through informal processes. One such implementation of this imperative of design is the creation of an AI Ethics Board with a real cross-functional membership, as suggested in Section 5.2.

The capability of incident response is an aspect that is not always heavily invested: organizations must be prepared to effectively respond to the occurrence of AI ethics incidents (places where AI systems generate harmful, unfair, or legally non-compliant results). Successful incident response needs to have clear protocols on how to detect the incident (including both whistleblower channels as well as automated anomaly detection), analyze the severity of the incident, contain instituted immediate harms, communicate transparently with the societal stakeholders affected, implement remediation and learn on incidents to avoid reoccurring related harms.(Mehdi & Naz, 2025)

8. IMPLEMENTATION ROADMAP

8.1 A Step-by-step Process to Ethical AI Governance.

The adoption of an ethical AI governance framework of the organization IS is better implemented in the form of a phased, iterative program, which cannot be implemented as a one-time project. The following roadmap shows a step-by-step approach to developing ethical AI governance capabilities within an 18 months perspective with clear milestones, activities and success criteria at every stage:

This roadmap is descriptive, but not prescriptive. The right speed of the implementation, the type of activity in each stage, the relative activity of most governance dimensions, and the cultural orientation of organizations will differ significantly depending on the size, sector, opposition, current AI maturity, and organizational culture. Nevertheless, the phased organizational structure based on foundation-building through the framework design, piloting, scaling, and continuous evaluation, reflects the tested organization approach to change management that balances the urgency of ethical AI governance with organizational realities of resource constraints, change capacity.(Murikah et al., 2024)

8.2 Technology Infrastructure to Ethical Governance.

Organizational IS needs ethical AI governance to support such technology infrastructure that can facilitate the actual implementation of governance requirements. This infrastructure involves a number of subcategories of tools and platforms that need to be chosen, implemented and integrated with core IS architecture.

Registries of AI models include central documentation of all AI models deployed in organizational IS, including specifications, training data provenance, performance characteristics, fairness audit results, and ownership. An effective oversight is a precondition of a working model registry: without a systematic documentation and tracking of model system, a governance of AI systems is impossible. Simple spreadsheet-based inventories in maturing governance environments can be considered simple model registries, even though the situation may be more complex than this simplistic scenario.(Chigbu & Makapela, 2025)

Fairness monitoring systems are self-monitoring evaluation and monitoring systems of AI model outputs to evaluate the evidence of demographic bias. The modern fairness monitoring systems are interrelated with AI deployment pipelines to signal an outlier in output distributions between demographic groups that are safeguarded. The best approach involves these tools being set up with fairness thresholds, which consider the organizational values and legal needs instigated but not arbitrary default.

The privacy management system can promote the following workflows: data subject rights, consent management, data retention enforcement, and privacy impact assessment. In an organization where the volume of personal data and the frequency of its requests are at all levels of the scope of the obligations with the data subjects rights, automated privacy management platforms are necessary to effectively comply with data subject rights requirements - manual compliance processes simply cannot be scaled to levels of the scope of the obligations to the data subject present in large consumer-facing organizations.

Explainable toolkit Explanation generation abilities provide and allow generation of explanations of decisions of AI models in a way that can be understood by the user. The choice of what methods are to be used in explanation must be informed by the requirements to be met by the use case in terms of explanation, the technical ability of the intended consumers and the regulatory demands that may be imposed on the AI application.(Zaidan et al., 2026)

8.3 Culture and Change Management.

The framework of technical governance and the supporting technologies are required but not alone to help in effective ethical AI governance. It is also important to foster an organizational culture in which ethical AI practice is a professional value, not an obligation to adhere to a Code of Conduct. As with change, visible senior leadership commitment - boards and women and men who publicly and consistently champion ethical AI principles, including in those cases where ethical requirements restrict short-term commercial interests. It entails introducing the ethical AI aspects in performance management systems including the AI developers and data scientists and the IS managers. It needs to salute and applaud ethical AI win stories as well as productivity win stories. It also involves the establishment of the psychological safety the workplace where the employees feel confident enough to speak about any ethical issues without fear of having their careers ruined.

The ethical AI governance through change management should also respond to the concerns and interests of those direct and immediate beneficiaries of the AI-enabled IS. Workers who believe that AI systems are stalking them, assessing them unjustly, or stealing their professional judgment are not likely to welcome -and even may take action against -initiatives involving AI deployment. When organizations invest in the real dialogue with employees on AI governance, when they give employees meaningful input in the design of AI-enabled performance systems, and when they create strong mechanisms that would allow the employees to question the AI decisions that impact their careers, are better placed to gain the workforce trust and engagement that underlies true productivity gains.(Eastwood et al., 2026)

9. CONCLUSION

This chapter has maintained that not only are there no restraints on AI-enabled productivity but prevailing patterns show ethics, privacy, and governance are not drivers of it, but rather constitutive components of any, real, durable, and stakeholder-valid productivity in the organizational information systems. The fact that the measurement of productivity in AI-enabled environments is not merely incomplete, but is systematically misleading, providing productivity metrics that overstate organizational value creation, and understate organizational risk.

The proposed Ethical Productivity Index (EPI) in this chapter presents a viable framework on how to incorporate the ethical quality assessment in the organizational productivity measurement. The EPI would give a single, interpretable composite metric that would reflect the real value-adjusted productivity of AI-enabled IS. The four-layer architectural framework - Governance, Ethics and Privacy, Information Systems, and Productivity Measurement - offers an organizational design template into which ethical governance is to be implanted into IS architecture since the very base of the IS architecture.

The implementation roadmap given in this chapter recognizes the complexity within an organization to ensure that true ethical AI governance is realized. The development of the ethics literacy, maturity of data governance, cross-functional collaboration structures, and incident response capabilities needed to achieve successful governance is a long-term, multi-year initiative that requires senior leadership investment, multi-function cross-collaborative structure, and organization learning. The entity-building to framework-design-piloting-scaling-onwards-and-assessment cycling business complexity gives a structured process through the business complexity.

There are some key themes, which will have to be discussed in more detail than it is feasible to do within the limits of this chapter. It is an area of future research that should be put into priority so that future industry-specific EPI frameworks can be developed, to the best of the specific ethical concerns, regulatory imperatives, and productivity relationships of particular industries. The empirical support of the EPI in an organizational field setting, through longitudinal studies that trace the relationship between the investment of an ethical governance in the organization and its performance over time, would greatly augment the evidentiary base of the framework. Expanding the framework to tack this emerging AI governance issues, such as the governance of generative AI systems, agentic AI systems that operate with greater autonomy than conventional AI tools, and AI systems that operate across organizational and jurisdictional boundaries, are all critical frontiers to both research and practice.

After all, the main message of this chapter is at once the simplest one: those organizations, which view ethical AI governance as a strategic investment rather than a compliance cost, will be in a better position to not just experience the productivity benefits that AI promises, but also enjoy trust, resilience and legitimacy that characterizes sustainable organizational performance, as opposed to being driven by short-term efficiency that is extractive in nature and thus has to be surrendered by the organization to gain the advantages that it comes with. The need to consider ethics, privacy, and governance issues when the AI-enabled information system is ever getting more and more inherent in organizational life, is not a choice but a necessity, not only to ensure organizational sustainability but also to ensure regulatory compliance and to ensure human prosperity, as well.

REFERENCES.

Agbabiaka, O., Ojo, A., & Connolly, N. (2025). Requirements for trustworthy AI-enabled automated decision-making in the public sector: A systematic review. *Technological Forecasting and Social Change, 215*, 124076. Advance online publication. DOI: 10.1016/j.techfore.2025.124076

Autili, M., Corsi, R., De Sanctis, M., Inverardi, P., & Pelliccione, P. (2025). Ethics Label for Digital Systems to Promote Transparency and User Awareness. *Journal of Systems and Software, 112752*. Advance online publication. DOI: 10.1016/j.jss.2025.112752

Bokhari, S. A. A. (2026). Artificial intelligence, governance, and economic growth: Toward a new theory of digital developmentalism. *Social Sciences & Humanities Open, 13*, 102842. Advance online publication. DOI: 10.1016/j.ssaho.2026.102842

Chigbu, B. I., & Makapela, S. L. (2025). AI in education, sustainability, and the future of work: An integrative review of industry 5.0, education 5.0, and work 5.0. *Journal of Open Innovation, 11*(4), 100645. Advance online publication. DOI: 10.1016/j.joitmc.2025.100645

Díaz-Rodríguez, N., Del Ser, J., Coeckelbergh, M., López de Prado, M., Herrera-Viedma, E., & Herrera, F. (2023). Connecting the dots in trustworthy Artificial Intelligence: From AI principles, ethics, and key requirements to responsible AI systems and regulation. *Information Fusion, 99*, 101896. Advance online publication. DOI: 10.1016/j.inffus.2023.101896

Eastwood, C., Lim, N., Durie, R., Dela Rue, B., Bifet, A., & Reed, C. (2026). JDS Communications® TBC; TBC Mini-Review Animal Nutrition and Farm Systems Integrating Agentic artificial intelligence into pasture-based dairy systems: Applications, governance, and future directions. https://creativecommons.org/licenses/by/4.0/

Evangelista, E., & Salman Bukhari, S. M. (2026). From ethical principles to executable governance: A policy-as-code framework for trustworthy AI in higher education. *Computers and Education: Artificial Intelligence, 10*, 100594. Advance online publication. DOI: 10.1016/j.caeai.2026.100594

Hodzic, S., Stevic, A., & Matthes, J. (2026). Generative AI in practice: An umbrella review of risks, benefits, ethics, and future directions across major domains. *Technology in Society, 87*, 103331. Advance online publication. DOI: 10.1016/j.techsoc.2026.103331

Jafarinezhad, O., Zhang, Q., Rezai, R., Noaeen, M., Shachak, A., Far, B., & Shakeri, Z. (2026). Centralized pooling and federated learning for Canadian patient-level data sharing in multicenter medical AI: A scoping review. *Artificial Intelligence in Medicine, 178*, 103422. DOI: 10.1016/j.artmed.2026.103422 PMID: 42066521

Ji, Z., Lee, N., Frieske, R., Yu, T., Su, D., Xu, Y., Ishii, E., Bang, Y. J., Madotto, A., & Fung, P. (2023). Survey of Hallucination in Natural Language Generation. In ACM Computing Surveys (Vol. 55, Number 12). Association for Computing Machinery. DOI: 10.1145/3571730

Liao, S. M., Haykel, I., Cheung, K., & Matalon, T. (2025). Navigating the complexities of AI and digital governance: The 5W1H framework. *Journal of Responsible Technology, 23*, 100127. Advance online publication. DOI: 10.1016/j.jrt.2025.100127

Madanchian, M., & Taherdoost, H. (2025). Criteria for AI Adoption in HR: Efficiency vs. Ethics. *Procedia Computer Science, 258*, 233–241. DOI: 10.1016/j.procs.2025.04.261

Mehdi, N., & Naz, T. (2025). Governing the intelligent factory – Transforming labor law through an open-standards framework for AI governance in industry 4.0. In Journal of Open Innovation: Technology, Market, and Complexity (Vol. 11, Number 4). Elsevier B.V. DOI: 10.1016/j.joitmc.2025.100690

Monteiro, N., & Singh, V. (2025). The wheel of artificial intelligence governance. In *Sustainable Futures* (Vol. 10). Elsevier Ltd., DOI: 10.1016/j.sftr.2025.101279

Murikah, W., Nthenge, J. K., & Musyoka, F. M. (2024). Bias and ethics of AI systems applied in auditing - A systematic review. *Scientific African, 25*, e02281. Advance online publication. DOI: 10.1016/j.sciaf.2024.e02281

Nayak, P. B., & Jagadeeswari, I. U. (2026). Organizational performance optimization: An AI-enabled framework for employee compensation and benefits management. *Research in Globalization, 12*, 100328. Advance online publication. DOI: 10.1016/j.resglo.2025.100328

Omotayo, A. O., Adediran, S. A., Omotoso, A. B., Olagunju, K. O., & Omotayo, O. P. (2025). Artificial intelligence in agriculture: ethics, impact possibilities, and pathways for policy. In *Computers and Electronics in Agriculture* (Vol. 239). Elsevier B.V., DOI: 10.1016/j.compag.2025.110927

Pesqueira, A., de Bem Machado, A., Bolog, S., Sousa, M. J., & Pereira, R. (2024). Exploring the impact of EU tendering operations on future AI governance and standards in pharmaceuticals. *Computers & Industrial Engineering, 198*, 110655. Advance online publication. DOI: 10.1016/j.cie.2024.110655

Rouzky, R., Sarrafzadeh, A., Sowells-Boone, E., Pasandi, H. B., & Goins, G. (2025). Data governance in smart farming: A systematic review of challenges and gaps. In *Information Processing in Agriculture*. China Agricultural University., DOI: 10.1016/j.inpa.2025.11.006

Saghafi, A., & Angelopoulos, S. (2025). Virtual virtues: A governance framework of moral consequentialism and deontological ethics for immersive virtual reality platforms. *The Journal of Strategic Information Systems*, *34*(4), 101936. Advance online publication. DOI: 10.1016/j.jsis.2025.101936

Sebastian, G. (2026). Digital shadow AI risk theory (DART): A framework for managing data disclosure and privacy risks of AI tools at work. *Technological Forecasting and Social Change*, *229*, 124697. Advance online publication. DOI: 10.1016/j.techfore.2026.124697

Socorro Márquez, F. O., Reyes Ortiz, G. E., & Torrez Meruvia, H. (2026). Philosophical leadership in education: Rethinking pedagogy in an AI-driven world. In *Social Sciences and Humanities Open* (Vol. 13). Elsevier Ltd., DOI: 10.1016/j.ssaho.2026.102699

Tunca, S. (2026). The innovation–compliance–perception framework as a lens for AI governance — NLP evidence from Meta's smart glasses and GDPR discourse. *International Journal of Information Management Data Insights*, *6*(1), 100408. Advance online publication. DOI: 10.1016/j.jjimei.2026.100408

Zaidan, E., Truby, J., Ibrahim, I. A., & Hoppe, T. (2026). Hybrid global governance for responsible and inclusive Artificial Intelligence: Proposing a new Sustainable Development Goal 18. *Technology in Society*, *85*, 103159. Advance online publication. DOI: 10.1016/j.techsoc.2025.103159

Zhang, Q., Gillenson, M. L., & Zhang, X. P. (2026). The impact of person-organization ethics fit on ethical performance of autonomous vehicles. *Computers in Human Behavior Reports*, *21*, 100953. Advance online publication. DOI: 10.1016/j.chbr.2026.100953

KEY TERMS AND DEFINITIONS

Algorithmic Fairness: The property of AI systems whereby outputs are equitable across demographic groups, assessed using metrics such as demographic parity, equalized odds, and individual fairness.

Automation Bias: The tendency of human decision-makers to over-rely on automated recommendations, deferring to AI outputs even when human judgment would lead to better decisions.

Data Minimization: The principle that only personal data strictly necessary for a specified purpose should be collected and processed, enshrined in GDPR Article 5(1)(c).

Ethical Productivity Index (EPI): A composite metric proposed in this chapter that combines conventional productivity measures with an Ethics Multiplier to produce a value-adjusted assessment of AI-enabled IS performance.

Privacy-by-Design: An approach to IS development that embeds privacy protections into system architecture from the earliest design stage, rather than adding them as post-hoc compliance measures.

Algorithmic Auditing: The systematic, independent examination of AI systems to assess their behavior, fairness, accuracy, and compliance with legal and ethical requirements.

Data Subject Rights: Legal rights granted to individuals whose personal data is processed, including rights of access, rectification, erasure, portability, and objection to automated decision-making.

Human-in-the-Loop: An AI system design pattern that maintains meaningful human oversight and intervention capacity in AI-driven decision processes, particularly for consequential decisions.

Chapter 10
The Evolution of Libraries in the Digital Age:
Beyond Brick and Mortar

Tolulope Balogun
University of South Africa, South Africa

Oluwole Olumide Durodolu
http://orcid.org/0000-0003-2734-8165
University of South Africa, South Africa

ABSTRACT

Libraries have long served as the custodians of knowledge, playing a pivotal role in the preservation and dissemination of information throughout human history. They have evolved over time, adapting to meet community needs. This research aims to explore how modern libraries have evolved from traditional physical spaces to dynamic digital entities. It will examine the integration of digital technologies in library services, the impact on user engagement and access to information, and the challenges and opportunities this transformation presents. The study will focus on several key areas: digital collections and archives, online library services, virtual reference systems, and the role of libraries in promoting digital literacy. By investigating these aspects, the research seeks to provide a comprehensive understanding of the modern library's function and significance in the digital age, emphasizing that libraries are no longer confined to their physical buildings but have become integral components of the global information infrastructure. This study offers an original contribution by repositioning the contemporary library not merely as a digitized extension of its traditional functions, but as a structurally reconfigured knowledge institution embedded within the global digital information ecosystem.

DOI: 10.4018/979-8-2600-0111-0.ch010

INTRODUCTION

Libraries have long served as the custodians of knowledge, playing a pivotal role in the preservation and dissemination of information throughout human history. One of the earliest and most illustrious examples of this role is the Library of Alexandria, established in the 3rd century BCE. This ancient institution was more than a mere repository of scrolls, as it was a symbol of intellectual pursuit and the collective effort to accumulate and safeguard the world's knowledge. The Library of Alexandria represented the epitome of what a library could achieve—a center for learning, scholarship, and the preservation of cultural heritage. Its eventual destruction, often attributed to the actions of Julius Caesar during the Siege of Alexandria, stands as a stark reminder of the fragility of knowledge repositories and the profound cultural losses that can occur when they are compromised (Lodha, 2024). The legacy of Alexandria endures, symbolizing the historical significance of libraries in advancing civilization.

Libraries have evolved over time, adapting to meet community needs. Traditionally, librarians served as gatekeepers, helping patrons navigate curated collections. Libraries also functioned as communal spaces, fostering shared knowledge and collective learning (Hapel, 2020). However, the advent of digital technology has transformed the function and perception of libraries. No longer confined to brick-and-mortar spaces, libraries have increasingly embraced digital formats, transforming themselves into dynamic entities that extend far beyond their physical walls. This transformation is not merely about digitizing existing collections but also involves reimagining the library as a versatile platform for information exchange, accessible to a global audience (Janes, 2013). The digitization of collections, online library services, and virtual reference systems have expanded libraries' reach, serving diverse user bases. Libraries promote digital literacy, ensuring users can navigate and utilize digital resources effectively, redefining their role in global information infrastructure (Jaeger et al, 2013).

AIM AND SCOPE

This aim of this paper is to discuss how modern libraries have evolved from traditional physical spaces to dynamic digital entities. It examines the integration of digital technologies in library services, the impact on user engagement and access to information, and the challenges and opportunities this transformation presents. It focuses on the following key areas: digital collections and archives, online library services, virtual reference systems, and the role of libraries in promoting digital literacy.

LITERATURE REVIEW

Historical Evolution of Libraries

Libraries have a rich history, tracing back to the early efforts to preserve and transmit knowledge, reflecting and fostering societal advancement. The Library of Alexandria, established in the 3rd century BCE, is often cited as the archetype of ancient libraries, symbolizing the aspirations of human culture to accumulate and safeguard knowledge across generations (Battles, 2004; Stephens, 2023). This institution was remarkable not only for its vast collection of texts but also for its role as a center of learning and scholarship, attracting scholars from across the Mediterranean. The destruction of the Library of Alexandria remains a potent symbol of the vulnerability of knowledge repositories to external forces. The library evolved over time, with medieval Europe's monasteries serving as custodians of knowledge, preserving classical texts and ensuring continuity during political and social instability (Clark, 2007). With the advent of the printing press in the 15th century, the role of libraries expanded significantly. The mass production of books made knowledge more accessible, and libraries began to emerge as public institutions, serving broader segments of society (Pettegree, 2017). The establishment of public libraries in the 19th century, such as the Boston Public Library in 1852, marked a significant milestone in the democratization of knowledge, providing free access to information for all citizens (Battles, 2004). The 20th century saw significant transformations in libraries, with the introduction of electronic media, microfilm, audio recordings, and computers, leading to a digital revolution and expanded multimedia resources (Candela, et al., 2012; Rubin & Rubin, 2020).

Digital Transformation in Libraries

The landscape of libraries is undergoing a profound transformation driven by evolving user demands and rapid technological advancements. This digital transformation encompasses a shift from traditional service models to hybrid approaches, which integrate distributed collections and data curation practices (Anuradha, 2018; Kempf, 2023). Libraries are increasingly adopting digital technologies to enhance various aspects of service delivery, management, and patron engagement, ultimately fostering greater utilization (Kari, 2020). The integration of digital technologies enables libraries to expand beyond their physical boundaries, broadening their reach and enhancing their relevance in the digital age. A significant component of this transformation involves the digitization of materials. Initiatives like Google Books and the Digital Public Library of America have not only increased the availability of digital resources but also facilitated the preservation of fragile materials. The shift toward digitization allows libraries to create comprehensive online collections that are accessible to a wider audience, thereby enhancing user engagement (Singh & Asif, 2019). Furthermore, libraries are implementing online services, such as databases and multimedia resources, which serve to broaden their user base and provide a more interactive experience. The transition to digital environments also includes the development of virtual reference systems that leverage technologies like chatbots and artificial intelligence. These innovations enhance the traditional reference desk experience by providing users with instant access to information and support, thus increasing library relevance in a technology-driven society (Kari, 2020). However, navigating this digital transformation is not without challenges. It requires a well-organized digital strategy to effectively address the technological and procedural changes involved (Anuradha, 2018). Librarians' roles are evolving as they become more embedded in user research workflows, necessitating a shift in skill sets and approaches to engage effectively with patrons (Kempf, 2023). As libraries continuously monitor and respond to the digital transformation, they face both opportunities and challenges in meeting the diverse information needs of their communities.

Challenges and Opportunities

While the digital transformation has brought many opportunities, it has also presented significant challenges for libraries. One of the primary challenges is the technological barrier, which includes the cost of acquiring and maintaining digital infrastructure, as well as the need for ongoing staff training. Many libraries, particularly those in underfunded or rural areas, struggle to keep pace with rapid technological advancements, which can exacerbate inequalities in access to information (Real et al., 2014; Thiele, 2016). Additionally, the digital divide remains a persistent issue, with certain populations lacking access to the necessary devices or internet connections to fully benefit from digital library services (Bertot, et al. 2012; Jaeger et al. 2012; Gautam, 2014). This divide is often driven by factors such as income, education, geographic location, and age, leading to disparities in access to digital resources and the skills needed to use them effectively (van Dijk, 2020). Financial constraints further complicate the adoption of digital technologies (Ullah et al., 2023; Breeding, 2010; Neal, 2014). While digital resources can reduce costs associated with physical collections, they require significant upfront investment in technology, digital content, and cybersecurity measures. Moreover, the shift to digital can lead to challenges in copyright management and the negotiation of licenses for digital materials, adding complexity to the librarian's role (Besek, 2003; Ferullo & Soules, 2012; Hirtle, et al., 2009).

Despite these challenges, the digital age also presents numerous opportunities for libraries to reinvent themselves and expand their impact. The increasing availability of open access resources, for example, offers libraries the chance to provide more equitable access to information, regardless of a user's location or economic status (Willinsky, 2006; Stevenson, 2009; Suber, 2012). Additionally, emerging technologies such as artificial intelligence and big data analytics have the potential to enhance library services, offering personalized recommendations and more sophisticated search capabilities (Adewojo & Dunmade, 2024; Priya & Ramya, 2024; Rao & Sahu, 2024). Libraries are also uniquely positioned to play a leading role in promoting digital literacy, helping users develop the skills needed to navigate an increasingly complex information landscape (Martin, 2008; Koltay, 2011; Koltay & Špiranec, 2017).

METHODOLOGY

This review of literature aims at discussing how modern libraries have evolved from traditional physical spaces to dynamic digital entities. The methodology for this review involved an efficient search and analysis of peer-reviewed articles, in terms of books, and conference papers published between 2003 to 2024. The main databases used were Google Scholar, Ebscohost, Web of Science, and Scopus, these databases were chosen as a result of their wide-ranging coverage of library and information science (LIS) literature.

A arrangement of keywords such as "Digital Libraries", "Digital Literacy", "Library Services", "Information Access", and Technology. Boolean operators AND and OR were deployed to enhance search strategy. Exclusion criteria included articles that did not directly relevant to the subject matter as captured in the aims of the study.

The preliminary search strategy generated 145 articles. After examining the titles and abstracts, 95 articles were carefully chosen for full-text review. Of these, 65 met the inclusion criteria and were included in the final compilation. Data extraction focused on key findings allied to the subject matter of evolution of libraries in the digital age, with special attention paid to modern libraries and how they have evolved from traditional and physical spaces to the more dynamic digital entities

DISCUSSION

Digital Collections and Archives

The evolution from physical to digital collections has redefined the traditional role of libraries, transforming them into custodians of both tangible and intangible cultural heritage. Libraries have embraced the digital realm by curating and managing vast collections of digital content, a process that involves intricate strategies for selection, digitization, and metadata creation. The transition is not merely about replicating physical collections in digital formats but involves the creation of born-digital content that is natively digital from its inception. This shift requires librarians to develop new competencies in digital curation, comprising everything from the selection of software tools for digitization to the application of metadata standards like Dublin Core and MARC 21, which are critical for ensuring discoverability and interoperability across platforms (Pasqui, 2024). Digital collection management requires a robust framework for long-term preservation, addressing challenges like format obsolescence and data corruption (Brown, 2013; Gladney, 2009). Initiatives like DPC and OAIS guide libraries, ensuring accessibility and authenticity. Sustainability and continuity are crucial in digital curation (Brown, 2013).

Ensuring broad access to digital collections while simultaneously preserving them for future generations presents a complex challenge for libraries. On one hand, libraries must adopt strategies that enhance accessibility, such as the implementation of open access repositories, digital lending platforms, and user-friendly interfaces that cater to diverse audiences (Mafungwa, 2017). For instance, the rise of digital libraries like the HathiTrust Digital Library and Europeana has democratized access to vast troves of digitized materials, enabling users worldwide to engage with content that was previously confined to physical archives (Gooding & Fulkerson, 2020). However, preserving digital content involves legal complexities, including copyright and digital rights management (Ferullo & Soules, 2012; Fisher, 2020). Libraries must negotiate licenses and access restrictions, potentially limiting long-term availability (Albitz, 2014; Walters, 2013). Balancing user needs and collections' enduring value requires a proactive approach that considers both immediate needs and collections' value.

Digital collections in libraries have shown significant benefits in user engagement and access. The National Library of Australia's Trove platform (National Library of Australia, n.d.), a searchable database of digitized content, has attracted millions of users annually. The New York Public Library's Digital Collections initiative, offering about 922,000 digitized items, has facilitated deep engagement with its collections (The New York Public Library, 2024). The integration of social media tools and digital exhibitions has further broadened its reach. In addition, the United Nations

Office at Geneva (UNOG) Library through its initiated the Total Digital Access to the League of Nations Project (LONTAD) provides access to about 15 million digitized materials related to the League of Nations (United Nations, n.d.). These case studies highlight the transformative power of digital collections in contemporary libraries, showing how well-considered expenditures on user experience and digital infrastructure may greatly increase information access while safeguarding cultural heritage for future generations.

Online Library Services

The digital revolution has enabled libraries to expand their services far beyond the physical limitations of their collections, offering a diverse array of online resources that cater to the needs of a global user base. Among the most significant developments is the provision of e-books, which have become a staple of modern library services. Many libraries now offer vast collections of e-books that can be borrowed and read on a variety of devices, providing users with convenient access to literature and scholarly works. Platforms such as OverDrive and Libby have played a crucial role in facilitating this shift, allowing libraries to lend digital content seamlessly (Miller, 2021). In addition to e-books, libraries have expanded their offerings to include online journals and databases, which are essential for academic research. Subscriptions to databases like JSTOR, ProQuest, and IEEE Xplore enable library patrons to access peer-reviewed articles, conference papers, and other scholarly materials from virtually anywhere in the world. This accessibility is particularly valuable for researchers and students, who can now engage with up-to-date information and conduct comprehensive literature reviews without the need to visit a physical library (Harboe-Ree, 2020). Furthermore, libraries have embraced multimedia resources as part of their online services, offering access to digital archives of music, film, and art. The inclusion of multimedia resources broadens the scope of what libraries can offer, supporting not only traditional literacy but also digital and media literacy. For instance, the British Library's Sounds Archive provides access to a vast collection of sound recordings, while the Smithsonian Institution offers online access to its extensive multimedia collections, showcasing the intersection of technology and cultural heritage (Smithsonian Institution, 2022; Durodolu, 2018, Durodolu, Adekanye & Olorunfemi, 2013).

The advent of online library services has fundamentally transformed how users interact with libraries, shifting the focus from physical spaces to digital platforms. A key aspect of this transformation is the development of user-friendly interfaces that enhance the user experience (UX) (Bignoli & Stara, 2020). Modern libraries prioritize the design of intuitive and accessible websites and applications, which are essential for navigating the vast array of online resources. These platforms often include personalized services, such as tailored recommendations based on a user's borrowing history or search behavior, which further enhance engagement and satisfaction (Borgman, 2017). For example, discovery layers in online catalog systems enable users to search across multiple databases simultaneously, while libraries integrate social media tools for dynamic content engagement, making services more relevant and fostering deeper connections with users (Breeding, M. (2015). Personalization and interactivity have become central to the online library experience, with libraries increasingly offering services such as virtual reference systems, where users can chat with librarians in real-time, and personalized alerts for new publications in areas of interest. These innovations have not only enhanced user engagement but have also democratized access to library services, making them available to a broader audience irrespective of geographical constraints.

As libraries continue to expand their online services, ensuring accessibility and inclusivity has become a critical priority. Libraries are committed to providing equitable access to digital resources, recognizing the diverse needs of their user communities. To this end, many libraries have adopted the Web Content Accessibility Guidelines (WCAG), which provide a framework for making web content more accessible to people with disabilities (Billingham, 2014). Efforts to enhance accessibility include the implementation of screen reader compatibility, keyboard navigation, and closed captioning for video content. Libraries are also increasingly offering materials in multiple formats, such as audiobooks and braille e-books, to cater to users with different needs. Additionally, many libraries have developed partnerships with organizations that specialize in accessible technology, such as Bookshare, which provides digital books for individuals with print disabilities (Turner, 2018; Beaumon, 2011). However, inclusivity extends beyond physical disabilities to encompass a broader spectrum of user needs, including those related to language and socioeconomic status. Libraries have made significant strides in offering multilingual resources and ensuring that their online services are available to users from diverse linguistic backgrounds (Stiller et al., 2013). Furthermore, many libraries provide free or low-cost access to digital resources, ensuring that financial barriers do not hinder access to information (Real et al., 2014). These efforts reflect a commitment to the core mission of libraries: to serve as inclusive institutions that provide equitable access to knowledge for all members of society.

Virtual Reference Systems

The evolution of reference services in libraries has been shaped by the growing influence of digital technology, transitioning from traditional in-person consultations to sophisticated virtual reference systems. Historically, reference services were confined to physical interactions, where patrons would visit the library to seek assistance from a librarian. These consultations typically involved face-to-face conversations, during which the librarian would guide the patron in locating relevant resources, navigating catalog systems, and answering specific queries. The traditional reference desk was a cornerstone of library services, emphasizing personal interaction and the librarian's role as a knowledge intermediary (Cassell & Hiremath, 2023). The advent of the internet in the late 20th century initiated a shift towards more accessible and flexible reference services. The introduction of email and asynchronous communication methods allowed libraries to extend their reference services beyond physical boundaries, enabling users to submit inquiries remotely. This transition marked the beginning of virtual reference services, which expanded further with the development of real-time chat systems in the early 2000s. These early chat-based reference systems offered a new level of immediacy, allowing users to interact with librarians in real-time, mirroring the in-person experience while offering the convenience of remote access (Casey, 2004). Over time, virtual reference systems have continued to evolve, incorporating a range of digital tools and platforms that facilitate synchronous and asynchronous communication (Hase et al., 2014; Alenzuela & Kamilova, 2018). The integration of these technologies has enabled libraries to provide more dynamic and responsive services, meeting the needs of a diverse and geographically dispersed user base.

Modern virtual reference systems adopt a variety of technologies to deliver timely and accurate information to users. Among the most prominent tools are chatbots, which use artificial intelligence (AI) to handle routine queries and provide instant responses. These AI-driven systems can assist with a wide range of inquiries, from locating resources within the library's catalog to answering frequently asked questions about library services. Chatbots are particularly effective in managing high volumes of queries, freeing up human librarians to focus on more complex and specialized inquiries (Ehrenpreis & DeLooper, 2022). In addition to chatbots, libraries have increasingly integrated video conferencing tools into their virtual reference systems, enabling users to have face-to-face consultations with librarians from any location. Platforms such as Zoom, Microsoft Teams, and Google Meet have become essential components of virtual reference services, particularly during the COVID-19 pandemic, when physical access to libraries was restricted. Complex and more interactive consultations are possible with video conferencing, as librarians may share screens, walk through search techniques, and give individualized advice in real time (Hurst, 2020). AI and machine learning technologies are also playing an increasingly important role in enhancing virtual reference services. These technologies enable the automation of certain aspects of information retrieval, such as personalized recommendations based on user behavior and preferences. By analyzing patterns in user queries, AI systems can suggest relevant resources or anticipate user needs, thereby improving the overall efficiency and accuracy of the reference service (Hanson & Okorie, 2024).). The effectiveness of these technologies in virtual reference systems is evident in their ability to provide users with rapid, accurate, and personalized responses, thereby enhancing the user experience. However, successful integration requires continuous adaptation and training for librarians to manage and utilize these tools effectively.

The rise of virtual reference systems has transformed librarians' roles, necessitating proficiency in various digital tools and platforms (Ullah et al., 2023). They now need to use chat systems, video conferencing software, and AI-driven tools to deliver effective reference services. This shift emphasizes digital literacy, guiding users through complex online databases and digital archives. Strong communication skills are essential for remote assistance. The integration of AI and machine learning has created new roles, including data analysis and some form of literacy in algorithms. Librarians must understand AI systems' limitations and biases to ensure accurate information and address ethical considerations (Saeidnia, 2023).

The Role of Libraries in Promoting Digital Literacy

Digital literacy involves using digital technologies effectively, critically, and critically, including tools, online research, evaluation, and communication in digital environments. In the digital age, these skills are essential for individuals to participate fully in society, access information, and engage with the digital economy. The significance of digital literacy is evident in its impact on education, employment, civic participation, and personal empowerment. Without these skills, individuals are at a significant disadvantage, facing barriers to accessing information, services, and opportunities that are increasingly available only through digital means (Jaeger et al., 2012). Libraries play a crucial role in promoting digital literacy, educating users about digital tools and information navigation. They provide access to technology and training, empowering users to become informed, critical, and engaged participants in the digital landscape, bridging the digital divide and promoting social inclusion (Jaeger et al., 2012).

Libraries have implemented a wide range of programs and initiatives aimed at promoting digital literacy among their communities. These programs often include workshops, online courses, and community outreach efforts tailored to meet the diverse needs of their user base. One common approach is the offering of workshops and training sessions on various aspects of digital literacy. These workshops cover topics such as basic computer skills, internet safety, online research techniques, and the use of specific software or digital tools. For example, the New York Public Library (NYPL) offers a series of digital literacy workshops that cater to different skill levels, from beginner to advanced (The New York Public Library, 2024). These workshops provide hands-on training and are often conducted in multiple languages to serve the library's diverse community. In addition to in-person workshops, many libraries have expanded their digital literacy offerings to include online courses and tutorials. These resources are available on library websites and are designed to be self-paced, allowing users to learn at their own convenience. The British Library, for instance, offers a range of online tutorials on topics such as online privacy, digital creativity, and e-commerce, which are accessible to users around the world (British Library, n.d.). Community outreach is another critical component of libraries' digital literacy initiatives. Libraries frequently collaborate with local schools, community centers, and other organizations to extend their digital literacy programs to underserved populations. For example, the Chicago Public Library's "CyberNavigators" program provides digital literacy training to residents in underserved neighborhoods, with a particular focus on seniors and low-income individuals. (Chicago Public Library Foundation, 2024). The program includes one-on-one mentoring and group classes, with the goal of increasing participants' confidence and competence in using digital tools (Urban Libraries Council, 2024).

The effectiveness of library-led digital literacy programs can be observed across different user groups, including students, professionals, and the elderly. Research has shown that these programs have a significant impact on improving digital skills, particularly among populations that may have limited access to technology and training. For students, digital literacy programs offered by libraries are crucial in supporting academic success (Rafi et al., 2019). Libraries provide students with the skills needed to conduct online research, evaluate sources, and use digital tools for learning and collaboration (Bowles-Terry, 2012). Rafi et al. (2019) in their study found that students who participated in library-led digital literacy programs demonstrated improved academic performance and greater confidence in using digital technologies. Professionals also benefit from digital literacy programs, particularly in the context of career development and job searching. Libraries offer training on the use of professional networking platforms, online job boards, and digital portfolios, which are essential tools in today's job market (Johnson, et al. 2020). For the elderly, digital literacy programs provided by libraries play a vital role in reducing social isolation and improving quality of life. Many seniors face challenges in adapting to new technologies, and library programs help bridge this gap by offering tailored training that addresses their specific needs. Community-based ICT training programs like "Senior Planet" at the New York Public Library for example, can support active aging by improving older adults' technology skills and social connectedness (Gardner et al., 2012). Library-led digital literacy programs significantly enhance individuals' digital competence and confidence, contributing to the development of an informed and digitally literate society through accessible and inclusive education.

Future Opportunities for Libraries in the Digital Age

Despite the challenges, the digital age also presents significant opportunities for libraries to further transform their services through emerging technologies. One of the most promising areas is the use of artificial intelligence (AI) in library operations. AI can be leveraged to improve cataloging and classification systems, personalize user experiences through recommendation algorithms, and enhance virtual reference services with AI-driven chatbots that can provide instant assistance to users. AI also offers opportunities for more advanced data analytics, enabling libraries to better understand user behavior and tailor services to meet specific needs (Cox et al., 2021). Big data is another area where libraries can capitalize on emerging technologies (Adewojo & Dunmade, 2024; Borgman, 2017). Libraries generate and have access to vast amounts of data related to user interactions, resource usage, and collection management. By applying big data analytics, libraries can gain insights into trends and patterns that can inform decision-making and improve service delivery. For example, big data can help libraries identify which resources are most in demand, optimize space utilization, and develop targeted outreach programs (Bamigbola, 2023; Ashikuzzaman, 2024). This data-driven approach allows libraries to operate more efficiently and effectively, maximizing their impact on the communities they serve. Virtual reality (VR) and augmented reality (AR) also offer exciting possibilities for libraries (Marshall et al., 2019). IFLA, 2023; Library Technology, 2024). These technologies can create immersive learning experiences, allowing users to explore digital environments in new and engaging ways. For instance, Oculus Rift and HTC Vive, are common VR devices in libraries typically available for in-library use (Greene & Groenendyk, 2021). Libraries can use Virtual reality to offer virtual tours of historical sites, interactive exhibits, or even virtual classrooms where users can participate in workshops and seminars remotely. Augmented reality can enhance the physical library experience by overlaying digital information onto physical books or exhibits, providing users with additional context and resources as they interact with the library's collections.

Discuss future and emerging trends. Provide insight about the future of the book's theme from the perspective of the chapter focus. Viability of a paradigm, model, implementation issues of proposed programs, etc., may be included in this section. If appropriate, suggest future research opportunities within the domain of the topic.

CONCLUSION

The evolution of libraries from traditional physical spaces to dynamic digital entities highlights their ongoing relevance in the information age. As libraries adapt to technological advancements, they are redefining their roles, broadening access to knowledge, and enhancing user experiences through digital technologies. This transformation presents challenges such as financial constraints and the digital divide but also opportunities for innovation. Libraries have successfully navigated the complexities of digital collections management, ensuring long-term preservation and accessibility. The expansion of online services has democratized access to information, and the integration of AI and multimedia resources has personalized and improved user experiences. Libraries also play a crucial role in promoting digital literacy, bridging the digital divide, and fostering social inclusion. As they continue to embrace emerging technologies like AI, big data, virtual reality, and augmented reality, libraries remain vital institutions that safeguard cultural heritage and empower individuals in the digital age.

ACKNOWLEDGMENT

The authors express their sincere gratitude to the journal editors and anonymous reviewers for their valuable assistance in reviewing and publishing this paper.

REFERENCES

Adewojo, A. A., & Dunmade, A. O. (2024). From big data to intelligent libraries: Leveraging analytics for enhanced user experiences. *Business Information Review*, *41*(3), 02663821241264707. DOI: 10.1177/02663821241264707

Albitz, B. (2014). *Licensing and managing electronic resources*. Elsevier.

Alenzuela, R., & Kamilova, Y. (2018). Synchronous and Asynchronous Engagement in Virtual Library Services as Learning Support Systems from the Perspectives of Post-Graduate Students: A Case Study. [JIStaP]. *Journal of Information Science Theory and Practice*, *6*(1).

Anuradha, P. (2018). Digital transformation of academic libraries: Opportunities and challenges. *IP Indian Journal of Library Science and Information Technology*, *3*(1), 8–10.

Ashikuzzaman, M. D. (2024). The Applications of Big Data in Libraries. Library and Information Science Network. https://www.lisedunetwork.com/the-applications-of-big-data-in-libraries/

Bamigbola, A. A. (2023). *BIG DATA" Revitalizing Librarianship: Impact On Librarians*. Library Philosophy & Practice.

Battles, M. (2004). *Library: An unquiet history*. WW Norton & Company.

Beaumon, B. (2011). Bookshare: Making accessible materials available worldwide. In *World Library and Information Congress: 77th IFLA General Conference and Assembly. San Juan, Puerto Rico.*

Bertot, J. C., Gorham, U., Jaeger, P. T., & Taylor, N. G. (2012). Public Libraries and the Internet 2012: Key findings, recent trends, and future challenges. *Public Library Quarterly*, *31*(4), 303–325. DOI: 10.1080/01616846.2012.732479

Besek, J. (2003). Copyright Issues Relevant to the Creation of a Digital Archive. *De Gruyter*, *32*(3), 86–97. DOI: 10.1515/MFIR.2003.86

Bignoli, C., & Stara, L. (2020). *Responding to rapid change in libraries: a user experience approach*. American Library Association.

Billingham, L. (2014). Improving academic library website accessibility for people with disabilities. *Library Management, 35*(8/9), 565–581. DOI: 10.1108/LM-11-2013-0107

Borgman, C. L. (2017). *Big data, little data, no data: Scholarship in the networked world*. MIT press.

Breeding, M. (2010). Automation Marketplace 2010: The New Frontier. *Library Journal, 135*(6), 22–28.

Breeding, M. (2015). The future of library resource discovery. *Information Standards Quarterly, 27*(1), 24–30. DOI: 10.3789/isqv27no1.2015.04

British Library. (n.d.). Learning at the Library. https://support.bl.uk/Page/Learning

Brown, A. (2013). *Practical digital preservation: A how-to guide for organizations of any size*. Facet Publishing.

Candela, L., Castelli, D., & Pagano, P. (2012). History, evolution, and impact of digital libraries. In *Organizational Learning and Knowledge: Concepts, Methodologies, Tools and Applications* (pp. 837-866). IGI Global. DOI: 10.4018/978-1-60960-783-8.ch301

Casey, A. M. (2004). A Historical Overview of Internet Reference Services for Distance Learners. *Internet Reference Services Quarterly, 9*(3/4), 5–17. Advance online publication. DOI: 10.1300/J136v09n03_02

Cassell, K. A., & Hiremath, U. (2023). *Reference and information services: An introduction*. American Library Association.

Chicago Public Library Foundation. (2024). Bridge the Digital Divide. https://cplfoundation.org/impact/bridge-the-digital-divide/

Clark, J. M. (2007). *The Care of Books: An Essay on the Development of Libraries and Their Influence on Civilization*. Cambridge University Press.

Durodolu, O. O. (2018). Secondary School Teachers' Perceptions of Information Literacy Skills. *Mousaion, 36*(1). Advance online publication. DOI: 10.25159/0027-2639/3873

Durodolu, O.O, Adekanye, A. E (and) Olorunfemi, Y. D (2013). Information literacy skills of arts subject teachers in Lagos state senior secondary schools Nigeria. IOSR Journal of Humanities and Social Science (IOSR-JHSS). Volume 14, Issue 6. Pp. 66-75. https://uzspace.unizulu.ac.za/items/37fdd5bf-9ca0-48b1-919c-db4acc4aec48

Ehrenpreis, M., & DeLooper, J. (2022). Implementing a chatbot on a library website. *Journal of Web Librarianship, 16*(2), 120–142. DOI: 10.1080/19322909.2022.2060893

Ferullo, D. L., & Soules, A. (2012). Managing Copyright in a Digital World. [IJ-DLS]. *International Journal of Digital Library Systems, 3*(4), 1–25. DOI: 10.4018/ijdls.2012100101

Fisher, K. (2020). Copyright and Preservation of Born-digital Materials: Persistent Challenges and Selected Strategies. *the american archivist, 83*(2), 238-267.

Gardner, P. J., Kamber, T., & Netherland, J. (2012). "Getting turned on": using ICT training to promote active ageing in New York city. *The journal of community informatics, 8*(1).

Gautam, D. K. (2014). Impact of digital divide and public libraries. *IOSR Journal of Humanities and Social Science, 19*(12), 59–63. DOI: 10.9790/0837-191245963

Gladney, H. (2009). Long-term preservation of digital records: Trustworthy digital objects. *The American Archivist, 72*(2), 401–435. DOI: 10.17723/aarc.72.2.g513766100731832

Gooding, P., & Fulkerson, N. (2020). Towards a Global Dataset of Digitised Texts: Final Report of the Global Digitised Dataset Network.

Greene, D., & Groenendyk, M. (2021). An environmental scan of virtual and augmented reality services in academic libraries. *Library Hi Tech, 39*(1), 37–47. DOI: 10.1108/LHT-08-2019-0166

Hanson, E. D., & Okorie, U. U. (2024). The roles of Artificial Intelligence in library automation: the prospects and challenges. https://www.globalacademicstar.com/download/article/the-roles-of-artificial-intelligence-in-library-automation-the-prospects-and-challenges.pdf

Hapel, R. (2020). Building a contemporary public library through community engagement: A personal journey. *Public Library Quarterly, 39*(5), 391–409. DOI: 10.1080/01616846.2020.1772621

Hase, V. L., Dhawle, G. U., & Dahibhate, N. B. (2014). Reference and information services in the digital era. *Asian Journal of Multidisciplinary Studies, 2*(6), 18–25.

Hirtle, P. B., Hudson, E., & Kenyon, A. T. (2009). Copyright and cultural institutions: Guidelines for digitization for US libraries, archives, and museums. *Peter B. Hirtle, Emily Hudson, and Andrew T. Kenyon, Copyright And Cultural Institutions: Guidelines For Digitization For Us Libraries, Archives, And Museums, Ithaca, NY: Cornell University Library Press, Forthcoming, U of Melbourne Legal Studies Research Paper*, (434).

Hurst, E. J. (2020). Web Conferencing and Collaboration Tools and Trends. *Journal of Hospital Librarianship, 20*(3), 266–279. DOI: 10.1080/15323269.2020.1780079

International Federation of Library Associations and Institutions (IFLA). (2023, June). Augmented Reality in Libraries https://www.ifla.org/news/augmented-reality-in-libraries/

Jaeger, P. T., Bertot, J. C., Thompson, K. M., Katz, S. M., & DeCoster, E. J. (2012). The intersection of public policy and public access: Digital divides, digital literacy, digital inclusion, and public libraries. *Public Library Quarterly, 31*(1), 1–20. DOI: 10.1080/01616846.2012.654728

Janes, J. (Ed.). (2013). *Library 2020: Today's leading visionaries describe tomorrow's library*. Scarecrow Press.

Johnson, E. M., Lehoahoa, E., Lehoahoa, P. S., & Urquhart, R. (2020). *Increasing digital platform use to help youth find work*. RTI Press. DOI: 10.3768/rtipress.2020.pb.0023.2005

Kari, K. (2020). Digital transformation of information and its impact on libraries. [WJIR]. *World Journal of Innovative Research, 9*(1), 26–30.

Kempf, K. (2023). Moving Libraries toward Digital Transformation. *The International Information & Library Review, 55*(3), 233–240. DOI: 10.1080/10572317.2023.2231715

Koltay, T. (2011). The media and the literacies: Media literacy, information literacy, digital literacy. *Media Culture & Society, 33*(2), 211–221. DOI: 10.1177/0163443710393382

Koltay, T., & Špiranec, S. (2017). Libraries meet research 2.0: Literacies and services. In *Research 2.0 and the Impact of Digital Technologies on Scholarly Inquiry* (pp. 32–52). IGI Global. DOI: 10.4018/978-1-5225-0830-4.ch003

Library Technology. (2024). Augmented Reality and Virtual Reality in Libraries. https://www.lib.pacificu.edu/augmented-reality-and-virtual-reality-in-libraries/

Lodha Genius Programme. (2024). The Evolving Role of Libraries in the Digital Age. Retrieved on 03/06/2024, from https://www.linkedin.com/pulse/evolving-role-libraries-digital-age-lodha-genius-programme-xuhsc/

Mafungwa, T. (2017). *The adoption of technology to enhance innovative user services at CALICO libraries.*

Marshall, D. H., DuBose, J., & Archer, P. (2019). Mixed reality lab at Mississippi state university libraries. *Public Services Quarterly, 15*(1), 51–58. DOI: 10.1080/15228959.2018.1554466

Martin, A. (2008). Digital literacy and the "digital society". *Digital literacies: Concepts, policies and practices, 30*(151), 1029-1055.

National Library of Australia. (.n.d.). Trove. https://trove.nla.gov.au

Neal, J. G. (2014). Advancing from kumbaya to radical collaboration: redefining the future research library. In *Repackaging Libraries for Survival* (pp. 66–76). Routledge.

Pasqui, V. (2024). Digital curation and long-term digital preservation in libraries. *JLIS. it, 15*(1), 109-125.

Pettegree, A. (2017). *The book in the Renaissance.* Yale University Press. DOI: 10.12987/9780300168358

Priya, S., & Ramya, R. (2024). Future Trends and Emerging Technologies in AI and Libraries. *Applications of Artificial Intelligence in Libraries*, 245-271.

Rafi, M., JianMing, Z., & Ahmad, K. (2019). Technology integration for students' information and digital literacy education in academic libraries. *Information Discovery and Delivery, 47*(4), 203–217. DOI: 10.1108/IDD-07-2019-0049

Rao, S., & Sahu, S. C. (2024). The Influence of Artificial Intelligence on Library Services: Enhancing Access, Discovery, and User Engagement. *Academic Libraries*, 350.

Real, B., Bertot, J. C., & Jaeger, P. T. (2014). Rural public libraries and digital inclusion: Issues and challenges. *Information Technology and Libraries, 33*(1), 6–24. DOI: 10.6017/ital.v33i1.5141

Rubin, R. E., & Rubin, R. G. (2020). *Foundations of library and information science.* American Library Association.

Saeidnia, H. R. (2023). Ethical artificial intelligence (AI): Confronting bias and discrimination in the library and information industry. *Library Hi Tech News.* Advance online publication. DOI: 10.1108/LHTN-10-2023-0182

Singh, K. K., & Asif, M. (2019). Emerging trends and technologies for digital transformation of libraries. *IP Indian Journal of Library Science and Information Technology*, *4*(2), 41–43.

Stephens, W. (2023). *How Writing Made Us Human, 3000 BCE to Now*. JHU Press. DOI: 10.56021/9781421446646

Stevenson, S. (2009). Digital divide: A discursive move away from the real inequities. *The Information Society*, *25*(1), 1–22. DOI: 10.1080/01972240802587539

Stiller, J., Gäde, M., & Petras, V. (2013). Multilingual access to digital libraries: The Europeana use case/Mehrsprachiger Zugang zu Digitalen Bibliotheken: Europeana/ Accès multilingue aux bibliothèques numériques: Le cas d'Europeana. *Information-Wissenschaft & Praxis*, *64*(2-3), 86–95. DOI: 10.1515/iwp-2013-0014

Suber, P. (2012). *Open access*. The MIT Press. DOI: 10.7551/mitpress/9286.001.0001

The New York Public Library. (2024). About The New York Public Library Digital Collections. https://digitalcollections.nypl.org/about

Turner, B. (2018). Benetech global literacy services: Working towards a 'born accessible'world. *Learned Publishing*, *31*(1), 25–29. DOI: 10.1002/leap.1141

Ullah, A., Usman, M., & Khan, M. K. (2023). Challenges in delivering modern library services in the 21st century. *International Journal of Social Science Exceptional Research*, *2*(6), 146–151. https://www.allsocialsciencejournal.com/uploads/archives/20231109154831_B-23-27.1.pdf. DOI: 10.54660/IJSSER.2023.2.6.146-151

United Nations. (n.d.).LONTAD: Total Digital Access to the League of Nations Archives. https://libraryresources.unog.ch/lontad

Urban Libraries Council. (2024). The CyberNavigator Program at CPL. https://www.urbanlibraries.org/innovations/the-cybernavigator-program-at-cpl

Van Dijk, J. (2020). *The digital divide*. John Wiley & Sons.

Walters, W. H. (2013). E-books in academic libraries: Challenges for acquisition and collection management. *portal. Portal (Baltimore, Md.)*, *13*(2), 187–211. DOI: 10.1353/pla.2013.0012

Willinsky, J. (2006). *The access principle: The case for open access to research and scholarship*. MIT Press.

Chapter 11
The Institutional Data Supply Chain in Multi-Ranking Systems:
A Case Study of a Turkish Research University

Canan Hazal Akarsu
http://orcid.org/0000-0003-1692-7727
Istanbul University-Cerrahpasa, Turkey

Melike Solak Altuntas
http://orcid.org/0009-0009-3366-8799
Istanbul University-Cerrahpasa, Turkey

Tarik Kucukdeniz
http://orcid.org/0000-0002-6670-1809
Istanbul University-Cerrahpasa, Turkey

ABSTRACT

This chapter explores how colleges balance the demands of international rankings with their own data. Research typically focuses on how rankings affect university tactics. The daily grind, how teams actually collect, arrange, and present data, gets less attention. The paper examines how information moves between departments prior to reaching ranking agencies using an example from a Turkish research institution. Not everything is going smoothly. Different teams employ different approaches, which results in a lot of headaches and repetitive effort. Nonetheless, informal co-

DOI: 10.4018/979-8-2600-0111-0.ch011

operation is how people manage to get things done. The research refers to this as a "institutional data supply chain", a novel perspective that not only clarifies the procedure but also provides some useful suggestions for improving data management.

INTRODUCTION

Over the past two decades, global university ranking systems have expanded rapidly. The Academic Ranking of World Universities (ARWU) in 2003 was the first major global ranking. It started a trend that has grown into an ecosystem of more than 25 ranking systems, each with its own methods, indicators, and data needs (Hazelkorn, 2015; Shin et al., 2011). The Times Higher Education (THE) World University Rankings, Quacquarelli Symonds (QS) World University Rankings, AppliedHE World University Rankings, Higher Education Ranking (HE), ARWU, regional benchmarking platforms such as the European Higher Education Sector Observatory (EHESO) (European Education and Culture Executive Agency, 2024), and numerous national and thematic rankings now form a complex web of evaluation that shapes institutional strategy, resource allocation, and public perception worldwide (Hazelkorn, 2017; Marginson and van der Wende, 2007). The proliferation of these systems has been accompanied by sustained debate over their quality and methodological transparency: the Berlin Principles on Ranking of Higher Education Institutions set out widely cited criteria against which ranking methodologies should be evaluated (International Ranking Expert Group (IREG), 2006), and alternative multidimensional approaches—most prominently U-Multirank—have sought to address the limitations of single-score league tables by comparing institutions across multiple performance dimensions (van Vught and Ziegele, 2012). THE Impact Rankings alone attracted submissions from more than 2,500 universities in 2025 (Times Higher Education, 2025), illustrating the scale of institutional engagement with ranking systems. As an illustrative estimate, even if each of these institutions spends only 200 person-hours on a single submission—a figure consistent with the scale of data processing documented in this study— the total annual effort for one ranking system would exceed 500,000 person-hours. The resulting effort points to a substantial yet largely invisible organizational commitment.

The behavioral consequences of rankings for universities are well documented. Espeland and Sauder (2007) established the foundational concept of ranking reactivity, defined as public performance to change the social worlds they are supposed to simply mirror. Subsequent work has demonstrated how rankings function as "engines of anxiety" (Espeland and Sauder, 2016), reshape institutional governance (Hazelkorn, 2015), create discursive resilience that sustains their influence even amid criticism (Hamann and Ringel, 2023), and generate both strategic responses and institutional fatigue (Proserpio et al., 2024). In the Global South, rankings have been shown to drive gaming behaviors and impose Western university models on diverse institutional traditions (Bayanbayeva, 2025).

However, this comprehensive literature on ranking effects has left a significant gap regarding ranking processes. While the literature demonstrates why universities react to rankings and what behavioral distortions result, remarkably little is known about how institutions actually organize, process, and manage the data that feeds into ranking submissions. The internal organizational machinery—the people, templates, databases, validation procedures, and transformation workflows that convert raw institutional data into ranking-ready outputs—remains largely unexamined in the higher education literature. This omission has important consequences. The lack of understanding of what is referred to in this study as the institutional data supply chain leads to several problems. Ranking agencies design reporting requirements without being aware of the burden they impose on universities. University leaders allocate resources without fully understanding the complexity created by multiple ranking processes. In addition, the substantial interpretive labor embedded in ranking data remains invisible, and the resources required to sustain it are correspondingly underrecognized in institutional staffing and budgeting models (Whistle, 2017).

The scale of this blind spot is striking given that institutions may calculate upwards of 500 metrics in any given reporting year (Whistle, 2017), that data governance has been identified as the top strategic issue facing higher education institutions (Grajek and Milhans, 2024), and that institutional research offices have evolved from compliance-oriented functions to strategic intelligence units (Botha et al., 2024; Volkwein, 2008). The organizational complexity of managing these parallel data flows— what Power (1997) might recognize as an instance of the "audit society" penetrating deeply into institutional operations—has not been empirically examined. Recent work has begun to examine ranking production processes from the perspective of ranking agencies themselves (Barron, 2023) and the broader datafication of universities (Komljenovic et al., 2024), but the internal organizational machinery through which individual institutions manage multi-ranking data submissions has not been empirically investigated.

This research addresses this gap by developing the institutional data supply chain as an analytical framework for understanding how universities manage multi-directional information flows across heterogeneous ranking systems. The framework draws on supply chain management theory to model the multi-stage transformation of institutional data from departmental collection through central processing to ranking submission. Beyond filling a scholarly gap, this framework aims to make visible what has been invisible: the organizational costs of ranking participation, the interpretive labor hidden behind seemingly objective numbers, and the structural challenges that the current multi-ranking ecosystem imposes on universities. Theoretically, the framework extends ranking reactivity theory (Espeland and Sauder, 2007) by revealing the material infrastructure—the templates, databases, and transformation workflows—through which rankings reshape institutional operations, connecting the behavioral dynamics of reactivity to their concrete organizational enactment. The study is grounded in an insider case study at Istanbul University-Cerrahpasa (IUC), a Turkish research university that simultaneously participates in 14 ranking systems through a dedicated Corporate Data Management Office (CDMO)—providing a perspective from the Global South, where institutions face the dual burden of satisfying both domestic accountability requirements and international ranking expectations.

This chapter is primarily a conceptual contribution, not an institutional case description or a how-to guide. The IUC case is used to develop, illustrate, and stress-test the institutional data supply chain framework rather than to argue for the generalizability of any specific organizational arrangement. The practical implications that follow from the framework are accordingly presented as derivatives of the conceptual contribution, not as the chapter's main object. The argument is also explicitly ambivalent about the framework's normative valence: Building a more efficient supply chain is shown to ease institutional compliance with rankings while simultaneously deepening institutional entanglement with the very evaluation regimes that generate the burden.

The central research question is: **How does a research university organize, process, and manage institutional data flows across multiple, heterogeneous ranking systems?** Three sub-questions guide the analysis:

1. What organizational structures and processes constitute the institutional data supply chain?
2. How is raw departmental data transformed into ranking-ready submissions?
3. What challenges arise from simultaneous participation in 14 ranking systems with different data requirements?

The research proceeds as follows. Section Background reviews four converging literatures— institutional research, ranking reactivity, data governance, and supply chain management— to identify the specific gap this study addresses. Section Main Focus of the Chapter presents the institutional data supply chain as a conceptual framework and derives four analytical propositions. Section Methodology describes the insider case study methodology and its distinctive epistemic advantages. Section Findings presents the empirical findings organized around the five stages of the supply chain. Section Discussion evaluates the propositions against the evidence. Section Solutions and Recommendations discusses theoretical and practical implications, and Sections Future Research Directions and Conclusions conclude with recommendations for institutions, ranking agencies, and policymakers.

BACKGROUND

This study sits at the intersection of four bodies of literature that have developed largely independently: institutional research, ranking reactivity, data governance in higher education, and supply chain management. This section reviews each stream and identifies the specific gap that the institutional data supply chain framework is designed to address.

Institutional Research: From Compliance to Strategic Intelligence

The field of institutional research (IR) was most influentially theorized by Volkwein (1999). His "four faces" framework defines the roles played by IR professionals: information authority, policy analyst, spin doctor, and scholar-researcher. Later studies added a fifth dimension to this framework. In this view, IR is also seen as a knowledge manager. In this role, raw data is transformed into actionable organizational intelligence (Volkwein, 2008). Terenzini (1993) described IR work as consisting of three levels of organizational intelligence: technical/ analytical, contextual, and issues intelligence. The global spread of IR practices was examined by Webber and Calderon (2015), whose comparative study showed that IR structures vary significantly across national contexts. In the United States, the Association for Institutional Research (AIR) has tracked the evolving function of IR offices, finding that while the majority remain in traditional compliance-reporting roles, a growing minority are embracing institutional effectiveness and strategic analytics functions (Calderon and Mathies, 2013). More recently, Botha et al. (2024) examined IR capacity building across four regional associations (AIR, EAIR, SAAIR, HEIR). The study argues for the need for more advanced approaches informed by systems thinking. The evolution toward data analytics has been further documented by Webber and Zheng (2020), who examined how big data capabilities can support organizational functions from admissions to strategic planning. However, the IR literature has mainly focused on the functions performed by IR offices. It has paid less attention to the operational workflows through which data is managed. In particular, the specific challenge of serving multiple external ranking systems at the same time has not been sufficiently addressed.

The closest the literature comes to an operational focus is in discussions of reporting burden (Whistle, 2017). However, these analyses remain at an aggregate level. They measure time and cost but do not map actual data flows. Ironically, as the IR field has shifted its focus from compliance to strategic intelligence, the basic data management work that is still essential for external reporting has received less, not more, scholarly attention. In this process, it has become largely invisible within the field's own upward trajectory.

Ranking Reactivity and the Sociology of Quantification

While the IR literature explains the functions of data management, a separate line of research has examined the broader institutional dynamics that generate the need for such work. The theoretical basis for understanding how institutions respond to rankings was established by Espeland and Sauder (2007), who identified two mechanisms that drive reactivity: self-fulfilling prophecy and commensuration. Commensuration refers to the process of making qualitatively different entities comparable through a common metric (Espeland and Stevens, 1998).Their longitudinal study of U.S. law school rankings demonstrated how rankings reshape the institutions they measure, transforming ordinal positions into organizational goals. This framework was extended by Espeland and Sauder (2016), which documented rankings as "engines of anxiety" that generate pervasive behavioral effects across institutional hierarchies. Hazelkorn (2015, 2017) drew attention to the policy dimension of ranking influence. Their work shows that rankings have evolved from a statistical and technical phenomenon into a geopolitical instrument that drives competition at institutional, national, and global levels. Shin et al. (2011) provided a comprehensive analysis of ranking methodologies and their differential impacts, arguing that rankings induce short-termism and resource reallocation toward maximizing relative positions. The discursive dynamics of rankings were examined by Hamann and Ringel (2023), who showed that rankings sustain their influence through the shared discursive efforts of both supporters and critics. In addition, Brankovic et al. (2023) analyzed the institutionalization patterns of ranking systems. Sauder and Espeland (2009) further demonstrated how rankings create "tight coupling" between organizational structures and external evaluation criteria, generating isomorphic pressures that reshape internal processes.

Rankings can also be situated within a broader scholarly tradition on the social con- sequences of quantification. This tradition has established three insights relevant to the present study. First, audit and accountability rituals reshape organizational behavior by making certain activities visible at the expense of others (Power, 1997), transforming institutions into performers of their own metrics (Strathern, 2000). Second, the historical drive toward "trust in numbers" (Porter, 1995) produces what Muller (2018) called "metric fixation." This refers to the widespread belief that quantitative indicators can replace professional judgment. However, composite indicators such as rankings, much like GDP, may hide as much as they reveal (Vernon et al., 2018). Third, performance indicators are not merely descriptive but constitutive: they actively shape the phenomena they purport to measure (Dahler-Larsen, 2014).

Parallel concerns have been articulated within the research-evaluation community itself: the Leiden Manifesto for research metrics sets out ten principles for the responsible use of quantitative indicators in research assessment, warning explicitly against over-reliance on narrow bibliometric measures (Hicks et al., 2015), and the San Francisco Declaration on Research Assessment (DORA) calls on universities, funders, and publishers to move away from journal-level metrics as proxies for research quality (DORA, 2012). Together, these works establish that rankings are not neutral measurement tools but active agents that reconfigure organizational priorities, and that the responsible-metrics movement has produced explicit normative standards against which ranking-driven data practices can be assessed. The present study uses these insights as more than background scaffolding: Power's notion of audit infrastructure, Strathern's account of performative accountability, and Muller's concept of metric fixation each return in the analysis of the IUC supply chain to interpret specific empirical patterns—respectively, the verification work that the CDMO performs on behalf of ranking agencies, the reorganization of internal data collection around external audit categories, and the path dependency that emerges once an institution professionalizes its ranking submissions (see Section Solutions and Recommendations)

Other recent work has examined ranking dynamics in specific regional contexts. Proserpio et al. (2024) documented how "ranking fever" has given way to "ranking fatigue" among academic leaders in East Asia, with leaders disbelieving in rankings yet continuing to engage with them. In the Global South, Bayanbayeva (2025) identified strategic gaming techniques in Kazakhstan's centralized higher education system. Moreover, the ranking ecosystem continues to grow. The emergence of sustainability-focused rankings—including the THE Impact Rankings (which evaluate universities against the United Nations Sustainable Development Goals), QS Sustainability (which assesses environmental, social, and governance performance), Green Mentors Global Green University Ranking (which include space, air, earth, energy, water topics) and UI GreenMetric (the Universitas Indonesia World University Rankings on sustainability, organised around six environmental and campus domains)—and regional evaluation systems has further reinforced this trend. As a result, universities are not only maintaining existing data flows but also continuously creating new ones. This makes the lack of systematic research on institutional data management increasingly significant. While the quantification literature establishes these dynamics at the theoretical level, recent empirical work has begun to examine how ranking production actually operates. Barron (2023) used institutional ethnography to examine the transnational coordination through which rankings are produced, tracing the data work performed by ranking agencies, bibliometric providers, and institutional contacts. However, Barron's analysis focused on the production side of rankings, namely how ranking agencies collect and process data. In contrast, the institutional submission side was not addressed. In particular, it did not examine how a single university internally manages the data flows that feed into multiple ranking submissions. More broadly, the ranking reactivity literature has mainly focused on outcomes and behaviors, that is, what institutions do and why they respond in certain ways, while largely overlooking how these processes actually operate.

It is known that institutions invest resources in ranking improvement, but not what the data management infrastructure looks like, how data flows through it, or what organizational challenges arise from the multi-ranking environment. This methodological focus on perceptions, strategies, and discourses has largely left the material infrastructure of ranking data management unexamined. This infrastructure includes templates, databases, validation workflows, and transformation processes.

Data Governance in Higher Education

The reactive dynamics described above generate concrete data demands, yet the governance literature that should address those demands has developed separately. Data governance in higher education has emerged as a growing concern, with the EDUCAUSE 2025 Top 10 identifying "the data-empowered institution" as the leading strategic issue (Grajek and Milhans, 2024). Guy (2025) proposed a Structurational Data Governance Model applying Giddens's structuration theory to analyze the recursive relationship between data governance structures and data practices in higher education. Earlier work by Jim and Chang (2018) documented the fragmented state of data governance across institutions. Data governance frameworks typically prescribe data quality standards, stewardship roles, and lifecycle management procedures. While these principles are relevant, they assume a relatively stable set of data users and definitions. However, this assumption no longer holds when a university must meet the requirements of multiple external ranking agencies at the same time. This is because each agency uses different indicator definitions, time frames, and evidence requirements.

Industry and practitioner frameworks have also contributed to this space, emphasizing that data transformation in higher education is strategy-led and technology-enabled but ultimately people-driven. de Oliveira et al. (2025) presented a case study of an integrated analytics ecosystem for institutional strategic transformation. The NORC at the University of Chicago produced landmark methodological reviews of both domestic and international ranking systems (Barari et al., 2024, 2025), identifying data quality limitations and subjective methodological decisions as cross-cutting issues.

Komljenovic et al. (2024) identified seven dimensions of university datafication: aspirational, technological, legal, commercial, organizational, ideological, and existential. The study also argues that transforming universities into data-driven organizations requires substantial effort to ensure interoperability across digital systems. While their broad framework encompasses multiple forms of institutional data, it does not trace ranking specific data flows or map the internal transformation pipeline that converts raw departmental data into ranking submissions. More broadly, the data governance literature in higher education has remained largely generic. It addresses data management principles but does not sufficiently focus on the very practical and specific challenge of managing data flows that must simultaneously meet the requirements of 14 external ranking agencies with different indicator definitions, time requirements, and evidence standards.

The Data Supply Chain: A Cross-Disciplinary Framework

None of the three preceding strands of literature provides an operational model for the multi-stage data transformation process required by ranking participation. Supply chain management (SCM), defined as the coordination of material, information, and financial flows across organizational boundaries (Lambert and Cooper, 2000; Mentzer et al., 2001; Tirpan, 2019), is used here as more than an evocative metaphor. It is treated as an analytical framework that contributes four specific elements which the adjacent traditions do not directly supply. First, SCM provides a stage-decomposition logic: it disciplines the analyst to disaggregate an apparently continuous data process into discrete value-adding transformations (Collection, Aggregation, Normalization, Transformation, Submission) that can be examined independently for their inputs, outputs, and bottlenecks. Second, SCM offers the concept of postponement or delayed differentiation (Mentzer et al., 2001): customization to downstream consumers is deferred to the latest feasible stage, a pattern that the present study identifies in the way IUC maintains undifferentiated institutional data upstream and only diverges into ranking specific formats at the Transformation stage. Third, SCM supplies a fan-out architecture appropriate to a single producer serving many heterogeneous consumers, a configuration that data governance and infrastructure studies have not formalized for the ranking submission context. Fourth, SCM brings with it a capacity, throughput, and consolidation-ratio vocabulary that allows the labor and material costs of ranking participation to be characterized in process-metric terms rather than only as discursive or behavioral effects. By contrast, data governance (Guy, 2025; Komljenovic et al., 2024) contributes the principles and roles that should govern such a chain; institutional ethnography (Rankin, 2017; Smith, 2005) contributes the analytical lens on textually mediated coordination at each stage; and infrastructure studies (Bowker and Star, 1999; Leonelli and Tempini, 2020; Star and Ruhleder, 1996) contribute the recognition that classification choices are consequential. SCM is therefore positioned in this study as the operational backbone of the framework, into which these adjacent perspectives are integrated. The concept of a "data supply chain" has also gained traction in industry and legal scholarship (e.g., Reyes and Parella, 2026), where it describes the journey of raw data through processing stages to emerge as finished data products.

In education, Williamson (2018) documented the "hidden architecture" of big data in- frastructure in universities. The study revealed complex assemblages of human and nonhuman actors. The Integrated Tertiary Educational Supply Chain Management (ITESCM) model applied supply chain concepts to the education and research delivery process (Chowdhury et al., 2025). However, these applications have focused on the educational process (student as product) rather than the data management process (ranking submission as product). Bowker and Star (1999) provided a complementary perspective through their analysis of classification systems as infrastructure, demonstrating that the categories through which data is organized are not neutral containers but consequential choices that shape what can be known, communicated, and compared—an insight directly relevant to how ranking indicators structure institutional data collection.

The science and technology studies (STS) literature on data practices offers additional theoretical resources. Borgman (2015) demonstrated that data rarely stand alone but require extensive contextual work—software, protocols, metadata—to become usable, a dynamic clearly observable in ranking data management. Star and Ruhleder (1996) showed that infrastructure becomes visible only upon breakdown, a pattern directly applicable to institutional data processes that surface only when a definitional inconsistency forces reprocessing. Leonelli and Tempini (2020) introduced the concept of "data journeys" to trace how data travels across institutional spaces and disciplinary boundaries. The present study adopts the "supply chain" rather than "journey" metaphor because it foregrounds the production logic, quality checkpoints, and fan-out architecture that distinguish ranking data management from the more open-ended movement of research data.

Institutional ethnography (IE) offers a complementary analytical resource. Smith (2005) introduced the concept of ruling texts—standardized documentary instruments that coordinate the work of dispersed organizational actors toward institutionally consequential ends. While Barron (2023) applied IE to trace the production-side coordination of ranking data, the concept of ruling texts has not been applied to the submission-side instruments—collection templates, portal interfaces, data request forms—through which individual universities organize their data management work.

Identifying the Gap

The four strands of literature reviewed above converge on a shared blind spot. To the best of the authors' knowledge, no published study has empirically mapped the full internal data workflow through which universities collect, reconcile, validate, and submit data to multiple ranking agencies simultaneously. The convergence of the four traditions on this absence is not coincidental: each contributes one component that the others cannot supply, yet none has assembled them into a single traceable workflow. The IR literature describes the functions that data offices perform but not the ranking specific workflows through which those functions are operationalized. The ranking reactivity and quantification literature theorize behavioral and constitutive effects of measurement but stop short of the organizational infrastructure through which those effects are materially enacted. The data governance literature provides principles and roles but lacks ranking specific applications. The supply chain literature provides the conceptual machinery for staged transformation but has not been applied to university ranking data flows. The institutional data supply chain proposed in this study is the organizational mechanism that links these four contributions into a single object of empirical analysis. The practical consequences of leaving this object unexamined are significant: stakeholders across the ranking ecosystem—agencies, university leaders, and policymakers—currently operate without an empirical understanding of the internal processes through which ranking data is produced. This study addresses this gap by introducing the institutional data supply chain as a framework that integrates insights from all four streams to map the journey of institutional data from departmental origins to ranking outputs. In this way, the study responds to calls for research that goes beyond simply documenting ranking effects and instead examines the organizational mechanisms through which ranking systems enter institutional life (Brankovic et al., 2023; Sauder and Espeland, 2009).

MAIN FOCUS OF THE CHAPTER

Drawing on supply chain management theory (Lambert and Cooper, 2000; Mentzer et al., 2001) and adapting it to the higher education context, this research proposes the institutional data supply chain as an analytical framework for understanding how universities manage ranking-related information flows. Before presenting the model, it is worth explaining why a supply chain metaphor is appropriate and what analytical work it performs. Several alternative framings might be considered. A data pipeline metaphor captures the sequential processing stages but obscures the bidirectional flows (requirements flowing upstream, feedback flowing laterally) that characterize ranking data management. An information architecture framing emphasizes structural design but underplays the dynamic, process-oriented character of data work. Bowker and Star (1999) provide a compelling account of classification systems as infrastructure, which captures the invisibility and taken-for-grantedness of data processes, yet infrastructure studies tend to emphasize stability rather than the cyclical, deadline-driven transformation work that ranking submissions demand. The "data journey" metaphor (Leonelli and Tempini, 2020) explains the movement of data across institutional spaces. However, it emphasizes an open-ended form of movement rather than the goal-oriented, deadline-driven, and quality-controlled transformation process that characterizes ranking data management. By contrast, the supply chain metaphor is preferred because it highlights three key features that distinguish this type of data management. These are: (a) a multi-stage transformation process with distinct value-added activities at each stage, (b) multiple heterogeneous consumers, namely ranking agencies, with different requirements served from a common upstream source, and (c) multi-directional flows operating at the same time, with data moving downstream, requirements moving upstream, and feedback flowing in both directions.

The metaphor also has limitations. Unlike commercial supply chains driven by market demand, ranking data flows operate under quasi-coercive pressure: non-participation carries reputational risks (Hazelkorn, 2015). Moreover, the supply chain framing may inadvertently depoliticize a power-laden process, obscuring the asymmetry between agencies who define indicators and universities who bear compliance costs. Supply chain concepts are therefore used in this study as an adapted analytical lens rather than as a fully equivalent management model, retained for their analytical utility while remaining attentive to these limitations.

The Five-Stage Model

The institutional data supply chain comprises five stages (see Figure 1)

1. **Collection (Upstream):** Raw data is collected from organizational units such as faculties, departments, institutes, and administrative offices. Standardized templates and data request tools are used in this process. This stage involves designing collection instruments, distributing them to data providers, and receiving unit-level responses in varied formats.
2. **Aggregation (Mid-stream):** Unit-level submissions are consolidated into institutional master datasets. Individual faculty or departmental data files are merged, deduplicated, and organized into coherent institutional records. This stage reduces data volume while preserving granularity.
3. **Normalization (Mid-stream):** Aggregated data is matched with institutional meta-data frameworks and ranking-specific indicator definitions. Author names are standardized, departmental codes are made consistent across systems, and the data is classified according to both institutional taxonomies and external classification schemes. Examples of institutional taxonomies include faculty-

department mappings, while external classification schemes include journal quartile tiers and ISCO- 08 (International Standard Classification of Occupations) codes.

4. **Transformation (Downstream):** Normalized institutional data is reformatted to meet the specific requirements of each ranking system. The same underlying data, namely staff counts, student numbers, publication metrics, and financial figures, is reorganized into different templates, indicator formats, and evidence packages required by each ranking agency.
5. **Submission (Downstream):** Finalized data packages are uploaded to ranking agency portals, accompanied by supporting evidence documentation, narrative sections, and verification materials. Quality checks, version control, and submission status tracking occur at this stage.

The transitions between stages are defined by the nature of the data transformation performed. The Collection-to-Aggregation boundary is crossed when unit-level data files are merged into a single institutional record. The Aggregation-to-Normalization boundary is marked by the application of external classification schemes or metadata standards to the aggregated data. The Normalization-to-Transformation boundary occurs when normalized data is restructured to meet a specific ranking system's format requirements. The Transformation-to-Submission boundary is reached when data packages are finalized for portal upload. In practice, these boundaries may be crossed iteratively rather than sequentially as noted in the limitations.

Three Flow Types

Analogous to physical supply chains where material, information, and cash flow in different directions (Lambert and Cooper, 2000), the institutional data supply chain features three concurrent flows. The analogy is structural rather than exact: while data flow maps readily onto material flow, and requirements flow parallels the information flow of customer specifications, the feedback flow does not correspond directly to the financial flow of classical supply chains. Rather, feedback represents a second information channel— performance data flowing back from ranking outcomes to inform upstream decisions—that has no precise SCM analog, consistent with the observation that institutional data supply chains operate outside market mechanisms (Hazelkorn, 2015).

- **Data Flow (Downstream):** Raw departmental data moves toward ranking ready outputs through the five transformation stages.
- **Requirements Flow (Upstream):** The specifications set by ranking agencies, including indicator definitions, submission templates, evidence require-

ments, and deadlines, move backward through the supply chain. These elements shape data collection tools and data processing decisions.

- **Feedback Flow (Bidirectional):** Ranking results and performance analyses feed back into the system, informing strategic adjustments to data collection priorities, template designs, and institutional investment decisions.

The "One Source, Many Outputs" Principle

A defining feature of the institutional data supply chain is the one-source, many-outputs principle. According to this principle, the same underlying institutional data, such as faculty counts, student demographic information, and publication records, must be reformatted and restructured differently for each ranking system. This creates a fan-out architecture in which upstream stages serve multiple downstream branches, each with its own transformation requirements. The term "fan-out" is borrowed from systems engineering, where it describes the number of downstream consumers that a single output source can serve.

In supply chain management theory, the practice of maintaining undifferentiated products upstream and deferring market-specific customization to downstream stages is known as postponement or delayed differentiation (Mentzer et al., 2001). The institutional data supply chain shows this pattern. Raw institutional data remains in a common format throughout the Collection and Aggregation stages. Ranking-specific differentiation appears only at the Transformation stage. This postponement structure is efficiency enhancing, minimizing redundant data collection while maximizing flexibility to serve diverse downstream consumers.

This principle has a critical corollary. Because the same source data must be interpreted

through different classificatory lenses (Bowker and Star, 1999), the transformation process is not merely technical but inherently interpretive. Deciding whether a researcher counts as "faculty" (for THE, which uses full-time equivalents, or FTE) or "academic staff" (for QS, which uses head count, or HC) requires classificatory judgment that shapes the institutional portrait each ranking produces. The institutional data supply chain is therefore not a neutral channel of transfer. Rather, it is an active site of commensuration (Espeland and Stevens, 1998). In this space, qualitatively different institutional realities are made comparable through the discipline of standardized indicators.

Analytical Propositions

The framework generates four analytical propositions that guide the empirical investigation:

1. **Transformation complexity is hypothesized to grow more than linearly with the number of ranking systems:** each additional ranking system introduces not only one additional output but also reconciliation demands against each existing system's definitions. With n systems sharing k common data elements, the number of pairwise definitional reconciliation tasks is structurally proportional to $n(n - 1)/2 \times k$, which is consistent with super-linear—rather than strictly linear—scaling. Direct empirical measurement of this scaling, including marginal cost per additional system, is left to future comparative research.
2. **Upstream data collection is shaped by downstream requirements:** ranking agency indicator definitions propagate backward through the supply chain, determining what data is collected and how it is organized at the departmental level.
3. **The supply chain generates its own labor demands:** the normalization and transformation stages require specialized knowledge work—what Bowker and Star (1999) called "invisible work"—that is neither recognized in institutional staffing models nor captured in ranking methodology discussions.
4. **The supply chain instantiates a power asymmetry:** ranking agencies define the requirements. In other words, they determine what should be reported, how it should be formatted, and when it should be submitted. Universities, by contrast, bear the full cost of compliance. Their ability to negotiate indicator definitions or reporting timelines is also quite limited (Hazelkorn, 2015).

Figure 1. The institutional data supply chain: A five-stage model with three concurrent flow types

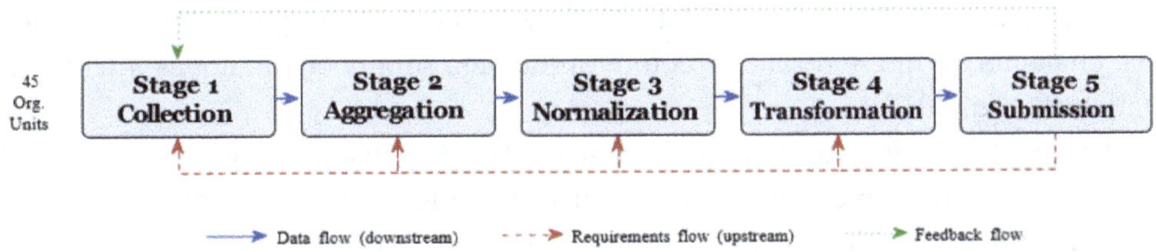

METHODOLOGY

Research Design: Insider Case Study Informed by Institutional Ethnography

This study employs an insider case study design (Stake, 1995; 1995; Yin, 2018) enriched by analytical concepts drawn from Dorothy Smith's institutional ethnography (IE) (Smith, 2005, 2006; Smith and Griffith, 2022). From IE, the study borrows two key analytical sensibilities: attention to how textually mediated practices—forms, templates, reports, data systems—coordinate activity across multiple organizational sites (Rankin, 2017), and the concept of "ruling texts" (Smith, 2005) —standardized instruments that coordinate the work of dispersed organizational actors toward institutionally consequential ends. While the study does not constitute a full IE in Smith's sense, it is animated by IE's core insight that institutional coordination is accomplished through texts, and that these texts deserve empirical scrutiny.

The case of Istanbul University-Cerrahpasa (IUC) was selected as what Stake (1995) terms an "instrumental" case and what Yin (2018) termed a "revelatory case": the insider position that enables this study is precisely what makes the phenomenon observable, providing access to a complete documentary trail—from data request template to ranking portal submission—that would be inaccessible to an external researcher. IUC is analytically valuable because it participates simultaneously in 14 ranking systems, providing sufficient complexity to observe the full range of data supply chain challenges, and because the recent establishment of the CDMO (October 2023) means that both the creation and ongoing operation of data management infrastructure could be documented. The study operates within an interpretive-qualitative paradigm; quantitative measures reported in the findings—file counts, type distributions, consolidation ratios—serve as descriptive process metrics that characterize the scale and structure of the data supply chain, not as inferential statistics (Yin, 2018).

This methodology is designed to be transferable. Any institution with a centralized or semi-centralized data management function could conduct a comparable study by: (a) cataloguing all files involved in a single annual ranking cycle (incoming and submitted), (b) mapping the transformation path for each ranking system from data request to portal submission, (c) constructing a cross-system indicator matrix to identify definitional incon- sistencies, and (d) documenting the organizational coordination required at each stage. The five-stage framework provides a structured template for organizing such an analysis, while the specific findings would necessarily reflect each institution's unique organizational configuration.

The insider dimension is essential to this study. As the founding Director of the CDMO, the authors occupies a unique vantage point at the center of the institutional data supply chain, with direct access to data flows, decision rationales, and practical challenges that would be inaccessible to an external researcher (Brannick and Coghlan, 2007; Unluer, 2012). Insider status confers epistemic privileges—deep contextual knowledge, access to tacit processes—alongside risks such as naturalization of local practices and difficulty achieving analytical distance (Costley et al., 2010; Merton, 1972). To manage these risks, the authors relied on documentary evidence rather than personal recollection, maintained a research diary, and sought to present findings that include challenges and limitations rather than only success narratives.

Case Context: Istanbul University-Cerrahpasa

Istanbul University-Cerrahpasa (IUC) is a public research university in Istanbul, Turkey, with roots dating to 1933. It is one of 23 institutions designated as "research universities" by the Council of Higher Education (YOK) out of 209 universities in Turkey, currently classified in the A2 performance tier (ranked 17th nationally). The university comprises 2,829 academic staff and 34,598 students from 71 countries, organized across 9 faculties, 6 institutes, 5 vocational schools, and numerous research centers.

The CDMO was established by Senate Decision dated 26 October 2023 (Session 54, Decision No. 2), formalized through a directive grounded in Law No. 2547 on Higher Education. The office reports directly to the Rector and is mandated to: (a) ensure data quality, consistency, and integrity across the university; (b) implement data governance policies and standards; (c) provide analytics and decision support; (d) monitor and manage university ranking submissions; (e) build institutional data literacy; and (f) facilitate interdepartmental data collaboration. The office coordinates data flows from 24 academic units and 21 administrative units to 14 external ranking and evaluation systems.

The CDMO model represents one organizational configuration—a centralized, rector-reporting data office. Universities with distributed IR functions, where ranking data is managed by individual faculties or by multiple administrative units without central coordination, would likely exhibit different supply chain architectures. Three structural differences can be anticipated. First, in distributed configurations the Aggregation stage is typically performed in parallel by several office-level actors rather than in a single hub, with the consequence that downstream Normalization must reconcile heterogeneous unit-level interpretations rather than apply a single institutional schema; this lengthens the chain and increases the likelihood of definitional drift between units. Second, distributed governance tends to displace the Normalization and Transformation stages toward the individual ranking submissions, so that the same data element may be interpreted multiple times within the same institution—an outcome that the centralized IUC model avoids through its master metadata file and consolidated personnel database. Third, distributed configurations are more vulnerable to the temporal-misalignment challenge (Section Findings) because submission cycles operate without a single calendar-keeping authority. The five- stage framework is designed to accommodate both centralized and distributed configurations, as the stages describe functional transformations rather than organizational positions; the IUC case should therefore be read as documenting one configuration in depth, not as an exhaustive account of how all universities organize ranking data work. The methodological implications of this scope decision are revisited in Section Solutions and Recommendations.

At the time of this study, IUC actively submitted data to 14 primary ranking and evaluation systems: THE World University Rankings, THE Impact Rankings, QS World University Rankings, QS Sustainability Rankings, Round University Ranking (RUR), UI GreenMetric, Green Mentors, AppliedHE World University Rankings, HE Ranking, URAP (University Ranking by Academic Performance), YOK Phase 1 and Phase 2 national evaluations, TUIK (Turkish Statistical Institute) reporting, and the European Higher Education Sector Observatory (EHESO). EHESO is not a global ranking in the conventional sense but a benchmarking and reporting platform launched in 2024 by the European Education and Culture Executive Agency (EACEA), which compiles indicator data from approximately 3,500 European higher education institutions to support cross-institutional comparison and policy monitoring (European Education and Culture Executive Agency, 2024). It is included in this study because, from a data supply chain perspective, it imposes the same kind of structured indicator submission and evidence requirements as the other systems. Additionally, the university participates in the Research University Program and the Entrepreneurial and Innovative University Index, which draw substantially on data already collected for the primary systems. This study focuses on the 14 primary systems that require dedicated data collection and submission workflows.

Data Sources

The study draws on three categories of data collected between January 2024 and February 2026:

Document Analysis (Primary Source): A corpus of over 3,800 files (with the exact count varying as the 2026 collection cycle was still in progress at the time of writing) was analyzed, including data collection templates distributed to academic and administrative units (General Data Request forms); completed unit submissions organized by year and ranking system; submitted data packages formatted for each ranking agency; institutional metadata files (master indicator lists, department mapping tables, program registries); ranking portal outputs and confirmation documents; and internal correspondence related to data collection and submission.

Process Mapping: As part of the CDMO's mandate, systematic documentation was maintained of data workflows across two full annual collection cycles (2024 and 2025) and the initial stages of a third (early 2026). This included direct observation of data transformation processes, recording of decision points and challenges, and documentation of the complete path from data request issuance to ranking portal submission for each ranking system.

Organizational Records: The CDMO directive, senate decisions, staff recruitment documents, quality assurance protocols, satisfaction survey instruments, and strategic analysis reports provided institutional context for understanding how the data supply chain is embedded in organizational structures and governance frameworks.

The file corpus was not sampled but analyzed comprehensively, as the complete documentary trail—from data request templates through unit submissions to final ranking portal uploads—constitutes the object of study. However, depth of analysis varied purposefully: all files were catalogued and classified by type, source, and stage in the supply chain, while detailed content analysis focused on documents that most clearly illustrated the transformation process (e.g., consolidated data files, normalization scripts, multi-version analysis files, and cross-system mapping tables). This approach follows IE's emphasis on tracing how texts coordinate activity rather than coding for thematic content Rankin (2017).

Analysis Approach

Analysis proceeded through four iterative phases between mid-2024 and early 2026, with phases overlapping as new data became available with each ranking cycle, following Bowen (2009) on document analysis as a qualitative method and Rankin (2017) on conducting analysis in IE. Process maps were initiated during the first ranking cycle (2024) and refined through the second (2025). The file corpus was organized in a structured hierarchical archive by year, ranking system, and data type, with systematic file naming conventions encoding the source unit, ranking system, data type, and version number.

Phase 1: Process mapping. For each of the 14 ranking systems, the complete data flow was traced from initial request to final submission, documenting what data enters the system (incoming data), what transformations occur at each stage, and what exits (submitted data). These maps were constructed directly from the documentary trail itself, rather than from retrospective accounts. This trail included file names, folder structures, version histories, and cross references between files. This approach is consistent with IE's emphasis on following texts instead of relying on participants' own accounts of their work (Smith, 2005).

Phase 2: Cross-system comparison. The 14 data flow maps were compared to identify patterns of indicator overlap, definitional inconsistency, and format variation. This involved creating a master indicator matrix. The matrix was used to track how the same institutional data element, such as "number of academic staff," was defined, scoped, and formatted differently across ranking systems.

Phase 3: Document analysis. Following Bowen (2009), key documents were examined across four dimensions. These documents included data collection templates, metadata files, normalization scripts, correspondence, and submission confirmations. The analysis focused on: (a) the data elements they contained or requested, (b) the transformations they documented or required, (c) the definitional specifications they imposed, and (d) the organizational coordination they revealed. For each ranking system, key transformation decisions—where institutional data was reinterpreted, reclassified, or reformatted to match ranking-specific requirements—were identified and documented. The goal was to understand the standardization and classification decisions embedded in these texts. Bowker and Star (1999) referred to this as the "politics of classification" inherent in every effort of standardization.

Phase 4: Framework integration. The analyses from Phases 1 to 3 were integrated into the five-stage supply chain framework. This framework was used in two ways. First, it was applied deductively as an organizing structure derived from supply chain theory. Second, it was used inductively, allowing the data to reveal stages, challenges, and dynamics that had not been anticipated by the framework. For example, the "one source, many outputs" principle, while formalized in the framework (Section Main Focus of the Chapter) was initially identified through inductive observation of how the same personnel database was reformatted differently for THE, QS, and RUR submissions, and was subsequently elevated to a framework component.

Trustworthiness and Ethical Considerations

Trustworthiness was pursued through four strategies aligned with Lincoln and Guba (1985). Credibility was strengthened through prolonged engagement (over two years across two complete ranking cycles) and triangulation across data sources (templates, submissions, correspondence, and metadata). Transferability is supported by thick description of the institutional context and data processes. Dependability was addressed through systematic documentation: all data flows were reconstructed from the documentary record rather than personal recollection, and the complete file corpus was organized in a hierarchical archive constituting an audit trail. Confirmability rests on the documentary evidence itself: the templates, spreadsheets, portal submissions, and correspondence cited in the findings are institutional records rather than researcher-generated interpretations. Reflexivity and bias management received explicit attention given the insider position. Three procedures were used to mitigate the risks of naturalisation and confirmation bias. First, analytical interpretations were reconstructed exclusively from the documentary record (file names, version histories, folder structures, and templates) rather than from personal recollection, so that the evidentiary chain could in principle be reproduced by another analyst working with the same corpus. Second, factual descriptions of work- flows and unit-level processes were cross-checked with CDMO team members responsible for the relevant stages—a form of member checking that surfaced corrections to draft descriptions of the bibliometric normalization and aggregation pipelines. Third, the supply chain framework was applied both deductively and inductively, so that stages and challenges not anticipated by the framework—for example, the inductive emergence of the "one source, many outputs" principle—could enter the analysis. The methodological limitations associated with single-analyst coding are acknowledged in Section Discussion.

Ethical considerations were addressed under the standards applicable to non-human subjects research. The study draws exclusively on institutional records and process observations conducted within the authors' professional mandate as Director of CDMO; no interviews, surveys, or other forms of human-subjects data collection were undertaken. Under Istanbul University-Cerrahpasa's research ethics framework, document-based studies of organizational processes that do not involve identifiable individual data fall outside the scope of mandatory ethics committee review, and the project was conducted on this basis. All findings are accordingly reported at the aggregate level; where team members contributed to specific data processes, their roles are described by function rather than by name. Confidential operational details—such as the internal file naming of personally identifiable records or named ranking-agency correspondence—have been excluded from the manuscript, with only descriptive features of the documentary trail retained.

FINDINGS

The findings are organized in three parts: the architecture of IUC's data supply chain, the five-stage transformation pipeline traced through specific examples, and the cross-system challenges that emerge from simultaneous participation in 14 ranking systems.

The Architecture of IUC's Data Supply Chain

The institutional data supply chain at IUC operates through a convergent and divergent architecture. On the input side, it follows a many to one structure. On the output side, it follows a one to many structure. CDMO stands at the center of this architecture (Figure 2). On the upstream side, 24 academic units and 21 administrative units converge their data flows into a single processing hub; on the downstream side, the CDMO distributes transformed outputs to 14 ranking and evaluation systems. This architecture is more complex than a simple hub and spoke: the CDMO is not merely a routing node but a transformation engine that actively reshapes data between input and output.

Figure 2. IUC's convergent-divergent data architecture: 45 organizational units feed data through the CDMO to 14 ranking systems. Within the CDMO, data flows through three processing stages: incoming data, processing metadata, and submitted outputs, corresponding to the five-stage pipeline described

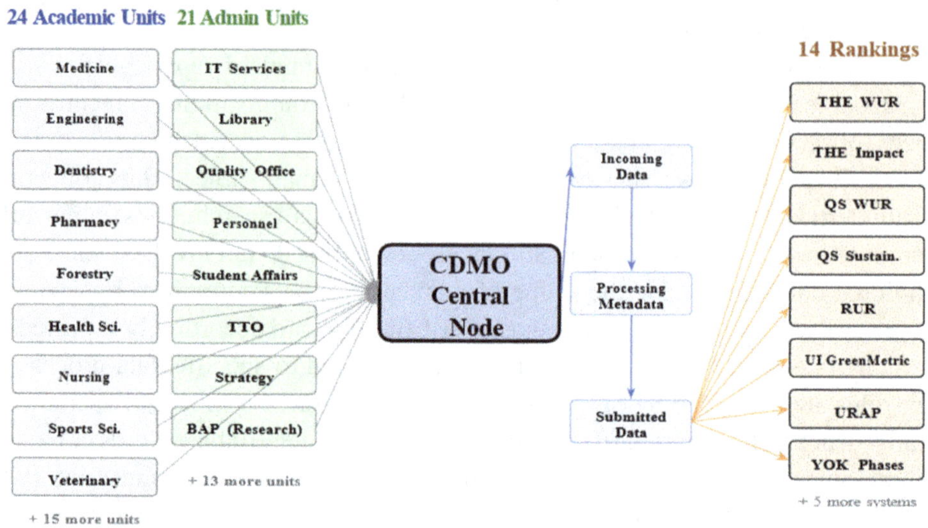

Data collection instruments. The data collection architecture employs three primary instruments. First, the annual General Data Request is a standardized Excel template distributed to all academic units. It is used to collect core institutional indicators such as student enrollment, faculty composition, research output, and international engagement. Second, specialized templates are used for specific ranking systems. The clearest examples are the sustainability evidence templates prepared for THE Impact Rankings, Green Mentors and UI GreenMetric. These templates require department-level documentation of activities linked to the 17 United Nations Sustainable Development Goals (SDGs). Third, the Faculty Report Card system collects internal performance indicators from each academic unit. This process is supported by evidence documentation across nine administrative categories.

Data organization. The data organization follows a three-level hierarchical structure: Year → Direction (incoming data / submitted data) → Ranking System. Incoming Data contains the raw submissions received from units. Submitted Data contains the processed outputs that are ready for ranking submission. This architectural distinction, which keeps both raw inputs and processed outputs, is important. It makes it possible to maintain audit trails, compare data across years, and reprocess data when ranking methodologies change. As shown in Figure 2, the three internal processing categories, incoming data, Processing Metadata, and submitted data, correspond to the five-stage model in the following way: Incoming data covers the Collection stage and the early part of Aggregation, meaning the raw inputs coming from units. Processing Metadata supports the Normalization and Transformation stages, including the master indicator lists, classification schemes, and department mappings that guide data processing. Submitted data represents the final outputs of the Transformation stage and the data packages that are ready for submission.

Scale of operations. The scale of the operation is substantial. In the 2024 cycle, the CDMO processed 1,075 incoming files totaling 2.1 GB, producing 408 submitted files totaling 540 MB. This yields a file-count consolidation ratio of 2.6:1, indicating that for every file submitted to a ranking agency, approximately 2.6 files were received from internal units. The volume consolidation ratio is higher (3.9:1), reflecting the compression of large data-centric input files into smaller, targeted output documents. Table 1 summarizes the quantitative dimensions of this transformation for the 2024 annual cycle, presented as a representative baseline from the full corpus of over 3,800 files spanning two complete cycles; the most notable pattern is the shift from data-centric inputs (Excel-dominant) to narrative and evidence centric outputs (Word-dominant), reflecting the interpretive work the supply chain performs. Data completeness varied across collection streams and organizational units. Data collection required persistent follow-up: 39 formal correspondence letters were issued to units during a single collection round in the 2026 cycle, and the CDMO maintained tracking documents such as "Sustainability Data Missing List" to monitor incomplete submissions. Precise response rates were not systematically recorded during the 2024 cycle. This gap shows the absence of standardized process metrics in institutional data management. The supply chain framework is designed to address exactly this problem.

Approximate institutional labor estimate. Although the present study did not deploy formal time-tracking instruments, an order of magnitude estimate of the institutional labor required to operate the supply chain can be derived from the documented process metrics. The 2024 cycle entailed the ingestion and validation of 1,075 incoming files, the production of 408 multi-stage outputs across 14 distinct ranking systems, eight successive versions of the bibliometric analysis file alone, 39 formal correspondence letters in a single collection round, and post-submission feedback exchanges with several ranking agencies. On a conservative reckoning that allows an average of four to six person-hours per processed file across collection, validation, normalization, transformation, and submission—weighted upward for evidence-heavy submissions (THE Impact, Green Mentors, UI GreenMetric) and downward for highly standardized submissions (URAP, TÜIK)—the institutional investment in ranking-related data work plausibly falls in the range of 4,000–6,000 person-hours per annual cycle. Roughly two-thirds of this effort is concentrated within the CDMO, equivalent to two to three full-time positions, while the remainder is distributed across designated representatives in the 45 contributing academic and administrative units. Expressed per ranking system, the implied average burden falls in the order of 400–600 person-hours, which is broadly aligned with—and dispersed around—the 200-hour-per-submission baseline used in the Introduction, once the substantial system-to-system variation documented in Section Findings is taken into account. These figures are offered as a transparent approximation rather than as a measured result, and direct time-tracking studies are identified in Section Future Research Directions as a priority for future research.

Table 1. Data transformation metrics across the institutional data supply chain (2024 cycle)

Metric	Incoming	Submitted
Total files	1,075	408
Total data volume	2.1 GB	540 MB
PDF documents	552 (51%)	223 (55%)
Excel spreadsheets	382 (36%)	39 (10%)
Word documents	40 (4%)	108 (26%)
Image files	37 (3%)	10 (2%)
Archives (ZIP/RAR)	40 (4%)	0 (0%)
URL references	0 (0%)	14 (3%)
Other	24 (2%)	14 (3%)

Note. *Several systems require multiple submission phases (e.g., YOK Phase 1 and Phase 2, THE portal data and evidence uploads), resulting in 15 distinct submission cycles across 14 primary systems. Other includes PowerPoint presentations, CSV data files, and HTML documents. No comparable institutional metrics have been published; these figures are offered as a baseline for future research.

File-count consolidation ratio 2.6: 1
Volume consolidation ratio 3.9: 1
Contributing units 45 (24 academic + 21 administrative) Ranking systems served 14
Major submission cycles 15 per year*

The Five-Stage Transformation Pipeline

Having described the architecture and scale of the data supply chain, this section traces the transformation process through each of its five stages, using specific examples from the 2024 and 2025 ranking cycles.

Stage 1: Collection

Data collection operates on an annual cycle with multiple parallel streams. Each academic unit receives the General Data Request template in the first quarter, with discipline specific variations for different faculties. The THE Impact Rankings collection is particularly complex: in the 2025 cycle, 36 different organizational units contributed sustainability evidence, with the Technical Sciences Vocational School alone providing 40 separate files. Engineering Faculty contributions were disaggregated across 14 individual departments (Chemical, Computer, Maritime Transportation Management, Mechanical, Civil, Metallurgical and Materials, Electric and Electronics, Environmental, Industrial, Geophysical, Geological, Mining Engineering, Engineering Sciences and Chemistry Department).

Collection challenges include variable response rates, format inconsistencies, and the need for persistent follow-up through formal correspondence to non-responsive units. The gap between initial data request and complete data receipt can span weeks, during which the CDMO must balance deadline pressure from ranking agencies against the operational realities of academic units whose primary mission is teaching and research, not data reporting.

Stage 2: Aggregation

Unit-level submissions are consolidated into master institutional datasets. The primary aggregation artifact is a consolidated Excel file that merges all academic unit responses into a single institutional record. For the YOK Phase 1 submission, 16 unit-level Excel submissions and supporting files were aggregated into excel spreadsheet.

Personnel data illustrates the aggregation challenge. As of October 2024, the institutional personnel database contains more than 19,445 individual records. This figure includes not only the 2,829 academic staff reported to ranking agencies, but all staff categories (academic, administrative, technical, and support). This comprehensive database requires standardized department-faculty mapping through reference files such as "Department-Faculty Matching". Successive data updates—from 17,908 rows in May 2024 to 19,445 rows by October 2024—demonstrate the dynamic nature of the aggregation process. This growth reflects cumulative record-keeping:

new appointments add rows while departed staff records are retained for historical reference, and seasonal variations (such as the academic year start in September) contribute to clustering of new entries.

Stage 3: Normalization

Normalization involves mapping raw institutional data against both internal metadata frameworks and external classification standards. The master metadata file contains 21 indicator sheets with over 3,400 records, serving as the institutional data dictionary that standardizes terminology, unit codes, and indicator definitions.

The bibliometric data pipeline provides a detailed illustration of normalization complexity. Starting with a Web of Science (WOS) export of 4,707 publication records, the normalization process involves: (a) Turkish character conversion for author names (e.g., the dotted/undotted i distinction—a frequent source of bibliometric matching failures, as international databases routinely conflate I/ı with İ/i); (b) key-based record linkage (implemented via spreadsheet lookup functions) against the institutional personnel database to link publications to faculty members; (c) department-unit mapping to assign each publication to its originating academic unit; and (d) journal quartile classification (Q1–Q4) using Journal Citation Reports data. This normalization involves both automated processing (Python-based matching scripts) and manual correction layers—the analysis file contains a dedicated worksheet for manual verification, named after the team member responsible for reconciling cases that automated matching could not resolve. The WOS analysis file iterated through eight versions (v5 through v12) during the 2024 processing cycle, with each version reflecting a successive round of automated matching and manual correction that incrementally increased the affiliation-matching rate. While the exact matching percentages at each version were not systematically recorded, the eight-version progression itself serves as a process metric: it quantifies the iterative human effort that automated bibliometric matching alone cannot eliminate, providing concrete evidence for the "invisible data labor" that the normalization stage demands.

Stage 4: Transformation

The transformation stage restructures normalized institutional data into the specific formats required by each ranking system. This is where the "one source, many outputs" principle operates most visibly—the postponement structure described in Section Main Focus of the Chapter where undifferentiated institutional data is maintained upstream and ranking-specific customization occurs only at this downstream stage. Table 2 summarizes the data requirements across the 14 primary ranking systems.

Table 2. Ranking systems and their data requirements at IUC, with approximate indicator counts and operational burden classification

System	Key Data Requirements	Format	Indicators (approx.)	Evidence-heavy?	Burden tier
THE WUR	Staff, students, finance, research, reputation	Portal	18	No	High
THE Impact	SDG evidence (17 goals), policies, metrics	Evidence + Portal	100+	Yes	Very High
QS WUR	Staff, students, programs, tuition, employment	Portal	20	No	High
QS Sustain.	ESG (Environmental, Social, Governance) metrics	Portal + Evidence	50+	Partial	Medium--High
RUR	Staff/students by discipline, finance, degrees	Excel + Portal	20 (×4 disc.)	No	High
UI GreenMetric	6 environmental domains, campus data	Evidence + Form	39	Yes	Very High
URAP	Publications, citations (automated)	Database	N/A	No	Low
YOK Phase 1	National monitoring indicators	Excel + Evidence	40+	Partial	Medium
YOK Phase 2	Research specialization data	Excel	25+	Partial	Medium
TUIK	National statistical reporting	Structured form	30+	No	Low--Medium
EHESO	Student experience, satisfaction, staff, students	Survey data + Portal	40+	No	Medium
AppliedHE	Student experience, satisfaction, staff, students	Survey data + Portal	10+	No	Low--Medium
HE	Staff, students, programs, tuition, employment	Google Forms	50+	No	Medium
Green Mentors	5 environmental domains, campus data	Portal + Evidence	50	Yes	Very High

For THE Impact Rankings, the transformation involves mapping dispersed institutional evidence to 17 SDG categories, with each evidence item coded using a standardized indicator system (e.g., "2.3.1," "16.3.2"). The 2025 submission produced 78 consolidated evidence items with paired DOCX and PDF versions, culminating in a "Consolidated Table" that serves as the master submission index.

For RUR, the same staff and student data submitted to THE and QS must be disaggregated by disciplinary area (Clinical & Health, Life Sciences, Engineering, Computer Science), with multi-year time series (2022–2025) for each indicator. The 2024 RUR submission (using reference-year 2023 data) recorded: 679 academic staff in Clinical & Health Sciences, 224 in Life Sciences, 276 in Engineering, and 20 in Computer Science—totaling 1,199 in these four RUR categories, which falls short of the 1,300 FTE reported to THE because RUR's four disciplinary categories do not exhaustively cover all academic fields (e.g., staff in faculties such as Forestry, Nursing, or Sports Sciences are excluded from the disciplinary disaggregation).

Stage 5: Submission

The final stage involves uploading processed data to ranking agency portals, each with distinct interface requirements, verification processes, and documentation standards. The heterogeneity of submission mechanisms is itself a source of complexity: THE, AppliedHE and QS use web-based portal systems requiring manual data entry into structured forms; RUR accepts pre-formatted Excel workbooks; GreenMetric and Green Mentors combines online forms with evidence file uploads, HE Ranking use Google forms; and YOK Phase 1 requires a hybrid of structured data and supporting narrative documentation.

Submission status is tracked through file naming conventions that serve as a low- technology version control system: "finished" and "entered" suffixes indicate completed submissions, while version numbers (v1, v2) track revisions. The absence of an integrated submission management platform means that the CDMO relies on folder structures and file naming as the primary coordination mechanism—a practice that works but is fragile. In the 2025 THE Impact submission, for instance, 78 evidence items were organized in paired DOCX/PDF format with SDG-coded file names, requiring meticulous cross-referencing against the master submission index (Consolidated Table) to ensure completeness.

Post-submission, ranking agencies may request clarifications or revisions, initiating feedback loops that can extend for weeks. These interactions—which occur through email, portal messaging, or phone—are documented in the correspondence archive but represent an unpredictable labor demand that disrupts planned workflows.

To illustrate the concrete reality of the five-stage pipeline, consider a single, seemingly simple data element: the number of academic staff, as documented in the General Data Request responses and ranking submission files for the 2024 cycle. The journey begins at Stage 1, when the General Data Request template asks each faculty to report its personnel by rank and employment type. The Faculty of Medicine reports 892 academic staff; Engineering reports 187; Dentistry reports 156—and so on across 24 units, each submitting an Excel file with its own formatting conventions. At Stage 2 (Aggregation), these 24 unit-level files are merged into the consolidated personnel spreadsheet, cross-referenced against the institutional personnel database maintained by the Human Resources department. At Stage 3 (Normalization), the aggregate figure must be interpreted through different classificatory lenses: THE requires full-time equivalents (FTE), so part-time staff are fractionally counted; QS requires head count (HC), so every individual counts as one regardless of appointment fraction; RUR requires staff disaggregated by four disciplinary areas. At Stage 4 (Transformation), the same underlying personnel data produces: "1,300" for the THE portal (FTE), "2,829" for the QS portal (HC), and four discipline-specific rows for RUR. A single institutional fact—how many people teach and research here—thus becomes at least four different numbers, each "correct" within its own definitional frame. This illustrates why the transformation challenge requires classificatory judgment, not merely technical formatting: it requires decisions about what counts, for whom, and under which definitions. Table 3 summarizes this divergence.

Table 3. How a single institutional attribute—academic staff—produces different figures across ranking systems (2024 cycle)

System	Count basis	Reported figure	Scope
THE WUR	FTE	1,300	All academic staff (fractional)
QS WUR	Head count	2,829	All academic staff (individual)
RUR	HC by discipline	1,199	Four disciplinary areas only

Note. All three figures derive from the same institutional personnel database. Differences reflect classificatory choices (FTE vs. HC), scope boundaries (all fields vs. four disciplines), and definitional frames imposed by each ranking system.

Cross-System Challenges

Analysis across all 14 ranking systems revealed four structural challenges inherent in the institutional data supply chain.

Definitional inconsistency. The same concept is defined differently across ranking systems. "Faculty" is counted as full-time equivalents (FTE) for THE, head count (HC) for QS, and by discipline-specific FTE for RUR. "International students" may include or exclude exchange students depending on the system. "Research income" encompasses different revenue categories across THE, RUR, and YOK definitions. These inconsistencies require the CDMO to maintain multiple parallel counts of ostensibly the same institutional attribute.

The "one source, many formats" problem. The "one source, many outputs" principle described in the conceptual framework (Section Main Focus of the Chapter) manifests operationally as a format proliferation challenge. Bibliometric data illustrates this most clearly. Publication and citation metrics are used by at least eight different ranking systems, yet each requires different scoping (timeframe, database source, field normalization), formatting (aggregate counts vs. per-capita ratios vs. percentile ranks), and contextual framing (standalone metrics vs. discipline-adjusted indicators).

Temporal misalignment. Ranking systems request data from different reference periods—THE WUR 2026 uses 2023 data, QS uses a rolling five-year window, RUR requests four consecutive years simultaneously, and YOK uses the most recent academic year. With several systems requiring multiple submission phases, the CDMO manages 15 distinct submission cycles per year, requiring multi-year dataset maintenance and clear versioning.

Invisible data labor. The human effort required to operate the institutional data supply chain is substantial yet largely invisible. The 2024 cycle involved processing over 1,000 files, issuing dozens of formal correspondence letters, conducting iterative data validation (eight versions of a single analysis file), and maintaining hybrid automated-manual processing workflows. This labor constitutes what Bowker and Star (1999) termed "invisible work"—essential organizational activity that is neither recognized nor resourced in proportion to its significance.

Taken together, these four challenges reflect a structural feature of the multi-ranking environment: the most widely shared data elements—academic staff counts, student enrollment, and publication metrics—are paradoxically the most definitionally inconsistent, as each system applies its own classification scheme to these seemingly standard concepts. The four challenges are neither equally consequential nor independent. Definitional inconsistency operates as the root challenge: because the same institutional attribute is defined differently across systems, the supply chain is forced to maintain multiple parallel representations of the same data, which is what generates the operational manifestation captured by the "one source, many formats" problem. These two challenges, in turn, drive invisible data labor: the iterative validation, manual reconciliation, and version-by-version refinement that the normalization and transformation stages require would be substantially reduced if upstream definitions were harmonized. Temporal misalignment compounds the burden by spreading the same labor across an effectively continuous submission cycle and by forcing recomputation of historical figures under each system's evolving reference window. In this sense, definitional inconsistency is the most consequential of the four challenges because addressing it would relax pressure on the other three; harmonization at the indicator-definition level would have larger systemic effects than improvements at any single supply-chain stage.

The operational burden is also not evenly distributed across the 14 ranking systems. At one end, URAP relies entirely on bibliometric databases and imposes negligible direct burden on the CDMO. TÜIK reporting is intermediate: the indicators are largely standardized and the submission instrument is a structured form, which limits transformation work. Evidence-heavy systems impose the highest burden: the THE Impact Rankings require the assembly, SDG coding, and consolidation of evidence items drawn from dozens of organizational units, Green Mentors and UI GreenMetric similarly combines structured indicators with extensive documentary evidence. Among the research-focused rankings, RUR, AppliedHE and HE Ranking are the most demanding because it requires disciplinary disaggregation of staff, students, and finance into four categories whose membership is not natively recorded in institutional systems, while THE WUR and QS WUR are demanding primarily through the depth of their definitional specifications rather than through evidence volume. YOK Phase 1 and Phase 2 occupy an intermediate position: they are nationally mandated and high-stakes, but their indicator definitions are more aligned with institutional record-keeping than international rankings. Taken together, evidence-based and disaggregation-based systems—THE Impact, GreenMetric, RUR—account for a disproportionately large share of the CDMO's annual workload, and any institution seeking to reduce reporting burden would benefit most from automation and standardization targeted at these systems specifically.

DISCUSSION

The findings address the three sub-questions posed in the Introduction. The first question— what organizational structures and processes constitute the institutional data supply chain—is answered by the convergent-divergent architecture and the five-stage pipeline documented in Section Findings. The second question—how raw departmental data is transformed into ranking-ready submissions—is illustrated most concretely by the academic staff trace, which follows a single data element from 24 unit-level Excel files through aggregation, normalization, and transformation into three different numbers for three different ranking systems. The third question is addressed by the cross-system analysis in Section Findings, which establishes that definitional inconsistency is the root challenge from which the other three derive and that evidence-based and disaggregation-based systems impose a disproportionate share of the operational burden.

SOLUTIONS AND RECOMMENDATIONS

Theoretical Implications

This study provides an empirical mapping of the institutional data workflow through which a university collects, reconciles, and submits data to multiple ranking systems simultaneously—an area that, to the best of the authors' knowledge, has not previously been documented in this level of operational detail. The institutional data supply chain framework that emerges from this mapping makes four contributions to higher education scholarship.

First, it bridges the gap between ranking reactivity theory and organizational practice. Espeland and Sauder (2007) established that rankings reshape institutions through reactivity and commensuration, but their framework operates at the behavioral and perceptual level—how rankings change what people value, pursue, and attend to. The institutional data supply chain reveals the organizational infrastructure through which reactivity is materially enacted. Rankings do not simply influence perceptions. They also generate concrete organizational demands—templates to complete, databases to query, evidence to compile, portals to navigate—that require dedicated staffing, standardized processes, and substantial institutional investment. The five-stage model (Collection → Aggregation → Normalization → Transformation → Submission) provides an analytical vocabulary for describing this infrastructure that the reactivity literature currently lacks. Where Barron (2023) traced how ranking agencies coordinate data production from the supply side, the present study maps the corresponding organizational infrastructure through which individual universities respond to those production requirements—the supply and demand sides of the same data transaction.

Second, it extends supply chain theory to the domain of higher education data management. While Mentzer et al. (2001) and Lambert and Cooper (2000) established the conceptual architecture of supply chain management—material flows, information flows, and cash flows operating across organizational boundaries—and while Williamson (2018) documented the "hidden architecture" of data infrastructure in universities, neither tradition has addressed the specific challenge of managing data flows to multiple external consumers (ranking agencies) with heterogeneous requirements. The institutional data supply chain adapts supply chain concepts to capture a distinctive feature of university data management: the fan-out architecture where a single upstream data source must be transformed into multiple downstream outputs with different formats, definitions, and evidence standards. The three-flow model (data, requirements, and feedback) parallels the classical supply chain while capturing the unique bidirectional dynamics of ranking participation. The findings also corroborate Star and Ruhleder's (1996) observation that infrastructure becomes visible only upon breakdown: the CDMO's data management processes surfaced as objects of analysis precisely because the inconsistencies between ranking systems' definitions forced explicit reclassification work that would otherwise remain invisible.

Third, it reveals "ruling texts" in action. Borrowing from institutional ethnography (Smith, 2005; Smith and Griffith, 2022), the findings demonstrate that ranking submission templates and portal interfaces function as ruling texts—standardized instruments that coordinate the work of dispersed organizational actors toward institutionally consequential ends. The General Data Request template, distributed annually to 45 units, literally structures what data is collected, how it is formatted, and when it is due. The ranking agency portals further specify the transformation requirements, creating textually mediated coordination that extends the authority of ranking agencies deep into institutional operations. This finding demonstrates the value of applying IE concepts to a domain—university ranking data management—that has not been previously examined through this analytical lens.

Fourth, it connects ranking participation to the broader dynamics of audit culture. Power (1997) argued that the rise of auditing and verification rituals transforms organizations by making certain activities visible and auditable at the expense of others. The institutional data supply chain is precisely such a verification infrastructure: it makes certain institutional attributes (publication counts, staff ratios, revenue figures) legible to external audiences while rendering invisible the interpretive labor required to produce those numbers. Strathern (2000) warned that accountability demands generate their own performative effects—institutions begin to organize themselves around what can be measured and reported rather than around educational or research missions. The findings of this study provide granular evidence for this dynamic: the CDMO's data collection instruments are shaped not by what the institution needs to know about itself but by what ranking agencies ask it to report. Muller (2018) described this phenomenon as "metric fixation," and the data supply chain is the organizational infrastructure through which metric fixation is operationalized.

Fifth, and most distinctively, the framework frames the institutional data supply chain as an ambivalent organizational response rather than as a neutral management solution. The four preceding contributions describe what the supply chain is and what it does; this fifth contribution concerns what the supply chain means for the institutions that build it. A central tension runs through the empirical findings: the same infrastructure that allows IUC to absorb the burden of multi-ranking participation also draws the institution more deeply into the ranking regimes that generate that burden. By professionalizing the submission process and standardizing the underlying data work, the CDMO makes ranking participation less costly at the margin. Lower marginal cost in turn reinforces the institutional commitment to rankings: as compliance becomes routinized, exit from any single ranking system becomes harder to justify against the sunk investment in personnel, processes, and institutional knowledge. Sauder and Espeland (2009) documented this dynamic with U.S. law school rankings, where tight coupling between organizational infrastructure and ranking criteria produced path dependency that militated against selective withdrawal even when individual rankings were criticized internally. The IUC findings give granular evidence for the same dynamic at the operational layer: once the General Data Request template, the consolidated personnel database, and the bibliometric normalization pipeline are in place, their existence becomes an argument for continued participation in all the systems they feed.

The supply chain therefore needs to be understood simultaneously as a form of organizational capacity and as a form of deeper entanglement with external evaluation regimes. As a capacity, it equips an institution to coordinate complex external reporting demands that would otherwise overwhelm dispersed faculty-level efforts. As an entanglement, it shifts internal data practices into alignment with externally defined indicator categories, so that what counts as a measurable institutional attribute is increasingly determined by what ranking agencies have decided to ask. This is consistent with Strathern's (2000) account of accountability infrastructures generating their own performative effects and with the concerns articulated by the responsible-metrics movement (DORA, 2012; Hicks et al., 2015): efficient compliance can crowd out the institutional capacity to articulate what the university wants to know about itself, independent of what it has been asked to report.

Two observations made possible by the insider position deserve specific attention here, because they show how the entanglement dynamic operates in administrative practice rather than only at the strategic level. First, the institutional staff who design the data collection instruments come over time to think through ranking categories. The General Data Request template asks faculties to report personnel in categories that mirror THE and QS rather than categories that match the institution's own organizational chart; over successive cycles, the institutional chart itself begins to be described, internally, in ranking-aligned terms. Second, the boundary between "data the institution needs about itself" and "data ranking agencies require" erodes in everyday work: when a faculty submits its annual personnel return, it submits a return whose structure was determined by external indicator definitions, with the consequence that internal strategic analysis is increasingly conducted on data that was scoped for external evaluation. These observations are not arguments against ranking participation; they are arguments for treating the supply chain as an analytically ambivalent object, capable of supporting either deeper compliance or evidence-based resistance depending on how its outputs are mobilized.

This ambivalence has direct implications for how universities should reason about supply chain investments. By making visible the true cost and complexity of multi-ranking compliance, the framework can support evidence-based arguments for selective participation, indicator harmonization, or even strategic withdrawal from systems whose burden exceeds their informational value. But the same visibility can also be deployed to justify the further build-out of compliance infrastructure as a competitive necessity. Which path institutions take is not a question the framework itself can settle; it is a question the framework helps institutions ask more clearly.

Before evaluating the propositions, a methodological note on the scope of these contributions is warranted. This study employs what Yin (2018) termed a "revelatory case"—an instance where the researcher has access to a phenomenon previously inaccessible to scientific investigation. The insider position that enables this study is precisely what makes the phenomenon observable; the trade-off between depth and breadth is thus a feature of the research design, not merely a limitation. The goal is analytic generalization— extending the institutional data supply chain framework as a theoretical proposition that can be tested, refined, or disconfirmed through subsequent cases—rather than statistical generalization from a sample to a population.

Returning to the analytical propositions advanced in Section Main Focus of the Chapter the findings—presented by supply chain stage and cross-system challenge, as the empirical evidence cross-cuts multiple propositions simultaneously—provide support for all four.

Proposition 1 (transformation complexity is hypothesized to grow more than linearly) finds qualitative support in the cross-system challenges: each additional ranking system introduces not merely one more output but new definitional inconsistencies that compound with existing systems. The same personnel data produces three legitimately different figures across ranking systems, requiring pairwise reconciliation. The reconciliation demands are structurally consistent with super-linear growth—pairwise definitional reconciliation tasks scale proportionally to $n(n-1)/2 \times k$ for n systems sharing k common data elements—but the present study does not directly measure marginal complexity per additional system, and the proposition is therefore offered as a structural hypothesis to be tested rather than as an empirical finding. Temporal misalignment further compounds this complexity: because ranking systems request data from different reference periods, the CDMO must maintain and reconcile multi-year versions of the same institutional datasets, adding a temporal dimension to the definitional reconciliation that each additional system demands. Direct empirical verification through comparative multi-institutional research would be required to confirm the scaling exponent.

Proposition 2 (downstream requirements shape upstream collection) is evident through out the data supply chain. The General Data Request template is structured around ranking indicator definitions rather than institutional information needs, with its categories mirroring what THE, QS, and YOK require rather than what the institution needs to know about itself. The bibliometric normalization pipeline further illustrates this dynamic: WOS publication data is scoped by timeframe, normalized by field, and classified by journal quartile specifically because downstream ranking systems require these parameters—requirements that propagate backward to determine what data is extracted, how it is processed, and which matching criteria are applied.

Proposition 3 (the supply chain generates its own labor demands) is substantiated by the invisible data labor findings: the eight-version iteration of the WOS bibliometric analysis file, the 39 formal correspondence letters required to extract unit-level data in a single collection round, and the hybrid automated-manual processing workflows that characterize ranking data management.

Proposition 4 (the supply chain instantiates a power asymmetry) is demonstrated by the unidirectional character of requirements flow: ranking agencies determine indicator definitions, data formats, temporal reference frames, and submission deadlines, while universities absorb the full organizational cost of compliance without meaningful opportunities to negotiate these parameters.

Practical Implications

The theoretical analysis above establishes that the institutional data supply chain is simultaneously a material infrastructure, an interpretive process, a system of textually mediated coordination, and a mechanism of audit compliance. These characteristics carry direct practical implications for four distinct audiences: university leaders, ranking agencies, institutional researchers, and policymakers. The implications for each group are signposted separately below so that readers approaching this chapter from different professional vantage points can identify the takeaways most relevant to their work.

For university leaders, the five-stage model can serve as a maturity assessment framework: institutions can evaluate whether each stage is standardized or ad hoc, automated or manual, documented or tacit—with lower maturity at any stage creating vulnerability to staff turnover, data quality errors, and deadline failures. The IUC case demonstrates that a centralized data management office can effectively coordinate multi-ranking submissions. Beyond external reporting, the same infrastructure could be re-purposed for institutional self-knowledge—strategic planning, resource allocation, and internal benchmarking. The framework also identifies which stages are most amenable to technological intervention: Collection benefits from digital form systems, Aggregation from database integration tools, and Normalization from scripting and, increasingly, artificial intelligence. The Transformation stage, however, requires interpretive judgment, making full automation premature.

For ranking agencies, the empirical evidence of reporting burden calls for greater attention to indicator harmonization. The finding that the same bibliometric data is reformatted for eight different ranking systems—each with different scoping, formatting, and contextualization requirements—suggests significant potential for reducing institutional burden through coordinated data standards. A concrete step would be the adoption of a Common Data Standard for university rankings, analogous to the U.S. Common Data Set initiative, that harmonizes core indicator definitions (such as "academic staff," "international students," and "research income") across systems. The Berlin Principles on Ranking of Higher Education Institutions (International Ranking Expert Group (IREG), 2006), already provide a methodological foundation for such harmonization, and the Leiden Manifesto (Hicks et al., 2015) and DORA (DORA, 2012) supply complementary norms for responsible use of the underlying research metrics; alignment with these established standards would lend additional legitimacy to harmonization efforts.

For institutional researchers, the supply chain framework provides both a diagnostic tool and a professional vocabulary. The four-step analytical procedure described in the Methodology—cataloguing files in an annual cycle, mapping transformation paths, constructing a cross-system indicator matrix, and documenting stage-level coordination— offers a structured starting point for any IR office wishing to audit its own ranking-related operations. The five-stage taxonomy provides a shared language with which institutional researchers can describe their work to internal stakeholders who otherwise treat data submission as an undifferentiated activity. The framework also responds to a gap identified in the data governance literature, where existing frameworks have remained generic (Guy, 2025; Jim and Chang, 2018), it gives the IR profession a ranking-specific application of governance concepts that can support evidence-based requests for staffing, automation investment, and institutional recognition of the normalization and transformation work documented in Section Findings.

For policymakers, particularly in the Global South, the findings highlight the resource implications of multi-ranking participation. The Turkish experience, where 23 research universities must satisfy both domestic accountability requirements (YOK, TUIK) and international ranking expectations, illustrates a dual burden that creates an equity paradox: institutions that most need visibility through rankings are least equipped to manage the data infrastructure that ranking participation demands, risking reinforcement rather than reduction of existing hierarchies in global higher education. National quality assurance agencies could reduce this burden by aligning domestic reporting indicators with international ranking frameworks where conceptually appropriate, and universities considering centralized data offices should ensure the mandate includes explicit authority to request data from academic units.

FUTURE RESEARCH DIRECTIONS

Several limitations should be acknowledged. As a single-case study at a centralized Turkish public university, the findings may not generalize to institutions with distributed IR functions or different resource contexts. The insider positionality carries inherent bias risks, mitigated through systematic reliance on documentary evidence and transparent reporting of challenges. The study captures only formal data flows—informal coordination through phone calls, corridor conversations, and messaging is not represented in the documentary record. The five-stage model imposes linearity on what is in practice an iterative process, and the CDMO's early operational phase (established October 2023) may have amplified certain challenges while obscuring others that emerge with maturity. There is also an inherent circularity in the researcher having designed aspects of the system being analyzed, mitigated by using the framework both deductively and inductively. Additionally, differential unit compliance introduces a selection effect: the institutional portrait presented to ranking agencies is shaped by which units respond as much as by actual performance. Future research should prioritize comparative multi-institutional studies to test the framework's generalizability, cost quantification to establish the economic burden of multi-ranking participation (Whistle, 2017), and longitudinal analysis of how data supply chains mature as automation tools transform normalization and transformation workflows.

CONCLUSION

This research developed the institutional data supply chain as an analytical framework for understanding how universities manage information flows across multiple ranking systems. Through an insider case study (Yin, 2018) at Istanbul University-Cerrahpasa, informed by concepts from institutional ethnography, a mapping of the five-stage transformation pipeline was constructed—Collection, Aggregation, Normalization, Transformation, and Submission—through which raw data from 45 organizational units is converted into ranking-ready submissions for 14 external evaluation systems. The empirical findings reveal that this process involves over 1,000 data files per annual cycle, a 2.6:1 file-count consolidation ratio, and substantial labor in the form of an iterative validation, cross-system reconciliation, and multi-format transformation. A single institutional attribute—the number of academic staff—produces legitimately different figures across ranking systems (1,300 FTE for one, 2,829 HC for another), demonstrating that the transformation process is fundamentally interpretive rather than merely technical. The cross-system analysis further establishes that the structural challenges of multi-ranking participation are hierarchically organized rather than parallel: definitional inconsistency operates as the root challenge, the operational manifestations of which are documented in Section Findings. These findings address the three research sub-questions posed in the Introduction and provide empirical support for the analytical propositions derived from the framework.

This framework makes an important contribution to higher education scholarship. It brings together four strands of literature—institutional research, ranking reactivity, data governance, and supply chain management—that have previously developed in isolation. It extends Espeland and Sauder's (2007) reactivity theory by revealing the organizational infrastructure through which ranking influence is materially enacted and adapts supply chain management concepts to capture the distinctive "one source, many outputs" architecture of university data management. Additionally, it demonstrates the analytical value of institutional ethnography's "ruling texts" concept (Smith, 2005) for understanding how ranking templates coordinate dispersed organizational work and provides granular evidence for the audit culture dynamics (Power, 1997) through which ranking participation reshapes institutional priorities. Most distinctively, the framework treats the institutional data supply chain as an ambivalent organizational response rather than as a neutral management solution: building a more efficient supply chain simultaneously increases institutional capacity to manage ranking demands and deepens institutional entanglement with the evaluation regimes that generate those demands. This ambivalence is, in our view, the chapter's most original contribution and is developed at length in Section Solutions and Recommendations.

Ranking systems continue to grow in number and become more diverse. Sustainability and impact rankings are now being added to the traditional research-focused systems. As a result, the organizational demands on institutional data management will become even greater. The institutional data supply chain framework provides universities with a diagnostic tool for assessing their readiness—though as noted in the Discussion, the same infrastructure that enables efficient compliance may also deepen institutional entanglement with ranking systems, creating path dependencies that constrain future strategic choices. It provides ranking agencies with evidence for harmonizing core indicator definitions—a Common Data Standard analogous to existing national initiatives—to reduce institutional reporting burden, and policymakers with insight into the resource implications of the ranking ecosystem.

Future research should prioritize comparative studies across diverse institutional types to test the framework's generalizability, cost quantification to establish the economic burden of multi-ranking participation, and investigation of how emerging automation tools may transform normalization and transformation workflows. The descriptive metrics presented here—the number of files, type distributions, and consolidation ratios—provide a foundation for quantifying this process. Consequently, understanding the institutional data supply chain is not merely a matter of organizational analysis. It is also a prerequisite for moving from passive compliance to strategic engagement with the ranking ecosystem. While the infrastructure that enables such agency may also deepen institutional entanglement with ranking systems, as discussed above, this very visibility equips university leaders to make evidence-based decisions about which rankings to prioritize, where to invest in automation, and when the organizational costs of participation outweigh its reputational benefits.

FUNDING

This research received no external funding.

CONFLICT OF INTEREST

The authors are academic staff serving at the Corporate Data Management Office (CDMO) of the institution under study. To mitigate insider research bias, three safeguards were implemented: (i) grounding interpretations strictly in documentary records, (ii) validating workflow descriptions with CDMO team members, and (iii) balancing deductive and inductive framework applications. Operational challenges are reported alongside standard practices to ensure an objective evaluation.

ETHICAL APPROVAL AND CONFIDENTIALITY

This study relies solely on institutional document analysis and process mapping within the authors' professional mandate, involving no human subjects, interviews, or surveys. To protect data privacy, all metrics are aggregated or reported at the faculty level, with internal staff designated only by functional roles. Under the university's framework, such data-exempt organizational studies are immune to mandatory ethics committee review.

USE OF AI-ASSISTED TOOLS

All conceptual analyses, framework design, and empirical interpretations are entirely the authors' own. General-purpose AI tools were utilized exclusively for language editing and reference formatting support; no automated tools were used to generate substantive content, synthesize data, or draft findings. The authors assume full scholarly responsibility for the manuscript.

DATA AVAILABILITY

The institutional data analyzed in this study contains proprietary information belonging to Istanbul University-Cerrahpasa. Anonymized process maps and template structures can be made available upon reasonable request to the corresponding author, subject to institutional approval.

REFERENCES

Barari, S., Newsom, E., Park, J. E., & Paddock, S. M. (2024). *College ranking systems: A methodological review. Final report*. Chicago, IL: NORC at the University of Chicago.

Barari, S., Park, J. E., & Paddock, S. (2025). *International college ranking systems: A methodological review. Final report*. Chicago, IL: NORC at the University of Chicago.

Barron, G. R. S. (2023). How university rankings are made through globally coordinated action: A transnational institutional ethnography in the sociology of quantification. *Higher Education, 86*(4), 809–826. DOI: 10.1007/s10734-022-00903-y

Bayanbayeva, A. (2025). Strategic response or gaming the rankings? Unravelling the strategies behind global university rankings manipulation in the higher education context of Kazakhstan. *Higher Education*. Advance online publication. DOI: 10.1007/s10734-025-01512-1

Borgman, C. L. (2015). *Big Data, Little Data, No Data: Scholarship in the Networked World*. MIT Press. DOI: 10.7551/mitpress/9963.001.0001

Botha, J., Webber, K., Williams, J., Calderon, A., Klemencič, M., Wooldridge, A., & Chirikov, I. (2024). Building capacity in institutional research: Collaboration and complementarity? *Tertiary Education and Management, 30*(2), 129–145. DOI: 10.1007/s11233-024-09139-0

Bowen, G. A. (2009). Document analysis as a qualitative research method. *Qualitative Research Journal, 9*(2), 27–40. DOI: 10.3316/QRJ0902027

Bowker, G. C., & Star, S. L. (1999). *Sorting Things Out: Classification and Its Consequences*. MIT Press. DOI: 10.7551/mitpress/6352.001.0001

Brankovic, J., Hamann, J., & Ringel, L. (2023). The institutionalization of rankings in higher education. *Higher Education, 86*(4), 719–731. DOI: 10.1007/s10734-023-01018-8

Brannick, T., & Coghlan, D. (2007). In defense of being "native": The case for insider academic research. *Organizational Research Methods, 10*(1), 59–74. DOI: 10.1177/1094428106289253

Calderon, A. J., & Mathies, C. (2013). Institutional research in the future: Challenges within higher education and the need for excellence in professional practice. *New Directions for Institutional Research, 2013*(157), 77–90. DOI: 10.1002/ir.20040

Chowdhury, S. A., Sharmin, R., Al-Amin, M., & Shifat, M. N. (2025). Integrating an educational supply chain model in the higher education sector: Meeting the 21st century workforce demands in Bangladesh. *Frontiers in Education, 10*, 1521309. DOI: 10.3389/feduc.2025.1521309

Costley, C., Elliott, G., & Gibbs, P. (2010). *Doing Work Based Research: Approaches to Enquiry for Insider-Researchers*. SAGE Publications. DOI: 10.4135/9781446287880

Dahler-Larsen, P. (2014). Constitutive effects of performance indicators: Getting beyond unintended consequences. *Public Management Review*, *16*(7), 969–986. DOI: 10.1080/14719037.2013.770058

de Oliveira, T. H. M., de Castro Neto, M., Costa, E. G., Simoes, M. Q., & Sousa, C. (2025, October). Rewiring governance: Building a data-centric ecosystem for higher education strategic (and digital) transformation. In *Proceedings of the Future Technologies Conference* (pp. 38-60). Cham: Springer Nature Switzerland.

DORA. (2012). San francisco declaration on research assessment. *Declaration on Research Assessment*, San Francisco. Retrieved May 13, 2013, from https://sfdora.org/read/

Espeland, W. N., & Sauder, M. (2007). Rankings and reactivity: How public measures recreate social worlds. *American Journal of Sociology*, *113*(1), 1–40. DOI: 10.1086/517897

Espeland, W. N., & Sauder, M. (2016). *Engines of Anxiety: Academic Rankings, Reputation, and Accountability*. Russell Sage Foundation.

Espeland, W. N., & Stevens, M. L. (1998). Commensuration as a social process. *Annual Review of Sociology*, *24*(1), 313–343. DOI: 10.1146/annurev.soc.24.1.313

European Education and Culture Executive Agency. (2024). *European Higher Education Sector Observatory (EHESO)*. European Commission, EACEA. Retrieved 2016, from https: //national-policies.eacea.ec.europa.eu/eheso

Grajek, S., and Milhans, J. (2024). 2025 EDUCAUSE Top 10: Restoring Trust. EDUCAUSE *Review (Online)*.

Guy, I. (2025). Conceptual framework of data governance and data organization in higher education: Application of the structurational model of technology. In *Proceedings of the Association for Information Science and Technology*. DOI: 10.1002/pra2.1436

Hamann, J., & Ringel, L. (2023). The discursive resilience of university rankings. *Higher Education*, *86*(4), 845–863. DOI: 10.1007/s10734-022-00990-x

Hazelkorn, E. (2015). *Rankings and the Reshaping of Higher Education: The Battle for World-Class Excellence* (2nd ed.). Palgrave Macmillan. DOI: 10.1057/9781137446671

Hazelkorn, E. (2017). *Global Rankings and the Geopolitics of Higher Education: Under- standing the Influence and Impact of Rankings on Higher Education, Policy and Society*. Routledge.

Hicks, D., Wouters, P., Waltman, L., de Rijcke, S., & Rafols, I. (2015). Bibliometrics: The leiden manifesto for research metrics. *Nature*, *520*(7548), 429–431. DOI: 10.1038/520429a PMID: 25903611

International Ranking Expert Group (IREG). (2006). *Berlin principles on ranking of higher education institutions. IREG Observatory on Academic Ranking and Excellence*, Berlin. Retrieved 2006, from https://ireg-observatory.org/en/berlin-principles/

Jim, C. K., & Chang, H. C. (2018). The current state of data governance in higher education. *Proceedings of the Association for Information Science and Technology*, *55*(1), 198–206. DOI: 10.1002/pra2.2018.14505501022

Komljenovic, J., Sellar, S., & Birch, K. (2024). Turning universities into data-driven organisations: Seven dimensions of change. *Higher Education*, *89*(5), 1369–1386. DOI: 10.1007/s10734-024-01277-z

Lambert, D. M., & Cooper, M. C. (2000). Issues in supply chain management. *Industrial Marketing Management*, *29*(1), 65–83. DOI: 10.1016/S0019-8501(99)00113-3

Leonelli, S., & Tempini, N. (Eds.). (2020). *Data Journeys in the Sciences*. Springer. DOI: 10.1007/978-3-030-37177-7

Lincoln, Y. S., & Guba, E. G. (1985). *Naturalistic Inquiry*. SAGE Publications. DOI: 10.1016/0147-1767(85)90062-8

Marginson, S., & van der Wende, M. (2007). To rank or to be ranked: The impact of global rankings in higher education. *Journal of Studies in International Education*, *11*(3–4), 306–329. DOI: 10.1177/1028315307303544

Mentzer, J. T., DeWitt, W., Keebler, J. S., Min, S., Nix, N. W., Smith, C. D., & Zacharia, Z. G. (2001). Defining supply chain management. *Journal of Business Logistics*, *22*(2), 1–25. DOI: 10.1002/j.2158-1592.2001.tb00001.x

Merton, R. K. (1972). Insiders and outsiders: A chapter in the sociology of knowledge. *American Journal of Sociology*, *78*(1), 9–47. DOI: 10.1086/225294

Muller, J. Z. (2018). *The Tyranny of Metrics*. Princeton University Press.

Porter, T. M. (1995). *Trust in Numbers: The Pursuit of Objectivity in Science and Public Life*. Princeton University Press.

Power, M. (1997). *The Audit Society: Rituals of Verification*. Oxford University Press.

Proserpio, L., Kandiko Howson, C., & Lall, M. (2024). The university ranking game in East Asia: The sensemaking of academic leaders between pressures and fatigue. *Asia Pacific Education Review*.

Rankin, J. (2017). Conducting analysis in institutional ethnography: Guidance and cautions. *International Journal of Qualitative Methods, 16*(1), 1–11. DOI: 10.1177/1609406917734472

Reyes, C., & Parella, K. (2026). Data supply chains. SSRN Working Paper.

Sauder, M., & Espeland, W. N. (2009). The discipline of rankings: Tight coupling and organizational change. *American Sociological Review, 74*(1), 63–82. DOI: 10.1177/000312240907400104

Shin, J. C., Toutkoushian, R. K., & Teichler, U. (2011). *University Rankings: Theoretical Basis, Methodology and Impacts on Global Higher Education*. Springer. DOI: 10.1007/978-94-007-1116-7

Smith, D. E. (2005). *Institutional Ethnography: A Sociology for People*. AltaMira Press. DOI: 10.5040/9798216409632

Smith, D. E. (2006). *Institutional Ethnography as Practice*. Rowman & Littlefield. DOI: 10.5040/9798216402855

Smith, D. E., & Griffith, A. I. (2022). *Simply Institutional Ethnography: Creating a Sociology for People*. University of Toronto Press. DOI: 10.3138/9781487528072

Stake, R. E. (1995). *The Art of Case Study Research*. SAGE Publications.

Star, S. L., & Ruhleder, K. (1996). Steps toward an ecology of infrastructure: Design and access for large information spaces. *Information Systems Research, 7*(1), 111–134. DOI: 10.1287/isre.7.1.111

Strathern, M. (2000). The tyranny of transparency. *British Educational Research Journal, 26*(3), 309–321. DOI: 10.1080/713651562

Terenzini, P. T. (1993). On the nature of institutional research and the knowledge and skills it requires. *Research in Higher Education, 34*(1), 1–10. DOI: 10.1007/BF00991859

Times Higher Education. (2025). *Impact Rankings*. Retrieved in 2025, from https://www.timeshighereducation.com/impactrankings

Tirpan, O. (2019). Analyzing the enablers for turkish defence industry supply chains: An interpretive structural modeling approach. *International Journal of Economics and Financial Issues*, *9*(3), 205–212. DOI: 10.32479/ijefi.8085

Unluer, S. (2012). Being an insider researcher while conducting case study research. *The Qualitative Report*, *17*(29), 1–14.

van Vught, F. A., & Ziegele, F. (Eds.). (2012). *Multidimensional Ranking: The Design and Development of U-Multirank*. Springer. DOI: 10.1007/978-94-007-3005-2

Vernon, M. M., Balas, E. A., & Momani, S. (2018). Are university rankings useful to improve research? A systematic review. *PLoS One*, *13*(3), e0193762. DOI: 10.1371/journal.pone.0193762 PMID: 29513762

Volkwein, J. F. (1999). The four faces of institutional research. *New Directions for Institutional Research*, *1999*(104), 9–19. DOI: 10.1002/ir.10401

Volkwein, J. F. (2008). The foundations and evolution of institutional research. *New Directions for Higher Education*, *2008*(141), 5–20. DOI: 10.1002/he.289

Webber, K. L., & Calderon, A. J. (2015). *Institutional Research and Planning in Higher Education: Global Contexts and Themes*. Routledge. DOI: 10.4324/9781315777726

Webber, K. L., & Zheng, H. Y. (2020). *Big Data on Campus: Data Analytics and Decision Making in Higher Education*. Johns Hopkins University Press. DOI: 10.1353/book.78960

Whistle, W. (2017). *How higher education data reporting is both burdensome and inadequate*. Technical report, Third Way.

Williamson, B. (2018). The hidden architecture of higher education: Building a big data infrastructure for the 'smarter university'. *International Journal of Educational Technology in Higher Education*, *15*(1), 1–26. DOI: 10.1186/s41239-018-0094-1

Yin, R. K. (2018). *Case Study Research and Applications: Design and Methods* (6th ed.). SAGE Publications.

KEY TERMS AND DEFINITIONS

Aggregation Stage: The mid-stream stage at which unit-level submissions are consolidated into institutional master datasets through merging, deduplication, and structural reorganization.

Collection Stage: The upstream stage at which raw data is gathered from organizational units (faculties, departments, institutes, administrative offices) through standardized templates and data request instruments.

Definitional Inconsistency: The structural condition in which ostensibly equivalent indicators (for example, "academic staff") are defined differently across ranking systems, requiring institutions to maintain multiple parallel representations of the same underlying data.

Five-Stage Model: An analytical decomposition of the institutional data supply chain into five sequential value-adding stages: Collection, Aggregation, Normalization, Transformation, and Submission. Each stage performs a distinct function in converting raw departmental inputs into ranking-ready outputs.

Institutional Data Supply Chain: An organizational mechanism through which raw institutional data is collected from internal units, consolidated, classified against standardized definitions, restructured to meet the requirements of multiple external evaluation systems, and submitted to those systems. The concept adapts supply chain management theory to the context of university ranking data management.

Invisible Data Labor: The specialized interpretive and reconciliation work—performed at the Normalization and Transformation stages—that is required to convert institutional data into ranking-ready outputs but is typically neither recognized in institutional staffing models nor accounted for in ranking methodology discussions.

Normalization Stage: The mid-stream stage at which aggregated data is mapped against both internal institutional metadata frameworks and external indicator classification schemes (such as journal quartile tiers or occupational classifications).

One Source, Many Outputs Principle: The structural property of the institutional data supply chain by which the same underlying institutional data source yields multiple, legitimately different outputs across ranking systems, owing to differences in indicator definitions, scope boundaries, and formatting requirements.

Postponement (Delayed Differentiation): A supply chain management concept, applied here to data management, denoting the practice of maintaining undifferentiated upstream data and deferring system-specific customization to the latest feasible downstream stage.

Submission Stage: The terminal stage at which transformed data is uploaded to ranking agency portals or other reporting instruments, subject to verification and post-submission revision requests.

Compilation of References

Aarthi, S. Ravikumar, Sapayev Odilbek Uglu, V., Sottarov, A., & Singh, A. (2025). The privacy paradox. In *User-Centric Cybersecurity Implications for Sustainable Digital Transformation* (pp. 223–256). IGI Global Scientific Publishing. DOI: 10.4018/979-8-3373-3171-3.ch007

Aarthi, S., Ravikumar, R. N., Sobirova, K., & Mamadiyarov, Z. (2025). Empowering a sustainable future through digital learning and the SDGs. In *Harnessing E-Learning to Create a Sustainable Future* (pp. 145–172). IGI Global Scientific Publishing., DOI: 10.4018/979-8-3373-0112-9.ch006

Abdulgafar, A. A., Michael Oluwaseyi, A., Popoola, R., Anuoluwapo Rachael, A., & Chinonyerem, C. A. (2025). Human Factors Engineering and AI for optimizing human-machine interaction in industrial systems. *Asian Journal of Advanced Research and Reports*, *19*(10), 1–15. DOI: 10.9734/ajarr/2025/v19i101164

Åberg, P., Arenö, E., & Alvinius, A. (2021). Organizational challenges in the public sector: A qualitative study of the Swedish Armed Forces and elderly care. *Qualitative Sociology Review*, *17*(3), 34–54. DOI: 10.18778/1733-8077.17.3.02

Aboshi, S., Thomas, D. R., & Moshfeghi, Y. (2025). The ethics of psychological manipulation in adversarial conversational AI: Confronting the recognition-behaviour gap. In *Proceedings of the 7th ACM Conference on Conversational User Interfaces* (pp. 1–6). DOI: 10.1145/3719160.3737616

Abraham, D., Leon, L., Nakatsu, R., Przasnyski, Z., & Seal, K. (2004). The alignment of organizational incentives with organizational goals across IT adoption stages. In *Proceedings of the Americas Conference on Information Systems*.

Adewojo, A. A., & Dunmade, A. O. (2024). From big data to intelligent libraries: Leveraging analytics for enhanced user experiences. *Business Information Review*, *41*(3), 02663821241264707. DOI: 10.1177/02663821241264707

Agbabiaka, O., Ojo, A., & Connolly, N. (2025). Requirements for trustworthy AI-enabled automated decision-making in the public sector: A systematic review. *Technological Forecasting and Social Change, 215*, 124076. Advance online publication. DOI: 10.1016/j.techfore.2025.124076

Agote-Garrido, A., Martín-Gómez, A. M., & Lama-Ruiz, J. R. AgoteGarrido. (2023). Manufacturing system design in Industry 5.0: Incorporating sociotechnical systems and social metabolism for humancentered, sustainable, and resilient production. *Systems, 11*(11), 537. DOI: 10.3390/systems11110537

Aisyah, P. N., & Dp, R. T. (2025). Artificial Intelligence and Cloud-Based Accounting Information Systems: Enhancing financial reporting reliability and cybersecurity in the digital era. *Jurnal Ekonomi Dan Bisnis Digital, 4*(3), 203–222. DOI: 10.55927/ministal.v4i3.14519

Akintola, A. S. O., Fawehinmi, Y., Aiyenitaju, O., Chinemerem, B., & Emmanuella, O. (2025). Digital transformation in telehealth: A systematic review of user trust, privacy, and regulatory governance in AI-powered remote monitoring systems. *Journal of Scientific Research and Reports, 31*(11), 163–182. DOI: 10.9734/jsrr/2025/v31i113658

Al Naqbi, H., Bahroun, Z., & Ahmed, V. (2024). Enhancing work productivity through generative artificial intelligence: A comprehensive literature review. [Publisher Full Text.]. *Sustainability (Basel), 16*(3), 1166. DOI: 10.3390/su16031166

Alassaf, N. (2025). From abstraction to realization: A diagrammatic BIM framework for conceptual design in architectural education. *Sustainability (Basel), 17*(19), 8853. DOI: 10.3390/su17198853

Albitz, B. (2014). *Licensing and managing electronic resources*. Elsevier.

Alderfer, C. (1972). *Existence, relatedness and growth: Human needs in organizational settings*. Free Press.

Aldhafeeri, F. M. (2025). Governing artificial intelligence in radiology: A systematic review of ethical, legal, and regulatory frameworks. *Diagnostics (Basel), 15*(18), 2300. DOI: 10.3390/diagnostics15182300 PMID: 41008671

Alenzuela, R., & Kamilova, Y. (2018). Synchronous and Asynchronous Engagement in Virtual Library Services as Learning Support Systems from the Perspectives of Post-Graduate Students: A Case Study. [JIStaP]. *Journal of Information Science Theory and Practice, 6*(1).

Allan, B.A., Batz-Barbarich, C., Sterling, H. M., & Tay, L. (2019). Outcomes of Meaningful Work: A Meta-Analysis. Journal of Management Studies, Special Issue: Meaningful Work: Prospects for the 21st Century, 56(3), 500-528. https://doi.org/ DOI: 10.1111/joms.12406

Allan, B. A., Duffy, R. D., & Douglass, R. (2015). Meaning in life and work: A developmental perspective. *The Journal of Positive Psychology*, *10*(4), 323–331. DOI: 10.1080/17439760.2014.950180

Altmann, E. M., & Trafton, J. G. (2002). Memory for goals: An activation-based model. *Cognitive Science*, *26*(1), 39–83.

Anderson, J., Frank, L. E., & Spahn, A. (Eds.). (2025). *The ethics of behaviour change technologies: Beyond nudging and persuasion*. Bloomsbury Publishing. DOI: 10.5040/9798881847432

Aneesh, A. (2009). Global Labor: Algocratic Modes of Organization. *Sociological Theory*, *27*(4), 347–370. DOI: 10.1111/j.1467-9558.2009.01352.x

Ang, K. C. S., Sankaran, S., & Liu, D. (2025). Advancing sociotechnical systems theory: New principles for human-robot team design and development. *Applied Ergonomics*, *129*, 104604. Advance online publication. DOI: 10.1016/j.apergo.2025.104604 PMID: 40753964

Anuradha, P. (2018). Digital transformation of academic libraries: Opportunities and challenges. *IP Indian Journal of Library Science and Information Technology*, *3*(1), 8–10.

Arigbabu, A. T., Olaniyi, O. O., Adigwe, C. S., Adebiyi, O. O., & Ajayi, S. A. (2024). Data governance in AI - enabled healthcare systems: A case of the Project Nightingale. *Asian Journal of Research in Computer Science*, *17*(5), 85–107. DOI: 10.9734/ajrcos/2024/v17i5441

Arlinghaus, A., & Nachreiner, F. (2014). Health effects of supplemental work from home in the European Union. *Chronobiology International*, *31*(10), 1100–1107. DOI: 10.3109/07420528.2014.957297 PMID: 25229274

Asha, M., & Kumar, A. (2025). Interface design and employee well-being in the digital workplace: The role of basic psychological need satisfaction. *Asian Journal of Interdisciplinary Research*, *8*(3), 29–40.

Ashikuzzaman, M. D. (2024). The Applications of Big Data in Libraries. Library and Information Science Network. https://www.lisedunetwork.com/the-applications-of-big-data-in-libraries/

Atiase, V. Y., Kolade, O., & Liedong, T. A. (2020). The emergence and strategy of tech hubs in Africa: Implications for knowledge production and value creation. *Technological Forecasting and Social Change, 161*, 120307. DOI: 10.1016/j.techfore.2020.120307

Autili, M., Corsi, R., De Sanctis, M., Inverardi, P., & Pelliccione, P. (2025). Ethics Label for Digital Systems to Promote Transparency and User Awareness. *Journal of Systems and Software, 112752*. Advance online publication. DOI: 10.1016/j.jss.2025.112752

Ayyagari, R., Grover, V., & Purvis, R. (2011). Technostress: Technological antecedents and implications. *Management Information Systems Quarterly, 35*(4), 831–858. DOI: 10.2307/41409963

Baethge, A., & Rigotti, T. (2013). Interruptions to workflow: Their relationship with irritation and satisfaction. *Journal of Organizational Behavior, 34*(6), 855–875.

Bailey, C., Yeoman, R., Madden, A., Thompson, M., & Kerridge, G. (2018). A Review of the Empirical Literature on Meaningful Work: Progress and Research Agenda. Human Resource Development Review, 18(1), 83-113. (Original work published 2019)DOI: 10.1177/1534484318804653

Bailey, B. P., & Konstan, J. A. (2006). On the need for attention-aware systems: Measuring effects of interruption on task performance, error rate, and affective state. *Computers in Human Behavior, 22*(4), 685–708. DOI: 10.1016/j.chb.2005.12.009

Bala, H., & Bhagwatwar, A. (2018). Employee dispositions to job and organization as antecedents and consequences of information systems use. *Information Systems Journal, 28*(4), 650–683. DOI: 10.1111/isj.12152

Balakrishnan, S., Arunkumar, A., John, E. P., Savitha, S., Chandra, K., & Subrahmanyam, S. (2025). Exploring the influence of family supportive benefits on work-life balance and job embeddedness through internal motivation in IT sectors. *Revista Latinoamericana de la Papa, 26*(1), 441–453. https://dialnet.unirioja.es/servlet/articulo?codigo=10627881

Ball, K. (2021). *Electronic monitoring and surveillance in the workplace: Literature review and policy recommendations*. Publications Office of the European Union., DOI: 10.2760/451453

Bamigbola, A. A. (2023). *BIG DATA" Revitalizing Librarianship: Impact On Librarians*. Library Philosophy & Practice.

Bandura, A., Barbaranelli, C., Caprara, G. V., & Pastorelli, C. (1996). Mechanisms of moral disengagement in the exercise of moral agency. *Journal of Personality and Social Psychology*, *71*(2), 364–374. DOI: 10.1037/0022-3514.71.2.364

Barari, S., Newsom, E., Park, J. E., & Paddock, S. M. (2024). *College ranking systems: A methodological review. Final report*. Chicago, IL: NORC at the University of Chicago.

Barari, S., Park, J. E., & Paddock, S. (2025). *International college ranking systems: A methodological review. Final report*. Chicago, IL: NORC at the University of Chicago.

Barocas, S., & Selbst, A. D. (2016). Big data's disparate impact. *California Law Review*, *104*(3), 671–732.

Barron, G. R. S. (2023). How university rankings are made through globally coordinated action: A transnational institutional ethnography in the sociology of quantification. *Higher Education*, *86*(4), 809–826. DOI: 10.1007/s10734-022-00903-y

Barsky, A. (2011). Investigating the effects of moral disengagement and participation on unethical work behavior. *Journal of Business Ethics*, *104*(1), 59–75. DOI: 10.1007/s10551-011-0889-7

Bastiaansen, C. A. J., & Wilderom, C. P. M. (2022). Agile and generic work values of British vs Indian IT workers: A culture-clash case. *Journal of Strategy and Management*, *15*(3), 353–376. DOI: 10.1108/JSMA-03-2021-0071

Battles, M. (2004). *Library: An unquiet history*. WW Norton & Company.

Baumeister, R. F., Vohs, K. D., & Tice, D. M. (2007). The strength model of self-control. *Current Directions in Psychological Science*, *16*(6), 351–355. DOI: 10.1111/j.1467-8721.2007.00534.x

Bayanbayeva, A. (2025). Strategic response or gaming the rankings? Unravelling the strategies behind global university rankings manipulation in the higher education context of Kazakhstan. *Higher Education*. Advance online publication. DOI: 10.1007/s10734-025-01512-1

Beaumon, B. (2011). Bookshare: Making accessible materials available worldwide. In *World Library and Information Congress: 77th IFLA General Conference and Assembly. San Juan, Puerto Rico*.

Bedmutha, A. S.Akangsha Sunil Bedmutha. (2025). Adaptive Cognitive Reality: AI-driven personalized reality for optimized human potential. *International Journal of Computational and Experimental Science and Engineering, 11*(4). Advance online publication. DOI: 10.22399/ijcesen.4496

Bertot, J. C., Gorham, U., Jaeger, P. T., & Taylor, N. G. (2012). Public Libraries and the Internet 2012: Key findings, recent trends, and future challenges. *Public Library Quarterly, 31*(4), 303–325. DOI: 10.1080/01616846.2012.732479

Besek, J. (2003). Copyright Issues Relevant to the Creation of a Digital Archive. *De Gruyter, 32*(3), 86–97. DOI: 10.1515/MFIR.2003.86

Bhushan, N. (2025). Artificial intelligence (AI) and its role in enhancing the well-being of employees in the public sector: A systematic review. *International Journal of Scientific Research and Modern Technology, 13*, 13. Advance online publication. DOI: 10.38124/ijsrmt.v4i12.1060

Bignoli, C., & Stara, L. (2020). *Responding to rapid change in libraries: a user experience approach.* American Library Association.

Billingham, L. (2014). Improving academic library website accessibility for people with disabilities. *Library Management, 35*(8/9), 565–581. DOI: 10.1108/LM-11-2013-0107

Björck, A., Vogel, B., Pugnetti, C., & Lopez, M. (2025). Advancing cyber crisis readiness: Context, microfoundations and the role of leadership. *Journal of Communication Management (London)*, •••, 1–20. DOI: 10.1108/JCOM-01-2025-0006

Bobrytska, V. I., Krasylnykova, H. V., Protska, S. M., Skyrda, T. S., Krasylnykov, S. R., & Chkhalo, O. M. (2025). Digitalisation in higher education: A systematic review of its impact on health, cognition, and social interaction. *International Journal of Learning Teaching and Educational Research, 24*(5), 339–359. DOI: 10.26803/ijlter.24.5.18

Bodker, S., Dindler, C., Iversen, O. S., & Smith, R. C. (2022). *Participatory design.* Springer., DOI: 10.1007/978-3-031-02235-7

Bokhari, S. A. A. (2026). Artificial intelligence, governance, and economic growth: Toward a new theory of digital developmentalism. *Social Sciences & Humanities Open, 13*, 102842. Advance online publication. DOI: 10.1016/j.ssaho.2026.102842

Boos, A. K. (2024). Conceptualizing automated decision-making in organizational contexts. *Philosophy & Technology, 37*(3), 1–30. DOI: 10.1007/s13347-024-00773-5 PMID: 39027378

Borgman, C. L. (2015). *Big Data, Little Data, No Data: Scholarship in the Networked World*. MIT Press. DOI: 10.7551/mitpress/9963.001.0001

Borgman, C. L. (2017). *Big data, little data, no data: Scholarship in the networked world*. MIT press.

Borsato, M., Lattanzio, S., & Newnes, L. (2025). Leveraging motivational theories to enhance engagement and productivity in manufacturing digitalisation projects. In *Transdisciplinarity for a better world* (pp. 409–418). IOS Press. DOI: 10.3233/ATDE251113

Botha, J., Webber, K., Williams, J., Calderon, A., Klemencič, M., Wooldridge, A., & Chirikov, I. (2024). Building capacity in institutional research: Collaboration and complementarity? *Tertiary Education and Management*, *30*(2), 129–145. DOI: 10.1007/s11233-024-09139-0

Bouchon-Meunier, B. (2021). Ethics, diversity and consciousness in AI [president's message]. *IEEE Computational Intelligence Magazine*, *16*(3), 3–4. DOI: 10.1109/MCI.2021.3084388

Bowen, G. A. (2009). Document analysis as a qualitative research method. *Qualitative Research Journal*, *9*(2), 27–40. DOI: 10.3316/QRJ0902027

Bowker, G. C., & Star, S. L. (1999). *Sorting Things Out: Classification and Its Consequences*. MIT Press. DOI: 10.7551/mitpress/6352.001.0001

Boztas, C., Ghadafi, E., & Ibrahim, R. (2025). Metaverse architectures: A comprehensive systematic review of definitions and frameworks. *Future Internet*, *17*(7), 283. DOI: 10.3390/fi17070283

Brankovic, J., Hamann, J., & Ringel, L. (2023). The institutionalization of rankings in higher education. *Higher Education*, *86*(4), 719–731. DOI: 10.1007/s10734-023-01018-8

Brannick, T., & Coghlan, D. (2007). In defense of being "native": The case for insider academic research. *Organizational Research Methods*, *10*(1), 59–74. DOI: 10.1177/1094428106289253

Breeding, M. (2010). Automation Marketplace 2010: The New Frontier. *Library Journal*, *135*(6), 22–28.

Breeding, M. (2015). The future of library resource discovery. *Information Standards Quarterly*, *27*(1), 24–30. DOI: 10.3789/isqv27no1.2015.04

British Library. (n.d.). Learning at the Library. https://support.bl.uk/Page/Learning

Brodowicz, D. P.SGH Warsaw School of Economics. (2025). From smart to agentic environments: AI and innovative technologies transforming learning, work and urban living. *E-Mentor, 111*(4), 54–61. DOI: 10.15219/em111.1720

Brown, A. (2013). *Practical digital preservation: A how-to guide for organizations of any size*. Facet Publishing.

Brown, T. B., Mann, B., Ryder, N., Subbiah, M., Kaplan, J., Dhariwal, P., Neelakantan, A., Shyam, P., Sastry, G., Askell, A., Agarwal, S., Herbert-Voss, A., Krueger, G., Henighan, T., Child, R., Ramesh, A., Ziegler, D. M., Wu, J., Winter, C., & Amodei, D. (2020). *Language models are few-shot learners* (Vol. 33). Advances in Neural Information Processing Systems, https://arxiv.org/abs/2005.14165

Bruckler, M., Wietschel, L., Messmann, L., Thorenz, A., & Tuma, A. (2024). Review of metrics to assess resilience capacities and actions for supply chain resilience. *Computers & Industrial Engineering, 192*, 110176. DOI: 10.1016/j.cie.2024.110176

Brunyé, T. T., Mitroff, S. R., & Elmore, J. G. (2026). Artificial intelligence and computer-aided diagnosis in diagnostic decisions: 5 questions for medical informatics and human-computer interface research. *Journal of the American Medical Informatics Association : JAMIA, 33*(2), 543–550. DOI: 10.1093/jamia/ocaf123 PMID: 41101774

Brynjolfsson, E., & McAfee, A. (2014). *The second machine age*. W. W. Norton & Company.

Cajochen, C., Frey, S., & Anders, D.. (2011). Evening exposure to LED-backlit screens affects circadian rhythms. *Journal of Applied Physiology, 110*(5), 1432–1438. DOI: 10.1152/japplphysiol.00165.2011 PMID: 21415172

Caldeira, R., & Infante-Moro, A. (2025). The importance of ethics in organisations, their leaders, and sustainability. *Administrative Sciences, 15*(9), 372. DOI: 10.3390/admsci15090372

Calderon, A. J., & Mathies, C. (2013). Institutional research in the future: Challenges within higher education and the need for excellence in professional practice. *New Directions for Institutional Research, 2013*(157), 77–90. DOI: 10.1002/ir.20040

Candela, L., Castelli, D., & Pagano, P. (2012). History, evolution, and impact of digital libraries. In *Organizational Learning and Knowledge: Concepts, Methodologies, Tools and Applications* (pp. 837-866). IGI Global. DOI: 10.4018/978-1-60960-783-8.ch301

Carayon, P., Hoonakker, P., & Hundt, A. S. (2021). Human factors and ergonomics in health care and patient safety. In Salvendy, G. (Ed.), *Handbook of human factors and ergonomics* (5th ed., pp. 1674–1700). Wiley. DOI: 10.1002/9781119636113.ch53

Casalino, N., Armenia, S., & Di Nauta, P. (2021). Inspiring the organizational change and accelerating the digital transition in public sector by systems thinking and system dynamics approaches. In *International KES Conference on Smart Education and Smart E-Learning* (pp. 197–214). Springer. DOI: 10.1007/978-981-16-2834-4_17

Caschera, M. C., & Guzzo, T. (2026). User-centred interaction design for enhancing professional well-being in healthcare environments. *Health Care, 14*(5), 637. PMID: 41827591

Casey, A. M. (2004). A Historical Overview of Internet Reference Services for Distance Learners. *Internet Reference Services Quarterly, 9*(3/4), 5–17. Advance online publication. DOI: 10.1300/J136v09n03_02

Cassell, K. A., & Hiremath, U. (2023). *Reference and information services: An introduction.* American Library Association.

Chang, A. M., Aeschbach, D., Duffy, J. F., & Czeisler, C. A. (2015). Evening use of light-emitting devices negatively affects sleep. *Proceedings of the National Academy of Sciences of the United States of America, 112*(4), 1232–1237. DOI: 10.1073/pnas.1418490112 PMID: 25535358

Chauhan, A., Sarkar, D., Verma, G. S., Rastogi, H., Adapa, K., & Duggal, M. (2025). Evaluating trustworthiness in AI-Based diabetic retinopathy screening: Addressing transparency, consent, and privacy challenges. *BMC Medical Ethics, 26*(1), 140. DOI: 10.1186/s12910-025-01265-7 PMID: 41107928

Chicago Public Library Foundation. (2024). Bridge the Digital Divide. https://cplfoundation.org/impact/bridge-the-digital-divide/

Chigbu, B. I., & Makapela, S. L. (2025). AI in education, sustainability, and the future of work: An integrative review of industry 5.0, education 5.0, and work 5.0. *Journal of Open Innovation, 11*(4), 100645. Advance online publication. DOI: 10.1016/j.joitmc.2025.100645

Chowdhury, S. A., Sharmin, R., Al-Amin, M., & Shifat, M. N. (2025). Integrating an educational supply chain model in the higher education sector: Meeting the 21st century workforce demands in Bangladesh. *Frontiers in Education, 10*, 1521309. DOI: 10.3389/feduc.2025.1521309

Çitli, I. (2025). AI and the employee: Emerging organizational behavior trends for the future of work. In *The future of work and work design.*

Clark, J. M. (2007). *The Care of Books: An Essay on the Development of Libraries and Their Influence on Civilization*. Cambridge University Press.

Colquitt, J. A., Conlon, D. E., Wesson, M. J., Porter, C. O. L. H., & Ng, K. Y. (2001). Justice at the millennium. *The Journal of Applied Psychology*, *86*(3), 425–445. DOI: 10.1037/0021-9010.86.3.425 PMID: 11419803

Conz, E., & Magnani, G. (2020). A dynamic perspective on the resilience of firms: A systematic literature review and a framework for future research. *European Management Journal*, *38*(3), 400–412. DOI: 10.1016/j.emj.2019.12.004

Coron, C., & Porcher, S. (2026). Ethical considerations in algorithm construction: Evidence from two human-resources algorithms. M@n@gement,, 29(1), 7-20. DOI: 10.37725/mgmt.2025.9830

Costley, C., Elliott, G., & Gibbs, P. (2010). *Doing Work Based Research: Approaches to Enquiry for Insider-Researchers*. SAGE Publications. DOI: 10.4135/9781446287880

Cruz, G. V., Liberacka-Dwojak, M., Wiłkość-Dębczyńska, M., Terzioğlu, M. A., Farchione, T., Lecomte, T., & Khazaal, Y. (2025). Perceived digital well-being scale in the United States and United Kingdom: Psychometric validation study. *JMIR Mental Health*, *12*(1), e78334. DOI: 10.2196/78334 PMID: 41166607

Csikszentmihalyi, M. (1990). *Flow: The psychology of optimal experience*. Harper & Row.

Čvokić, D. D. (2025). The unintended consequences of algorithmic transparency on trust: A multi-disciplinary analysis. *Acta Scientifica Balcanica*, *6*(1), 22–40. DOI: 10.63356/asb.2025.002

Daassi, M., Daassi, C., & Favier, M. (2006). Integration visualization techniques in groupware interfaces. In *Encyclopedia of Virtual Communities and Technologies* (pp. 279–284). IGI Global., DOI: 10.4018/978-1-59140-563-4.ch053

Dafoe, A. (2018). AI governance: a research agenda. *Governance of AI Program, Future of Humanity Institute, University of Oxford: Oxford, UK, 1442*, 1443.

Daft, R. L., & Lengel, R. H. (1986). Organizational information requirements and media richness. *Management Science*, *32*(5), 554–571. DOI: 10.1287/mnsc.32.5.554

Dahler-Larsen, P. (2014). Constitutive effects of performance indicators: Getting beyond unintended consequences. *Public Management Review*, *16*(7), 969–986. DOI: 10.1080/14719037.2013.770058

Davenport, T. H., & Prusak, L. (1998). *Working knowledge: How organizations manage what they know*. Harvard Business Press.

Davenport, T. H., & Ronanki, R. (2018). Artificial intelligence for the real world. *Harvard Business Review*, *96*(1), 108–116.

De Bloom, J., Vaziri, H., Tay, L., Kujanpää, M., & Kinnunen, U. (2020). Effects of vacation and recovery. *Journal of Occupational Health Psychology*, *25*(5), 1–14.

de Oliveira, T. H. M., de Castro Neto, M., Costa, E. G., Simoes, M. Q., & Sousa, C. (2025, October). Rewiring governance: Building a data-centric ecosystem for higher education strategic (and digital) transformation. In *Proceedings of the Future Technologies Conference* (pp. 38-60). Cham: Springer Nature Switzerland.

Dhand, S., Pandey, A., Mishra, S., Sharma, K., Kadanga, A., Rawat, A., Kumari, V., Yadav, M., & Chand, B.-U.-N. (2025). Role of Artificial Intelligence in enhancing employee well-being at the workplace. In *Advances in Computational Intelligence and Robotics* (pp. 25–46). IGI Global Scientific Publishing. DOI: 10.4018/979-8-3373-1270-5.ch002

Dhand, S. (2025). Human-centric digital workplace: Designing for employee well-being and productivity. In *Human-centric, sustainable, and resilient organizations in the digital age* (pp. 125–146). IGI Global Scientific Publishing.

Di Maggio, M., Ratnadiwakara, D., & Carmichael, D. (2021). Invisible Primes: Fintech Lending with Alternative Data. Harvard Business School Working Paper, No. 22-024.

Díaz-Rodríguez, N., Del Ser, J., Coeckelbergh, M., López de Prado, M., Herrera-Viedma, E., & Herrera, F. (2023). Connecting the dots in trustworthy Artificial Intelligence: From AI principles, ethics, and key requirements to responsible AI systems and regulation. *Information Fusion*, *99*, 101896. Advance online publication. DOI: 10.1016/j.inffus.2023.101896

Dinev, T., & Hart, P. (2006). Privacy concerns and trust in information systems. *Management Information Systems Quarterly*, *30*(1), 61–88.

Diniz, P., Marques, I. C. P., & Pereira, Â. M. (2025). Leadership, human-centred management and organisational culture: Pathways to well-being and innovative work based on a systematic review. *Sustainability (Basel)*, *17*(24), 11181. DOI: 10.3390/su172411181

DORA. (2012). San francisco declaration on research assessment. *Declaration on Research Assessment*, San Francisco. Retrieved May 13, 2013, from https://sfdora.org/read/

Dubey, A., Sinha, A., & Raj, A. (2024). Navigating the digital divide in India: A comprehensive guide. *Humanities & Social Sciences Reviews*, *12*(2), 16–24. DOI: 10.18510/hssr.2024.1223

Durodolu, O.O, Adekanye, A. E (and) Olorunfemi, Y. D (2013). Information literacy skills of arts subject teachers in Lagos state senior secondary schools Nigeria. IOSR Journal of Humanities and Social Science (IOSR-JHSS). Volume 14, Issue 6. Pp. 66-75. https://uzspace.unizulu.ac.za/items/37fdd5bf-9ca0-48b1-919c-db4acc4aec48

Durodolu, O. O. (2018). Secondary School Teachers' Perceptions of Information Literacy Skills. *Mousaion*, *36*(1). Advance online publication. DOI: 10.25159/0027-2639/3873

Dutta Roy, T. P. (2025). Bioethics artificial intelligence advisory (BAIA): An agentic artificial intelligence (AI) framework for bioethical clinical decision support. *Cureus*, *17*(3), e80494. DOI: 10.7759/cureus.80494 PMID: 40083589

Dzindolet, M. T., Pierce, L. G., Beck, H. P., & Dawe, L. A. (2002). The perceived utility of human and automated aids in a visual detection task. *Human Factors*, *44*(1), 79–94. DOI: 10.1518/0018720024494856 PMID: 12118875

Eastwood, C., Lim, N., Durie, R., Dela Rue, B., Bifet, A., & Reed, C. (2026). JDS Communications® TBC; TBC Mini-Review Animal Nutrition and Farm Systems Integrating Agentic artificial intelligence into pasture-based dairy systems: Applications, governance, and future directions. https://creativecommons.org/licenses/by/4.0/

Ebojoh, S., & Högberg, K. (2024). Exploring leadership in the hybrid workplace. [IJAC]. *International Journal of Advanced Corporate Learning*, *17*(4), 16–41. DOI: 10.3991/ijac.v17i4.50857

Economics, S. K. K. N. U. (2025). of, Grynevych, L., Kniazieva, O., University, O. S. A., Pedorenko, D., & University, P. S. T. (2025). Analysis of the impact of marketing strategy on the formation of the components of the information and logistics system of a trading enterprise. *Ukrainian Journal of Applied Economics and Technology*, *2025*(3), 12–15. DOI: 10.36887/2415-8453-2025-3-1

Effoduh, J. O., Akpudo, U. E., & Kong, J. D. (2024). Toward a trustworthy and inclusive data governance policy for the use of artificial intelligence in Africa. *Data & Policy*, *6*, e34. DOI: 10.1017/dap.2024.26

Ehrenpreis, M., & DeLooper, J. (2022). Implementing a chatbot on a library website. *Journal of Web Librarianship*, *16*(2), 120–142. DOI: 10.1080/19322909.2022.2060893

Eilouti, B. (2023). A framework for integrating ergonomics into architectural design. *Ergonomics in Design*, *31*(1), 4–12. DOI: 10.1177/1064804620983672

El Arab, R. A., Al Moosa, O. A., Sagbakken, M., Ghannam, A., Abuadas, F. H., Somerville, J., & Al Mutair, A. (2025). Integrative review of artificial intelligence applications in nursing: Education, clinical practice, workload management, and professional perceptions. *Frontiers in Public Health, 13*(1619378), 1619378. DOI: 10.3389/fpubh.2025.1619378 PMID: 40823249

Endsley, M. R. (1995). Toward a theory of situation awareness. *Human Factors, 37*(1), 32–64. DOI: 10.1518/001872095779049543

Eppler, M. J., & Mengis, J. (2004). The concept of information overload: A review of literature from organization science, accounting, marketing, MIS, and related disciplines. *The Information Society, 20*(5), 325–344. DOI: 10.1080/01972240490507974

Epstein, E. G., & Hamric, A. B. (2009). Moral distress, moral residue, and the crescendo effect. *The Journal of Clinical Ethics, 20*(4), 330–342. DOI: 10.1086/JCE200920406 PMID: 20120853

Espeland, W. N., & Sauder, M. (2007). Rankings and reactivity: How public measures recreate social worlds. *American Journal of Sociology, 113*(1), 1–40. DOI: 10.1086/517897

Espeland, W. N., & Sauder, M. (2016). *Engines of Anxiety: Academic Rankings, Reputation, and Accountability*. Russell Sage Foundation.

Espeland, W. N., & Stevens, M. L. (1998). Commensuration as a social process. *Annual Review of Sociology, 24*(1), 313–343. DOI: 10.1146/annurev.soc.24.1.313

European Commission. (2021). *Industry 5.0: Towards a sustainable, human-centric and resilient European industry*. Publications Office of the European Union., DOI: 10.2777/308407

European Education and Culture Executive Agency. (2024). *European Higher Education Sector Observatory (EHESO)*. European Commission, EACEA. Retrieved 2016, from https: //national-policies.eacea.ec.europa.eu/eheso

Evangelista, E., & Salman Bukhari, S. M. (2026). From ethical principles to executable governance: A policy-as-code framework for trustworthy AI in higher education. *Computers and Education: Artificial Intelligence, 10*, 100594. Advance online publication. DOI: 10.1016/j.caeai.2026.100594

Fafrowicz, M., Marek, T., Karwowski, W., & Schmorrow, D. (Eds.). (2012). *Neuroadaptive systems: Theory and applications*. CRC Press. DOI: 10.1201/b13019

Farid, A., A. (. (2024). An approach for enhancing architectural performance-based design assessment in terms of sustainability. *Engineering Research Journal (Shoubra), 53*(1), 170–180. DOI: 10.21608/erjsh.2023.243056.1235

Faryabi, M., & Tajvidi, M. (2012). Investigation the effect of investment in information technology on organization productivity. *Iranian Journal of Information Processing and Management, 27*(1), 340–352.

Fawzy Eid, M. (2024). Using artificial intelligence in electronic health record systems to mitigate physician burnout: A roadmap. *Journal of Healthcare Management, 69*(4), 244–254. DOI: 10.1097/JHM-D-24-00094 PMID: 38976785

Ferullo, D. L., & Soules, A. (2012). Managing Copyright in a Digital World. [IJDLS]. *International Journal of Digital Library Systems, 3*(4), 1–25. DOI: 10.4018/ijdls.2012100101

Finbite. (2024). *Sustainable development & digital waste reduction*. Finbite. https://finbite.eu/en/digital-waste/

Fisher, K. (2020). Copyright and Preservation of Born-digital Materials: Persistent Challenges and Selected Strategies. *the american archivist, 83*(2), 238-267.

Floridi, L., Cowls, J., & Beltrametti, M.. (2018). AI4People—An ethical framework for artificial intelligence. *Minds and Machines, 28*(4), 689–707. DOI: 10.1007/s11023-018-9482-5 PMID: 30930541

Floridou, G. A., Katre, F., & Jeuken, E. (2025). A digital tool for assessing well-being at the workplace and in personal life: Development and validation of the Quan Well-Being Index. *JMIR Formative Research, 9*, e73713. DOI: 10.2196/73713 PMID: 40779765

Forcellini, M., & Gracikova, E. (2025). From cognitive bias to algorithmic influence: Theoretical shifts in behavioral finance. *Journal of Behavioral Economics and Policy, 1*(1), 20–27. DOI: 10.55121/jbep.v1i1.766

Forster, E. M. (1909). The Machine Stops. In The Eternal Moment and Other Stories. Sidgwick & Jackson. Available at chrome-extension://efaidnbmnnnibpcajpcglclefindmkaj/https://www.cs.ucdavis.edu/~koehl/Teaching/ECS188/PDF_files/Machine_stops.pdf

Fousiani, K., Cremer, L. R., Çetin, M., & Raeder, S. (2026). When algorithmic managers fail to fulfill their promises: The role of anthropomorphism in shaping justice perceptions. *PLoS One, 21*(2), e0340860. DOI: 10.1371/journal.pone.0340860 PMID: 41719274

Gao, S., Jia, Y., Liu, B., & Mu, W. (2025). Algorithmic monitoring increases unethical behavior in gig workers: The mediating role of moral disengagement. *Information Technology & People*, *38*(6), 2506–2530. DOI: 10.1108/ITP-07-2023-0693

García-Ruiz, P., & Rocchi, M. (2026). Can work be meaningful under algorithmic management? A MacIntyrean perspective. *Business Ethics Quarterly*, *36*(1), 3–30. DOI: 10.1017/beq.2025.5

Gardner, P. J., Kamber, T., & Netherland, J. (2012). "Getting turned on": using ICT training to promote active ageing in New York city. *The journal of community informatics, 8*(1).

Gautam, D. K. (2014). Impact of digital divide and public libraries. *IOSR Journal of Humanities and Social Science*, *19*(12), 59–63. DOI: 10.9790/0837-191245963

Gephart, R. P.Jr. (2002). Introduction to the brave new workplace: Organizational behavior in the electronic age. *Journal of Organizational Behavior*, *23*(4), 327–344. DOI: 10.1002/job.143

Gholami, B. (2025). Pathways to innovation: Empowering change with systems and design thinking. In *Mastering innovation in business* (pp. 21–46). IGI Global.

Giorgi, G., Lecca, L. I., Alessio, F., Finstad, G. L., Bondanini, G., Lulli, L. G., Arcangeli, G., & Mucci, N. (2020). COVID-19-related mental health effects in the workplace: A narrative review. *International Journal of Environmental Research and Public Health*, *17*(21), 7857. DOI: 10.3390/ijerph17217857 PMID: 33120930

Gladney, H. (2009). Long-term preservation of digital records: Trustworthy digital objects. *The American Archivist*, *72*(2), 401–435. DOI: 10.17723/aarc.72.2.g513766100731832

González-Reyes, C., Ficapal-Cusí, P., & Torrent-Sellens, J. (2026). AI and organizational leadership: Bibliometric review and future trends. *Journal of Organizational Change Management*, •••, 1–35. DOI: 10.1108/JOCM-03-2025-0291

Gonzalez, V. M., & Mark, G. (2004). Constant, constant, multi-tasking craziness. CHI Proceedings. DOI: 10.1145/985692.985707

Gooding, P., & Fulkerson, N. (2020). Towards a Global Dataset of Digitised Texts: Final Report of the Global Digitised Dataset Network.

Gorodetsky, V. I., Samoylov, V. V., & Trotskii, D. V. (2015). The reference ontology of collective behavior of autonomous agents and its extensions. *Journal of Computer and Systems Sciences International*, *54*(5), 765–782. DOI: 10.1134/S1064230715030089

Grajek, S., and Milhans, J. (2024). 2025 EDUCAUSE Top 10: Restoring Trust. EDUCAUSE *Review (Online)*.

Gram-Hansen, S. B. (2021). Defining features of behavior design: Considering context. In *International Conference on Persuasive Technology* (pp. 308–319). Springer International Publishing. DOI: 10.1007/978-3-030-79460-6_24

Greene, D., & Groenendyk, M. (2021). An environmental scan of virtual and augmented reality services in academic libraries. *Library Hi Tech*, *39*(1), 37–47. DOI: 10.1108/LHT-08-2019-0166

Guy, I. (2025). Conceptual framework of data governance and data organization in higher education: Application of the structurational model of technology. In *Proceedings of the Association for Information Science and Technology*. DOI: 10.1002/pra2.1436

Hacker, J., vom Brocke, J., Handali, J., Otto, M., & Schneider, J. (2019). Virtually in this together. *Information Systems Journal*, *29*(1), 3–45.

Hamann, J., & Ringel, L. (2023). The discursive resilience of university rankings. *Higher Education*, *86*(4), 845–863. DOI: 10.1007/s10734-022-00990-x

Hanson, E. D., & Okorie, U. U. (2024). The roles of Artificial Intelligence in library automation: the prospects and challenges. https://www.globalacademicstar.com/download/article/the-roles-of-artificial-intelligence-in-library-automation-the-prospects-and-challenges.pdf

Han, Z., Song, G., Zhang, Y., & Yan, L. (2025). Enhancing employees' workplace well-being through workplace digitization: Exploring the mediating roles of job demands and digital anxiety. *Frontiers in Psychology*, *16*, 1642489. DOI: 10.3389/fpsyg.2025.1642489 PMID: 40787118

Hapel, R. (2020). Building a contemporary public library through community engagement: A personal journey. *Public Library Quarterly*, *39*(5), 391–409. DOI: 10.1080/01616846.2020.1772621

Haque, A. (2025). Responsible artificial intelligence (AI) in healthcare: A paradigm shift in leadership and strategic management. *Leadership in Health Services (Bradford, England)*, *38*(4), 644–656. DOI: 10.1108/LHS-01-2025-0018 PMID: 40911384

Hase, V. L., Dhawle, G. U., & Dahibhate, N. B. (2014). Reference and information services in the digital era. *Asian Journal of Multidisciplinary Studies*, *2*(6), 18–25.

Hazelkorn, E. (2015). *Rankings and the Reshaping of Higher Education: The Battle for World-Class Excellence* (2nd ed.). Palgrave Macmillan. DOI: 10.1057/9781137446671

Hazelkorn, E. (2017). *Global Rankings and the Geopolitics of Higher Education: Under- standing the Influence and Impact of Rankings on Higher Education, Policy and Society*. Routledge.

Held, V. (2005). *The ethics of care: Personal, political, and global*. Oxford University Press. DOI: 10.1093/0195180992.001.0001

Hevner, A. R., March, S. T., Park, J., & Ram, S. (2004). Design science in information systems research. *Management Information Systems Quarterly*, *28*(1), 75–105. DOI: 10.2307/25148625

Hicks, D., Wouters, P., Waltman, L., de Rijcke, S., & Rafols, I. (2015). Bibliometrics: The leiden manifesto for research metrics. *Nature*, *520*(7548), 429–431. DOI: 10.1038/520429a PMID: 25903611

Hirtle, P. B., Hudson, E., & Kenyon, A. T. (2009). Copyright and cultural institutions: Guidelines for digitization for US libraries, archives, and museums. *Peter B. Hirtle, Emily Hudson, and Andrew T. Kenyon, Copyright And Cultural Institutions: Guidelines For Digitization For Us Libraries, Archives, And Museums, Ithaca, NY: Cornell University Library Press, Forthcoming, U of Melbourne Legal Studies Research Paper*, (434).

Hochschild, A. R. (1983). *The managed heart: Commercialization of human feeling*. University of California Press.

Hodzic, S., Stevic, A., & Matthes, J. (2026). Generative AI in practice: An umbrella review of risks, benefits, ethics, and future directions across major domains. *Technology in Society*, *87*, 103331. Advance online publication. DOI: 10.1016/j.techsoc.2026.103331

Horsthofer-Rauch, J., Guesken, S. R., Weich, J., Rauch, A., Bittner, M., Schulz, J., & Zaeh, M. F.HorsthoferRauch. (2024). Sustainability-integrated value stream mapping with process mining: State of the art and future directions. *Production & Manufacturing Research*, *12*(1), 2334294. DOI: 10.1080/21693277.2024.2334294

Hou, M., Zhu, H., Zhou, M., & Arrabito, G. R. (2011). Optimizing operator–agent interaction in intelligent adaptive interface design: A conceptual framework. *IEEE Transactions on Systems, Man, and Cybernetics. Part C, Applications and Reviews*, *41*(2), 161–178. DOI: 10.1109/TSMCC.2010.2052041

Hurst, E. J. (2020). Web Conferencing and Collaboration Tools and Trends. *Journal of Hospital Librarianship*, *20*(3), 266–279. DOI: 10.1080/15323269.2020.1780079

Hutsaliuk, O., & Shainovskyi, R. (2025). Decision-making in selecting information and analytical systems for corporate IT cluster enterprises. *Herald of the Economic Sciences of Ukraine*, (2(49)), 152. DOI: 10.37405/1729-7206.2025.2(49).152-165

Ilie, A.-C. (2026). Human ethics vs. algorithmic ethics: The limits of automating moral decision-making. *Theoretical and Applied Economics, 33*(1), 219–240.

Illgen, K. M., & Thomas, O. (2025). Towards the operationalization of digital well-being in the world of new work: Development of a taxonomy. In *INFORMATIK 2025* (p. 843). Gesellschaft für Informatik.

Independent researcher New Haven CT 06511 USA, B. I. at A. A., Mokashi, S. P., Naik, S., & Solutions Consultant San Francisco CA 94103 USA, S. (2025). Cognitive-aware shift scheduling in smart manufacturing: An AI framework for reducing burnout and fatigue and investigating the impact of. *Frontiers in Emerging Artificial Intelligence and Machine Learning, 02*(08), 16–29. DOI: 10.37547/feaiml/Volume02Issue08-03

Infosys. (2023). *Infosys integrated annual report 2022-23*. Infosys Limited.

International Federation of Library Associations and Institutions (IFLA). (2023, June). Augmented Reality in Libraries https://www.ifla.org/news/augmented-reality-in-libraries/

International Ranking Expert Group (IREG). (2006). *Berlin principles on ranking of higher education institutions. IREG Observatory on Academic Ranking and Excellence*, Berlin. Retrieved 2006, from https://ireg-observatory.org/en/berlin-principles/

Islam, F. A. S. (2025). Artificial intelligence-powered carbon market intelligence and blockchain-enabled governance for climate-responsive urban infrastructure in the Global South. *Journal of Engineering Research and Reports*, *27*(7), 440–472. DOI: 10.9734/jerr/2025/v27i71585

Ismanov, I., Qayumov, N., Mukhamadjonova, D., & Akhmadaliyev, B. (2024, April). AI and cost management: Strategies for reducing expenses and improving profit margins in business. In *2024 International Conference on Knowledge Engineering and Communication Systems (ICKECS)* (Vol. 1, pp. 1-7). IEEE. DOI: 10.1109/ICKECS61492.2024.10616761

Jaeger, P. T., Bertot, J. C., Thompson, K. M., Katz, S. M., & DeCoster, E. J. (2012). The intersection of public policy and public access: Digital divides, digital literacy, digital inclusion, and public libraries. *Public Library Quarterly*, *31*(1), 1–20. DOI: 10.1080/01616846.2012.654728

Jafarinezhad, O., Zhang, Q., Rezai, R., Noaeen, M., Shachak, A., Far, B., & Shakeri, Z. (2026). Centralized pooling and federated learning for Canadian patient-level data sharing in multicenter medical AI: A scoping review. *Artificial Intelligence in Medicine, 178*, 103422. DOI: 10.1016/j.artmed.2026.103422 PMID: 42066521

Janes, J. (Ed.). (2013). *Library 2020: Today's leading visionaries describe tomorrow's library*. Scarecrow Press.

Jarrahi, M. H. (2019). In the age of the smart artificial intelligence: AI's dual capacities for automating and informating work. *Business Information Review, 36*(4), 178–187. DOI: 10.1177/0266382119883999

Jarvenpaa, S. L., & Lang, K. R. (2005). Managing the paradoxes of mobile technology. *Information Systems Management, 22*(4), 7–23. DOI: 10.1201/1078.10580530/45520.22.4.20050901/90026.2

Ji, Z., Lee, N., Frieske, R., Yu, T., Su, D., Xu, Y., Ishii, E., Bang, Y. J., Madotto, A., & Fung, P. (2023). Survey of Hallucination in Natural Language Generation. In ACM Computing Surveys (Vol. 55, Number 12). Association for Computing Machinery. DOI: 10.1145/3571730

Jia, X., Chowdhury, M., Prayag, G., & Hossan Chowdhury, M. M. (2020). The role of social capital on proactive and reactive resilience of organizations post-disaster. *International Journal of Disaster Risk Reduction, 48*, 101614. DOI: 10.1016/j.ijdrr.2020.101614

Jim, C. K., & Chang, H. C. (2018). The current state of data governance in higher education. *Proceedings of the Association for Information Science and Technology, 55*(1), 198–206. DOI: 10.1002/pra2.2018.14505501022

Johnson, E. M., Lehoahoa, E., Lehoahoa, P. S., & Urquhart, R. (2020). *Increasing digital platform use to help youth find work*. RTI Press. DOI: 10.3768/rtipress.2020.pb.0023.2005

Just, N., & Latzer, M. (2016). Governance by Algorithms: Reality Construction by Algorithmic Selection on the Internet (2017). Media, Culture & Society, 39(2), 238-258; , Available at *SSRN*: https://ssrn.com/abstract=3871903DOI: 10.1177/0163443716643157

Kahneman, D. (2011). *Thinking, fast and slow*. Farrar, Straus and Giroux.

Karasek, R. (1979). Job demands, job decision latitude, and mental strain. *Administrative Science Quarterly, 24*(2), 285–308. DOI: 10.2307/2392498

Kari, K. (2020). Digital transformation of information and its impact on libraries. [WJIR]. *World Journal of Innovative Research*, *9*(1), 26–30.

Kasar, P. (2025). There is a problem, but not a responsibility gap. *Ethics and Information Technology*, *27*(4), 1–11. DOI: 10.1007/s10676-025-09851-4

Kellogg, K. C., Valentine, M. A., & Christin, A. (2020). Algorithms at work: The new contested terrain of control. *The Academy of Management Annals*, *14*(1), 366–410. DOI: 10.5465/annals.2018.0174

Kempf, K. (2023). Moving Libraries toward Digital Transformation. *The International Information & Library Review*, *55*(3), 233–240. DOI: 10.1080/10572317.2023.2231715

Khavandi, S., Zaghloul, F., Higham, A., Lim, E., de Pennington, N., & Celi, L. A. (2023). Investigating the impact of automation on the health care workforce through autonomous telemedicine in the cataract pathway: Protocol for a multicenter study. *JMIR Research Protocols*, *12*, e49374. DOI: 10.2196/49374 PMID: 38051569

Kiemde, S. M. A., & Kora, A. D. (2022). Towards an ethics of AI in Africa: Rule of education. *AI and Ethics*, *2*(1), 35–40. DOI: 10.1007/s43681-021-00106-8

Kim, K. H., Payne, G. T., & Tan, J. A. (2006). An examination of cognition and affect in strategic decision-making. *The International Journal of Organizational Analysis*, *14*(4), 277–294. DOI: 10.1108/19348830610849709

Kirsh, D. (2000). A few thoughts on cognitive overload. *Intellectica*, *30*(1), 19–51. DOI: 10.3406/intel.2000.1592

Klein, G. (2007). Performing a premortem. *Harvard Business Review*, *85*(9), 18–19.

Koltay, T. (2011). The media and the literacies: Media literacy, information literacy, digital literacy. *Media Culture & Society*, *33*(2), 211–221. DOI: 10.1177/0163443710393382

Koltay, T., & Špiranec, S. (2017). Libraries meet research 2.0: Literacies and services. In *Research 2.0 and the Impact of Digital Technologies on Scholarly Inquiry* (pp. 32–52). IGI Global. DOI: 10.4018/978-1-5225-0830-4.ch003

Komljenovic, J., Sellar, S., & Birch, K. (2024). Turning universities into data-driven organisations: Seven dimensions of change. *Higher Education*, *89*(5), 1369–1386. DOI: 10.1007/s10734-024-01277-z

Konjen, H. (2025). Algorithmic management and the future of human work: Implications for autonomy, collaboration, and innovation (No. arXiv:2511.14231v1). arXiv.

Kushlev, K., & Dunn, E. W. (2015). Checking email less frequently reduces stress. *Computers in Human Behavior, 43*, 220–228. DOI: 10.1016/j.chb.2014.11.005

Lambert, D. M., & Cooper, M. C. (2000). Issues in supply chain management. *Industrial Marketing Management, 29*(1), 65–83. DOI: 10.1016/S0019-8501(99)00113-3

Langenbucher, K., & Corcoran, P. (2021). Responsible AI Credit Scoring – A Lesson from Upstart.com. In Avgouleas, E., & Marjosola, H. (Eds.), *Digital Finance in Europe: Law, Regulation, and Governance*. De Gruyter., DOI: 10.1515/9783110749472-006

Latour, B. (2005). *Reassembling the Social: An Introduction to Actor-Network-Theory*. Oxford University Press. DOI: 10.1093/oso/9780199256044.001.0001

Ledro, C., Nosella, A., & Vinelli, A. (2022). Artificial intelligence in customer relationship management: Literature review and future research directions. *Journal of Business and Industrial Marketing, 37*(13), 48–63. DOI: 10.1108/JBIM-07-2021-0332

Lee, J. D., & See, K. A. (2004). Trust in automation. *Human Factors, 46*(1), 50–80. DOI: 10.1518/hfes.46.1.50.30392 PMID: 15151155

Lehdonvirta, V. (2018). Flexibility in the gig economy: Managing time on three online piecework platforms. *New Technology, Work and Employment, 33*(1), 13–29. DOI: 10.1111/ntwe.12102

Leonardi, P. M., & Treem, J. W. (2020). Behavioral visibility: A new paradigm for organization studies in the age of digitization, digitalization, and datafication. *Organization Studies, 41*(12), 1601–1625. DOI: 10.1177/0170840620970728

Leonelli, S., & Tempini, N. (Eds.). (2020). *Data Journeys in the Sciences*. Springer. DOI: 10.1007/978-3-030-37177-7

Lepisto, D. A., & Pratt, M. G. (2016). Meaningful work as realization and justification: Toward a dual conceptualization. Organizational Psychology Review, 7(2), 99-121. (Original work published 2017).DOI: 10.1177/2041386616630039

Leroy, S. (2009). Why is it so hard to do my work? *Organizational Behavior and Human Decision Processes, 109*(2), 168–181. DOI: 10.1016/j.obhdp.2009.04.002

Liao, S. M., Haykel, I., Cheung, K., & Matalon, T. (2025). Navigating the complexities of AI and digital governance: The 5W1H framework. *Journal of Responsible Technology, 23*, 100127. Advance online publication. DOI: 10.1016/j.jrt.2025.100127

Library Technology. (2024). Augmented Reality and Virtual Reality in Libraries. https://www.lib.pacificu.edu/augmented-reality-and-virtual-reality-in-libraries/

Li, M., Cheng, S., & Lu, M. (2024). Impact of information technology capabilities on organizational resilience: The mediating role of social capital. *Humanities & Social Sciences Communications*, *11*(1), 1424. DOI: 10.1057/s41599-024-03951-0

Lima, S. A.Sungida Akther Lima. (2024). Algorithmic fairness in HRM balancing AI-driven decision making with inclusive workforce practices. *Journal of Information Systems Engineering & Management*, *9*(4s), 2760–2769. DOI: 10.52783/jisem.v9i4s.13251

Lincoln, Y. S., & Guba, E. G. (1985). *Naturalistic Inquiry*. SAGE Publications. DOI: 10.1016/0147-1767(85)90062-8

Lindebaum, D., Vesa, M., & Courpasson, D. (2020). Insights from 'the machine stops' to better understand rational assumptions in algorithmic decision-making and its implications for organizations. *Academy of Management Review*, *45*(1), 247–260. DOI: 10.5465/amr.2018.0181

Lips-Wiersma, M., & Morris, L. (2009). Discriminating between 'meaningful work' and the 'management of meaning'. *Journal of Business Ethics*, *88*(3), 491–511. DOI: 10.1007/s10551-009-0118-9

Lips-Wiersma, M., & Wright, S. (2012). Measuring the meaning of meaningful work: Development and validation of the Comprehensive Meaningful Work Scale (CMWS). *Group & Organization Management*, *37*(5), 655–685. DOI: 10.1177/1059601112461578

Li, Q., Abdul Ghani Azmi, I., & Norman, A. A. (2025). Enhancing sustainable innovation through workplace well-being and digital capability: A systematic literature review toward responsible and cleaner consumption. *Cleaner and Responsible Consumption*, *18*, 100305. DOI: 10.1016/j.clrc.2025.100305

Lodha Genius Programme. (2024). The Evolving Role of Libraries in the Digital Age. Retrieved on 03/06/2024, from https://www.linkedin.com/pulse/evolving-role-libraries-digital-age-lodha-genius-programme-xuhsc/

Lozovetska, V., Pavlov, Y., & Fedorenko, L. (2024). Meaningful work literature meta-review. Multidisciplinary Science Journal, 6, 2024ss0740. DOI: 10.31893/multiscience.2024ss0740

Luo, J. (2025). AI empowers enterprise agility and performance: Research trends and implications for future research. *Business Information Review*, *42*(4), 238–257. DOI: 10.1177/02663821251384881

Madanchian, M., & Taherdoost, H. (2025). Criteria for AI Adoption in HR: Efficiency vs. Ethics. *Procedia Computer Science, 258*, 233–241. DOI: 10.1016/j.procs.2025.04.261

Mafungwa, T. (2017). *The adoption of technology to enhance innovative user services at CALICO libraries.*

Mago, B., Ishaq Almaazmi, K., Jafar Almaazmi, A., Mohammed Falaha, K., & Dahi Almidfaa, E. (2022). Modeling situational IT ethics in UAE. *International Journal for Global Academic & Scientific Research, 1*(2), 21–35. DOI: 10.55938/ijgasr.v1i2.10

Marginson, S., & van der Wende, M. (2007). To rank or to be ranked: The impact of global rankings in higher education. *Journal of Studies in International Education, 11*(3–4), 306–329. DOI: 10.1177/1028315307303544

Mark, G., Gonzalez, V. M., & Harris, J. (2005). No task left behind? Examining the nature of fragmented work. *Proceedings of the SIGCHI Conference on Human Factors in Computing Systems*, 321-330. DOI: 10.1145/1054972.1055017

Mark, G., Gudith, D., & Klocke, U. (2008). The cost of interrupted work: More speed and stress. *Proceedings of the SIGCHI Conference on Human Factors in Computing Systems*, 107-110. DOI: 10.1145/1357054.1357072

Mark, G., Voida, S., & Cardello, A. (2012). A pace not dictated by electrons. CHI Proceedings. DOI: 10.1145/2207676.2207754

Marshall, D. H., DuBose, J., & Archer, P. (2019). Mixed reality lab at Mississippi state university libraries. *Public Services Quarterly, 15*(1), 51–58. DOI: 10.1080/15228959.2018.1554466

Marsh, E., Perez Vallejos, E., & Spence, A. (2024). Overloaded by information or worried about missing out on it: A quantitative study of stress, burnout, and mental health implications in the digital workplace. *SAGE Open, 14*(3), 21582440241268830. DOI: 10.1177/21582440241268830

Martela, F., & Pessi, A. B. (2018). Significant work is about self-realization and broader purpose: Defining the key dimensions of meaningful work. *Frontiers in Psychology, 9*, 363. Advance online publication. DOI: 10.3389/fpsyg.2018.00363 PMID: 29632502

Martin, A. (2008). Digital literacy and the "digital society". *Digital literacies: Concepts, policies and practices, 30*(151), 1029-1055.

Maslow, A. H. (1965). Humanistic science and transcendent experiences. *Journal of Humanistic Psychology, 5*(2), 219–227. DOI: 10.1177/002216786500500211

Mateescu, A., & Nguyen, A. (2019). Explainer: Algorithmic management in the workplace. Data & Society Research Institute. Available at https://datasociety.net/wp-content/uploads/2019/02/DS_Algorithmic_Management_Explainer.pdf?utm_source=chatgpt.com

Ma, Y., Li, X., Hu, S., Liu, S., & Cheong, K. H. (2025). Trustworthy AI in education: Framework, cases, and governance strategies. *Innovation and Emerging Technologies*, *12*(2550026), 2550026. Advance online publication. DOI: 10.1142/S2737599425500264

Mazmanian, M., Orlikowski, W. J., & Yates, J. (2013). The autonomy paradox: The implications of mobile email devices for knowledge professionals. *Organization Science*, *24*(5), 1337–1357. DOI: 10.1287/orsc.1120.0806

Mehdi, N., & Naz, T. (2025). Governing the intelligent factory – Transforming labor law through an open-standards framework for AI governance in industry 4.0. In Journal of Open Innovation: Technology, Market, and Complexity (Vol. 11, Number 4). Elsevier B.V. DOI: 10.1016/j.joitmc.2025.100690

Mentzer, J. T., DeWitt, W., Keebler, J. S., Min, S., Nix, N. W., Smith, C. D., & Zacharia, Z. G. (2001). Defining supply chain management. *Journal of Business Logistics*, *22*(2), 1–25. DOI: 10.1002/j.2158-1592.2001.tb00001.x

Merton, R. K. (1972). Insiders and outsiders: A chapter in the sociology of knowledge. *American Journal of Sociology*, *78*(1), 9–47. DOI: 10.1086/225294

Meske, C. (2019). Digital workplace transformation: On the role of self-determination in the context of transforming work environments.

Methuku, V., & Kamatala, S. (2025). Intelligent systems and organizational intelligence: A literature review and conceptual framework. In *2025 6th International Conference on Data Intelligence and Cognitive Informatics (ICDICI)* (pp. 1–8). IEEE. DOI: 10.1109/ICDICI66477.2025.11135342

Microsoft. (2022). *Microsoft Work Trend Index 2022: Great expectations — Making hybrid work work*. Microsoft Corporation. https://www.microsoft.com/en-us/worklab/work-trend-index/great-expectations-making-hybrid-work-work

Milanez, A., Lemmens, A., & Ruggiu, C. (2025). Algorithmic management in the workplace: New evidence from an OECD employer survey. OECD ARTIFICIAL INTELLIGENCE PAPERS February 2025 No. 31. Available at https://www.oecd.org/content/dam/oecd/en/publications/reports/2025/02/algorithmic-management-in-the-workplace_3c84ed6d/287c13c4-en.pdf

Minkkinen, M., & Mäntymäki, M. (2023). Discerning between the "easy" and "hard" problems of AI governance. *IEEE Transactions on Technology and Society*, *4*(2), 188–194. DOI: 10.1109/TTS.2023.3267382

Mishra, R., & Jadeja, D. (2025). A literature review on the impact of AI-enhanced HRIS on employee retention and engagement. In *Intersecting natural language processing and FinTech innovations in service marketing* (pp. 11–20). DOI: 10.4018/979-8-3693-9944-6.ch002

Miszczynski, M., Pieczka, A., & Klimek, J. (2026). The algorithm's middlemen: Resistance, compliance and managerial contradictions in Amazon's warehouses in Poland. Critical Perspectives on International Business, ahead-of-print. DOI: 10.1108/cpoib-05-2025-0109

Mokoagow, M. S., Sukmana, O., & Yumitro, G., & Nurudin. (2026). Max Weber's social action and rationality: An analysis of bureaucracy and rationalization processes in modern organizations. International Journal of Economics. *Management and Social Science*, *9*(1), 1–20.

Molino, M., Cortese, C. G., & Ghislieri, C. (2020). The promotion of technology acceptance and work engagement in industry 4.0: From personal resources to information and training over time. *International Journal of Environmental Research and Public Health*, *17*(7), 2438. DOI: 10.3390/ijerph17072438 PMID: 32260142

Monsell, S. (2003). Task switching. *Trends in Cognitive Sciences*, *7*(3), 134–140. DOI: 10.1016/S1364-6613(03)00028-7 PMID: 12639695

Monteiro, N., & Singh, V. (2025). The wheel of artificial intelligence governance. In *Sustainable Futures* (Vol. 10). Elsevier Ltd., DOI: 10.1016/j.sftr.2025.101279

Morato, O., & Nunes, D. J. C. (2023). The use of behavioral design on technological platforms and their regulatory initiatives: A study of the Hook model. *Revista Justiça e Direito*, *37*, 207.

Muller, J. Z. (2018). *The Tyranny of Metrics*. Princeton University Press.

Murikah, W., Nthenge, J. K., & Musyoka, F. M. (2024). Bias and ethics of AI systems applied in auditing - A systematic review. *Scientific African*, *25*, e02281. Advance online publication. DOI: 10.1016/j.sciaf.2024.e02281

Naqshbandi, M. M., Kabir, I., Ishak, N. A., & Islam, M. Z. (2024). The future of work: Work engagement and job performance in the hybrid workplace. *The Learning Organization*, *31*(1), 5–26. DOI: 10.1108/TLO-08-2022-0097

Narayan, P., Kedia, G., & Tiwari, S. (2025). Digital Sustainability and it's implications in the era of 5.O. In *Integrating Management Principles with Business Analytics Concepts and Applications* (pp. 82–91). QTanalytics India. DOI: 10.48001/978-81-980647-9-0-7

Narayanan, H., & Shankar, S. L. (2025). Cortisol levels and their association with workplace stress in IT workers. *National Journal of Community Medicine, 16*(8), 824–830. Advance online publication. DOI: 10.55489/njcm.160820255534

National Institution for Transforming India Aayog. (2018). *National strategy for artificial intelligence* (#AIforAll). Government of India. https://www.niti.gov.in/sites/default/files/2023-03/National-Strategy-for-Artificial-Intelligence.pdf

National Library of Australia. (.n.d.). Trove. https://trove.nla.gov.au

Nayak, P. B., & Jagadeeswari, I. U. (2026). Organizational performance optimization: An AI-enabled framework for employee compensation and benefits management. *Research in Globalization, 12*, 100328. Advance online publication. DOI: 10.1016/j.resglo.2025.100328

Neal, J. G. (2014). Advancing from kumbaya to radical collaboration: redefining the future research library. In *Repackaging Libraries for Survival* (pp. 66–76). Routledge.

Neves, I. B. S., Vianna, F. R. P. M., & Sutil, B. N. (2021). Algocracy: A critical analysis on management mediated by algorithms. Contextus - Revista Contemporânea de Economia e Gestão, 19, 246-256. DOI: 10.19094/contextus.2021.67949

Newport, C. (2016). *Deep work: Rules for focused success in a distracted world*. Grand Central Publishing.

Norman, D. A. (2013). *The design of everyday things*. Basic Books.

Nussbaumer, A., Pope, A., & Neville, K. (2023). A framework for applying ethics-by-design to decision support systems for emergency management. *Information Systems Journal, 33*(1), 34–55. DOI: 10.1111/isj.12350

O'Neil, C. (2016). *Weapons of math destruction*. Crown Publishing.

Ojika, F. U., Owobu, W. O., Abieba, O. A., Esan, O. J., Ubamadu, B. C., & Darao-jimba, A. I. (2022). The role of artificial intelligence in business process automation: A model for reducing operational costs and enhancing efficiency. *International Journal of Multidisciplinary Research and Growth Evaluation, 3*(1), 842–860.

Okuboye, A. (2021). Cross-cultural variability in workforce optimization: A bpm perspective on remote and hybrid teams. *International Journal of Multidisciplinary Futuristic Development, 2*(1), 15–24. DOI: 10.54660/IJMFD.2021.2.1.15-24

Oluwafemi, I. O., Clement, T., Adanigbo, O. S., Gbenle, T. P., & Adekunle, B. I. (2021). A review of ethical considerations in AI-driven marketing analytics: Privacy, transparency, and consumer trust. *International Journal of Multidisciplinary Research and Growth Evaluation*, *2*(2), 428–435. DOI: 10.54660/.IJMRGE.2021.2.2.428-435

Omotayo, A. O., Adediran, S. A., Omotoso, A. B., Olagunju, K. O., & Omotayo, O. P. (2025). Artificial intelligence in agriculture: ethics, impact possibilities, and pathways for policy. In *Computers and Electronics in Agriculture* (Vol. 239). Elsevier B.V., DOI: 10.1016/j.compag.2025.110927

Paas, F., Renkl, A., & Sweller, J. (2004). Cognitive load theory: Instructional implications of the interaction between information structures and cognitive architecture. *Instructional Science*, *32*(1/2), 1–8. DOI: 10.1023/B:TRUC.0000021806.17516.d0

Pacheco, P. O., & Coello-Montecel, D. (2023). Does psychological empowerment mediate the relationship between digital competencies and job performance? *Computers in Human Behavior*, *140*, 107575. DOI: 10.1016/j.chb.2022.107575

Palaniappan, K. (2025). The future of enterprise software: Enabling human-AI collaboration in the age of trillion-scale data. *European Modern Studies Journal*, *9*(5), 190–196. DOI: 10.59573/emsj.9(5).2025.18

Pandit, S., Ravikumar, R. N., Joshi, N., Pandit, S., Kishore, S., & Aarthi, S. (2025). Retrieval-Augmented Generation (RAG) for enterprise intelligence. In *Leveraging LLMs for Business Innovation* (pp. 69–106). IGI Global Scientific Publishing. DOI: 10.4018/979-8-3373-3912-2.ch003

Parasuraman, R., & Riley, V. (1997). Humans and automation. *Human Factors*, *39*(2), 230–253. DOI: 10.1518/001872097778543886 PMID: 18689061

Pasqui, V. (2024). Digital curation and long-term digital preservation in libraries. *JLIS. it*, *15*(1), 109-125.

Pasupuleti, M. K. (2024). *AI-driven leadership: Crisis management and virtual organizations in the digital age*. National Education Services., DOI: 10.62311/nesx/rb978-81-981179-1-5

Pasupuleti, M. K. (2024). *Human Factors and Ergonomics*. National Education Services., DOI: 10.62311/nesx/rb978-81-974226-6-9

Pesqueira, A., de Bem Machado, A., Bolog, S., Sousa, M. J., & Pereira, R. (2024). Exploring the impact of EU tendering operations on future AI governance and standards in pharmaceuticals. *Computers & Industrial Engineering*, *198*, 110655. Advance online publication. DOI: 10.1016/j.cie.2024.110655

Pettegree, A. (2017). *The book in the Renaissance*. Yale University Press. DOI: 10.12987/9780300168358

Picard, R. W. (1997). *Affective computing*. MIT Press. DOI: 10.7551/mitpress/1140.001.0001

Ponomarov, S. Y., & Holcomb, M. C. (2009). Understanding the concept of supply chain resilience. *International Journal of Logistics Management*, *20*(1), 124–143. DOI: 10.1108/09574090910954873

Porter, T. M. (1995). *Trust in numbers: The pursuit of objectivity in science and public life*. Princeton University Press.

Porter, T. M. (1995). *Trust in Numbers: The Pursuit of Objectivity in Science and Public Life*. Princeton University Press.

Pothuganti, S. K., Ramachandra, G. P., & Devi, V. R. (2025). The impact of technostress on employee engagement and wellbeing: The moderating role of perceived organizational support. *Personnel Review*, *44*(5). Advance online publication. DOI: 10.1177/01672533251331503

Power, M. (1997). *The Audit Society: Rituals of Verification*. Oxford University Press.

Praharaj, A., & Chhatoi, B. P. (2025). Enterprise resource planning (ERP) in business: A contextual snapshot. *Global Knowledge, Memory and Communication*. Advance online publication. DOI: 10.1108/GKMC-07-2024-0453

Pratt, M. G., & Ashforth, B. E. (2003). Fostering Meaningfulness in Working and at Work. In Cameron, K. S., Dutton, J. E., & Quinn, R. E. (Eds.), *Positive Organizational Scholarship: Foundations of a New Discipline* (pp. 309–327). Berret-Koehler.

Priya, S., & Ramya, R. (2024). Future Trends and Emerging Technologies in AI and Libraries. *Applications of Artificial Intelligence in Libraries*, 245-271.

Proserpio, L., Kandiko Howson, C., & Lall, M. (2024). The university ranking game in East Asia: The sensemaking of academic leaders between pressures and fatigue. *Asia Pacific Education Review*.

Puppala, A. (2025). Cognitive Load Analysis in AI-Augmented BI Dashboards: Understanding the Impact of Artificial Intelligence on User Comprehension, Trust, and Decision-Making Efficiency. *Journal of Computer Science and Technology Studies*, *7*(6), 207–213.

Rafi, M., JianMing, Z., & Ahmad, K. (2019). Technology integration for students' information and digital literacy education in academic libraries. *Information Discovery and Delivery*, *47*(4), 203–217. DOI: 10.1108/IDD-07-2019-0049

Rai, A. (2020). Explainable AI: From black box to glass box. *Journal of the Academy of Marketing Science*, *48*(1), 137–141. DOI: 10.1007/s11747-019-00710-5

Raisch, S., & Krakowski, S. (2021). Artificial intelligence and management: The automation-augmentation paradox. *Academy of Management Review*, *46*(1), 192–210. DOI: 10.5465/amr.2018.0072

Rajkumar, N., Nachiappan, B., Mathews, A., Radha, V., Viji, C., & Kovilpillai, J. A. (2024). Industry 5.0: The human-centric future of manufacturing. In Sharmila, V. (Eds.), *Challenges in information, communication and computing technology* (pp. 562–567). CRC Press., https://www.taylorfrancis.com/books/9781003559085/chapters/10.1201/9781003559085-97 DOI: 10.1201/9781003559085-97

Rakhra, A. K., & Mann, D. D. (2018). Design and evaluation of individual elements of the interface for an agricultural machine. *Journal of Agricultural Safety and Health*, *24*(1), 27–42. DOI: 10.13031/jash.12410 PMID: 29528604

Rankin, J. (2017). Conducting analysis in institutional ethnography: Guidance and cautions. *International Journal of Qualitative Methods*, *16*(1), 1–11. DOI: 10.1177/1609406917734472

Rao, S., & Sahu, S. C. (2024). The Influence of Artificial Intelligence on Library Services: Enhancing Access, Discovery, and User Engagement. *Academic Libraries*, 350.

Rathinavel, P., Ravikumar, R. N., Aarthi, S., Habib, M., Salaeva, N., & Pardaev, J. (2025). Augmenting human capabilities. In *Advances in Computational Intelligence and Robotics* (pp. 1–30). IGI Global Scientific Publishing. DOI: 10.4018/979-8-3373-2372-5.ch001

Rausch, L., Burtscher, J., Ruedl, G., Schindelwig, K., Steidl-Müller, L., & Mohr, M. (2024). How to embrace interdisciplinarity in sport science – An approach at the ÖSG Congress Innsbruck 2024. *Current Issues in Sport Science (CISS)*, *9*(4), 001. DOI: 10.36950/2024.4ciss001

Ravid, D. M., Tomczak, D. L., White, J. C., & Behrend, T. S. (2020). EPM is not for everyone. *The Journal of Applied Psychology*, *105*(6), 585–606.

Ravikumar, & Aarthi, S. (2025a). AI-driven climate resilience. In *Advances in Computational Intelligence and Robotics* (pp. 207–238). IGI Global Scientific Publishing. DOI: 10.4018/979-8-3373-5540-5.ch007

Ravikumar, & Aarthi, S. (2025a). Cognitive collaboration. In *Advances in Computational Intelligence and Robotics* (pp. 125–158). IGI Global Scientific Publishing. DOI: 10.4018/979-8-3373-7416-1.ch006

Ravikumar, & Aarthi, S. (2026). Synergizing innovation. In *Advances in Computational Intelligence and Robotics* (pp. 59–90). IGI Global Scientific Publishing. DOI: 10.4018/979-8-3373-7620-2.ch003

Ravikumar, A. S., Kurbanova, N., Sevdim, K. E., Zaynitdinovna, B. D., & Jumaniyazova, N. (2026). Bridging knowledge and policy. In *Advances in Computational Intelligence and Robotics* (pp. 119–150). IGI Global Scientific Publishing. DOI: 10.4018/979-8-3373-7620-2.ch005

Ravikumar, R. N., & Aarthi, S. (2025b). Augmented decision-making. In *Advances in Computational Intelligence and Robotics* (pp. 227–258). IGI Global Scientific Publishing. DOI: 10.4018/979-8-3373-7416-1.ch009

Ravikumar, R. N., & Aarthi, S. (2025c). Human-AI synergy for organizational resilience. In *Advances in Computational Intelligence and Robotics* (pp. 287–322). IGI Global Scientific Publishing. DOI: 10.4018/979-8-3373-7416-1.ch011

Ravikumar, R. N., Aarthi, S., & Mamadiyarov, Z. (2026). Building the foundations of augmented organizations through AI empowerment. In *Advances in Computational Intelligence and Robotics* (pp. 101–130). IGI Global Scientific Publishing. DOI: 10.4018/979-8-3373-8607-2.ch006

Ravikumar, R. N., Aarthi, S., Sapayev, V., & Esanov, A. (2026). Generative artificial intelligence for visual branding and creative automation in modern marketing ecosystems. In *Advances in Computational Intelligence and Robotics* (pp. 1–32). IGI Global Scientific Publishing. DOI: 10.4018/979-8-3373-4506-2.ch001

Razaghzadeh Bidgoli, M., Raeesi Vanani, I., & Goodarzi, M. (2024). Predicting the success of startups using a machine learning approach. *Journal of Innovation and Entrepreneurship*, *13*(1), 80. DOI: 10.1186/s13731-024-00436-x

Real, B., Bertot, J. C., & Jaeger, P. T. (2014). Rural public libraries and digital inclusion: Issues and challenges. *Information Technology and Libraries*, *33*(1), 6–24. DOI: 10.6017/ital.v33i1.5141

Reyes, C., & Parella, K. (2026). Data supply chains. SSRN Working Paper.

Rifkin, J. (1995). *The End of Work: The Decline of the Global Labor Force and the Dawn of the Post-Market Era*. G. P. Putnam's Sons.

Rosenblat, A., & Stark, L. (2016) Algorithmic Labor and Information Asymmetries: A Case Study of Uber's Drivers International Journal of Communication, 10, 27. Available at *SSRN*: https://ssrn.com/abstract=2686227 or DOI: 10.2139/ssrn.2686227

Rosso, B. D., Dekas, K. H., & Wrzesniewski, A. (2010). On the Meaning of Work: A Theoretical Integration and Review. *Research in Organizational Behavior, 30*, 91–127. DOI: 10.1016/j.riob.2010.09.001

Rouzky, R., Sarrafzadeh, A., Sowells-Boone, E., Pasandi, H. B., & Goins, G. (2025). Data governance in smart farming: A systematic review of challenges and gaps. In *Information Processing in Agriculture*. China Agricultural University., DOI: 10.1016/j.inpa.2025.11.006

Rubin, R. E., & Rubin, R. G. (2020). *Foundations of library and information science*. American Library Association.

Rubinstein, J. S., Meyer, D. E., & Evans, J. E. (2001). Executive control of cognitive processes. *Journal of Experimental Psychology*, *27*(4), 763–797. PMID: 11518143

Sadeghi, S., & Hoseinpour Jajarm, M. (2025). Evaluating the performance of architectural structures using NLP-enhanced fuzzy logic. *Engineering, Construction, and Architectural Management*, •••, 1–18. DOI: 10.1108/ECAM-07-2025-1214

Saeidnia, H. R. (2023). Ethical artificial intelligence (AI): Confronting bias and discrimination in the library and information industry. *Library Hi Tech News*. Advance online publication. DOI: 10.1108/LHTN-10-2023-0182

Saghafi, A., & Angelopoulos, S. (2025). Virtual virtues: A governance framework of moral consequentialism and deontological ethics for immersive virtual reality platforms. *The Journal of Strategic Information Systems*, *34*(4), 101936. Advance online publication. DOI: 10.1016/j.jsis.2025.101936

Sang, L. T., Ravikumar, R. N., Aarthi, S., & Ben, T. L. (2025). Optimizing sales and inventory performance using AI and business intelligence in POS environments. In *Advances in Computational Intelligence and Robotics* (pp. 259–290). IGI Global Scientific Publishing. DOI: 10.4018/979-8-3373-4392-1.ch011

Sarker, S., Xiao, X., Sarker, S., & Ahuja, M. (2012). Managing employees' use of mobile technologies to minimize work-life balance impacts. *MIS Quarterly Executive*, *11*(4), 143–157. https://ir.library.louisville.edu/faculty/359/

Sauder, M., & Espeland, W. N. (2009). The discipline of rankings: Tight coupling and organizational change. *American Sociological Review*, *74*(1), 63–82. DOI: 10.1177/000312240907400104

Schafheitle, S. D., Weibel, A., Ebert, I. L., Kasper, G., Schank, C., & Leicht-Deobald, U. (2020). No stone left unturned? Toward a framework for the impact of datafication technologies on organizational control. *Academy of Management Discoveries*, *6*(3), 455–487. DOI: 10.5465/amd.2019.0002

Sebastian, G. (2026). Digital shadow AI risk theory (DART): A framework for managing data disclosure and privacy risks of AI tools at work. *Technological Forecasting and Social Change*, *229*, 124697. Advance online publication. DOI: 10.1016/j.techfore.2026.124697

Shah, I. (2025). AI-driven price discrimination: Strategic applications, ethical challenges, and regulatory implications. *International Science Journal of Management. Economics & Finance*, *4*(5), 33–50. DOI: 10.46299/j.isjmef.20250405.04

Shin, J. C., Toutkoushian, R. K., & Teichler, U. (2011). *University Rankings: Theoretical Basis, Methodology and Impacts on Global Higher Education*. Springer. DOI: 10.1007/978-94-007-1116-7

Shin, Y. (2025). Toward human-centered artificial intelligence for users' digital wellbeing: Systematic review, synthesis, and future directions. *JMIR Human Factors*, *12*(1), e69533. DOI: 10.2196/69533 PMID: 40928842

Shreha, S. A., Ravikumar, R. N., & Aarthi, S. (2025). Neuro-symbolic AI and Behavioral Intelligence. In *Advances in Computational Intelligence and Robotics* (pp. 121–152). IGI Global Scientific Publishing. DOI: 10.4018/979-8-3373-5012-7.ch005

Shreha, S. A., Ravikumar, R. N., & Aarthi, S. (2026). Precision medicine, genomics, and health equity challenges and opportunities. In *Advancing Equity in Global Healthcare Systems* (pp. 321–354). IGI Global Scientific Publishing., DOI: 10.4018/979-8-3373-1330-6.ch012

Sihotang, D. S. (2026). Digital Twins as an Enabler of Cognitive Enterprise Architecture: Reconfiguring Organizational Systems and Decision Intelligence. In *Transforming Physical Assets to Cognitive Enterprises With Digital Twins* (pp. 289–320). IGI Global Scientific Publishing. DOI: 10.4018/979-8-3373-9998-0.ch010

Singh, K. K., & Asif, M. (2019). Emerging trends and technologies for digital transformation of libraries. *IP Indian Journal of Library Science and Information Technology*, *4*(2), 41–43.

Singh, V. K., & Gupta, R. (2025). From Taylorism to algorithmic management: How technological evolution reshapes foundational management principles. International Journal of Latest Technology in Engineering, Management &. *Applied Sciences (Basel, Switzerland)*, *14*(8), 1–15. DOI: 10.51583/IJLTEMAS.2025.1408000206

Smith, D. E. (2005). *Institutional Ethnography: A Sociology for People*. AltaMira Press. DOI: 10.5040/9798216409632

Smith, D. E. (2006). *Institutional Ethnography as Practice*. Rowman & Littlefield. DOI: 10.5040/9798216402855

Smith, D. E., & Griffith, A. I. (2022). *Simply Institutional Ethnography: Creating a Sociology for People*. University of Toronto Press. DOI: 10.3138/9781487528072

Socorro Márquez, F. O., Reyes Ortiz, G. E., & Torrez Meruvia, H. (2026). Philosophical leadership in education: Rethinking pedagogy in an AI-driven world. In *Social Sciences and Humanities Open* (Vol. 13). Elsevier Ltd., DOI: 10.1016/j.ssaho.2026.102699

Sonnentag, S., & Fritz, C. (2015). Recovery from job stress. *Annual Review of Organizational Psychology*, *2*, 1–26.

Sonnentag, S., & Fritz, C. (2015). Recovery from job stress: The stressor-detachment model as an integrative framework. *Journal of Organizational Behavior*, *36*(S1), S72–S103. DOI: 10.1002/job.1924

Sousa, N. M. T. (2025). Integration of artificial intelligence in the digital preservation of academic repositories and scientific data in higher education libraries. *Digital Library Perspectives*, ●●●, 1–21. DOI: 10.1108/DLP-06-2025-0074

Stake, R. E. (1995). *The Art of Case Study Research*. SAGE Publications.

Stanovich, K. E., & West, R. F. (2000). Individual differences in reasoning. *Behavioral and Brain Sciences*, *23*(5), 645–665. DOI: 10.1017/S0140525X00003435 PMID: 11301544

Stark, D., & Vanden Broeck, P. (2024). Principles of algorithmic management. *Organization Theory*, *5*(2), 1–24. DOI: 10.1177/26317877241257213

Star, S. L., & Ruhleder, K. (1996). Steps toward an ecology of infrastructure: Design and access for large information spaces. *Information Systems Research*, *7*(1), 111–134. DOI: 10.1287/isre.7.1.111

Steger, M. F., Dik, B. J., & Duffy, R. D. (2012). Measuring Meaningful Work: The Work and Meaning Inventory (WAMI). *Journal of Career Assessment*, *20*(3), 322–337. DOI: 10.1177/1069072711436160

Stephens, W. (2023). *How Writing Made Us Human, 3000 BCE to Now*. JHU Press. DOI: 10.56021/9781421446646

Stevenson, S. (2009). Digital divide: A discursive move away from the real inequities. *The Information Society*, *25*(1), 1–22. DOI: 10.1080/01972240802587539

Stiller, J., Gäde, M., & Petras, V. (2013). Multilingual access to digital libraries: The Europeana use case/Mehrsprachiger Zugang zu Digitalen Bibliotheken: Europeana/Accès multilingue aux bibliothèques numériques: Le cas d'Europeana. *Information-Wissenschaft & Praxis*, *64*(2-3), 86–95. DOI: 10.1515/iwp-2013-0014

Stock, O., Guerini, M., & Pianesi, F. (2016). Ethical dilemmas for adaptive persuasion systems. *Proceedings of the AAAI Conference on Artificial Intelligence*, *30*(1), •••. DOI: 10.1609/aaai.v30i1.9803

Strathern, M. (2000). The tyranny of transparency. *British Educational Research Journal*, *26*(3), 309–321. DOI: 10.1080/713651562

Suber, P. (2012). *Open access*. The MIT Press. DOI: 10.7551/mitpress/9286.001.0001

Subrahmanyam, S. (2025). AI and Automation: The Intersection of Human Autonomy and Machine Learning. In Tsvasman, L. (Ed.), *Cybernetic Leadership for Sustainable Innovation* (pp. 237–262). IGI Global Scientific Publishing., DOI: 10.4018/979-8-3373-2484-5.ch009

Subrahmanyam, S. (2026a). Building Applied Models From Multiple Sources. In Hai-Jew, S. (Ed.), *Building Applied Models for Problem Solving* (pp. 27–62). IGI Global Scientific Publishing., DOI: 10.4018/979-8-3373-3301-4.ch002

Subrahmanyam, S. (2026b). Building Trust in the Age of Intelligent Machines: Rethinking Human-Robot Synergy. In Anshari, M., Ordóñez de Pablos, P., & Almunawar, M. (Eds.), *Driving Organizational Transformation Through Human-Robotic Collaboration* (pp. 237–272). IGI Global Scientific Publishing., DOI: 10.4018/979-8-3373-3404-2.ch008

Subrahmanyam, S. (2026c). Entrepreneurship and Startup Business in the Age of AI. In Almasradi, R., & Awad, A. (Eds.), *Innovative Approaches to AI-Supported Hybrid and Remote Workplaces* (pp. 159–192). IGI Global Scientific Publishing., DOI: 10.4018/979-8-3373-7416-1.ch007

Suhud, U., Allan, M., Hoo, W., Azinuddin, M., Madhavedi, S., Mukhibad, H., & Sihotang, D. (2026). Digitally literate, habitually engaged: Unpacking sustainable urge to travel in coffee tourism. *International Journal of Data and Network Science*, *10*(2), 925–938. DOI: 10.5267/j.ijdns.2025.11.006

Suhud, U., Boonkaew, S., Sihotang, D. S., Azinuddin, M., & Aujirapongpan, S. (2025). Bridging Social Responsibility and Sustainability: A Case Study of Modelling Tourist Citizenship Behaviour in Indonesia. *International Journal of Sustainable Development and Planning*, *20*(12), 5381–5393. DOI: 10.18280/ijsdp.201229

Sull, D., Sull, C., & Zweig, B. (2022). Toxic culture is driving the great resignation. *MIT Sloan Management Review*, *63*, 1–9. https://sloanreview.mit.edu/article/toxic-culture-is-driving-the-great-resignation/

Sunyaev, A., Avital, M., & Lacity, M. C. (2026). From ideology to design: Toward purposeful decentralization of information systems governance. *Journal of Information Technology, 41*(1), 2–14. Advance online publication. DOI: 10.1177/02683962261430919

Supriyadi, T., Sulistiasih, S., Rahmi, K. H., Pramono, B., & Fahrudin, A. (2025). The impact of digital fatigue on employee productivity and well-being: A scoping literature review. *Environment and Social Psychology, 10*(2), 1–13. DOI: 10.59429/esp.v10i2.3420

Sweller, J. (1988). Cognitive load during problem solving: Effects on learning. *Cognitive Science, 12*(2), 257–285. DOI: 10.1207/s15516709cog1202_4

Sweller, J. (2011). Cognitive load theory. *Psychology of Learning and Motivation, 55*, 37–76. DOI: 10.1016/B978-0-12-387691-1.00002-8

Sweller, J., Ayres, P., & Kalyuga, S. (2011). *Cognitive load theory*. Springer. DOI: 10.1007/978-1-4419-8126-4

Sylqa, D. A. (2025). Enhancing organizational performance through quality information systems in internationally engaged enterprises. *Journal of Risk Analysis and Crisis Response, 15*(1), 11–11. DOI: 10.54560/jracr.v15i1.568

Tabatabaei, E. M., & Khalili, S. (2025). Cognitive hybridization: Redefining human identity at the interface of neuroscience and artificial intelligence: A narrative review. *Journal of Advanced Biomedical Sciences*. DOI: 10.18502/jabs.v16i1.20125

Tarafdar, M., Tu, Q., Ragu-Nathan, B. S., & Ragu-Nathan, T. S. (2007). The impact of technostress on role stress and productivity. *Journal of Management Information Systems, 24*(1), 301–328. DOI: 10.2753/MIS0742-1222240109

Tata Steel. (2023). *Tata Steel integrated report and annual accounts 2022-23*. Tata Steel Limited. https://www.tatasteel.com/investors/integrated-report-2022-23/

Technology, E. (2026). Digital technologies as the basis of a constructive business environment in large industrial enterprises. *Problemi Ekonomìki, 4*(66), 230–238. DOI: 10.32983/2222-0712-2025-4-230-238

Technology, O. N. U. (2025). The role of the marketing complex in the formed logistics system of enterprise. *Economic Herald of the Donbas*, (2 (80)), 50–55. DOI: 10.12958/1817-3772-2025-2(80)-50-55

Ter Hoeven, C. L., van Zoonen, W., & Fonner, K. L. (2016). The practical paradox of technology: The influence of communication technology use on employee burnout and engagement. *Communication Monographs*, *83*(2), 239–263. DOI: 10.1080/03637751.2015.1133920 PMID: 27226694

Terenzini, P. T. (1993). On the nature of institutional research and the knowledge and skills it requires. *Research in Higher Education*, *34*(1), 1–10. DOI: 10.1007/BF00991859

Thaler, R. H., & Sunstein, C. R. (2008). *Nudge*. Yale University Press.

Thao, N. V. H., & Mai Dr, L. T. T. (2025). Optimizing employee motivation in the era of artificial intelligence: Evidence from MH Raroma, a digital creative enterprise in Vietnam. *International Journal of Innovative Science and Research Technology*, (IJISRT25OCT658), 1196–1206. DOI: 10.38124/ijisrt/25oct658

The New York Public Library. (2024). About The New York Public Library Digital Collections. https://digitalcollections.nypl.org/about

Thota, S. (2025). A scalable microservices-based architecture for AI-driven Salesforce Cloud applications. *American International Journal of Computer Science and Technology*, *7*, 92–103. DOI: 10.63282/3117-5481/AIJCST-V7I6P110

Times Higher Education. (2025). *Impact Rankings*. Retrieved in 2025, from https://www.timeshighereducation.com/impactrankings

Tirpan, O. (2019). Analyzing the enablers for turkish defence industry supply chains: An interpretive structural modeling approach. *International Journal of Economics and Financial Issues*, *9*(3), 205–212. DOI: 10.32479/ijefi.8085

Trist, E. L., & Bamforth, K. W. (1951). Some social and psychological consequences of the longwall method of coal-getting: An examination of the psychological situation and defences of a work group in relation to the social structure and technological content of the work system. *Human Relations*, *4*(1), 3–38. DOI: 10.1177/001872675100400101

Tronto, J. C. (1993). *Moral boundaries: A political argument for an ethic of care*. Routledge.

Trstenjak, M., Benešova, A., Opetuk, T., & Cajner, H. (2025). Human factors and ergonomics in Industry 5.0—A systematic literature review. *Applied Sciences (Basel, Switzerland)*, *15*(4), 2123. DOI: 10.3390/app15042123

Tsamados, A., Aggarwal, N., Cowls, J., Morley, J., Roberts, H., Taddeo, M., & Floridi, L. (2022). The ethics of algorithms: Key problems and solutions. *AI & Society*, *37*(1), 215–230. DOI: 10.1007/s00146-021-01154-8

Tsamados, A., Floridi, L., & Taddeo, M. (2025). Human control of AI systems: From supervision to teaming. *AI and Ethics*, *5*(2), 1535–1548. DOI: 10.1007/s43681-024-00489-4 PMID: 40352578

Tudose, A. (2025). Understanding organizational stress in the era of digital transformation. In *European Conference on Innovation and Entrepreneurship* (pp. 865–871). Academic Conferences International Limited. DOI: 10.34190/ecie.20.1.3849

Tunca, S. (2026). The innovation–compliance–perception framework as a lens for AI governance — NLP evidence from Meta's smart glasses and GDPR discourse. *International Journal of Information Management Data Insights*, *6*(1), 100408. Advance online publication. DOI: 10.1016/j.jjimei.2026.100408

Turner, B. (2018). Benetech global literacy services: Working towards a 'born accessible'world. *Learned Publishing*, *31*(1), 25–29. DOI: 10.1002/leap.1141

Turner, B. (2025). Workplace democracy, algorithmic management, and epistemic agency. *Critical Review of International Social and Political Philosophy*, •••, 1–25. DOI: 10.1080/13698230.2025.2588074

Udupa, A. N., Majmudar, A. A., & Tran, L. (2024). A systematic review of neurological airway respiratory cardiovascular other-surgical severity (NARCO-SS) score as a pediatric perioperative scoring system. *Paediatric Anaesthesia*, *34*(5), 396–404. DOI: 10.1111/pan.14846 PMID: 38300020

Ullah, A., Usman, M., & Khan, M. K. (2023). Challenges in delivering modern library services in the 21st century. *International Journal of Social Science Exceptional Research*, *2*(6), 146–151. https://www.allsocialsciencejournal.com/uploads/archives/20231109154831_B-23-27.1.pdf. DOI: 10.54660/IJSSER.2023.2.6.146-151

United Nations. (n.d.).LONTAD: Total Digital Access to the League of Nations Archives. https://libraryresources.unog.ch/lontad

University, E. (2025). The algorithm for integrating digital technologies into enterprise management system. *Bìznes Ìnform*, *3*(566), 67–75. DOI: 10.32983/2222-4459-2025-3-67-75

University, L. N. T., & Topalov, V. (2025). Development of the information security system for small business entities. *Business Navigator*, (4(81)). Advance online publication. DOI: 10.32782/business-navigator.81-34

Unluer, S. (2012). Being an insider researcher while conducting case study research. *The Qualitative Report*, *17*(29), 1–14.

Urban Libraries Council. (2024). The CyberNavigator Program at CPL. https://www.urbanlibraries.org/innovations/the-cybernavigator-program-at-cpl

Uriasiev, M., & Voloschuk, L. (2026). Digital transformation of information support for enterprise financial flow management. *Economic Scope*, (209), 319–329. DOI: 10.30838/EP.209.319-329

Van Dijk, J. (2020). *The digital divide*. John Wiley & Sons.

van Vught, F. A., & Ziegele, F. (Eds.). (2012). *Multidimensional Ranking: The Design and Development of U-Multirank*. Springer. DOI: 10.1007/978-94-007-3005-2

Vanden Abeele, M. M. P., & Nguyen, M. H. (2022). Digital wellbeing in an age of mobile connectivity: An introduction to the special issue. *Mobile Media & Communication*, *10*(2), 174–189. Advance online publication. DOI: 10.1177/20501579221080899

Vargas-Hernandez, J. G., & Vargas-González, O. C. (2025). Digital organizational culture: A literature review and analysis. In *Knowledge sharing and fostering collaborative business culture* (pp. 277–296). DOI: 10.4018/979-8-3373-0710-7.ch015

Veldurthi, A. K. (2025). Ethical considerations in AI-driven financial decision-making. *European Journal of Computer Science and Information Technology*, *13*(31), 49–64. DOI: 10.37745/ejcsit.2013/vol13n314964

Venkatesh, V., Thong, J. Y. L., & Xu, X. (2016). Unified theory of acceptance and use of technology: A synthesis and the road ahead. *Journal of the Association for Information Systems*, *17*(5), 328–376. DOI: 10.17705/1jais.00428

Vernon, M. M., Balas, E. A., & Momani, S. (2018). Are university rankings useful to improve research? A systematic review. *PLoS One*, *13*(3), e0193762. DOI: 10.1371/journal.pone.0193762 PMID: 29513762

Vial, G. (2019). Understanding digital transformation: A review and a research agenda. *The Journal of Strategic Information Systems*, *28*(2), 118–144. DOI: 10.1016/j.jsis.2019.01.003

Vignola, E. F., Baron, S., Abreu Plasencia, E., Hussein, M., & Cohen, N. (2023). Workers' Health under Algorithmic Management: Emerging Findings and Urgent Research Questions. *International Journal of Environmental Research and Public Health*, *20*(2), 1239. DOI: 10.3390/ijerph20021239 PMID: 36673989

Vohs, K. D., & Baumeister, R. F.. (2008). Decision fatigue. *Journal of Personality and Social Psychology*, *94*(5), 883–898. DOI: 10.1037/0022-3514.94.5.883 PMID: 18444745

Volkwein, J. F. (1999). The four faces of institutional research. *New Directions for Institutional Research*, *1999*(104), 9–19. DOI: 10.1002/ir.10401

Volkwein, J. F. (2008). The foundations and evolution of institutional research. *New Directions for Higher Education*, *2008*(141), 5–20. DOI: 10.1002/he.289

Walenta, D. C., & Koppe, T. (2025). Exploring sociotechnical alignment and productivity: Post-pandemic insights. In *Proceedings of the Pacific Asia Conference on Information Systems*.

Walters, W. H. (2013). E-books in academic libraries: Challenges for acquisition and collection management. *portal. Portal (Baltimore, Md.)*, *13*(2), 187–211. DOI: 10.1353/pla.2013.0012

Walter, Y. (2024). Digital psychology: Introducing a conceptual impact model and the future of work. *Trends in Psychology*, •••, 1–37. DOI: 10.1007/s43076-024-00408-w

Wang, B., Liu, Y., Qian, J., & Parker, S. K. (2021). Achieving effective remote working during the COVID-19 pandemic: A work design perspective. *Applied Psychology*, *70*(1), 16–59. DOI: 10.1111/apps.12290 PMID: 33230359

Wang, Y. (2026). Algorithmic decision-making in organizations: A systematic review toward an integrated tension alignment framework. *Organizational Management Journal*, *23*(1), 115–131. DOI: 10.1108/OMJ-11-2024-2342

Warkentin, M., & Mutchler, L. (2014). Behavioral information security management. In *Computing handbook: Information systems and information technology*. DOI: 10.1201/b16768-62

Webber, K. L., & Calderon, A. J. (2015). *Institutional Research and Planning in Higher Education: Global Contexts and Themes*. Routledge. DOI: 10.4324/9781315777726

Webber, K. L., & Zheng, H. Y. (2020). *Big Data on Campus: Data Analytics and Decision Making in Higher Education*. Johns Hopkins University Press. DOI: 10.1353/book.78960

Weill, P., & Woerner, S. L. (2018). *What's your digital business model?: Six questions to help you build the next generation enterprise*. Harvard Business Review Press.

Whistle, W. (2017). *How higher education data reporting is both burdensome and inadequate*. Technical report, Third Way.

Whitney, P., Thompson, S., Wolf, K., & Brothers, A. (2009). Bayesian assessments of likelihood, consequence and risk for comparing scenarios. In *Behavior Representation in Modeling and Simulation Conference*.

Wiggin, T. (2025). Weaponizing the Workplace: How Algorithmic Management Shaped Amazon's Antiunion Campaign in Bessemer, Alabama. *Socius: Sociological Research for a Dynamic World*, *11*, 11. DOI: 10.1177/23780231251318389

Willcocks, L. P. (2024). Automation, digitalization and the future of work: A critical review. *Journal of Electronic Business & Digital Economics*, *3*(2), 184–199. DOI: 10.1108/JEBDE-09-2023-0018

Williamson, B. (2018). The hidden architecture of higher education: Building a big data infrastructure for the 'smarter university'. *International Journal of Educational Technology in Higher Education*, *15*(1), 1–26. DOI: 10.1186/s41239-018-0094-1

Willinsky, J. (2006). *The access principle: The case for open access to research and scholarship*. MIT Press.

Yin, R. K. (2018). *Case Study Research and Applications: Design and Methods* (6th ed.). SAGE Publications.

Zaidan, E., Truby, J., Ibrahim, I. A., & Hoppe, T. (2026). Hybrid global governance for responsible and inclusive Artificial Intelligence: Proposing a new Sustainable Development Goal 18. *Technology in Society*, *85*, 103159. Advance online publication. DOI: 10.1016/j.techsoc.2025.103159

Zeng, J., & Kaye, D. B. V. (2022). From content moderation to visibility moderation: A case study of platform governance on TikTok. *Policy and Internet*, *14*(1), 79–95. DOI: 10.1002/poi3.287

Zhang, M. J. (2005). An empirical assessment of the performance impacts of IS support for knowledge management. In *International Conference on Electronic Business Proceedings*.

Zhang, Q., Gillenson, M. L., & Zhang, X. P. (2026). The impact of person-organization ethics fit on ethical performance of autonomous vehicles. *Computers in Human Behavior Reports*, *21*, 100953. Advance online publication. DOI: 10.1016/j.chbr.2026.100953

Zhan, Y., & Wang, Y. (2025). Network dynamics between digital media use and depressive symptomatology: A computational phenotyping approach using ecological momentary assessment. *Psychiatry Research*, •••, 116896. PMID: 41411707

Zhao, Y., & Siau, K. (2018). Cognitive neuroscience in information systems research. In *Applications of neuroscience: Breakthroughs in research and practice* (pp. 158–175). DOI: 10.4018/978-1-5225-5478-3.ch009

Zhao, G., & Yim, J. (2025). Towards usability-driven optimization: A human-in-the-loop approach to interface evaluation. *Edelweiss Applied Science and Technology, 9*(12), 630–643. DOI: 10.55214/2576-8484.v9i12.11407

Zhao, W. X., Zhou, K., Li, J., Tang, T., Wang, X., Hou, Y., Min, Y., Zhang, B., Zhang, J., Dong, Z., Du, Y., Yang, C., Chen, Y., Chen, Z., Jiang, J., Ren, R., Li, Y., Tang, X., Liu, Z., & Wen, J.-R. (2023). A survey of large language models. arXiv. https://arxiv.org/abs/2303.18223

Zhu, Z. Y. (2025). Ethical AI governance in urban governance: Normative, descriptive and prescriptive challenges and opportunities of autonomous vehicles. *Transforming Government, 19*(4), 914–932. DOI: 10.1108/TG-06-2025-0191

Zuboff, S. (2019). *The age of surveillance capitalism*. PublicAffairs.

Zuboff, S. (2019). *The age of surveillance capitalism: the fight for a human future at the new frontier of power*. PublicAffairs.

About the Contributors

Houssem Chemingui is an Assistant Professor of Information Systems at Brest Business School, France. He earned his PhD in Computer Science from Université Paris 1 Panthéon-Sorbonne, where his doctoral research focused on advanced approaches to software configuration and process-oriented decision support systems. His research lies at the intersection of artificial intelligence, data analytics, and software engineering, with a particular emphasis on guided product configuration and decision support for complex organizational processes. His work addresses several application domains, including business process management, logistics, and higher education, exploring how intelligent systems can enhance decision-making and organizational performance. He has published and presented his research in international conferences and scientific venues, and maintains active collaborations with both academic institutions and industry partners. He also serves as a reviewer for academic journals published by Elsevier and Springer. Through his research and teaching activities, he aims to bridge theoretical contributions and their practical implementation in real-world contexts.

***

Canan Hazal Akarsu is an academic staff member at Istanbul University-Cerrahpaşa. Her research focuses on artificial intelligence, machine learning, industrial engineering, optimization, scheduling, and supply chain management. In her academic work, she concentrates on production planning problems, heuristic algorithms, and data-driven decision-making methods, and she has publications in both national and international journals. She also contributes to projects and book chapters related to sustainable higher education and data governance.

Nilufar Aminova is an Associate Professor in the Department of Valuation and Investments at Tashkent State University of Economics, Uzbekistan. She has a strong academic background in finance, with specialization in investment analysis, asset valuation, and financial management. Her research interests include capital markets, portfolio management, valuation methodologies, and the application of modern financial tools for investment decision-making. She is actively engaged in teaching and curriculum development, equipping students with both theoretical knowledge and practical insights into financial markets. Dr. Aminova has contributed to academic research through publications and participation in conferences, promoting advancements in finance and investment studies. She also supports industry–academia collaboration initiatives to enhance the practical relevance of financial concepts. Her work contributes to strengthening financial education, investment strategies, and economic development in the evolving global financial ecosystem.

Pardaev Anvar is a faculty member in the Department of Economics at Termez University of Economics and Service, Uzbekistan. He is actively involved in teaching and research in the field of economics, with a focus on economic development, financial systems, and applied economic analysis. His academic interests include macroeconomic and microeconomic theory, policy evaluation, and the use of analytical tools to understand economic trends and decision-making processes. He contributes to curriculum development and student mentoring, fostering critical thinking and practical skills among learners. Pardaev has participated in academic research activities, including publications and collaborative projects that support knowledge dissemination and innovation. His work emphasizes the integration of theoretical concepts with real-world economic challenges, contributing to the advancement of economic education and sustainable development initiatives.

Eshniyozov Asadbek is a faculty member in the Department of Economics at Termez University of Economics and Service, Uzbekistan. He is actively engaged in teaching and research in the field of economics, with a focus on economic development, financial systems, and applied economic analysis. His academic interests include macroeconomic and microeconomic studies, economic policy evaluation, and the use of modern analytical tools to understand market dynamics and decision-making processes. He contributes to curriculum development and student mentoring, fostering analytical thinking and practical skills among learners. Eshniyozov has participated in academic research activities, including publications and collaborations that support innovation and knowledge dissemination. His work emphasizes bridging theoretical concepts with real-world economic challenges, contributing to the advancement of economic education and sustainable development.

Deniz Dirik is a Professor of Management at Manisa Celal Bayar University's Faculty of Economics and Administrative Sciences. She completed her PhD in

Organizational Behavior. Her research interests cover as effective leadership, power in organizations, gender at the workplace, and perceived organizational politics, among others. She has been teaching Organizational Behavior and Organization Theory, Contemporary Management, Global Business and Human Resource Management at undergraduate and graduate levels. Her recent scholarship has increasingly focused on university-industry collaborations, entrepreneurial ecosystems, startup co-founders' experiences of meaningful work, and sustainability-oriented leadership. Her work has been published in peer-reviewed journals including Journal of Global Entrepreneurship Research, Higher Education Research & Development, International Journal for Educational and Vocational Guidance, and Current Psychology. In addition to her academic research and teaching, she actively engages in science communication through her YouTube channel "Akademik Diyaloglar", where she creates original, evidence-based content that makes scholarly insights accessible to wider public audiences.

Agung Wahyu Handaru is an Associate Professor in the Department of Management at Universitas Negeri Jakarta, Indonesia. His research focuses on human resource management, organisational behaviour, leadership, entrepreneurship, and strategic management. He has extensive experience in academic research, teaching, and supervision across undergraduate, master's, and doctoral levels. He has published widely in national and international peer-reviewed journals and contributed to numerous academic collaborations and research projects. His scholarly work covers topics such as transformational leadership, job satisfaction, organisational commitment, employee performance, entrepreneurship, and digital business transformation. He has also contributed to books and other academic publications in management and business research.

Sevil Işık Özder received her PhD in Business Administration from Gebze Technical University, Türkiye. She is an interdisciplinary scholar in management information systems, with research interests in digital transformation, generative artificial intelligence, organizational learning, skills renewal, technology adoption, big data analytics, and data-driven decision-making. Her work examines how emerging technologies shape organizational capabilities, governance processes, risk perceptions, and decision behavior in business and digital market contexts. She has contributed to studies on big data analytics adoption, artificial intelligence in organizations, corporate governance, and institutional performance. She also has experience in gifted and talented education, mentoring students, and coordinating educational projects that connect research, leadership, innovation, and practice.

Nasiba Jumaniyazova is a faculty member in the Department of Psychology at Mamun University, Khiva, Uzbekistan. She has a strong academic background in psychology, with a focus on human behavior, cognitive processes, and mental health. Her areas of interest include developmental psychology, educational psychology, and psychological assessment, with an emphasis on understanding individual and group behavior in academic and social contexts. She is actively engaged in teaching and mentoring students, supporting their academic and personal development through evidence-based psychological approaches. Nasiba participates in research activities, publications, and academic collaborations that contribute to the advancement of psychological sciences. Her work emphasizes the application of psychological principles to real-world challenges, promoting well-being, effective learning environments, and the overall development of individuals and communities.

Kehinde Tola Benjamin is a Lecturer in the Department of History and International Studies at Redeemer's University. He is a historian and researcher whose work spans history, international relations, and global development studies. He obtained a Bachelor of Arts degree in History and Strategic Studies from the University of Lagos and a Master of Science degree in International Relations from Covenant University, where he graduated with distinction. He is currently pursuing a Ph.D. in History and International Studies at Redeemer's University, Ede, Osun State. Kehinde's research focuses on contemporary global issues at the intersection of history, technology, and international policy. His areas of specialization include cyber diplomacy, digital governance, climate action, peace studies, and foreign relations. He has published research articles in reputable local and international journals, contributing to scholarship on Africa's role in global affairs. In 2025, he was selected as a Fellow of the Ife Institute of Advanced Studies, in recognition of his academic promise and interdisciplinary engagement.

Tarık Küçükdeniz is a faculty member at the Department of Industrial Engineering, Istanbul University–Cerrahpaşa. He completed his bachelor's, master's, and doctoral studies in Industrial Engineering at Istanbul University. His research focuses on production and operations management, optimization, queuing theory, stochastic modeling, scheduling, supply chain management, and applications of artificial intelligence. He has contributed to numerous national and international publications and research projects, making significant academic contributions in his field. (AVESIS profile: https://avesis.iuc.edu.tr/tkdeniz)

Mirzayev Bobur is the Head of the Department of Finance at Alfraganus University, Tashkent, Uzbekistan. He has extensive academic and administrative experience in the field of finance, with expertise in financial management, investment analysis, and economic policy. His research interests include capital markets, corporate finance, and the application of modern financial technologies in decision-making processes. As a departmental leader, he plays a key role in curriculum development, academic planning, and fostering a research-oriented environment. He is actively involved in teaching and mentoring students, supporting their academic and professional growth in finance-related disciplines. Mirzayev has contributed to scholarly research through publications and participation in academic conferences. His work emphasizes bridging theoretical knowledge with practical financial applications, contributing to the advancement of financial education and institutional development.

Ravikumar R. N. is currently a Postdoctoral researcher at Universiti Malaysia Perlis, Malaysia. Also, working as an Assistant Professor in the Department of Computer Engineering at Marwadi University, Rajkot, Gujarat. He has 14 years of national and international teaching experience. He completed his PhD at Amity University, Rajasthan, M.E at VMRF Deemed University, B.E at Anna University, Chennai. He is the co-founder of the Research Activities Club at Marwadi University and trains students on research activities, which leads to the various publications. He has published numerous research articles in Scopus, SCI journals, Book chapters, and Conference papers. Also, he hold several patents and authored books. His specialization is ML, DL, Federated Learning, Recommendation Systems, and Optimization Techniques.

Nazirjon Rajabov is affiliated with the Department of International Scientific Journals and Ratings at Alfraganus University, Tashkent, Uzbekistan. He is actively involved in academic publishing and research evaluation, contributing to the improvement of scholarly communication and research quality. His areas of expertise include journal indexing, citation analysis, research metrics, and academic performance evaluation based on international standards. He supports researchers in enhancing the visibility and impact of their work through guidance on publication strategies and indexing platforms. Rajabov also participates in academic collaborations and institutional initiatives aimed at strengthening research output and global academic presence. His work contributes to promoting high-quality research practices, improving institutional rankings, and fostering international integration in the academic community.

Aarthi S is a dedicated Assistant Professor in Computer Science with over six years of teaching experience. She is currently pursuing her Ph.D. at Marwadi University, Gujarat, and holds an M.Phil. and MCA from Bharathiar University, Tamil Nadu. Throughout her academic career, Aarthi has specialized in programming languages such as C++, Java, and C, and contributed to research in recommender systems and AI-related data privacy. She has published journal articles, contributed to book chapters, and actively participated in technical workshops. Known for her student mentorship and engagement in academic events, Aarthi remains committed to fostering innovation and excellence in computer science education.

I**Gautam Shivaraj**, with a comprehensive academic background including a Bachelor's in Mechanical Engineering, Master of Engineering Management (Australia), MBA and also pursuing Ph.D., brings an impressive 07 years of teaching experience alongside a brief stint in the industry of 5 years. Currently serving as an Assistant Professor at the Adarsh Institute of Management and Information Technology in Bangalore, Karnataka, India, he has distinguished himself in the academic and research fields. Prof.Gautam Shivaraj professional journey is a testament to his dedication to academia, research, in the evolving world.

Doni Sugianto Sihotang is a doctoral student in Marketing at Jakarta State University, Indonesia. His academic background includes a Bachelor's degree in Social Anthropology from Universitas Sumatera Utara and a Master's degree in Marketing Management from Jakarta State University. His interdisciplinary training allows him to merge cultural perspectives with marketing and behavioral research methods. His research interests include consumer behavior, digital marketing, tourism marketing, artificial intelligence in marketing, and behavioral analytics. He has contributed to several peer-reviewed publications on topics such as consumer decision-making, destination branding, technology adoption, and sustainable tourism development. He has received multiple academic awards, including the BIMA DRTPM Research Grant from the Indonesian Ministry of Education and the PMDSU Fast-Track Scholarship for outstanding young researchers. His work aims to advance interdisciplinary research that combines anthropology, marketing, and emerging technologies to better understand consumer behavior and digital innovation in developing economies.

Melike Solak is a Ph.D. student in the Mathematics Department at Istanbul University. Since 2024, she has been a data scientist in the Corporate Data Management Office at Istanbul University-Cerrahpaşa. Her research interests include machine learning, stability analysis, nonlinear systems, and artificial neural networks.

Satya Subrahmanyam is a distinguished academic leader, researcher, and institutional strategist with over 28 years of experience in higher education, business research, leadership and management. He holds two PhDs and a Postdoctoral qualification from the Polytechnic Institute of Leiria, Portugal. Currently serving as

Professor and Dean (Research) at Holy Spirit University of Kaslik (USEK), Lebanon, he spearheads research initiatives that enhance academic excellence and institutional reputation. He played a pivotal role in the development of the Catholic University in Erbil, Kurdistan, where he established new departments, led research programs, and collaborated on international educational projects. As a founding member and Managing Partner of Vignan Institute of Technology and Management, India, he contributed to its transformation into a premier institution. With expertise in AI-driven business strategies, HR analytics, and leadership in technology adoption, he has published extensively, guided PhD research, and led training programs in corporate and academic settings.

Usep Suhud is a Professor of Marketing at the Faculty of Economics, Universitas Negeri Jakarta, Indonesia. He earned his Bachelor's degree in Business Education from IKIP Jakarta, a Master's degree in Marketing Communication from Universitas Indonesia, and a PhD in Marketing from Edith Cowan University in Australia. His research interests include consumer behaviour, tourism marketing, sustainable tourism, digital marketing, and artificial intelligence in education and business. He has published extensively in international peer-reviewed journals indexed in Scopus and has authored several academic books on marketing and research methodology. Additionally, he has led and participated in various nationally and internationally funded research projects related to tourism, sustainability, and digital transformation. He is also active in community engagement and international collaborations, including research fellowships and academic partnerships.

Index

A

B

C

D

S

T

U

W

www.ingramcontent.com/pod-product-compliance
Lightning Source LLC
LaVergne TN
LVHW081544300926
849161LV00006B/1505

9798260001110